GREAT WAR
RAILWAYMEN

GREAT WAR RAILWAYMEN

Britain's railway company workers at war 1914–1918

JEREMY HIGGINS

FOREWORD BY MICHAEL PORTILLO
INTRO BY GENERAL THE LORD DANNATT GCB, CBE, MC, DL

UNIFORM
PRESS

Uniform Press Ltd
66 Charlotte Street
London W1T 4QE

A catalogue record for this book is available from
the British Library

5 4 3 2 1

ISBN 978-1-910500-00-2

Cover design Vivian@Bookscribe
Typeset by Vivian@Bookscribe

Printed and bound in Spain by Graphycems

Raising money for Army Benevolent Fund,
the Soldiers' Charity and
Railway Benefit Fund.

15th December 1915, Liverpool Station. NRM 1997–7059_HOR_F_1541.

CONTENTS

PART 3   STORIES OF RAILWAY COMPANIES AT WAR

APPENDICES

MAPS

DOES IT MATTER?

Does it matter? losing your legs?
For people will always be kind,
And you need not show that you mind
When the others come in after football
To gobble their muffins and eggs.

Does it matter? losing your sight?
There's such splendid work for the blind;
And people will always be kind,
As you sit on the terrace remembering
And turning your face to the light.

Do they matter? those dreams from the pit?
You can drink and forget and be glad,
And people won't say that you're mad;
For they'll know that you've fought for your country,
And no one will worry a bit.

Siegfied Sassoon

INSPIRATION

O n my commute to work on my first day back after six months of reservist service in Iraq, I stood looking vacantly at the Great Western Railway war memorial at Leamington Spa station.

I saw a huge list of names, but no story, and I began to wonder whether there was a story to tell. An idea was triggered that would launch me on a seven-year exploration into the history of over 12,500 railwaymen who died, and from that research to piece together a picture which would preserve the exploits of the typical railwayman who served and made the ultimate sacrifice. Although there are many memorials across the rail network, the brass plaques of names could give a scale of the sacrifice but no clue as to the contribution or suffering of the railwaymen concerned. Hopefully this work does.

Throughout the last seven years I have been driven by a dual purpose, to tell the story of fellow railwaymen who went to war, but also to raise money for two worthy charities. Firstly, as a member of the railway family, it is appropriate to raise money for the Railway Benefit Fund. Secondly, so many soldiers have been injured not just in the recent campaigns in Afghanistan and Iraq, but as far back and including the Second World War, and many require help and support so the Army Benevolent Fund (The Soldiers' Charity) is an essential choice to me. Any profits from this work will be distributed evenly to these great causes.

THIS BOOK IS DEDICATED TO:

All the railwaymen who served and especially those who did not return.

And the soldiers of 19 Light Brigade and the 26 who made the supreme sacrifice in Iraq in 2006/07.

Also the soldiers of 11 Light Brigade killed in Afghanistan in January and February 2010.

OPERATION TELIC 9
Iraq   1 November 2006 to 1 May 2007

			AGE
Kingsman Jamie Hancock	2nd Btn Duke of Lancaster's Regiment	6 Nov 2006	19
Marine Jason Hylton	539 Assault Sqn RM	12 Nov 2006	33
Corporal Ben Nowak	45 Commando	12 Nov 2006	27
SSgt Sharron Elliott	Intelligence Corps	12 Nov 2006	35
WO2 Lee Hopkins	Royal Signals	12 Nov 2006	35
Sgt Jonathon Hollingsworth	Parachute Regt	23 Nov 2006	35
Sgt Graham Hesketh	2nd Btn Duke of Lancasters Regt	28 Dec 2006	35
Sgt Wayne Rees	Queens Royal Lancers	7 Jan 2007	36
Kingsman Alex Green	2nd Btn Duke of Lancaster's Regiment	13 Jan 2007	21
Private Michael Tench	2nd Btn Light Infantry	21 Jan 2007	18
2nd Lt Jonathon Bracho-Cooke	2nd Btn Duke Of Lancaster's Regiment	5 Feb 2007	24
Pte Luke Simpson	1st Btn Yorkshire Regt	9 Feb 2007	21
Rifleman Daniel Coffey	2nd Btn the Rifles	27 Feb 2007	21
Pte Johnathon Wysoczan	1st Btn Staffordshire Regiment	3 Mar 2007	21
Kingsman Adam Smith	2nd Btn Duke of Lancaster's Regiment	5 Apr 2007	19
Pte Eleanor Dlugosz	Royal Army Medical Corps	5 Apr 2007	19
Cpl Kris O'Neill	Royal Army Medical Corps	5 Apr 2007	27
2nd Lt Joanna Yorke Dyer	Intelligence Corps	5 Apr 2007	24
Sgt Mark McLaren	Royal Air Force	15 Apr 2007	27
C/Sgt M L Powell	Parachute Regiment	15 Apr 2007	37
Tpr Kristen Turton	Queens Royal Lancers	19 Apr 2007	27
Cpl Ben Leaning	Queens Royal Lancers	19 Apr 2007	24
Kingsman Alan Jones	2nd Btn Duke of Lancaster's Regiment	23 Apr 2007	20
Pte Paul Domachie	2nd Btn the Rifles	29 Apr 2007	18
Major Nick Bateson	Royal Signals	1 May 2007	49

OPERATION HERRICK 11
Afghanistan   5 January and 16 February 2010

			AGE
Captain Daniel Reed	11 EOD Regiment Royal Logistics Corps	11 Jan 2010	31
Rifleman Luke Farmer	3rd Btn the Rifles	15 Jan 2010	19
Cpl Lee Brownson	3rd Btn the Rifles	15 Jan 2010	30
Rifleman Peter Aldridge	4th Btn the Rifles	22 Jan 2010	19
L/Cpl Daniel Cooper	3rd Btn the Rifles	24 Jan 2010	22
L/Cpl Graham Shaw	3rd Btn the Yorkshire Regiment	1 Feb 2010	27
Cpl Liam Riley	3rd Btn the Yorkshire Regiment	1 Feb 2010	21
Pte Sean McDonald	1st Btn Scots (Royal Scottish Borderers)	7 Feb 2010	26
Cpl John Moore	1st Btn Scots (Royal Scottish Borderers)	7 Feb 2010	22
WO2 David Markland	36th Engineer Regiment	8 Feb 2010	36
L/Cpl Darren Hicks	1st Btn Coldstream Guards	11 Feb 2010	29
L/Sgt Dave Greenhalgh	1st Btn Grenadier Guards	13 Feb 2010	25
Rifleman Mark Marshall	6th Btn the Rifles	14 Feb 2010	29
Kingsman Sean Dawson	2nd Btn the Duke of Lancaster's Regiment	14 Feb 2010	19
Sapper Guy Mellors	36th Engineer Regiment	15 Feb 2010	20

FORWARD THINKING, BUT NEVER FORGETTING

Joining together to remember the contribution of the railway industry 100 years ago.

 abellio greateranglia

 ARRIVA TrainCare

 worldline

 BRITISH TRANSPORT POLICE

Chiltern Railways
If you think our way, travel our way.

 crosscountry

c2c

 METRO

 Direct Rail Services

 EAST COAST

First Great Western

EAST MIDLANDS TRAINS

First TransPennine Express

 GB Railfreight PART OF EUROPORTE

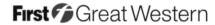 GRAND CENTRAL

 Heathrow Express The smarter way

ScotRail SCOTLAND'S RAILWAY

london midland

LOROL LONDON OVERGROUND RAIL OPERATIONS LTD

Merseyrail

 National Railway Museum

NetworkRail

RMT

 northern
a serco and abellio joint venture

southeastern.
working together to bring people together

SOUTHERN

SOUTH WEST TRAINS

Virgin trains

CLGR Limited
Railway Wheelset & Brake Limited

Thanks to the railway 'family' for helping to make this book possible and to support the aim of raising money for the Army Benevolent Fund and the Railway Benefit Fund.

FOREWORD

World War One was a railway war. Germany's Schlieffen plan was based on the rapid movement of its forces through Belgium and against France in the hope of knocking out its western enemy, so as to focus in Russia in the east. Conversely, Moscow hoped that its sparse rail network of non-standard gauge might offer a barrier against the Kaiser's onslaught. France's ability to use its rail network, especially two rings of tracks around Paris, enabled it to assemble an army that could be sent by train to the Battle of the Marne, where the German advance was turned back.

Britain used rail to move its expeditionary force to the continent with impressive speed and efficiency, so that it arrived in time to make a difference. Thereafter, our war fortunes oscillated as we at first struggled with, and then triumphantly mastered, the logistical challenges of moving men and munitions expeditiously to the front.

At home, Britain's railways had to cope with a supply chain that brought troops, horses, food and shells from around the Kingdom, through London to the channel ports, carried the wounded to British hospitals alongside men returning on leave, whilst continuing all the regular services for the civilian population. The rail companies managed to sustain the network despite a massive overnight depletion of their workforce as railwaymen answered Lord Kitchener's call to enlist. Something of a social revolution occurred as women filled some of the gaps.

The men who signed up, often in pals' battalions, were used mainly as ordinary soldiers, or in the Royal Navy or as airmen. As the strategic and tactical importance of railways became ever more apparent, a larger number was used in specialist roles, keeping the lines running, laying narrow gauge track close to the front and organising the supply of men and munitions.

Many railway stations in the United Kingdom have memorials to the railwaymen who died in the Great War. The lists are very long, because the railways were huge employers, and their workers responded in big numbers to the call of patriotic duty. Generally, hurrying to or from our train, we pass by their names without a glance.

Jeremy Higgins must often have done so too, until one day he, as a railwayman reservist returning from military duties in Iraq, began to investigate the list on the GWR memorial at Leamington Spa station. His work mushroomed as he unearthed the biographical details of thousands of fallen rail employees.

His extremely diligent investigations have restored identities to those men. Thanks to him we now know the names of some who were killed on the first day of the Battle of the Somme. We can put ages - some as young as 15 - to those who during the course of the war made the ultimate sacrifice. We learn of those drowned at sea, of one who was executed by the Germans and given a state funeral when his body was returned to Britain, and of air aces who survived numerous encounters with the enemy only to perish in pitiable accidents.

It helps us to understand why those station memorials are so numerous; because at the war's conclusion the country was in no doubt about how enormous had been the contribution to the war effort made by railwaymen and how huge had been the sacrifice.

In buying Jeremy Higgins's book you are making a donation to charitable institutions involved in service personnel's welfare. But you are also showing respect to the fallen; because here the anonymous names carved on war memorials are re-embodied. Paradoxically, as we learn of their deaths, they return to life.

Michael Portillo, Spring 2014

INTRODUCTION

Railways, Railwaymen and the First World War

The First World War was a tragedy for a myriad of reasons, and a tragedy of many dimensions. One of those dimensions was the role that railways played in that most awful of wars. When diplomacy in Europe failed in the six weeks between the assassination of the Archduke Ferdinand in Sarajevo on 28th June 1914 and the declaration of war between Great Britain and Germany on 4/5th August, the drumbeat to war was the clickety clack of the railways of Europe.

Knowing that the politicians might fail to achieve national objectives by negotiation, the generals had prepared over many years to achieve those same objectives by force. To get the armies to the right place at the right time, the means of transport selected by the General Staffs, principally in Germany, was the railway train. As all railwaymen know, the trains must run to schedule and the passengers – in this case, the soldiers – must be delivered to where they are needed on time. In 1914, when diplomacy broke down, war was declared, mobilisation was ordered and the trains began to roll. For Germany – paranoid about having to fight in both the east and the west simultaneously - this meant first a rapid deployment against France, a quick and decisive victory, to be followed by a switch east and another blow against Russia. The key to success were the railways. In this sense, the railways were a prime party to the tragedy.

But in every tragedy there is invariably a hero, and in the First World War the railways – and, more personally, the railwaymen that operated them – have a strong case to be called the hero. Once the opening moves of the war were completed, the fighting along the lines of the Western Front, as elsewhere, had to be sustained - troops continued to be moved, ammunition brought forward and casualties taken home. This was the role of the railways. It was vital, dangerous but, for some, unglamorous work. Track construction near to the front lines was essential, narrow gauge lines were the practical way to achieve success and getting these trains through to their destinations was the determined mission of those who ran them.

I grew up in the close company of my maternal grandfather, Frank Stanley Chilvers. He kept me spellbound by his stories of the railways – as a Royal Engineers officer from 1914 to 1918 running ammunition trains in France. As I write I have his three World War One medals beside me, including a clasp to show that he was Mentioned in Dispatches. And then as a senior officer of the old London North East Railway, the stories he told me were of keeping the trains running through East London during the Blitz and throughout the Second World War. Many young boys want to become an engine driver, but for me that was not good enough. I wanted to run the railways like my grandfather! Well, the dreams of many a young boy do not come to fruition. I did not run the railways but it was my privilege to run the Army for three years, during which time I was allowed to drive a military train, and I have the certificate to prove it!

I am, therefore, very pleased to write an introduction to this fascinating book about the railways in the First World War, the men who operated them and in the memory of the 20,000 railwaymen who lost their lives. One of my grandfather's stories was of sharing a cup of cocoa with a signalman in his dug in hut at a junction on the narrow gauge railway just behind the lines in France. My grandfather left the safety of the hut and had only walked a few yards when an artillery shell demolished the hut and killed the signalman. Such individual tragedies were commonplace in the First World War but for that man, his family and his friends that incident was a deep personal tragedy indeed.

This book is therefore a timely contribution to our commemoration of the First World War and the men and women of that generation who were caught up in its horror and intensity. I commend this book to the military historian and to the general reader alike. It is particularly appropriate that the proceeds from this book about railwaymen in the First World War are going to The Army Benevolent Fund – The Soldiers' Charity to help the needs of those who have served our country in more recent generations. Sadly, war and armed conflict are likely to remain a feature of our lives but even though modern technology has flown men through the sound barrier and put men on the Moon, railways will continue to be a part of our lives, as will the men and women who operate them.

I salute the memory of those who have served their country on the railways in war and peace – in the past, the present and in the future.

Richard Dannatt
General the Lord Dannatt GCB CBE MC DL
Chief of the General Staff 2006–2009

'A few youths of the carriage works decided that one morning they would join up, and they got together and shouted and shouted... in the next workshop... they had 20 or 30 of them then, they went and joined up and the same happened the next day and next until two or three hundred had joined up. Then the railway put on a special train and took them to Oxford'.[1]

Frank Gillard, ex-employee of L&NWR Wolverton works,
on volunteering in August 1914.

1   IWM Sound Archive, 6338, Frank Gillard

PREFACE

The war broke out at a time when the world's railway companies had transformed, or were transforming, much of the globe, but just before the internal combustion engine changed it again. It was at a time close to the pinnacle of the railway's scale and influence. Few industrial concerns were greater than the vast railway engineering works; railway engineering was at the forefront of technological expertise and sophistication.

British railway companies were some of the largest businesses in the country, with global reach. It was British investment and expertise, for example, that drove the development of much of Argentina as railways were constructed over that enormous country, providing access to mineral deposits in the hope of creating vast wealth. Domestically, the influence of companies like the Great Western Railway, London & North Western Railway, Great Eastern Railway and many others extended beyond railways into hotels, ships, ports and recognising the potential of motor vehicles, gradually into bus routes.

This book is about the contribution that the railway made to the Great War. Primarily it concerns British railway companies, or railways operated or utilised by Briton's overseas supporting the war effort. It also considers the part played by the railway of the Central Powers in the build up to conflict in Europe. Mainly though, it is a book about British railwaymen who died in the Great War. As part of the preparation for this book over 12,500 of the 20,000 who died have been researched and over 1,000 feature in this book. It is hoped that this gives some idea of the range, scope and scale of the effort that railway employees made in serving their country 100 years ago.

Chapter 1 sets the scene by looking at how the development of European railways revolutionised warfare, creating the conditions to sustain mass armies in the field, so changing the scale and identity of warfare and making world war a possibility. It also illuminates how railways may have contributed to the start of hostilities. Focusing on the railway in Britain, an appreciation is made of the nation's largest companies and the domination of one industry, the railway. The chapter then considers what that scale meant in terms of business complexity and potential supply of manpower in what would become a hugely expanded British army.

The book then splits into three parts, in Part 1 (chapters 2 to 7) it looks at the contribution of railwaymen in arms, looking first at the Army, through seven infantry battalions in which many railwaymen served; six on the Western Front and one overseas. Then it examines the role of military railway operations in sustaining the Western Front, for much of the war a largely static campaign, and Palestine which became a mobile one. Thereafter, the following chapters concern railwaymen known to have died serving with the RFC (Royal Flying Corps) or RAF (Royal Air Force) and with the Royal or Merchant Navies.

Part 2 (Chapters 8 to 10) looks at the contribution of railway organisations at home. It looks at the people from the big engineering works such as Derby and Swindon, to smaller stations and locomotive depots, considering the wealth of job roles from which the volunteers and conscripts came. Then it turns its attention to the close-knit communities and considers the effect of the loss on families at home. The final section of Part 2 recognises the gallantry amongst railwaymen.

The story then turns, in Part 3, to how the railway companies supported the war effort and in particular the output from the railway works, much of which was undertaken by women, many of them the wives of the men-folk fighting and dying overseas.

The book closes with four thought-provoking sections – railwaymen taken prisoner, the Quintinshill rail disaster, enemy railwaymen and railwaymen executed by firing squad.

CHAPTER I

BEFORE THE WAR

Although this is mainly a book about British railwaymen who made the supreme sacrifice in the Great War, the common denominator is of course the railway. It would be a mistake not to contextualise their sacrifice not only within the war that they fought, but also the global industry they had been a part of. So this opening chapter examines the entwined nature of the development of the railway from the 1840s alongside the evolution of warfare. Although many of the railwaymen who donned a uniform to fight for their country probably never realised it, if it wasn't for their industry the war that they fought would probably never have happened. Not at least in the way it did.

Strategic Development of European Railways before 1914

War before railways

'In the time of Frederick the Great (in the 1750s) an army of 100,000 men could be accompanied by 48,000 horses. Dry fodder was so bulky that it could only be transported by water'.[1] As a result, warfare tended to be limited to environments where armies could sustain themselves, since re-supply was a cumbersome and inefficient process. War was fought during the spring and summer so that soldiers could live off the land. 'Campaigning did not normally begin until the green grass grew'.[2] Food and fodder were the limiting factors rather than ammunition or other supplies. The lead in to war tended to be slow as the armies, subject to the coming conflict, marched to positions to commence warfare. There was in effect a cap on the size of a battle formation which equated to the amount that the local countryside could sustain and so armies tended to be small. Things had barely changed sixty of so years later during the Napoleonic era in the early 1800s. 'Although Napoleon was able to take advantage of the better road system that was beginning to be constructed in Europe by the end of the eighteenth century, and an increasing population density and thus a greater ability to support armies, he still held to the methods of his predecessors'.[3] Prior to the railway, armies were little changed from the days of Napoleon, Wellington and Frederick the Great. The advent of the railway infrastructure led to a significant change in the composition of armies and the strategy of how those armies could fight. 'With the railways came the modern age. The advent of the railway had a greater and more immediate impact than any other technological or industrial innovation before or since'.[4]

Early use of rail in conflict and deterrent to achieve political ends

It could be argued that the introduction of the world's first passenger railway service between Stockton and Darlington in 1833, only 18 years after Wellington defeated Napoleon at the Battle of Waterloo in 1815, changed warfare forever. As well as the commercial possibilities of moving freight and people, rail changed the way wars could and would be fought. Trains enabled the movement of manpower and supplies which meant that it was possible to mass larger armies and to mobilise

---

1   Thompson, J., *The Lifeblood of War. Logistics in Armed Conflict*, 26.
2   Thompson, 26.
3   Thompson, 27.
4   Neilson, K., and Otte, T.G., *Realpoltiik* in Railways and International Politics. Paths of Empire, 1848–1945, 1.

them rapidly, thus giving them greater reach. Armies were no longer limited to what they could forage from their immediate surroundings, removing the natural constraint on man and horsepower. Richard Trevithick's first steam locomotive had only come into service in 1804 and yet from that point and thereon for 100 years, the growth and expansion of the railway was phenomenal. It became a period of evolution, if not revolution, in how the expanding railroad could be used in attack and defence and in diplomacy to avoid war, or to deter would be aggressors.

The railway was used for its first significant movement of troops in 1846 when 14,500 Prussians were transported to attack Krakow. The Prussians had begun to understand the power of the railway in the concentration of force. Only four years later in October 1850 the Prussian's met their match during the Austro-Prussian conflict. The Austrians were able to mobilise and concentrate '75,000 men, 8,000 horses, 1,800 artillery pieces and 4,000 tons of supplies via a single track line from Hungary and Vienna to the Silesian frontier'.[5] This was achieved in only 26 days. This mobilisation by the Austrians was sufficient to dissuade the Prussians from hostile intent and for them to disengage. This became known as the Olmutz crisis, or the 'humiliation of Olmutz' and was the first example of the railway acting successfully as a deterrent for conflict. 'It also marked the birth of modern military transport and logistics'.[6]

The capabilities and opportunities of the railway in warfare and diplomacy were beginning to be understood by European powers. The next opportunity came with the Crimean War between 1853 and 1856. It was during this localised conflict, involving powerful global adversaries, that the value of the railway in sustaining a campaign was realised. The British built a short line between Balaclava, which was the main port, and Sevastopol which was besieged. 'At its peak it transported some 700 tons per diem. It proved vital in the allied logistics effort, bringing up heavy siege equipment'.[7] Russia switched onto the potential of the railway through the 'shock of the Crimean War'.[8] So, by 1860 a mere 45 years since Waterloo, the French, Prussians, Austro-Hungarians, Russians and British had all experienced warfare involving railways.

Railway developments across the globe

The power of the railway to unite, but also to incite, conflict within and between nations was becoming clear to those with the power to stimulate and finance rail expansion. 'As tracks expanded across countries they became a unifying force for nations, which in turn made conflict between them more likely since unification helped to forment nationalistic feelings'.[9] So on the one hand the railways created the conditions to enable control, but on the other they provided the means for subversion and revolution. The railways 'helped to spread revolutionary intent but made it easier to despatch the military to quell uprising'.[10]

It became clear that the railway had a key part to play in delivering imperial expansion and then protecting the acquired real estate. There was no railway in India in 1842 but the value of a developed system was such that by 1929 there were 41,000 miles. The railway network became synonymous with India and formed part of its protection. 'The superstructure of the Raj was bolted onto India's extensive railway network. The northwest frontier in turn, was defended by means of a series of strategic railways against the threat posed by Russian railways coming down from the Caspian Sea or Tashkent towards the Afghan and Persian borders.'[11]

It was not only in India that the British utilised the railway for strategic intent. 'The British Uganda railway (was) the one truly strategic railway project in tropical Africa. Control over the Uganda

5   Neilson, 10.
6   Neilson, 10.
7   Neilson, 10.
8   Neilson, 4.
9   Wolmar, C., *Engines of War: How Wars Were Won & Lost On The Railways*, xii.
10   Wolmar, 18.
11   Nielson, 8.

protectorate and the railway there was an integral part of British efforts to shield the Upper Nile Valley against the designs of other powers in order to keep British rule in Egypt on a firm footing'.[12]

The British were keen to defend their territories in the Sub-Continent and Africa and to expand elsewhere. Equally powers with Imperial ambition were keen to expand their stakes and their influence on areas which other nations considered to be their own backyards. This caused sensitivities and the potential for conflict and railway construction in such areas could be seen with aggressive intent. None more so than the proposed Berlin-Constantinople-Baghdad Railway which caused major tensions in relations between Germany, Britain and Russia. While Austro-Hungarian schemes for a line linking Bosnia with the Salonika railway caused frictions between Vienna and St Petersburg.[13] As Christian Wolmar said in *Engines of War*, 'that the heyday of the railways would also become the era of total war was no coincidence'.[14]

The American Civil War 1861–1865

It was the American Civil War between 1861 and 1865 where the railway had its first direct impact on the outcome of the war. The civil war was on an enormous scale, the North and the South fought across an area the size of Europe and within that area there were '10,000 military encounters of which 400 were serious enough to be deemed battles'.[15] The rail network across America was expansive, by the 1850s it was more than the rest of the world combined, and much of the network was concentrated in the North. The North used the railroad to move and concentrate troops more quickly than their opponents. The North also had a better understanding of logistics. 'Supplies were never to be forwarded until required and trains had to run to a schedule which they were not able to deviate even if they were half empty. The North had learnt that a delay in one part of the system almost invariably leads to holdups elsewhere. Priorities were established that 'the military should not interfere in running railways and that freight cars should be unloaded promptly'.[16] In stark contrast, the South did not have the same understanding of the war winning potential of the railroad: 'army officers were all too frequently ignorant of how delicately interlocked railroad operations were and consequently brought trains to a standstill amid chaos which might take days to sort out'.[17] The South lost.

Austro-Prussian War 1866

There followed a series of wars in 1864, 1866, and 1870–1871 on continental Europe that saw the art of railway logistics in supporting military ambition develop. The first war, the German-Danish war of 1864 occurred before the American Civil War had been concluded and the lessons of logistics management had not been fully applied by the attacking Germans; the name confusingly given to the Prussians and Austrians. The Germans mobilised 15,000 men and 4,600 horses in six days, but there was a considerable accumulation of victuals at the railheads which created inefficiency in the supply to the front lines. Although the mobilisation and concentration aspect of using railways in warfare had been successful, the ongoing re-supply had been a problem. The main stimulus to the development of railway logistics as a science was the chief of the Prussian General Staff, Field Marshall Helmuth von Moltke. Appointed in 1857 Moltke created a formidable central organisation tasked with developing staff processes and then rigidly applying those processes to battle. 'The use of railways would expedite mobilisation and deployment of the Army, and so optimise Prussia's chances of success'.[18]

---

12   Neilson, 8.
13   Neilson, 8.
14   Wolmar, 6.
15   Wolmar, 40.
16   Wolmar, 43.
17   Wolmar, 53.
18   Neilson, 11.

The Austro-Prussian War, also known as the German War of Unification, which followed in 1866 saw the side with the most extensive and organised railway network winning. The concentration of troops was completed within eight days. But despite Moltke's preparation and although the mobilisation was a success, there were still severe problems in respect to transportation. Supplies were rushed forward only to accumulate at railheads from where they could not be conveyed to the front lines. The railheads became blocked, the lines became blocked, goods rotted, and the Prussians overran their supply lines. But Moltke was able to combine his armies at the crucial moment giving him overwhelming force which achieved victory at Koniggratz.

Franco-Prussian War 1870–1871

The Prussians reappraised and by the next war with the French in 1870–1871 the Germans, as they had become, were determined to use the railway effectively. Learned from the experiences of the 1866 war were, the importance of co-ordination and the circulation of wagons to avoid trapped vehicles, and that there was a risk of congestion created by rushing stocks forward to the railheads only for them to block any onward distribution. 'If the German mobilisation was speedier and more efficient, the French had the better rail network. The French railways were better geared to war. There was a fuller integration of timetables; the lines were mostly double-track and had more rolling stock and faster trains. What logistical advantages could be derived from this were lost through the dispersal of the army.'[19]

Despite the advantages of the French, the Germans won the war, and a myth grew concerning the capabilities of Moltke's general staff. 'The 1870 war with France has often been described as the definitive event in rail warfare. The success of the highly trained and specialised Prussian general staff, Moltke's "demi gods", in speedily mobilising the troops and transporting them to the front created a legend, the "railway myth".'[20] Although the German plan was an improvement on their efforts in 1866 and built on their experiences still re-supply was chaotic, there was a shortage of rolling stock, wagons were not rotated efficiently with many stuck unproductive at railheads waiting to be unloaded. A lot of foodstuff rotted on vehicles at railheads. 'For all Moltke's emphasis on the railways, once the trains had disgorged their loads onto the battlefields, there was no more role for them. There was no proper transport and logistics co-ordination in the German army.'[21]

So, although the Germans won, the reason for their success was not in their skill in sustainment and wasn't especially in their abilities in mobilisation. It was because although France had a superior railway system their decision with respect to the strategic location of garrisons put themselves at a disadvantage when it came to warfare. 'The roots of France's defeat were political rather than military. Fear of domestic unrest persuaded Napoleon III to garrison regiments far away from their recruiting areas lest they be infected by local discontent.'[22]

Organisation of railways for maximum strategic advantage 1870–1890

'If the American Civil War was a first demonstration of military capabilities of the locomotive, it was the Prussian wars of 1866 and 1870–1871 that made the European Great Powers take note of railway warfare'.[23] There was a growing understanding of the power of the railway in providing military capability to mass, concentrate and supply forces. It was clear that in any future war the railway would proffer a major strategic advantage if logistics could be organised and co-ordinated.

---

19 Neilson, 12.
20 Neilson, 12.
21 Neilson, 13.
22 Neilson, 12.
23 Neilson, 11.

However, no side had yet mastered their planning. So began a railway-led arms race amongst the powers of Central Europe.

Laws enabling formal powers to control railways in wartime and to influence construction in peacetime were passed in Germany, France and Britain. In Germany in 1871 the constitution gave the military the right to supervise railway building and no new line could be built without the military general staff approving it. In the same year, in Britain, the Regulation of the Forces Act was passed. This Act was primarily concerned with increasing efficiency in the forces and modernisation. It was precipitated by Germany's victory over France and a belief that 'the Prussian system of professional soldiers with up-to-date weapons was far superior to the traditional system of gentlemen-soldiers that Britain used'.[24]

The so-called Cardwell Reforms made widespread and significant alterations to the Army. For instance, flogging was banned and the practice of purchasing commissions was ended. An important element of the Act, Section 19, gave the powerful right for the government to take control of the railway on mobilisation. A further act was passed in 1888, the National Defence Act, which gave the government the ability to prioritise shipments on the railway.

In Germany, Bismarck nationalised the Prussian Railway in 1879, better coordination with the military being one motive.[25] In so doing, it made 'the Prussian state the largest employer in Germany, responsible for some 700,000 people'.[26] This was important giving the military both greater control and certainty when it came to mobilisation. Additionally the workers of the nationalised industry were 'subject to almost military discipline and banned from trades union activities' which had a stabilising effect sociologically since as a direct result 'the railways also buttressed the existing political order in Imperial Germany'.[27] Meanwhile there was a growing realisation of the vulnerabilities of traditional fortifications and the opportunities derived by rail bound mobility. Moltke the elder, declaring 'build no more fortresses build railways'.[28] This was also recognised in France where, in 1885, General Derrecaigaix said 'a nation's first concern must be to cover its territory with a network of railways which will ensure the most rapid possible concentration.'[29]

Railway arms race

Railway expansion coincided with a growth in nationalism, of competition and fear between states, and rising territorial ambition. Nations continued working out how to utilise the railway to achieve their strategic and war aims. Increasingly wars involved the railway and new capabilities were learned which helped to sustain fighting. Railway construction also had the effect of adding to tensions between nations. The South African, or Boer, War of 1899–1901, was an expeditionary war and the railway was pivotal in providing the means for the Army to project inland from the base locations. Learning from earlier campaigns, the British in South Africa realised that to cover the large distances involved and to guarantee supply it was the railway that needed to control logistics and not the military. The lines of communication were poorly protected and vulnerable to Boer Kommando attack. In the Far East the extension of the Trans-Siberian railway made it possible for Russia and Japan to engage in warfare. The distances were such that until the railway was completed any significant conflict was impossible; as it was 'over one million men were transported over 5,500 miles of wasteland' during the Russo-Japanese war of 1904–05.[30]

---

24 Robert Ensor, *England, 1870-1914* (1936), 7-17. From Wikipedia.
25 Stevenson, D., War by timetable? The Railway Race Before 1914, Past & Present, No 162 (Feb.,1999), 163-194. – 171.
26 Neilson, 4.
27 Neilson, 4.
28 Stevenson, 173.
29 Stevenson, 174.
30 Wolmar, 111.

In Europe, where the rail network tripled in size between 1870 and 1914, Germany feared 'encirclement based upon the gradual driving together in agreements and alliances between France, Russia and Britain'.[31] As a result, and to combat this fear, the German railway network had grown rapidly. In 1850 there were only 115 miles of railway but by 1847 this had grown to 1,506 miles and by 1860 the mileage had doubled to 3,580. By the beginning of the Great War this would have grown to 22,744 miles.[32] The Russian railway network developed more slowly over a much bigger country and in 1861 extended only 1,408 miles, but after 1887 had grown to 17,776 miles. The growth rate over those years was much faster than the German network. The Germans were nervous of the Russians' intentions and 'the fact that three bursts of railway building activity coincided with periods of international tensions is suggestive of the strategic impetus behind Russia's railway programme'.[33] The Germans were also wholly suspicious of France's intent in funding the development and expansion of the Russian railway system. Especially as many of the lines being developed across this enormous country were in the west and directed towards Germany. 'Moltke described the Franco-Russia loan as "one of the most strategic blows that France has dealt us since the war of 1870–1871" and foresaw "a decisive turning point to Germany's disadvantage if France and Russian concentration becomes more simultaneous".'[34] The British also felt threatened, but by the German bankrolled ambitious proposal to create a Baghdad-Berlin railway it challenged Britain's supremacy in the east and the primacy of the British controlled Suez Canal as a trade route.[35]

The Germans, concerned with both French and Russian aspirations, considered the impact of fighting on more than one front (east and west). Of considerable importance was the ability to rapidly transport armies across Germany from east to west or vice versa, as well as the need for lateral movement north to south, effectively across the future fronts. The River Rhine was a natural barrier and fifteeen railway crossings were built. The Rhine crossings were linked by thirteen independent east-west routes and four north-south lateral routes across which armies could be transferred.[36] This network gave Germany a significant advantage over the French. According to Wolmar the funding of these crossings took precedent over all but the construction of battleships.[37] The French at the same time were developing their own railway mobilisation plans. Plan XVI of 1909 was reactive to German aggression and relied upon patience and then a combination of flexibility and speed. The plan was to wait until Germany was committed and their main axis was identified, then the French would manoeuvre to counter-strike at a point of weakness.[38] This plan was still not regarded as flexible enough by General Joffre who ordered plan XVII in 1911.[39] Railway construction continued at a pace. For many years prior to the outbreak of the Great War, both France and Germany constructed double tracks, flyovers, junctions, avoiding lines and sidings purely as contingency for future warfare.[40]

In 1870 there had been only thirteen routes from France and Germany to their common border. By 1913 this had increased to 29 with France having created sixteen and Germany thirteen. This number of routes could never be sustained by trade and was viewed in a mini Cold War as much a demonstration of hostile intent as the building of battleships. The historian David Stevenson concluded that this 'railway development was a precondition for the outbreak of war', and had it not been for its rail construction, Germany could not have contemplated risking a

31   Gilbert, M., First World War, 7.
32   Neilson, 3.
33   Neilson, 5.
34   Stevenson, 186.
35   Gilbert, 7.
36   Napier, C.S., Strategic Movement by Rail in 1914. Royal United Services Institution, Journal 80 (1935), 72.
37   Wolmar, 132.
38   Stevenson, 175.
39   Stevenson, 175.
40   Napier, 71.

war on two fronts and France could not have risked a re-run of the 1870 disaster.[41] So the railway construction made it possible for either side to consider engaging in a war.

In Britain, the Government had recognised the strategic potential of the railway in times of warfare, but the situation was different from mainland Europe. As an island nation, there was no brinksmanship of frontier dominance but the railway logistical challenge was in being able to transport Britain's then small volunteer army stationed at home anywhere across the island to counter the threat of invasion. Effective conveyance of soldiers obviated the need for thousands garrisoning empty coastline. As European conflict became more likely contingencies were developed and the railway company directors met government officials in secret to discuss ways that the rail fraternity could support the country in time of war. Somewhat surprisingly, despite the escalation in sabre rattling in mainland Europe, the War Office seemed slow in their contingency planning. It was only in 1911 that discussions were held with the War Railway Council regarding the potential of transporting the BEF to the continent.[42]

Lead up to war

The German military believed that once the French financed Russian railway construction passed a threshold, judged to be in 1916, then the balance of power would shift to Russia. Then it would be significantly more difficult, if not impossible, to defeat Russia when the railway lines were completed. Germany did not have the capacity to fight France and Russia concurrently but believed that if they could out mobilise France they could be swiftly defeated. Germany, using the new lateral rail corridors, would then swing her armies to the east and engage Russia. Time was of the essence because Germany considered they could not beat Russia if the Tsar's army had fully mobilised. Across mainland Europe there came to be a belief that a war-winning advantage would accrue to the side that mobilised and concentrated their army at key strategic positions most quickly. The railway, well prepared and organised and drilled, provided the means to achieve this advantage. In the environment of fear and distrust, intelligence agencies compared the capabilities of each other's networks and monitored construction and improvement, interpreting, and frequently misinterpreting and over-estimating capability.

As a result, detailed mounting plans were developed, probably driven in part to eliminate the failings of earlier railway mobilisation. These plans became so horrendously complex that once triggered there was little capacity to switch between a localised mobilisation and a general one. Meanwhile the military staffs were still trying to grapple with the discipline of railway logistics, trying to learn from the earlier conflicts and ensure that mistakes were not repeated in the event of war.

It became clear to the German military that the railway which was in quasi-military ownership would need to be carefully organised to ensure the effective and timely switch of forces from west to east. A mirror command system was initiated which came to the fore at the outbreak of war.[43] By 1914 the railway was divided into twenty-six line commands; each command headed by military and railway management. The 'apex of system was Eisenhahnabteilung (railway section) of the Prussian Great General Staff in Berlin' which was headed up by eighty staff officers. [44]

> 'Far from being unthinkable, continental war was viewed as a highly plausible, and by no means intolerable, outcome of international tensions. Europe had 20 million regular soldiers and reservists, and each nation developed plans for every contingency in which they might be deployed'.[45]

41   Stevenson, 190.
42   Stevenson, 171.
43   See Napier.
44   Stevenson, 172.
45   Hastings, M., *Catastrophe. Europe Goes to War 1914*, 26.

The Schlieffen plan

If the Germans were to invade France in a pre-emptive strike they had to consider where to do it. Much of the border was heavily fortified or the terrain was difficult and mountainous. The only gaps were where the French envisaged mounting a counter-strike and so to attack there would be a strategic folly. The only real option was to go around France. A plan was worked out by Field Marshall von Schlieffen who had taken over from Moltke as the Chief of the General Staff. The Plan, developed in secret in 1905, became known as the Schlieffen Plan, the invasion of Belgium designed to outflank the French defences, which would enable them to crush France before quickly switching their focus to the east. The Schlieffen Plan 'was the most important government document written in any country in the first decade of the twentieth century; it might be argued that it was to prove to be the most important official document of the last hundred years for what it caused to ensue on the field of battle'.[46]

Schlieffen's plan was to swing through Belgium then pivoting and moving to the south of Paris. The idea being to trap the French army in a pocket between their own fortress frontier and the advancing German army which would then close the gap where: 'they would be hammered in the rear on the anvil formed'.[47] Creating as John Keegan said, 'a great semi-circular pincer 400 miles in circumference, the jaws separated by 200 miles, (which) would close on the French army'.[48] Because of the imperative of then switching to defeat the Russians, Schlieffen wanted to avoid a 'wearing-out' war. His plan was clear: 'In the 42nd day since mobilisation the war in the west would be won.'[49]

The crux of Schlieffen's plan was the ability of the German railway to mobilise and concentrate the required number of troops, and then for sufficient troops to advance across Belgium and into France. But whilst the railway could mobilise sufficient numbers to the border and it was possible for troops to reach Paris in the allocated time, they would not be in sufficient number for victory unless 200,000 men advanced through Belgium. 'There was no room, his plan for a lightning victory was flawed at its heart.'[50] Although troops could be flooded into Belgium this 'would result in a useless traffic jam'.[51]

Schlieffen died in 1913 and Molkte's nephew took over as Chief of the General Staff. Some months later the assassination of Archduke Franz Ferdinand presented the opportunity for Germany to enact their war plan. Although war was not declared for another thirty-one days on, 1 August. The German railway-led mobilisation began on 6 August. 'This vast railway movement was a masterpiece of organisation, but when the deployment completed on 17 August, merged into the forward march, the friction of war soon revealed weaknesses in the German military machine and its control'.[52] Despite the flaws in the plan, the crossing of the Belgian border signalled the practical start of the World War and the unveiling of the Schlieffen plan, bringing Britain, who declared war on Germany on 4 August, into the war.

---

46   Keegan J., The First World War, 31.
47   Liddell Hart, B.H., *History Of The First World War*, 41.
48   Keegan, 34.
49   Keegan, 34.
50   Keegan, 39.
51   Keegan, 37.
52   Liddell Hart, 48.

The War

First railwaymen join the war effort

It was known that the British Army, even when including the 250,000 strong Territorial Army which had been extensively revamped a few years before, would be entirely insufficient for the industrial scale warfare likely, as large organised European armies clashed. A huge injection of manpower was required for Britain and the Empire to mount a successful war. Permission was soon given to create 'New Armies' of 100,000 men from volunteers aged between 18 and 30 (subsequently raised to 35). There was a terrific response and by the end of September there had been 761,000 volunteers and by 1915 some 145 infantry battalions, 70 artillery brigades, 48 engineer companies and 11 divisional artillery columns had been raised.[53]

Thousands of railwaymen responded to the call to arms in the first months of the war. Some were reservists or territorials, others volunteers. Amongst the first of those to volunteer was Sid Coles who had been a clerk in the stores account office at the London and North Western Railway (L & NWR) Wolverton works, 'There was an appeal for volunteers in August, most of the Wolverton boys were going into the Bucks battalion TA so I went with the Wolverton boys and was in within a fortnight'. [54] Hardie Henderson who had been a junior clerk in the Newcastle goods office learning the ropes of the business was 'caught up in the flow of human endeavour and found myself in a Drill Hall joining the Army the day after war was declared. I wanted to be there, the whole atmosphere of the company was so, I was just going along with the crowd'.[55] Coles found himself sleeping the following nights on the streets in Aylesbury along with many other volunteers until kitted out and then they moved on. Henderson, after a brief visit to the Drill Hall in Newcastle and attested into the 6th Northumberland Fusiliers, was sent with some new colleagues up to the stables of the Northumberland Hussars, spending two weeks feeding horses. The Army struggled initially to cope with the enormous spirit of national enthusiasm which was pressurising the recruiting Sergeants. But individuals were fashioned into soldiers and groups of men became platoons, as across the country men were training to 'words of command' so their battalions could take their place in the line. Up and down the country railwaymen like Coles and Henderson responded to their nation's initial call. Unlike many Coles and Henderson survived.

British railway companies

In 1907, the largest company in Britain was the General Post Office with 212,310 employees, but the second, third, fourth, fifth, sixth, seventh and ninth were all rail companies. Six railway companies in the top ten amounted to some 359,106 employees, L & NWR being the largest with 77,662, and nine companies in the top 20 totalled over half a million people.[56] The railway companies were both vertically and horizontally integrated, specialising not only in rail transportation but also ferry and omnibus operation. From the engineering perspective, the massive railway works of companies like the Great Western (GWR) at Swindon or the Midland at Derby, or L & NWR at Crewe, represented fully integrated complex and sophisticated factories capable of a massively wide range of engineering specialisms provided by a combination of a highly skilled technical workforce backed up by a plentiful supply of labour.

---

53   Carver, Field Marshall, Lord, *Britain's Army In The 20th Century*, 38.
54   IWM Sound Archive, 649, Sid Coles.
55   IWM Sound Archive, 11963, Hardie Henderson.
56   Jeremy, D.J., The Hundred Largest Employers in the United Kingdom, in Manufacturing and Non-Manufacturing Industries in 1907, 1935 and 1955. Business History 33 (1990-1991), 93-111.

The table below shows company size ranked by employees in 1907 and the amount who served, the percentage of the company size and the number who served.[57]

			Employees 1907	Served
1	GPO		212,310	75,000
2	London & North Western Railway	LNWR	77,662	31,744
3	Great Western Railway	GWR	70,014	25,460
4	Midland Railway	Midland	66,839	21,441
5	North East Railway	NER	47,980	18,339
6	Lancashire and Yorkshire Railway	L & Y	34,900	10,453
7	Fine Cotton Spinners		30,000	
9	Great Eastern Railway	GER	29,289	9,734
10	Royal Dockyards		25,580	
11	Great Central Railway	GCR	25,469	10,135
12	Armstrong Whitworth		25,000	

Contribution of railwaymen

As Hardie Henderson and Sid Coles were engaged in a significant period of training before Kitchener's armies deployed to the Front, the British Expeditionary Force (BEF), primarily made up of the regular army, were sent to France to engage the enemy. In the ranks were reservist soldiers who had pursued a career with the railway.

Amongst the first railwaymen to die was Private Fred Dale of 2nd Kings Own Scottish Borderers, from Newcastle who died on 23 August 1914. He had been a porter with North Eastern Railway (NER) at the Newcastle Forth goods yard. Amongst the last to die, on 11 November 1918, Armistice Day, was ex-Newcastle Forth clerk Henry Milburn serving with 2nd Seaforth Highlanders in Cambrai. The twenty-one-year-old had lived with his parents Joseph and Mary at 151 Rothbury Terrace, Heaton, Newcastle. In total over 180,000 men from railway companies enlisted (about the number of people currently employed in the rail industry). Between these two deaths and over four years over 20,000 railwaymen died. For 12,500 of the 20,000 the railway company, regiment and final resting place has been researched and this book is based upon those people. The vast majority, 11,200, were soldiers (of whom 8,500 were infantry, 67 cavalry, 878 artillerymen, 963 engineers and 143 medics) although there were also 500 sailors, 50 Royal Marines and 100 airmen. The numbers killed rose each year, peaking in 1918 at 3,500, nearly ten railwaymen killed for every day of the year. These numbers hide some pretty horrific days of battle, particularly the first day of the battle of the Somme on 1 July 1916, where at least 242 railwaymen were killed, although an insignificant number when compared against 59,000 British casualties on what remains the worst day of human carnage in British warfare. Over 1,800 died on the Somme, 1,800 at Ypres, over 800 in the hospitals in the rear

---

57 Ranked by the largest number of employees in UK manufacturing and non manufacturing industries in 1907
Numbers 1 = GPO 212,310.

zone of France, 69 died in Germany many of whom were prisoners, over a thousand died abroad, in Mesopotamia, Gallipoli, Palestine, Egypt, India, East Africa and even in Archangel in Russia. Nearly a thousand died in hospital in Britain or at home from wounds and some died in training.

Over 5,300 railwaymen were decorated, with at least seven Victoria Crosses (VC), 283 Military Crosses (MC), 2,517 Military Medals (MM), and many other medals and decorations being awarded to railwaymen from grateful nations. Given the size of the railway companies it seems unlikely that any other industry committed so many men to the British Army in the Great War.

The railway and railwaymen at home

Those railwaymen who were left at home continued to feed the war effort in a bewilderingly wide range of ways; from the operational railwaymen carting high quality coal from South Wales to the coaling stations across the country; to shipping millions of tons of munitions and logistic supplies, soldiers and sailors from one end of the country to another; and thousands of civilian workers to their employment supporting the war effort; to the engineering railwaymen building gun carriages, ambulance trains, vehicles, precision instruments, artillery fuses, and recycling millions of cartridge cases in the railway works.

The 12,500 upon whom this book is based

Railway employment

Nearly three quarters of the railwaymen came from forty roles, with; clerk (15.5%); porter (14%); labourer (10%); and cleaner (6%), amounting to 45% of all jobs.

There were many other trades or occupations in such a complicated industry as the railway. There were 34 horse lads, such as Leonard Edwards from GWR at Oxford who died on 17 April 1917 aged twenty-two serving with the Royal Army Medical Corps (RAMC). Twenty-eight blacksmiths, including Corporal Archibald Rudge from the Midland Railway at Bromsgrove who died serving with the 2/8th Worcesters in April 1918. Twenty-three timekeepers including Charles Cox from GWR at Bristol who died aged twenty-one whilst serving with the 8th Royal Berkshires. Fourteen chain horse lads, like A E Webb from Midland Railway's Northampton station, who died serving with the 4th Northamptons at Gaza. Charlie Harvie was a bill poster with the South Eastern and Chatham Railway (SECR) at New Cross but died serving with the 13th East Surrey's in 1917. John Booth, a key maker with the Lancashire and Yorkshire Railway (L & Y), died serving with the 8th Kings Royal Rifle Corps (KRRC). Donald Welham, a bolt maker with Great Eastern Railway (GER) at Stratford, died serving with 511 Field Company Royal Engineers (RE) in Ypres. Joseph Spriggs was a rough painter from 11 Station Terrace, Great Linford and worked at L & NWR's Wolverton works. He died serving with 7th Wiltshires in Salonika in April 1917. Leslie Burlton, who died serving with the 1st Royal Scots Fusiliers, had been a cleaner at the Hayes creosoting works. Amongst these unusual railway occupations there was also a cabinet maker, a French polisher, a screwer and a bottle washer, but the most unusual railwaymen were Basil Barker and William Turner. Both worked at Liverpool Street in the GER owned hotel as billiard markers. Walter had joined the Royal Field Artillery and was killed in January 1917 some five months before Basil who subsequently joined the 10th Londons. Both died aged twenty-one.

Work locations

A third of the railwaymen came from thirty-one locations, many were railway towns such as Derby, Swindon and York, or were large stations such as Sheffield or Bristol.

THE TOP JOBS IN THE 12,500

Clerk	1943	Striker	69
Porter	1750	Policeman	65
Labourer	1240	Loader	65
Cleaner (incl engine and carriage cleaners)	715	Wagon Repairer/Builder	64
		Sawyer/Carpenter/Joiner	62
Guards/Van guards	478	Carriage Washer	54
Fireman	368	Drayman	50
Platelayers	237	Greaser	50
Apprentice	195	Underman	49
Shunter	166	Telegraphist/Telephonist	49
Fitter	153	Ganger	47
Packer	152	Crane Driver	47
Machine Man	125	Boiler Maker	46
Car Man	119	Coal Man	46
Painter	102	Ticker Examiner	44
Number taker	86	Capstan Maker	44
Signalman	85	Sheet Dresser/Repairer	40
Carter	79	Trimmer	40
Messenger	77	Rullyman	40
Checker	71	Draughtsman	38
Coach Builder	71		
		74% of the 12,500	9221

NUMBERS OF WORKERS KILLED IN THE 12,500

1	Derby	441	17	Manchester	95
2	Swindon	428	18	Grimsby	94
3	Hull Station & Docks	263	19	Gateshead	91
4	York	212	20	Leeds	91
5	Birmingham	175	21	West Hartlepool	88
6	Darlington	165	22	Gorton	80
7	Crewe	157	23	Camden	80
8	Wolverton	144	24	Shildon	79
9	Newcastle	133	25	Nottingham	75
10	Bristol	131	26	London Marylebone	70
11	London Euston	131	27	Middlesborough	63
12	London Stratford	129	28	Newport	63
13	London St Pancras	114	29	Holyhead	61
14	London Bishopsgate	103	30	Reading	59
15	London Paddington	101	31	Wolverhampton	58
16	Sheffield	96			

Where they served

On land the units who lost most railwaymen included the 17th Northumberland Fusiliers, raised by the North Eastern Railway Company, the 1st, 2nd and 5th battalions of the Wiltshire Regiment, the 5th battalion Sherwood Foresters. At sea railwaymen served and died in many ships, including *HMS Aboukir*, *Cressy* and *Hogue* which were sunk by the same U-Boat within minutes; *HMS Good Hope* which was lost in the first defeat of the Royal Navy in nearly 100 years; and included capital ships at the Battle of Jutland, to minesweepers and submarines and patrol boats. In the Merchant Navy many of the railway's ferries continued plying their old routes as civilian non-combatants risking

German attack. Some were requisitioned and painted in grey, and others converted into temporary hospital ships. Twelve railway merchantmen met their end by torpedo, five were mined, one was captured, and three sunk in collisions one involving two ex-railway ferries. In the air over thirty railwaymen met their deaths from being shot down by the enemy, or in air accidents.

Ambulance trains being unloaded in France. NRM 1997–7059 HOR F 1752

PART ONE

STORY OF THE RAILWAYMEN AT WAR

CHAPTER TWO
ARMY RAILWAYMEN

The lions share of the railwaymen researched who died in the Great War, 94 per cent of the 12,500, served in the army, and 72 per cent of those served in the infantry.

Organisation of the British Army

By the end of the Great War there were five British armies fighting on the Western Front. Their make up varied over time and units were switched within armies and between armies. The construction of an army begins with the most basic unit, an infantry section.

The table below shows the hierarchy of an army. The fighting building block is the battalion, typically around 1,000 men at full strength.

An army would comprise something like 109 battalions, the current British Army amounts to some thirty battalions.

Battalions were created and recruited by regiments which were not, in the British Army at least, fighting entities but were administrative. A regiment would have a number of battalions. At the height of the Great War many regiments comprised over 20 battalions.

	Commander	Size
SECTION	Corporal	8–10 men
PLATOON	Second Lieutenant or Lieutenant	4 sections
COMPANY	Captain or Major	4 platoons
BATTALION	Lieutenant Colonel	4 companies
BRIGADE	Brigadier-General	4 battalions until winter 1917 then 3 battalions
DIVISION	Major-General	Usually 3 brigades
CORPS	Lieutenant-General	Usually 3 or 4 divisions
ARMY	General	Usually 4 corps

Ethos of the battalion

The role of an infantryman might be most simply described as to 'close with and destroy the enemy' (which is the US Marine Corps infantry squad motto), the most physical and bloody of roles requiring individual soldiers, where necessary, to sacrifice themselves for their mission, or more simply for their mates. Men fought, and continued to fight, for pride in their battalion. The British Army had been building *esprit de corps* for hundreds of years and in a uniform environment official elements of individualism which created identity were encouraged. Whether this was Battle Honours, uniform accoutrements acquired through heroic exploits over the centuries, or traditions acquired in similar ways. Battalions created battle winning individuality and identity which ultimately improved morale and gave men a staying power to persevere against all the odds. Even many 'New Army' battalions quickly created their own identities, often blending regimental tradition with idiosyncracies from their catchment. The Sherwood Foresters were proudly men from Nottinghamshire and Derbyshire, but the 5th Battalion was Derby's own battalion. Their identity was discrete from the other battalions, reflecting the social and employment mix of their host town. The 16th (Chatsworth Rifles) Sherwood Foresters, although formed in Derby, recruited mainly rural men from the north of the county, and the 17th Battalion (Welbeck Rangers) from the coalfields of north Nottinghamshire. Each battalion stressed both its similarity as part of the regimental family and its individuality which ensured a unique identity. The Army enhanced difference to build bonds. The rookie soldiers of the Kitchener battalions soon overlaid another dimension to their individual culture, that of the experience of combat. Almost despite the scale of carnage and loss, heroic stories were hardwired into the battalion psychy reinforcing that identity.

However, the cost of battle was such that by 1916 there was scarcely time to integrate new soldiers and build loyalty and a sense of brotherhood before the next battle drove the need to rebuild once more. The churn of men was enormous, some people lasted a few years, such as the Corporal in the Wiltshires who two years later was a Lieutenant Colonel in command of his battalion, nine ranks higher. But on the whole, a soldier's stay in a battalion was a short one before they were injured or killed. Many men were only slightly wounded, but by the time they returned to their battalion there may be few faces left that they recognised. Towards the end of the war, shortages resulted in soldiers being posted into battalions from other regiments. It wasn't rare for Scots to be posted into English County regiments, and cavalry regiments merged and their role changed. For example the South Nottinghamshire Hussars who fought most of the war on horseback in Palestine, were merged with the Warwickshire Yeomanry, transferred to the Machine Gun Corps and sent to the Western Front. But somehow the *esprit de corps*, characterised by a willingness to fight and die, seems to have been maintained, due at least in part to the fact that the average soldier was fighting not for the King, but for his mates, which was probably reason enough to fight.

Numbers of railwaymen in battalions

There is no way of knowing the precise number of railwaymen who served in any particular battalion but it is possible to estimate using a fairly simplistic yardstick. Overall 7.8 per cent of soldiers who served died (see page 295), but for railwaymen this was 11 per cent. The Great War statistics show that overall 2.37 times the number of people killed were injured. If it is accepted that say 10 per cent of the railwaymen who served in any particular battalion died then using the injured statistics it is possible to estimate the total number of railwaymen who both served and were injured. Of couse these are only rough approximations but serve to give a feel to the distribution of railwaymen within battalions.

Although many railwaymen were killed, many more endured the horror of war, survived, and returned to work with the railway, carrying with them their indelible memories, ultimately unless death intervened, until retirement sometime in the early 1960s. These figures suggest that in total nearly 50,000 railwaymen would have been injured, many of those would have made a full recovery and returned to the Front maybe to be wounded again or killed, but some incurred such crippling injury that when they returned home they never returned to the railway.

The selected battalions

In order to get a flavour of the experiences of the average railwaymen who served and died as

Numbers of railwaymen who died serving in battalions along with an estimate of the number who were injured and who served in those battalions.

		Killed	Estimate of served	Estimate of injured
17th	Northumberland Fusiliers (NER)	100	1,000	250
1st	Wiltshires	94	940	235
2nd	Wiltshires	68	680	170
5th	Wiltshires	57	570	140
5th	Sherwood Foresters	53	530	133
2nd	Kings Own Yorkshire Light Infantry	47	470	117
5th	Yorks and Lancaster	44	440	110
5th	Prince of Wales Own (W Yorks)	43	430	107
1st	Northamptonshire	42	420	105
1st	Grenadier Guards	41	410	103
4th	East Yorks	38	380	95
2nd	Essex	38	380	95
2nd	Grenadier Guards	38	380	95
96th	Light Railway Operating Company	37	370	93
2nd	Sherwood Foresters	37	370	93
1st	East Yorks	36	360	90
2nd	Oxfordshire & Buckinghamshire LI	36	360	90
2nd	Prince of Wales Own (W Yorks)	36	360	90
1st	Rifle Brigade	35	350	87
15th	Durham LI	34	340	85

infantry soldiers, six battalions, selected by the high number of railwaymen who died serving with them, are examined. The 1st and 2nd Wiltshires and the 1st and 2nd Northamptonshires along with the 5th Sherwood Foresters. The most populus battalion in terms of railwaymen who died in the Great War was the 17th Northumberland Fusiliers, a specialist 'pioneer' battalion, and their wartime experiences are quite different from the line infantry battalions. The experiences of the 5th Wiltshires is considered separately, from setting sail in 1915 bound for Gallipoli, until their return long after the war had ended. The aim is to follow the battalions throughout the war even though there are tracts of time when no railwaymen died, which may have indicated that they were lucky or that there were no railwaymen serving. An impression of the horrendous wastage rates is quickly gained as time and again battalions cease to exist as fit soldiers were turned into mass casualties.

In order to give an appreciation of the breadth of experiences of the railway soldiers some consideration is also given to military railway operations on the Western Front and the part the railway played in the Palestine operations (chapter 4), and to complete the picture a brief overview is made of the campaigns in Gallipoli, Mesopotamia, Salonika and Archangel (chapter 3).

The remainder of this chapter charts the activities of the six battalions, through the battles of the war on the Western Front. It tries to capture the essence of the time in major battles, and in the relative quiet times and to place those railwaymen who were killed. The picture is built up both from an analysis of the rolls of honour and the battalion war diaries, and subsequent accounts of the battle. In no way does this attempt to represent a history of the war although a lot of effort has been expended in trying to ensure that there are no glaring errors. It is important to remember that when the subject battalions were engaged they were always one of many, and at one point there were over 500 battalions on the Western Front. Hopefully, if nothing else, this work captures what the railwaymen, and indeed any other soldier, volunteer or otherwise, encountered and embraced in their war service.

Six battalions on the Western Front 1914–1918

1914

Mobilisation

Central to the Germans' mobilisation was activating their railway war plan. Soon after war was declared at the beginning of August 1914, the German railway network was dealing with unprecedented numbers at the start of the long planned mass build up. Some pre-positioning of rolling stock had begun prior to the declaration of war, and within hours full troop trains were on the move to the frontier. The German network carried two million troops, 118,000 horses and 400,000 tons of stores in the first twenty days of mobilisation. The thirteen key lines carried 660 trains per day over the first five days. The busiest bridge was in Cologne which experienced 2,150 mobilisation trains over 16 days in August, which was a train every ten minutes.[1] By the time the mobilisation was properly under way control of the German railway network had transferred directly to the Army Supreme Headquarters as planned.

In Britain, the regular battalions such as the 1st Wiltshires would have been busy with contingency planning in the lead up to war being declared. Training would have been ramped up and platoon NCOs, with a renewed sense of purpose, would be refreshing the drills of their sections, the officers would be involved in all aspects of organisation and preparation, pre-empting possible deployments, studying maps and thinking around the specifics of any likely conflict. The quartermaster would be demanding supplies and the adjutant filling manpower shortages from other battalions, or the mobilisation of territorials or reservists who would need to be rapidly integrated into a cohesive entity ready to deliver any task ordered.

The Call to Arms

Amongst the first to mobilise were Charles Kibblewhite, Percy Ricketts and Henry Jeffries, labourers at the Swindon Railway Works; William Manners a helper at the boilermakers workshop; George Tompkins a machineman from the wheel workshop; George Sawyer a stationary engine driver; and Thomas Porter a labourer at the carpenters workshop. These men along with colleagues Frank Parsons, H G Mildenhall and James Haines would have left the massive engineering works built to service the Great Western Railway. Possibly they fell in together at the work gates wearing their working clothes and marched, like the servicemen they had once been and would very shortly be again, out of the works, with cheers from their mates and applause from the bosses, maybe meeting up with Fred Weeks and H C Lawrence railway porters in Swindon. Proud men, with heads held high, mobilising with the 1st Wiltshires on 4 August and by the 13th they were in France and they would all be dead within weeks.

---

1   Napier, 82.

C Kibblewhite
Labourer
Swindon

Percy Ricketts
Labourer
Swindon

Henry Jeffries
Labourer
Swindon

George Sawyer
Engine driver
Swindon

H C Laurence
Porter
Swindon

Fred Weeks
Porter
Swindon

Another ex-railwayman, Thomas Painting, was in France by the 12 August with 3rd Kings Royal Rifle Corps (KRRC). He had left school aged eleven and a half and worked for WH Smith and Sons at a bookstall at Lichfield Trent Valley station, his father was a permanent way inspector.

Aged fourteen and a half he had moved into proper railway employment as a cart boy at Birmingham New Street before becoming a porter at Chester Road station between Birmingham and Sutton Coldfield. Seeking adventure he joined the army from the railway in 1907. Painting survived the war and was interviewed by the Imperial War Museum, his recollection sheds light on these early difficult weeks of the war.

The hastily prepared 3rd KRRC spent a few days in France before they marched towards battle. They had some administration to attend to, including the purchase of handkerchiefs.

'The commanding officer said we were not allowed to have white handkerchiefs so that we couldn't put up the white flag. We had to go and buy a red handkerchief.'[2]

'On the morning of the 21 August we started to march up to Mons, scorching hot. And the marching was terrible. The French roads were these cobbles, terrible to march on and as straight as a die. You could see for miles in front of you. The road seemed endless, very trying marching. We got up to Mons, about eleven o'clock in the morning on a scorching hot day. And we were told to take up out positions to the right of Mons… We dug some trenches there. And a battery of artillery, 70 Battery RFA were on a ridge to our front.'[3]

Slowing the advance the 1st Wiltshires and 1st Northamptons at Mons, Belgium

First contact was at Mons, Belgium, where battle began at 0830 on the 23 August, just two weeks after the first of 80,000 BEF troops had landed in France. By mid-afternoon the first battalions such as the 1st Royal West Kents, 1st Royal Scots Fusiliers and 2nd Kings Own Scottish Borderers, had been in contact and were withdrawing and the first railwaymen were dead. Fred Dale a thirty-year-old married man from the 2nd Kings Own Scottish Borderers who had been employed by the NER at Newcastle Forth; Lance Corporal Charles Hogg from the 1st Royal Scots Fusiliers, who had been a stableman with the L&NWR based in Euston; and Private Edwin Gomm, from the 4th Royal Fusiliers, who, aged thirty-five, had been with the GWR loco depot at Southall, was killed. As were William Valentine a former GER labourer at the Stratford Loco Depot and William Wilson, a former GER police constable from Liverpool Street both from the Royal West Kent's. They are commemorated on La Ferte memorial and were among 1,600 allied casualties that day. Less than a month after William Wilson died, his brother J T Wilson, serving with 2nd Oxfordshire

2   IWM Sound Archive, 212, Thomas Painting MBE MM.
3   IWM Sound Archive, 212, Thomas Painting.

and Buckinghamshire Light Infantry, was killed. Thomas and Emma Wilson of 25 Haildon Street, Homerton, London, would have been one of the first of the many to mourn their son's ultimate sacrifice.

William Valentine
GER

William Wilson
GER

Fred Dale
NER

The first British railwaymen had been killed in action, but so too had the first German railwaymen. Wilhelm Terwei, from the Westphalian town of Coesfeld was killed on 23 August. The following day one of his colleagues August Hummelt, an infantry corporal was injured and he died on 29 October (see page 300).

The men of the 3rd Kings Royal Rifle Corps were lucky. The nearby gun battery was engaged by the enemy who knocked out three of the guns but 'the gunners was jolly good. They crawled from one gun to the other and kept them going. And one gun that was knocked out they got in action again. And they were jolly good. We didn't get any infantry attack. We didn't get any rifle fire. Well we did but we didn't actually have to fire at them. You see, we got shelled at Mons, but nothing serious. The main attack came in on the left of the army'[4]

Only a few kilometres apart to the south of Mons, positioned to take on the battle as the first depleted battalions such as the 3rd Kings Royal Rifle Corps withdrew, were 1st Wiltshires and 1st Northamptons. The 1st Wiltshires had been furiously digging shell scrapes, hollows in the ground a soldier could lie in, knowing that they would be next to be engaged. Soon artillery rounds were falling around them. They would dig a lot more and be bombarded a lot more over the next four years. Bombardment helped focus the mind, there was a much higher chance of surviving artillery if you were dug in, and had some overhead cover. Infantrymen became good at digging. Further to the south-east the Northamptons could hear gunfire, but apart from that it was all quiet.

The following day the 1st Wiltshires were left as a rear guard as the retreat from Mons began, they took their first casualties, among four killed was Private Kibblewhite from Purton, Wiltshire, who just a few weeks before had marched out of the GWR Swindon works. In the same action the Wiltshires commanding officer had his horse shot from under him[5], and probably learnt that this wasn't the sort of war where sitting on a horse would assist his longevity; and after only one day in action the brigade commander was promoted to Major General, there was nothing like a bit of warfare to help promotion prospects. The Northamptons saw no action, but as they withdrew were caught up with streams of evacuating refugees and, due to a staff planning error causing massive congestion, it took twelve hours to march just fourteen miles.

The British troops kept falling back whilst fighting in an attempt to slow the enemy down. Units were out of place and the defence was disorganised. The Wiltshires and Northamptons were just two of many battalions, alternating between marching, establishing hasty defences, preparing to move and then marching again. The officers trying to find out what is going on but information was limited, incomplete, and often contradictory. The reservists, such as the ex-railwaymen, can hardly have been integrated into their platoons in the four weeks or so since mobilisation, but were expected to have acclimatised to the challenges of infanteering, trudging for many miles in heavy boots, short periods of intense fighting with bullet and bayonet, and long periods of sleep deprivation. It must have been tough enough for the hardened regulars, but even for men who were used to a

4   IWM Sound Archive, 212, Thomas Painting.
5   War Diary of the 1st Battalion Wiltshire Regiment August 1914 – May 1919, 2.

tough and physical factory life this was completely different. On 25 August, Thomas Painting with the 3rd Kings Royal Rifle Corps saw his first French troops: 'The cavalry were there with their cuirasses (metal armour worn around the chest) on, plumed helmets, the infantry with the red trousers, blue long jacket, wearing their war medals, going into war. They got pretty well shot up'.[6] It wasn't going to be a war of bright smart uniform and medal ribbons.

Trading space for time, blunting the enemy vanguard, the defence at Le Cateau

A more organised defence was needed, if only to improve morale. There was a thin line between withdrawing, a preferred military term, and retreating. Performance of an infanteer would hardly be enhanced by the perception that the enemy were getting the upper hand. The chosen defence line was between Le Cateau to Cambrai and here on 26 August it was hoped that the Germans could be stopped. Despite over 7,000 British casualties the Germans only conceded a slight delay. The Wiltshires, fighting midway between Le Cateau and Cambrai, suffered nearly 100 casualties, before they along with the rest of the British, were withdrawing again, throughout the rest of August.

The Northampton's account illustrates the conditions which were probably similar across the BEF stating 'weather very hot. Burning sun. Men are exhausted but marching well. Rations none too plentiful. Very little sleep'.[7] The Northamptons felt the stresses of continual reaction to a powerful enemy, retreating but not engaging. The regimental history recorded the feeling on 1 September: 'here we felt as if we're at last cornered and trapped, for we heard the guns firing from what seemed all around us... this continual retirement without fighting is undermining the morale of the men, making them lifeless and depressed'.[8] It is also recorded that the men were 'ragged, footsore, bearded, dirty and unkempt, gaunt-eyed through lack of sleep...' and the narrative continues, '... but upheld by that invincible spirit which is the glory of the British race'.[9] Whilst other battalions engaged in bloody, yet heroic, deeds this battalion has been tasked with nothing but retreat and psychologically that must have been damaging. The Wiltshires too had slogged, 220 miles in a little over two weeks, but they had been engaged in two of the opening actions of the war.

The first soldier of the Northamptons killed had been detailed to look after the battalion greatcoats in a village held by the French. When Germans attacked the French withdrew but escape was blocked by a machine gun, Private A Little was one of a group who stormed the machine gun, and was killed. Presumably the greatcoats were lost.

Pushed back to the Marne, and halting the enemy

In early September in the vicinity of the River Marne the French attacked the weak German flank giving the BEF the chance to about turn and help force the Germans back north as far as the River Aisne. Finally on 10 September the Northampton's made contact with the enemy for the first time, attacking a village called Priez, which cost them three men killed and 25 wounded, but their morale was strengthened because they had fought. The Germans withdrew to the east of the River Aisne selecting positions to put the attackers at a double disadvantage of attacking strongly defended positions uphill and having to resupply across a river which could be engaged by the enemy, demonstrating early in the war the German skill of making the best tactical use of ground.

On 13 September the Northamptons attacked a sugar factory on the outskirts of Troyon and suffered 105 casualties including Private Arthur Neville, the first railwaymen from the battalion to die. He had been employed by the Midland Railway as a boiler washer at Wellingborough. There

---

6   IWM Sound Archive, 212, Thomas Painting.
7   The Northamptonshire Regiment. 1914-1919, 22.
8   Northamptons, 24.
9   Northamptons, 24.

Map 1. The Western Front of the BEF

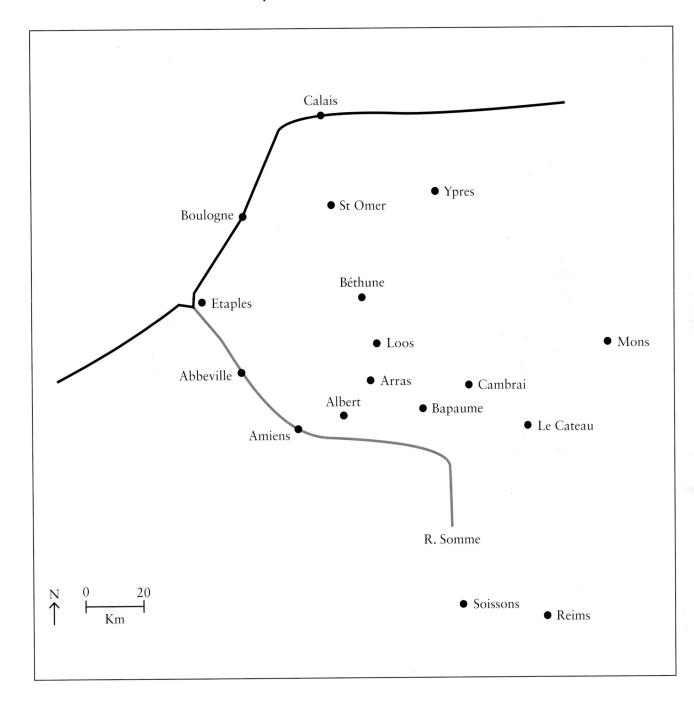

were at least six other railwaymen, all from the 2nd Kings Royal Rifle Corps, fighting alongside the Northamptons, killed in the same action.

Name	Rank	Btn	Regt	CWGC	Age	Rail Co	Location	Role
Walter Bedingham	Rfn	2nd	KRRC	La Ferte	30	LB&SCR		Sheeter
Joseph Ramsdell	Rfn	2nd	KRRC	La Ferte	35	Midland	Derby	Platers helper
Charles Raymond	Cpl	2nd	KRRC	La Ferte	32	SECR		Planer
Henry Remon	Rfn	2nd	KRRC	La Ferte		L&NWR	Broad St	Goods Porter
Henry Sutton	Sgt	2nd	KRRC	La Ferte	28	GCR	Annesley	

The Northamptons had to defend their position a few days later with a bayonet charge which although successful resulted in 161 casualties including at least three railwaymen.

William Bartlett	Pte	1st	Northamptons	La Ferte	L&NWR	Wolverton	Labourer
Arthur Mayes	L/Cpl	1st	Northamptons	La Ferte	Midland	Mansfield Woodhse	Porter
George Theobald	Pte	1st	Northamptons	La Ferte	Midland	Bedford	Labourer

Redeployed north, the 1st Wiltshires at Neuve Chapelle

Relieved on 21 September after a day of fighting near Soissons, the 1st Wiltshires were transported by rail, lorry, and a lot on foot, with little recovery time, until they deployed north of Bethune on 12 October. They occupied a number of trench positions eventually finding themselves caught up in the fighting at nearby Neuve Chapelle where they remained for the rest of October. When the battalion were relieved only five Officers and 200 men marched into the billets, 237 were injured, 157 missing and 71 killed. Amongst those killed were at least 16 railwaymen most from GWR, with one from SECR.

George Tompkins	Pte	1st	Wiltshires	Le Touret	Gt Western	Swindon	Machineman No18 Shop
George Sawyer	Pte	1st	Wiltshires	Le Touret	Gt Western	Swindon	Stationary Engine Driver
William Butcher	Pte	1st	Wiltshires	Le Touret	Gt Western	Wilton	Porter
William Manners	L/Cpl	1st	Wiltshires	Le Touret	Gt Western	Swindon	Helper V Shop
Percy Ricketts	Sgt	1st	Wiltshires	Le Touret	Gt Western	Swindon	Labourer
Frederick Weeks	Pte	1st	Wiltshires	Ration Farm	Gt Western	Swindon	Porter
H Lawrence	Pte	1st	Wiltshires	Le Touret	Gt Western	Swindon	Porter
Allen Massey	Pte	1st	Wiltshires	Le Touret	Gt Western	Birkenhead	Checker

Herbert Andrews	Sgt	1st	Wiltshires	Le Touret	Gt Western	West Drayton	Signalman
James Haines	Pte	1st	Wiltshires	Le Touret	Gt Western	Swindon	
Henry Jeffries	Pte	1st	Wiltshires	Le Touret	Gt Western	Swindon	Labourer
Stephen Pullen	Pte	1st	Wiltshires	Le Touret	Gt Western	SECR	Porter
Thomas Porter	Pte	1st	Wiltshires	Le Touret	Gt Western	Swindon	Labourer No 12 Shop
Arthur Crook	Pte	1st	Wiltshires	Le Touret	Gt Western	Swindon	Machineman
Ernest Castle	Pte	1st	Wiltshires	Le Touret	Gt Western	Landore	Examiner
Frank Parsons	Pte	1st	Wiltshires	Le Touret	Gt Western	Swindon	
Steven Pullen	Pte	1st	Wiltshires	Le Touret	SECR		Goods Porter

H C Sawyer *W B Butcher* *P T Ricketts* *F Weeks* *H R Jeffries* *A Massey* *G Sawyer* *W F G Manners*

First Battle of Ypres – 1st and 2nd Wiltshires, 1st Northamptons

The 2nd Wiltshires arrived at Zeebrugge in early October, spent two weeks marching to Ostend, but were forced backwards by the Germans, fighting, withdrawing, skirmishing, until Ypres. At Ypres the battalion was for a short time on the offensive pushing eastwards towards Menin. On 17 October to the east of Polygon Wood they experienced a prolonged attack during which Private Marchant, a thirty-four-year-old boilersmith's helper from GWR in Swindon, became the first railwaymen in the battalion to die. When it became clear that a German Corps was approaching from the east, 2nd Wiltshires were ordered to withdraw and to prepare defensive positions. By the 21st the battalion was under sustained attack and heavy artillery bombardment, they gained some protection from their trenches and were able to stop the hoards of Germans from over-running their positions. They had no telephone communications with headquarters and relied on runners for passing information. Often the information wasn't passed and the runner was never seen again. Gradually the battalion's fighting strength was reduced as the German onslaught continued. Eventually a runner got through and in a lull in the fighting on 23 October reinforcements were sent forward. The 300 Welsh Fusiliers who arrived at the dangerously exposed position were a needed boost. The Welsh had been sent forward without shovels and since they couldn't dig in and shovels couldn't be found they were then withdrawn. On the 24th, as the bombardment increased in intensity and accuracy, the Germans outflanked the battalion, attacked from the rear and overwhelmed them. The commanding officer and many others were captured, and the battalion strength reduced from 1,100 to only 450. Amongst those killed were Privates Chandler and Newton.

| Samuel Chandler | Pte | 2nd | Wiltshires | 24 | 10 | 14 | 21 | Menin Gate | Gt Western | Plymouth | Fireman |
| Sidney Newton | Pte | 2nd | Wiltshires | 24 | 10 | 14 | 33 | Menin Gate | Gt Western | Westbury | Shunter |

S Newton

W Patient

Only two platoons could be mustered compared to 12 a few days before. As the battle depleted, 2nd Battalion marched to the rear passing their sister battalion bound for the front. It is hard to imagine how the troops of the fighting strength 1st Battalion felt as they passed.

To the north of the Wiltshires and north of Ypres, on 21 October, the 1st Northamptons had been ordered to recapture a prominent mill and inn near the village of Pilchem. The mill was soon recaptured, but despite numerous attacks the inn did not fall. The battalion were also withdrawn on the 24th having suffered over 150 casualties including Private William Patient, a carriage washer from GER Stratford who was killed.

Thomas Painting and the 3rd Kings Royal Rifle Corps had fallen back with the withdrawal and whilst 1st Northamptons were fighting at Pilchem they were in support at nearby Passchendaele. On the 23rd they were sent up to Pilchem but Painting reports, 'we didn't have to do much' in contrast to the Northampton's experience just days before. At Polygon Wood on the 26th, after one particular action, Painting recalled: 'one of our sergeants, Sergeant Stott, he had 14 bullets through his clothes and he wasn't touched'.[10]

The British pulled back to Ypres, in what became the 1st Battle of Ypres, forced on the defensive, anxious to halt the German advance and consolidate their fragile positions, and so trench warfare began. The 3rd Kings Royal Rifle Corps were just one of the battalions trying to hold the line, and on the 27th they attacked from Zonnebeke ridge towards Passchendaele. 'We advanced a thousand yards under shellfire. Gerry then opened up with everything he could turn out. In my own platoon, which was fifty men, only seventeen of us got across. The others were all dead.'[11] The survivors managed to reach the German trenches which they occupied and attempted to defend. Casualties mounted but Painting recalls a particularly serious incident: 'The rations had come up. I got four canteens of rum one for each section, one canteen had a bullet hole in and we didn't know. We had to have a short rum ration. That was a very serious casualty that was'.[12] They held the trenches for four days until they were forced to withdraw on the 31 October, but not before they had been exposed to heavy and accurate shellfire: 'we had very heavy shelling and Gerry hit my platoon four times one morning with heavy shells. The first one hit the trench, blew it in. The last one found me at home. It blew the platoon's ammunition sky high, smashed my rifle in front of me, buried me in the trench, but didn't hurt me. They came and dug me out and what grieved me was my rations had gone.'[13] Only seven men of the platoon of 50 who had left Polygon Wood made it back, and they were almost immediately sent out to hold trenches along the Menin Road. Painting's seven men were quickly reduced to four. Painting was captured and made a prisoner of war.

To the south of the Wiltshires' former positions were the 1st Northamptons who took up defences on 30 October. They were soon forced into Shrewsbury Wood which they held, fighting off German attacks until relieved four days later. Another 100 men were casualties including three former railwaymen killed.

Charles Dove	Pte	1st	Northamptons	Menin Gate	Midland	Traffic	Peterborough	Boiler washer
Samuel Colburn	Pte	1st	Northamptons	Menin Gate	Midland	Goods	Leicester	Porter
Charles Cole	Sgt	1st	Northamptons	Menin Gate	Midland	Traffic	Chesterfield	Porter

10   IWM Sound Archive, 212, Thomas Painting.
11   IWM Sound Archive, 212, Thomas Painting.
12   IWM Sound Archive, 212, Thomas Painting.
13   IWM Sound Archive, 212, Thomas Painting.

By 5 November, 1st Wiltshires were alternating in and out of the line in the area around Ypres. Four or five days in the front line trench system and a similar amount doing labouring duties or getting some 'rest'. There wasn't much rest to be had. The periods of trench warfare, though static, involved much fighting, with a steady attrition rate of injured and killed. The 17 November, for example, involved the Germans shelling the trenchline then making an assault on the position. This was repelled with a bayonet charge which killed many of the enemy but the Wiltshires lost 11 killed, 5 railwaymen, and 15 wounded.

Charles Harman	Pte	1st	Wiltshires	Menin Gate	Gt Western	Swindon	Helper V Shop
Henry Penny	Pte	1st	Wiltshires	Menin Gate	Gt Western	Sheffield (Midland)	Drayman
Nelson Provis	Pte	1st	Wiltshires	Menin Gate	Gt Western	Swindon	Labourer
Lionel Coole	Pte	1st	Wiltshires	Menin Gate	Gt Western	Swindon	Apprentice (aged 18)
H E Slater		1st	Wiltshires	La Laiterie	Gt Western	Paddington	Pantry Boy

C Harman

On 9 November, the 1st Northamptons were moved to Polygon Wood and whilst advancing through the wood many were killed by heavy rifle and machine gun fire including the commanding officer and most of the officers. They had a torrid time in the wood, and on the 15 November when they were withdrawn, the battalion numbered only 350. Meanwhile their sister battalion, 2nd Northamptons, arrived in France on 5 November after a long trip from Egypt.

N Provis

Name	Rank		Unit	Died			Age	Place	Company	Location	Job
Walter Foskett	Pte	1st	Northamptons	9	11	14	28	Boulogne C	L & NWR	Kenton	Porter
Herbert Northfield	Pte	1st	Northamptons	10	11	14		Menin Gate	L & NWR	Peterborough	Underman
Thomas Johnson	Pte	1st	Northamptons	12	11	14	32	Boulogne	Midland	Belper	Labourer
Archie Shakeshaft	Pte	1st	Northamptons	12	11	14	25	Menin Gate	L & NWR	Wolverton	Labourer

The 2nd Wiltshires were quickly rebuilt, new drafts arrived, soldiers recovered from wounds, and officer resupply was resolved by the expediency of promoting fifty Privates from the 28th London Regiment and dispersing them across the brigade as 2nd Lieutenants, seemingly without too much training! The battalion were back in the trenches by the 8 November, after only two weeks, at Ploegsteert, or as the Tommy's called it 'Plug Street' where every three or four days they were relieved at the Front to spend a few days in shelters in the rear before returning for another few days in the sodden, muddy, miserable ground.

The First Battle of Ypres ended in the middle of November by which time the 1st and 2nd Wiltshires had each lost over 500 men and the 1st Northamptons over 650, the British 60,000.

The 1st Northamptons returned to the Front in style on 21 December in a fleet of London buses bound for Le Touret, to the north of Lens, where they immediately effected a night counter attack on completely unknown ground to re-capture some trenches. They were promptly withdrawn then committed to another fight only a few hours later, and two railwaymen were killed.

Richard Huntley	Pte	1st	Northamptons	Le Touret	Midland	Kettering	Labourer
George Maycock	Pte	1st	Northamptons	Le Touret	GCR	Woodford	Relayer

MENIN GATE

The Menin Gate in Ypres bears the names of more than 54,000 soldiers whose graves are not known. There are at least 589 railwaymen commemorated on the memorial, buried in graves of unknown soldiers, or their bodies smashed into unidentifiable parts by the incessant artillery fire, or simply lost in the mud and filth.

The first Christmas in the trenches

As Christmas approached the four battalions were in the line. Private Slater of 1st Wiltshires, a pantry boy from Paddington, was killed on Christmas Eve. Christmas Day for the 1st Wiltshires was spent in the trenches at Kemmel, near Ypres. The war diary states: 'In trenches. A thick fog all day. Practically no shelling on either side, but a little sniping in the trenches' [14] and 'Owing to the moonlight a good deal of difficulty in relieving fire trenches. Cold. Two killed, one wounded, one missing.'[15] A miserable festive season for those who thought it would all be over by Christmas. 2nd Wiltshires were also in the line. The Germans opposite them placed Christmas trees on their

14 1 Wiltshires War Diary, 23.
15 1 Wiltshires War Diary, 23.

trench parapets, complete with candles. The Wiltshiremen, clearly not quite in the Christmas mood, honed their marksmanship skills by taking pot shots at the candles. The Germans could be heard singing carols.[16] The 2nd Northamptons were in trenches in the Armentieres sector and the Germans precipitated a truce by chanting 'Play the game, play the game. If you don't shoot we won't shoot'.[17] In contrast, the 1st Northamptons spent the 25th out of the line and enjoyed a Christmas meal and a brief respite. For them war was temporarily suspended. Private Sawford, a former Midland wagon lifter from Wellingborough, died at home on Christmas Day, wounded in the earlier campaign, and is buried in Earls Barton in Northamptonshire. For the 2nd Wiltshires, Boxing Day began foggily and soldiers clambered out of their trenches with spades to make repairs. The fog lifted suddenly exposing troops from both sides involved in the same activity. Curiosity and the season of goodwill resulted in troops meeting, a truce was agreed and British and German alike took the opportunity to bury their dead who had been lost in No Man's Land.[18] The goodwill lasted until New Year's Eve when shots were fired further along the line. On New Year's Eve Private Christopher Hillier from 1st Wiltshires, a hydraulic forgemans assistant from Swindon, died.

The railwaymen occupying the trenches at the close of 1914 were largely reservists or territorials. Already a good number had been killed or wounded. You can only wonder of the hopes and wishes of the soldiers on both sides as they sheltered in their trenches from the elements as much as the enemy and pondered what the future might hold.

17th NORTHUMBERLAND FUSILIERS

Meanwhile, back at home another battalion full of railwaymen was in training. Not yet exposed to the horrors of the war.

The 17th Battalion Northumberland Fusiliers was, apart from the Post Office Rifles, the only battalion set up by a single company, the North Eastern Railway Company. It seems odd that they weren't formed into a specialist Royal Engineers Railway Regiment, but perhaps this was due to what must have been the pretty chaotic nature of army expansion in August 1914. The sheer scale of organisation and administration required must have been enormous. Regiments across the army were frantically forming new battalions. The number of battalions of Northumberland Fusiliers doubled in less than a month hence when the NER were granted permission to form a battalion they were given the number 17. The company management had already lost 2,000 keen men eager to serve the colours, and they thought that their workforce should be given the opportunity to serve together. Whether this was due to paternalistic or patriotic motivations is unclear, but within days there were over 3,000 volunteers.

Housing the expanding army was a tremendous problem, but not for this battalion, they used the warehousing at the recently opened NER owned King George Dock in Hull where the first detachment arrived on 22 September. The battalion then entered a long period of training for what was to be their specialist role, one of pioneer battalion to an infantry division.

The role of pioneers was to engage in general labouring tasks in support of infantry operations; often dangerous work carried out in contact with the enemy. Tasks involved digging; building or removing obstacles; improving roadways; demolition tasks; in fact anything which the commander on the ground needed to support the mission. Frequently this involved working as infantry soldiers, either in self defence, or to provide additional support in tight situations. Typically pioneers were expected to be jack of all trades and experts at them all.

16   1 Wiltshires War Diary, 27.
17   Northamptons, 74.
18   Scott Shepherd, W., The Second Battalion Wiltshire Regiment (99th) A record of their fight in the Great War, 1914-1918, 28.

1915

Winter trenches

What the immediate future held was more of the same, the old routine, alternating in and out of wet, muddy, cold and depressing trenches. The 1st Northamptons occupied trenches just a couple of miles from their sister battalion the 2nd Northamptons who had been in and out since early November soon after they had landed in France. The men of 1st Northamptons had had a miserable time with sickness and trench foot, and their adjutant wrote that wellington boots were great, so long as the mud wasn't too deep, but often it was, and then the best footware was waders.[19] Morale was high though in the 2nd Wiltshires despite their trenches being completely flooded, because they were working a four day shift system; they were up to full strength and because home leave was being granted. Being up to full strength made a tremendous difference. The number of fatigues and guard duties were the same but at half strength they came around twice as fast. So did the requirements for fighting patrols or wire cutting sorties into No Man's Land. The superstitious soldier had reason to think that the more squaddies there were the greater their likelihood of surviving.

In February 1915, the 5th Sherwood Foresters, a Territorial Army battalion from Derby, arrived in France. They had been mobilised immediately on war breaking out and many of their soldiers came from the Midland Railway's Derby Works.

Neuve Chapelle – 2nd Wiltshires and 2nd Northamptons

The first British offensive of the war took place at Neuve Chapelle on 10 March. The 2nd Northamptons attacked hard for little reward and received many casualties. The 2nd Wiltshires, one of many battalions that followed on in the afternoon, also experienced heavy casualties but made some headway and captured a German trench, only to be ousted and forced to capture it again the next day. By which time the situation was confused with sections, platoons and companies from different battalions mixed up together whilst fighting the enemy. Fighting continued until the 14th when the British worked out that they had insufficient artillery to achieve a breakthrough. The 2nd Wiltshires suffered 285 casualties, including 19 officers, of which 56 were killed. The 2nd Northamptons lost 414 of the 600 who started the battle, including 17 of their 19 officers. Less than two weeks later, 2nd Wiltshires were again in the forward trenches where they stayed until the end of March, when they could at last rebuild.

George Dangerfield	Pte	2nd Northamptons	14	3	15	21	Le Touret	Midland	Wellingborough	Labourer
Charles Smart	Pte	2nd Northamptons	14	3	15	21	Le Touret	Midland	Kettering	Labourer
Walter Watts	Pte	2nd Northamptons	14	3	15	21	Le Touret	GER	Continental steamers	Steward
Ernest Goldsborough	L/Cpl	2nd Wiltshires	10	3	15		Le Touret	Gt Western	Bristol	Fireman
Sidney Chanter	L/Cpl	2nd Wiltshires	11	3	15	25	Le Touret	Gt Western	Swindon	Machinist
Herbert Crocker	Pte	2nd Wiltshires	12	3	15	25	Le Touret	Gt Western	West London J	Porter
Albert Crook	Pte	2nd Wiltshires	12	3	15	17	Le Touret	Gt Western	Swindon	
Frederick Escott	Pte	2nd Wiltshires	12	3	15	21	Le Touret	Gt Western	Chippenham	Labourer
Edward Townsend	Sgt	2nd Wiltshires	12	3	15	27	Le Touret	Gt Western	Swindon	Forgemans Help
Thomas Gray	L/Cpl	2nd Wiltshires	13	3	15		Le Touret	Gt Western	Swindon	13 Shop

19 Northamptons, 80.

T C Gray   A Corbett   H Crocker   S Chanter   E A Townsend   F Escott   E Goldborough   W A Watts

2nd Battle of Ypres – 5th Sherwood Foresters, 22 April – 25 May

Since First Ypres ended it had been pretty calm in what was now called the Ypres Salient. Calm, but not quiet, with both sides engaged in 'aggressive patrolling' with a good number of Germans and British leaping out of their trenches to remind the other side they were still out there and with aggressive intent. Usually it meant returning with somewhat fewer soldiers than they started with. But sometimes there was success and information gained for no casualties. Each side maintained an uneasy routine without going on the offensive.

The 1st Wiltshires spent from late November until late March alternating in and out of the trenches, in their case around Kemmel, except for one day when they attacked a strongpoint at a place called Spanbroek Molen. The attack was unsuccessful and the battalion returned to their routine, having incurred 93 casualties including six railwaymen.

Herbert Lock	Pte	1st Wiltshires	12	3	15	32	La Laiterie	L & SWR		Shunter
Ernest Moulden		1st Wiltshires	12	3	15	41	Menin Gate	Gt Western	Swindon	Clerk
George Rainer	L/Cpl	1st Wiltshires	12	3	15	19	La Laiterie	GER	Bishopsgate	Clerk
Walter Shakespeare	Cpl	1st Wiltshires	12	3	15	20	Menin Gate	Gt Western	Swindon	Apprentice Boilermaker
W J Short	Pte	1st Wiltshires	12	3	15		La Laiterie	L & SWR		
Maynard Summers	L/Cpl	1st Wiltshires	12	3	15	27	Menin Gate	Gt Western	Swindon	Labourer

E G Moulden

The quiet routine changed on 22 April when the Germans attacked in force and used their new horror weapon, poison gas, in large quantities. Since the gas was heavier than air it tended to sink into the bottom of the trenches to asphyxiate those cowering at the bottom, so if you stood still, manned your parapet, stayed calm, you had more of a chance, there again you might have been hit by a bullet!

The only one of the featured battalions to be involved in the 2nd Battle of Ypres was the 5th Sherwood Foresters and their part was limited mainly to 26 being injured and four killed when the Germans detonated a mine below their positions. Although the battle petered out on 25 May having achieved a good many casualties and little else, the 5th Sherwood Foresters remained in the salient to hold the line for a further four months of comparative calm, but still the casualty rate ticked over.

W Shakespeare

SPECIAL BRIGADE ROYAL ENGINEERS

The cryptically named Special Brigade of the Royal Engineers specialised in poisoning the enemy by gas. Chemists and scientists on both sides devised ever more effective poison gases and more industrial means of delivery. Phosgene, unlike chlorine, could be inhaled for some time without awareness of damage, but when symptoms showed it was too late. The allies mixed chlorine and phosgene and called it 'White Star'.

At least 12 railwaymen served in the Special Brigade and all died in cemeteries behind the lines indicating they died of wounds. The horrific thought is that some of them might have accidentally gassed themselves.

Richard Moon	Cpl	25	6	16	29	Bertrancourt	L & SWR		
A V Garwood	Cpl	28	6	16	24	Le Fermont	GER	Ponders End	Booking Clerk
Frederick Lewis	Pnr	6	7	16		Vermelles	Barry Rail		Loco Fireman
George Hales	Pte	11	8	16	23	Etaples	L & NWR	Whitchurch	Booking Clerk
E Godfrey	Spr	17	8	16	22	Adanac	GCR	Sheffield	Clerk
Francis Sanderson	Lt	1	9	16	23	Heilly Station	GER	Stratford, Chemical Lab	
J C Beech	Pnr	17	4	17		Etaples	L & NWR	Walsall	Goods Porter
George Hall	Pte	6	5	17	27	Beaulencourt	Midland	Derby	Porter
George Hall	Spr	6	5	17	27	Beaulencourt	L & NWR	Crewe	Fitter
Robert Careswell	L/Cpl	15	11	17		Steenkerke	L & NWR	Camden	Clerk
S C Brown	Pnr	27	5	18		Longuenesse	SECR		Fireman
Walter Renshaw	Pnr	11	8	18	31	Pernois	L & Y		
C A Proud	Cpl	13	11	18		St Sever	L & NWR	Crewe	Draughtsman

Aubers Ridge, 9-15 May – 1st Northamptons

Whilst the Germans were still committed to their attack at Ypres, a little to the south and just a short way from Neuve Chapelle, an artillery bombardment on 9 May initiated the British attack on Aubers Ridge and signalled to the Germans that the British were coming. The infantrymen were expecting a 'devastating' artillery attack'[20] but after only 50 minutes the artillery lifted at just the point that the infantrymen went over the top. The 1st and 2nd Northamptons were confident and morale was high. The two battalions went over the top in different sectors but they suffered the same fate, they were mown down by German machine guns. Some of the 2nd Northamptons made the German trenches, but most of the attackers were killed or died in No Man's Land. Many other battalions suffered the same fate. The 'devastating artillery attack' didn't happen, as there was a critical shortage of shells.[21] Many of the injured were trapped until nightfall and fell prey to German marksmen. As night fell stragglers made their way back to the British trenches, stretcher bearers and private soldiers

20   There was a shortage of artillery at Aubers Ridge but it seems that the men of the 1st Northampton's were 'in good spirits and eager for the coming battle. Hopes ran high especially as regards the expected devastating effects of our heavy artillery'. Northamptons, 106.

21   1st and 2nd Northampton's suffered almost the worst casualty figures in the attack, only 2nd Rifle Brigade fared worse than 2nd Northamptons. The Northamptonshire Regiment account states 'the lives of many brave men were thrown away because the artillery preparation for this assault was insufficient,112. The artillery failure at Aubers Ridge resulted in the 'Shell Crisis' which precipitated the downfall of Asquith's government. See http://www.bbc.co.uk/news/mobile/magazine-17011607 for example.

alike took enormous risks bringing back injured comrades, and some died trying. The cost of the days fighting was: the 1st Northamptons had eight officers killed, including the last original officer who landed in France only ten months before, and nine wounded, with 540 casualties amongst the other ranks; of 2nd Northamptons 887 at the start of the day, 426 had been killed or wounded.[22] Although only a small proportion of the total, there were at least 17 railwaymen killed in the battle of Aubers Ridge. Because of the churn of soldiers since landing in France it is likely that many of these soldiers were not professional soldiers or ex-professionals on the reserve, but were Territorials or some of the first of Kitchener's volunteers.

Arthur Bird	Pte	1st	Northamptons		Le Touret	L & NWR	Northampton	Labourer
William Dolby	L/Cpl	1st	Northamptons	39	Le Touret	Midland	Peterborough	Labourer
Harry Haywood	Sgt	1st	Northamptons		Le Touret	LB & SCR		Constable
Frank Horne	L/Cpl	1st	Northamptons	21	Le Touret	GER	Continental steamers	Steward
James Letts	Sgt	1st	Northamptons	30	Le Touret	L & NWR	Rugby	Labourer
Thomas Mayes	Pte	1st	Northamptons		Le Touret	Midland	Kettering	Labourer
Cyril Ward	Sgt	1st	Northamptons	26	Rue-Petillon	L & NWR	Crewe	
Phillip Wright	Pte	1st	Northamptons	20	Le Touret	Midland	Kettering	Labourer
Percy Capon	Cpl	2nd	Northamptons	21	Ploegsteert	Midland	Wellingborough	Labourer
Albert Davis	Pte	2nd	Northamptons	26	Ploegsteert	L & NWR	Coventry	Fuelman
Joseph Hancock	Pte	2nd	Northamptons		Ploegsteert	Midland	Rushden	Porter
Ralph Murby	Pte	2nd	Northamptons		Ploegsteert	Midland	Wellingborough	Cleaner
Charles Pridham	L/Cpl	2nd	Northamptons		Ploegsteert	Midland	Kettering	Passed cleaner
Robert Kidman	Pte	1st	Northamptons	20	Bethune	GER	Steamers	Steward
Albert Spring	Pte	1st	Northamptons	28	Longuenesse	L & NWR	Bletchley	Labourer
Albert Pittam	Pte	1st	Northamptons	27	Chocques	L & NWR	Wolverton	Labourer

RC Kidman

Charles Reed

F H Horne

Festubert, 17-20th May – 2nd Wiltshires

As the attack at Aubers Ridge ended, ten kilometres away battalions massed to attack Festubert. 2nd Wiltshires were committed on 17 May, the second day of battle, just as the fine weather changed to rain and flooding made the going very difficult. The soldiers struggled across the open ground, fighting the enemy and the elements, and were halted by rifle and machine gun fire. The battle lasted three days with little or no gain. 2nd Wiltshires, by no means the worst affected battalion, still suffered 21 killed, at least four railwaymen, and 137 injured.

---

22   Northamptons, 118.

Henry Lynn	2nd	Wiltshires	Le Touret	Gt Western	Swindon	Labourer No 23 Shop
Bertrand Manners	2nd	Wiltshires	Le Touret	Gt Western	Swindon	Frame Builders Assistant
Isaac Watts	2nd	Wiltshires	Le Touret	Gt Western	Swindon	
Thomas Speed	2nd	Wiltshires	Le Touret	GCR	Ardwick	Loader

H T Lynn

Only three weeks later on 15 June, the 2nd Wiltshires, reinforced back to 1,000 men, were in a battle a mile south of Festubert at Givenchy. Surprise was compromised because the Germans had been able to tap into the allied telephone system and knew precisely when the attack was to happen.[23] The script seems to have been similar to many other battalions in many other battles. Courageous and heroic men attacked established German positions with men being cut to ribbons. The battalion was withdrawn after nightfall. Amongst the many to die in this abortive attack were at least four railwaymen from the GWR Works at Swindon.

Gilbert Dadge	Pte	2nd	Wiltshires	Le Touret	21	Smiths Apprentice
Percy Matthews	Pte	2nd	Wiltshires	Le Touret		Boilersmith V Shop
James Sims	Pte	2nd	Wiltshires	Le Touret	39	Striker No 14 Shop
Francis Wilkins	Pte	2nd	Wiltshires	Le Touret	28	Frame Builders Assistant

J W Sims

Ypres – 1st Wiltshires and 5th Sherwood Foresters

F J Wilkins

The 1st Wiltshires, near Ypres, in contrast had been having a comparatively quiet time with trench routine continuing, although Private Nelson Sprules from GWR at Swindon, and Private Sidney Clark, a draughtsman with SECR, were killed in the 'normal' business of trench warfare. All this was to change on the 16 and 17 June when the Wiltshires were involved in an attack on German trenches at Bellewaarde to the East of Ypres. The attack failed and cost 1st Wiltshires over 200 killed, wounded or missing. A follow up attack on the 22nd also failed and resulted in 26 further casualties.

P C Matthews

Francis Swansborough	Pte	1st	Wiltshires	Menin Gate	Swindon	
James Cole	Pte	1st	Wiltshires	Menin Gate	Swindon	Forgemans Assistant
Cecil Lang	Pte	1st	Wiltshires	Menin Gate	Swindon	Coach Builder
William Leggett	Pte	1st	Wiltshires	Menin Gate	Swindon	Coach Body Maker
Thomas Long	Pte	1st	Wiltshires	Menin Gate	Swindon	Labourer
Stanley Matthews	Pte	1st	Wiltshires	Menin Gate	Swindon	Forgemans Assistant
Harry Walton	Pte	1st	Wiltshires	Menin Gate	Swindon	Apprentice Boilermaker
Frank Newman	Pte	1st	Wiltshires	Menin Gate	Cardiff	Carriage Cleaner

F Newman

---

23   2nd Wiltshires, 45.

Around 1,500 metres from where 1st Wiltshires had been fighting was Sanctuary Wood, and on the 30 July the 5th Sherwood Foresters were one of many battalions dug in when the Germans mounted a fierce attack. The brunt of the attack was on the 8th Rifle Brigade, who suffered 488 casualties, with the Germans using flamethrowers for the first time. At least ten railwaymen died including three from the 8th Rifle Brigade – George Coley a boiler maker with L&NWR at Rugby, Arthur Gainford a loco cleaner from Barry Railway in South Wales, and Robert Marshall a 'case hardener' from GCR in Gorton. Two Sherwood Foresters from the Nottingham raised 7th Battalion died – C Clark and J Pottinger, who both worked in Nottingham, one for GCR and the other for Midland.

By contrast, the 2nd Wiltshires enjoyed a few weeks of mid-summer calm during some fine summer weather billeted in St Omer as the General Headquarters Reserve and then a few more weeks in a quiet section of trench-line. They even arranged a football match with 6th Wiltshires.[24]

Loos, 25 September – 8 October – 1st Northamptons and 2nd Wiltshires

The terrain around Loos was different to what the British had fought over so far, an industrial landscape dominated by slag heaps, headstocks and miners cottages with small settlements, fields and rivers interspersed. The 1st Northamptons were in the middle of this mining area, centred around a double set of headstocks called 'the Pylons' and two large slag heaps riddled with tunnels, trenchworks and strongpoints. The Battle of Loos began on 25 September and after four days of intense artillery bombardment 1st Northamptons began their attack. Gas released in support of the allied attack drifted back over their position, collected in hollow ground along the axis of advance effectively stalling the attack as the Northamptons were compelled to 'lie down in the open'[25] and subsequently suffered considerable loss. In this action Captain Montray Reed of the Northamptons won the VC, he was gassed and died in action. As the Regimental History of the Northamptonshire Regiment puts it 'Thus fell a gallant sportsman, and his death was one which every soldier can envy'.[26] You have to wonder whether this statement was truly reflective on what every soldier thought at the time. The Northamptons achieved the objective and dug in.

To the north-west of Loos was the demolished village of Vermelles around which 2nd Wiltshires had occupied positions since 9 September. The battalion did not feature in the initial attack. As battle commenced they slowly edged forward along crowded communication trenches loaded down with the extra paraphernalia required in the assault – ammunition, rations, water, bombs, flags, flares, wire cutters, picks and shovels. Eventually 2nd Wiltshires were committed to the fight and were soon into the former German front line trenches. Initially protected by a rise in the land, they soon cleared the hill top and were then fully exposed to German rifle and machine gun fire. They continued to advance as men were hit and fell. Eventually the attack petered out leaving the battalion in disarray and dead and wounded scattered along the forward edge of the hillside. Stretcher bearers and others were later to do a tremendous job in recovering many. Those still fighting, of whom just a few had reached a German emplacement, had to be hastily reorganised into an effective formation to move forward. Early on the following day the commanding officer had a quick 'shufti' with his binoculars, in order to assess the situation, and was promptly shot in the chest and killed. That night through wet, muddy and shell-damaged land, in complete darkness, and subject to ongoing artillery fire, 2nd Wiltshires were redeployed. Confusion reigned, but eventually positions were established. After more days of continuous rain and artillery bombardment the battalion were withdrawn on 1 October. They had suffered 415 casualties in five days, including at least eight railwaymen.

24   Wiltshires, 47.
25   Northamptons, 128.
26   Northamptons, 129.

The Northamptons similarly had paid a high price, they had dug in and withstood a number of counter attacks and held their ground until withdrawn on the 28 September. They lost 372 men.

Name	Rank	Bn	Regiment				Age	Battle	Railway	Station	Occupation
Joseph McMahon	Pte	2nd	Wiltshires	29	9	15		Loos	GER		Fitters Labourer
Thomas Leach	Pte	2nd	Wiltshires	26	9	15	20	Loos	Gt Western	Corsham	Porter
Arthur Selby	Pte	2nd	Wiltshires	26	9	15	35	Loos	Gt Western	Swindon	Fitters Labourer
John Vickery	L/Cpl	2nd	Wiltshires	26	9	15		Loos	Gt Western	Swindon	21A Carriage shop
Charles Whetham	Pte	2nd	Wiltshires	26	9	15	23	Loos	Gt Western	Swindon	Wagon Painter
Bert Winchurst	Pte	2nd	Wiltshires	26	9	15	19	Loos	Gt Western	Swindon	Labourer
William Joyce	Pte	2nd	Wiltshires	27	9	15	21	Loos	Gt Western	Swindon	Labourer
Charles Wiggall	Pte	2nd	Wiltshires	28	9	15		Loos	Gt Western	Swindon	Ass Examiner
Arthur Gregory	Pte	1st	Northamptons	25	9	15		Loos	Midland	Elmton & Creswell	Porter
Henry Pearson	Pte	1st	Northamptons	25	9	15		Loos	GCR	New Holland	Brakesman

Thomas Leech

F Wiggall

A H Selby

Ernest Thomson

After the battle the divisional commander, a Major General, spoke to the 2nd Wiltshires about their conduct. He made reference to their 'fine attack' on the 25th, that was the one which cost an enormous amount in manpower and achieved virtually nothing. He went on to say that: 'you were ordered to attack, and you advanced... in a straight line....' and that 'the only way to win is for everyone to be absolutely determined to go on, quite irrespectve of casualties'.[27]

5th Sherwood Foresters at Hohenzollern Redoubt

The men of the 5th Sherwood Foresters were well used to collieries, head stocks and slag heaps, many of them coming from a mining area, but probably had not anticipated attacking a fortified strong point built into one. Luckily the battalion only had a supporting part to play as the Midlanders from the 46th Division attacked Fosse 8 slag heap and the strong point known as The Hohenzollern Redoubt. The Division suffered 3,763 casualties when they attacked on 13 October, most within ten minutes of the start, but this was not a short engagement, those who survived fought hand to hand for over eighteen hours. But the attack failed and nothing, apart from wholesale carnage, was achieved. 6th North Staffords incurred 505 casualties mostly within metres of their trench-line, and the 5th South Staffords 319 casualties. Four battalions of the Lincolns and Leicesters suffered 64 officer casualties and 1,476 men. At least 25 railwaymen were killed but none were from the 5th Sherwood Foresters.

---

27 2nd Wiltshires, 61.

Map 2. North of Arras – Neuve Chapelle, Festubert, Loos

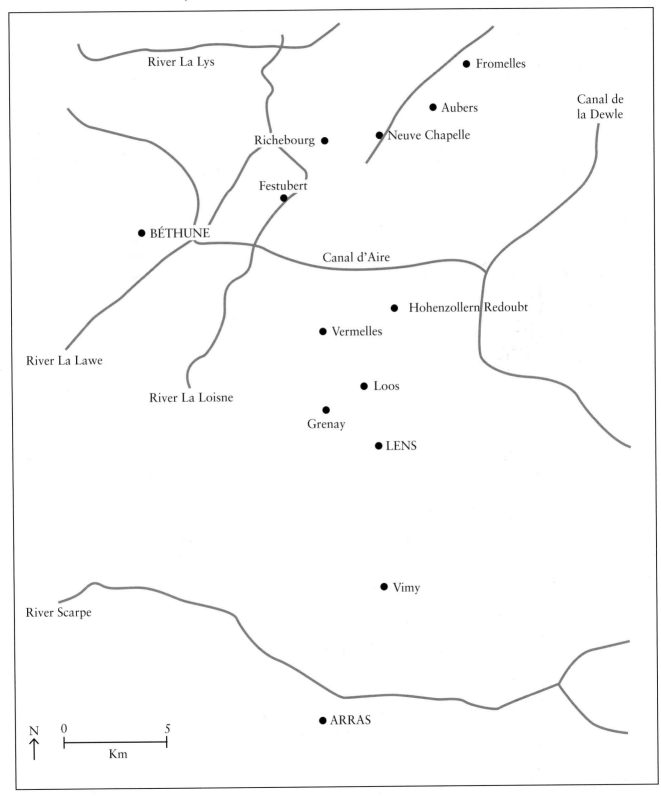

On 28 October the King inspected troops in a large ploughed field and shortly after inspecting the Sherwood Foresters he fell from his horse and was badly injured.

A second winter

Soon winter set in once again and the war of attrition was against the wet and cold as much as the Germans, as the troops alternated in and out of the trenches. For the 2nd Wiltshires their sick list was so long and the conditions so poor, that the periods of time in the trenches was shortened. They spent Christmas out of the line. The 1st Wiltshires spent the last months of 1915 at Ploegsteert and Christmas in the trenches, the war diary stating: 'the enemy was quiet all day' and 'the repair and drainage of trenches was carried out as usual'.[28] The 1st Northamptons in the now quiet Loos sector, spent Christmas in the trenches. The 2nd Northamptons also spent Christmas in the trenches, they had had a 'quiet' time since their mauling at Aubers Ridge in May and had spent time in and out of the line for nearly six months.

New Year for 1st Wiltshires was celebrated out of the line, and with the battalion being able to take a bath and enjoy a Christmas Dinner, but by the 3rd it was back to trenches of 'Plug Street'. The 5th Sherwood Foresters had been located very close to the enemy at Richbourg, just west of Neuve Chapelle, so close that there were frequent conversations between the sides. Morale would have improved when news spread that there was the prospect to escape the misery of mud and freezing conditions for the warmth of Africa, possibly bound for Gallipoli. December was spent out of the trenches and after a prolonged period at the Front the field cashiers were kept busy paying the Derby men their back pay, funding a hedonistic night or two on a 'run ashore' in Marseilles and all that the city could offer.

17th NORTHUMBERLAND FUSILIERS

The battalion began work as divisional pioneers on the 2 December. Teddy Marsden, who had worked at Hull West station, became the first fatality, killed by artillery on 23 December.

1916

On 2 January 1916, 17th Northumberland Fusiliers began work as a pioneer battalion in the Somme area working on engineering tasks in preparation for the 'big push' which included clearing and deepening trenches, building roadways, trench tramways and strengthening revetments. On the 26 January a shell landed in a communications trench killing five. Privates Lamming, a porter from Hull, Willans, an assistant signaller aged nineteen from Ferry Hill, Hodgson, a joiner from York, Reid a parcels porter from Newcastle, and a Private Swainson. On 5 February Corporal Sid Wade, aged twenty-five and a former joiner from Hull, was killed.

Hodgson   *Willans*   *Wade*   *Lamming*   *Swainson*   *Reid*

---

28   1ˢᵗ Wiltshires War Diary, 61.

2nd Wiltshires were also on the Somme holding trenches at Maricourt. The weather was miserably wet and cold and one company of the four was kept in billets in order to minimise weather related casualties, which was causing as much problem as the enemy (although usually of a less severe nature, the soldiers rarely died from trench foot or colds, but could die from complications associated with the conditions). But at least it was comparatively quiet since neither side were motivated for warfare when mere survival against the elements was tough enough.

The 1st Northamptons avoided some of the worst of the weather by being out of the line for a 'rest', this was a misnomer since even in peacetime the army doesn't 'rest'. During 'rest' battalions were constantly sending soldiers on fatigues or working parties. Whilst time in the line was characterised by dangerous patrols of No Man's Land, time spent out of the line involved a whole range of back-breaking tasks – digging, repairing and carrying. Yet, during this time, the soldiers relished these tasks because they got the blood pumping through the system, and the body, and particularly the feet, were warm. Standing around in trenches for hours and days caused the feet to rot, trench foot was rife, while hard physical work led to a functioning body. 'Rest' also meant training, and a bit of 'bull', and often some parading for the 'brass hats'. But it was a rest from vermin, lice, mud, enemy, cold, rain and putrid rotting flesh. By late February they were back in the trenches, in a different part of the Loos sector, and this time in the trenches on the slag heaps.

The men of the 5th Sherwood Foresters along with 46th Division had no such worries, they were located in the comparatively warm south of France waiting embarkation for Egypt. Some battalions reached Egypt by mid-January 1916 but pretty well instantly were 'about turned' and returned to France. The evacuation of Gallipoli meant that fewer troops were required in Egypt. The 5th Sherwood Foresters got no further than Marseilles and enjoyed an extended vacation. A good time was had by all and the war diary reports that on 31 January the battalion paraded for a VD inspection although the results are unknown.[29] By early February they were back in the battle area, initially training in the rear area of the Somme before being sent to Arras where they spent most of March and April, before returning to the Somme.

On 5 March the 2nd Wiltshires left Maricourt and marched through deep snow to the rear. B Company were sent to do some work on a light railway, and this must have been a welcome 'busman's holiday' to the railwaymen of the battalion. March and April were spent on fatigue duties, typically this involved hard manual work, often digging trenches, carrying defence stores such as corrugated iron, iron stakes and barbed wire towards the Front. As part of the preparation for the Battle of the Somme, over 7,000 miles of telephone cable were buried six feet below ground in order to protect the communications from artillery shell fire.[30] This was dug by hand by labour battalions and infantry battalions such as the Wiltshires.

By late April the 1st Wiltshires, who had spent the early part of the year training, had deployed, and like the 1st Northamptons were in the mining area of Loos, where they spent their longest trench stint of the war at 15 days, which cost 14 killed and 63 wounded. Private Cox a GCR relayer from Woodford Halse was killed on 31 May and Private Frank Althorpe, a cleaner with the Midland at Kettering, on the 20 June. According to Corrigan 'a battalion could expect, on average, to spend ten days a month in the trenches'.[31] So the 1st Northamptons had experienced a long duty in the trench line. This could have been in the fire trenches or in the second line support or reserve trench systems. According to Corrigan, 'There can be no doubt that regular rotation, never keeping men in the post of most danger for more than a few days at a time, made a very significant contribution to the fact that the British Army, alone amongst the major forces on the Western Front, never suffered a collapse of morale. Their time in the front line was short enough for them to see relief in sight'.[32]

29   The National Archives WO95/2695/1 War Diary 5th Sherwood Foresters.
30   Prior, R., & Wilson, T., Command On The Western Front. The Military Career Of Sir Henry Rawlinson 1914-1918, 156.
31   Corrigan, G., Mud, Blood and Poppycock. Britain and The First World War, 88.
32   Corrigan, 93.

Build up to the Battle of the Somme

The Somme campaign, a joint British and French attack, was planned in meticulous detail down to individual minutes of the enormous five-day barrage of 200,000 shells, and the detonation of a number of huge underground mines in the final sixty minutes before the assault. This was followed by the attack from 13 British divisions between Gommecourt in the north and Maricourt in the south, and the French Army further south.

Amongst the many battalions, artillery brigades, engineers and medical units who were establishing within the Somme area, were the 17th Northumberland Fusiliers who had spent February in Albert tasked with maintaining and improving the Somme roads and trackways. One Platoon was detached to nearby Corbie to work on a railway line for a time, which must have been a welcome relief and a reminder of times passed. On 15 March, Private Chatt, a gangman from Barnard Castle, was killed. On the 3 April one company working with a railway contruction company laid over a mile of broad gauge railway in a single day. On 7 May three Sergeants visited the Dorset Regiment to learn trench routine and were injured, a good indoctrination into trench reality. Private Brown, a 'reliefman' from Gateshead, was killed on 14 May whilst out wiring in No Man's Land.

In early May, 2nd Wiltshires were back in the Somme in the same portion of the line that they had left in the snow, alternating between the trenches and billets until they were withdrawn in early June to rehearse for the coming offensive. During this time precise attacks were practiced by everyone in the battalion. All drills were rehearsed again and again so that everyone was clear on the role they would have to play; so meticulous was the planning.

By the beginning of June the Northumberland Fusiliers pioneers were preparing logistics to support the forthcoming attack on Thiepval. Their role was to assist in opening up communications from the established British trench system by digging trenches, called saps, from the British trench-line into the captured land.

The artillery barrage commenced on 24 June as 2nd Wiltshires came into the line close to Carnoy looking out towards Montauban, an area they had come to know well. Their preparation for the attack involved regular patrolling of No Man's Land to keep the enemy out, to monitor the effect of the massive bombardment on German defences and in particular their barbed wire entanglement. Across the Somme battlefield many battalions were engaged in the same activity. It is unclear whether units accurately collated information indicating that the artillery was having limited effect on the German barbed wire, or whether negative information was disregarded. If the patrolling was successful then the units ought to have been aware that in many places the barbed wire remained effective and was going to be a formidable obstacle when the allied assault began.

By 30 June the 5th Sherwood Foresters were located at Foncquevillers on the northern edge of the Somme battlefield ready for the morning attack onto Gommecourt. The stage was set for the carefully planned, rehearsed and resourced set piece advance and break-through on the Somme. The 1st Wiltshires were redeploying to the Somme area tasked with following up on the gains made by the initial battalions, and the 1st Northamptons were still located in Loos.

The Battle of the Somme, Day One – 1 July 1916

The ground offensive began as the guns went quiet at 0730 on 1 July with simultaneous attacks involving 143 battalions, largely from Kitchener's volunteer army. The officers' whistles blew and troops all along the 16-mile Front clambered out of their trenches to take up their assault formation and head off equally spaced, at the requisite 100 paces per minute, towards the enemy.

In the north, 15 battalions in two waves from 46th (North Midland), and 56th (London) Divisions attacked German positions around the village of Gommecourt, the most northern of the Somme battles, conceived to fool the Germans that this was the main attack so that they shifted their reserves from where the main attack was going in to the south. The cohesion and fighting strength of the 5th Sherwood Foresters was destroyed in the first few minutes of the assault.

In the south, the 2nd Wiltshires were holding the front line trench from where the assaulting formations would form up. From the Wiltshires trenches 'well drilled khaki lines could be seen steadily advancing in perfect order'.[33] Unlike elsewhere on the Somme, progress was made and Montauban was secured. Further south were the 9th Devons who, having stepped out of their fire trenches, were cut to shreds from a cleverly positioned machine gun set up in the base of a fortified shrine in a graveyard on the edge of Mametz. The Company Commander, Captain Duncan Martin, knew of the machine gun's position and predicted that it would cause problems. Captain Martin and 121 of the battalion, including six railwaymen, were killed many without taking a step, falling straight back into the forward trench. This trench became their grave and is now known as the Devonshire Trench Commonwealth War Grave Cemetery.

9TH DEVONS						
Willie Best	Pte	22	Devonshire	GCR	London	Clerk
Horace Bill	CSM		Devonshire	Gt Western	Hockley	Carman
Henry Forrester	L/Cpl	25	Thiepval	GER	Police Dept	Police Constable
John Opie	Pte		Thiepval	Gt Western	Plymouth	Porter
Reginald Orsman	Pte	19	Devonshire	Caledonian	Dumbarton & Balloch	Lampman
Alfred Weston			Devonshire	GER	Stratford	Painter

The 17th Northumberland Fusiliers, in the centre, around Thiepval, spent the day supporting infantry and Royal Engineers as they attacked Leipzig Redoubt, a heavily fortified position dominating the surrounding area. The Fusiliers struggled through continuous fire across a No Man's Land of churned up soil, shell holes, barbed wire entanglements, craters and, in ever increasing numbers, dead bodies. One Platoon, number 9, stuck to their mission of establishing a communication sap. Pioneers were led over the top, in broad daylight, dodging from shell hole to shell hole, crawling past dead and wounded. Before forming up in the open, equally spaced along the line of the proposed sap, and with tremendous courage when you consider the carnage going on around them, got on their shovels and began to dig. The sap was successfully completed for only two pioneers injured, and was immediately used by the infantry as a safer route to their assaulting positions.

In the north, the 15 battalions attacking Gommecourt had suffered 4,580 casualties, but the Germans hadn't been fooled by the diversion. The 5th Sherwood Foresters

33 2nd Wiltshires, 81.

in the first wave of the attack lost 203 killed of which 17 were railwaymen and a total of 494 casualties from a strength of 724, nearly 70 per cent casualty rate on the day.

5TH SHERWOOD FORESTERS DEAD FROM 1 JULY 1916					
FA Alldred	Pte	24	Thiepval	Derby	Labourer
Joseph Bancroft	Pte		Thiepval	Nottingham	
A Bickerton	Pte	26	Gommecourt Wood	Derby	Wagon repairer
Ernest Derbyshire	Pte		Thiepval	Derby	Labourer
William Dumelow	L/Cpl	22	Thiepval	Derby	Coach body makers boy
Frank Frost	Pte		Thiepval	Derby	Coach Trimmer
Thomas Goodwin	CSM	32	Thiepval	Derby	Labourer
Victor Harrison	L/Cpl	21	Thiepval	Derby	Coach Finishers boy
Joseph Holmes	Pte	30	Thiepval	Derby	Labourer
George Hunt	Pte		Thiepval	Chaddesden	Shunter
Frederick Lewes	Capt	29	Thiepval	Hazelwood	Cadet
F Poyser	Pte		Thiepval	Derby	Wagon repairer
RE Rose	L/Cpl		Gommecourt Wood	Derby	Porter
H Shaw	Sgt	21	Foncquevillers	Hucknall	Porter
James Smith	Pte	19	Gommecourt	Derby	Machine Boy
George Webster	Pte		Thiepval	Derby	Hammerman
William Webster	Pte	23	Thiepval	Derby	Demurrageman
Frederick Whittingham	Pte	28	Thiepval	Westhouses	Holder up
Antony Wilcox	Pte	25	Thiepval	Derby	Striker

Across the Somme battlefront many battalions along the Front had been all but wiped out. Despite the meticulous planning, the day one objectives were not achieved. The General Staff had expected the Germans to crumble as a result of the almighty barrage. But the shock effect of artillery is achieved in the first few seconds. The longer the shelling goes on the more used to it recipients become, and as a massive generality if you survive the first couple of minutes then chances are you will survive. Perhaps suffering long term mental damage, but potentially still able to point and shoot a weapon. So when the artillery lifted on its pre-determined barrage the Germans came out of their deep bunkers, and whilst they were no doubt not in the best of conditions they fought and defended ferociously. The British infantry, marching in formation towards the Germans, presented a tremendous opportunity. Almost all the attacks were repulsed and at the end of the first day, the troops had marched forward at 100 paces per minute and there were 57,470 more allied casualties, nearly half of the injuries being inflicted in the first hour of the assault. The infantry suffered 50 per cent casualties and lost 75 per cent of their officers.

At least 240 railwaymen are known to have died on 1 July (see Appendix 7, page 320 for the full list) two thirds, have no known grave and are commemorated on the Thiepval memorial. They served in 88 infantry battalions. The highest railway death rate on the day was the 5th Sherwood Foresters (17), followed by the 10th Lincolnshires (10), the 11th Sherwood Foresters (7), 9th Devons

Q1103 IWM The 1st Wiltshires attacking near Thiepval, 7 August 1916

(6), 10th West Yorkshires (6). The Midland railway company lost, forty-nine men on the day. The spilt blood of the railwaymen was just a tiny fraction of the total blood soaking into the soil of the Somme, but you have to imagine the feeling of loss in towns and cities like Derby, and in places like the Midland works, where over the coming days the names of those lost would be shared across the remaining workforce and the families and friends back home.

The Somme, day two and beyond

What was left of the 5th Sherwood Foresters was withdrawn from the Somme on the 2 July and was moved to a quiet area near Bellacourt to the south west of Arras.

Even behind the lines it wasn't safe. On 2 July a group of 17th Northumberland Fusiliers resting and playing cards were hit by a shell which injured 28. Sergeant Sid Morris, a former number taker, and Private Val East, a wheelwright, both from West Hartlepool died of wounds. Added to the loss of Private Bays, who had worked in York as a wagon repairer who had been killed the day before and two former porters, Private Baldwinstone from Leeds, and Private Staples from Heslerton who were killed during the night whilst trying to bury infantrymen who had been killed in the assault in No Man's Land. Over the following days they worked to maintain roads and trenches for resupply and casualty evacuation through foul weather and ongoing enemy bombardment. The battalion supported infantry in the attack, joining them as they crossed No Man's Land along with engineers to fortify and harden captured strong points. They experienced many casualties from the cocktail of high explosive and gas shells.

RAILWAYMEN WHO DIED WITH THE 1ST WILTSHIRES, 5–8 JULY 1916 AT THE SOMME						
Arthur Reed	Pte	1st	Wiltshires	Thiepval	Swindon	Boilermakers Apprentice
Walter Trollope	Pte	1st	Wiltshires	Thiepval	Trowbridge	Mechanics Labourer
Arthur Dobson	Pte	1st	Wiltshires	Thiepval	Swindon	Machinist
Walter Preece	Pte	1st	Wiltshires	Thiepval	Hallatrow	
Edwin Whitman	Pte	1st	Wiltshires	Thiepval	Swindon	Dresser Foundry
George Gingell	Pte	1st	Wiltshires	Thiepval	Dauntsey	Slip Labourer
Philip Carter	Pte	1st	Wiltshires	Puchevillers	Swindon	Labourer
Henry Gibbs	Pte	1st	Wiltshires	Thiepval	Swindon	
Alfred Stevens	Pte	1st	Wiltshires	Puchevillers	Swindon	Painter

A Dobson

A E Reed

The 1st Wiltshires were fortunate to have spent 1 July in the rear area and by 3 July were formed up in Aveluy Wood behind the front line at Thiepval close to 17th Northumberland Fusiliers, and six or so miles to the north of 2nd Wiltshires. They took over from the remnants of battalions that had been wiped out over the first two days; occupying trenches on 4 July in the Leipzig Salient and the following day they took part in their first attack in this battle and captured a trench. The human loss was unremarkable in the Somme carnage, but still there were over 200 casualties including the commanding officer. A Captain Ogilvie took temporary command; he had been a Corporal only eighteen months before. Fighting over the next few days was intense, such that, when they were relieved, the battalion numbered only 200 soldiers.

Meanwhile the 1st Northamptons, who had been enjoying the relative comfort of the Loos slag heaps, were moved southwards on the 6 July towards the ongoing carnage down the road. The 2nd Northamptons were engaged in attacking Contalmaison on the 7 July until relieved on the 9th having incurred many hundreds of casualties with little positive having been achieved.

Attacks on Bernafay and Trones woods

To the east of Montauban, and the 2nd Wiltshires, there were two key woods. The first, Bernafay Wood, had been taken comparatively easily and it was assumed, wrongly, that Trones Wood would be equally straightforward. The plan was that in the early hours of the 8 July the 2nd Yorkshires would clear Trones Wood and the 2nd Wiltshires would then, from the safety of Trones Wood, attack a fortified farm. It didn't go according to plan. Between the two woods were several hundred metres of open fields. The Germans had sited their machine guns on a flank so that their arcs of fire cut down the fields between the woods, so that when any troops tried to cross the gap they would be engaged all the way across by the machine guns. Anyone making it across the gap could be picked off by the riflemen in the wood.

The 2nd Yorkshires attack failed with tremendous loss of life, but the 2nd Wiltshires crossed the open ground, penetrated the wood line, and engaged the enemy in hand to hand fighting. This became a battle not of company or even platoon commanders but of section leaders and individual soldiers fighting in the woodland. They tried to maintain the momentum of the attack even as casualties mounted and the bayonet was used to good effect. The battalion fought through the defences and, having gained a crucial foothold, began digging in to hold the ground and await reinforcements, which would have to cross the same machine gun exposed fields between the two woods. The battalion were only holding half of the wood, and their positions were exposed to sniper fire. Many officers became casualties. The 18th and 19th Manchesters, which included Privates Albert Ingram and Alfred Longshaw who suffered such a grizzly death (see page 301), were used to reinforce counter attacks but were fought off throughout the night. In the early hours of 9 July the 2nd Wiltshires were withdrawn. In 24 hours they had suffered a further 31 killed, 194 wounded and 14 missing.

Herbert Fowler	Pte	2nd	Wiltshires	8	7	16	24	Thiepval	Gt Western	Swindon	Coach Finisher
Archibald Smith	Pte	2nd	Wiltshires	8	7	16	26	Thiepval	Gt Western	Swindon	Machineman
Thomas Strange	Pte	2nd	Wiltshires	8	7	16	32	Thiepval	Gt Western	Swindon	

H J Fowler

After being relieved on the 7th the 1st Wiltshires were moved to Usna Hill which had been the start point for a major, and disasterous, attack a week previously on 1 July by the Tynesiders, and spent their time re-constituting and carrying out fatigues and working parties.

On the 14 July the British mounted an ambitious night attack from around Montauban gaining ground leading up to two woods which would gain notoriety by the sheer volume of human carnage and become imprinted in the minds of British people for 100 years, High Wood and Delville Wood. The 1st Northamptons were not in the initial attacks having arrived in the battered town of Albert on 10 July, but followed on along congested feeder trenches; eventually transiting the old front line on the edge of Mametz Wood; and over the next five days through continual gas and artillery bombardment forward into newly captured trenches. The Northamptons were generally not involved in fighting but tasked with holding previously captured trenches to provide strength in depth. They did take part in some set piece attacks which achieved little save for 268 casualties, which was pretty light compared to the average 'tariff' which was developing for battalions around the Somme.

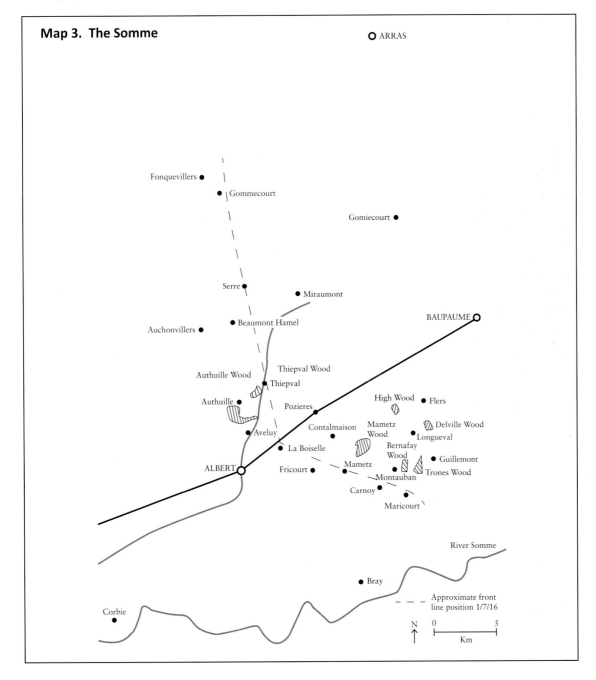

Map 3. The Somme

RAILWAYMEN WHO DIED IN BERNAFAY AND TRONES WOOD

It wasn't until 14 July that Trones Wood fell. Battalion after battalion were committed to fighting across the same exposed gap between the two woods. Those who got through into Trones Wood found dug in German infantry intent on holding every position right through the wood. Even when Trones Wood was captured it would still be the last resting place for many more soldiers killed trying to break out to capture the nearby village of Guillemont, which wasn't finally captured until 6 September.

There are seven railwaymen from seven battalions who are believed to have died in Bernafay Wood between 9 July and 19 October. All but one probably died in artillery bombardment whilst resting or in second line trenches in the area CWGC in brackets.

James Farr	6th	KOSB a Clerk from Great Western at Cardiff (Peronne Road)
Charles Jones	18th	Lancashire Fusiliers, a Labourer with the Midland at Skipton (Corbie)
Robert McGawley	20th	Lancashire Fusiliers, a L &NWR Caller off from Manchester (Thiepval)
Albert Kain	7th	DCLI, a GER Vanguard from Goodmans Yard (Thiepval)
William Keyte	1st	Grenadier Guards, a Midland Van Boy from Nottingham (Thiepval)
John Bagwell	7th	DCLI, a Porter for SECR (Bancourt)
Percy Allen	1st	Border regiment GER Porter Shunter from Trowse (Thiepval)

There are 17 railwaymen from eight battalions who are believed to have died in Trones Wood. Ten of whom were killed whilst the wood was fought over and 13 of the 17 have no known grave and are recorded on the Thiepval memorial. It is possible that their bodies were recovered after the wood was captured and are buried, but the burial site was lost, or more likely they were left as they fell during the fierce fighting and were blown to unrecognisable pieces in the ongoing artillery slaughter and remain buried in the wood, an eerie thought.

Kossak

Dale

Herbert Fowler	2nd	Wiltshires and from Great Western at Swindon (Thiepval)
Archibald Smith	2nd	Wiltshires and from Great Western at Swindon (Thiepval)
Thomas Strange	2nd	Wiltshires and from Great Western at Swindon (Thiepval)l
H Billington	18th	Manchester, Lancashire and Yorkshire Railway (Heath)
Lawrence Kossak	12th	Middlesex, GER Carriage Washer (Thiepval)
George Kesner	12th	Middlesex, Midland Railway, Porter at Darfield (Thiepval)
Horace Sawyer	6th	Northamptons, Great Northern Railway (Thiepval Bernafay Wood)
Sidney Glenn	6th	Northamptons, L& NWR, labourer (Thiepval)
Henry Reynolds	6th	Northamptons, L& NWR, labourer (Thiepval)
James Dale	7th	East Kent, GER Porter from Hackney Downs (Thiepval)
George Huggins	7th	East Kent, SECR (Corbie)
Cecil White	24th	Royal Fusiliers, from L&NWR at Crewe (Thiepval St Sever)
George Bettles	12th	KRRC and L&NWR, Liverpool Road (Thiepval)
Arthur Mountford	12th	KRRC and L&NWR, Coventry (Thiepval)
Charles Loose	1st	KSLI, a Sheetmaker from Cambrian Railways (Thiepval)

After 17 continuous days in the line, the 17th Northumberland Fusiliers were withdrawn on the 17 July. Pioneer battalions, unlike infantry, were not rotated and they had to maintain support for however long they were in the line. They were re-deployed to Loos to recover.

By 23 July, 2nd Wiltshires along with the 19th Manchesters formed up in Trones Wood ready to attack Guillemont to the east. The advance had been difficult; they struggled even getting to their start point. 'The roads were heavy with traffic, men, horses and wagons pressing forward and rearward each with their urgent duty to perform'.[34] Even before they got into Trones Wood their numbers were depleted by 45 men due to shellfire. The worst moment was when a lorry full of explosives was hit, injuring all but three in a passing platoon. The attack on Guillemont stalled almost before it started. Again there was open ground to cross and machine gunners wrought havoc. The Manchesters paid heavily and no substantial ground was made. The 2nd Wiltshires were not even used in the attack. So, the double entry book keeping of infantry warfare showed no attack and no ground taken and still 45 casualties. It wasn't the worst night by far, but for those who succumbed it was bad enough.

Slow Progress

Three weeks later on 15 August the 1st Northamptons returned to the line and the Germans had been pushed a further kilometre or so rearward, every single step fiercely fought over by one battalion or other. Elsewhere on the Somme the killing rate was as high but for little or no gain. In the distance the Northamptons could see High Wood, but their objective was the trench-line to their immediate front, believed to be lightly held, but just before the assault it was reinforced and the attack failed. The following day they captured the trench, but 204 casualties were incurred. When they marched to the rear after a week in the trenches their number was 374 lighter and they had lost seventeen of their officers. Only one railwayman is known to have been killed, but this may have been because most had already been killed or injured. He was L/Cpl Frederick Purcell, who was an L&NWR bricklayer from Bletchley. The Somme was consuming manpower at such an alarming rate that many regiments could no longer meet demand. The Northamptons had to be brought back up to strength with a big draft from the Norfolk Yeomanry.

The 1st Wiltshires were back into the trenches on the 18 August at Thiepval and the Leipzig Salient. For nine days they alternated between defence and assault, close quarter battles over the same very small piece of infected earth, with casualties mounting all the time. In those nine days there were 320 casualties. A week later the battalion attacked over the same ground and once again the defenders were able to deplete the attackers until they had insufficient 'bayonets' to see home the attack and so they withdrew.

By 9 September a rested and rebuilt 1st Northamptons were committed alongside numerous other battalions to attacking the splinters of what had been High Wood. The fight for this wood had been going on since mid-July and had consumed thousands of lives.

This latest attack could not penetrate the defences or capture any ground and after nightfall the men withdrew with 140 casualties, most of them killed, but no railwaymen were known to be amongst them. High Wood was finally cleared on 15 September on the same day that Tanks were used for the first time.

1st Northamptons returned to the Somme on 25 September but were finally withdrawn after three days and took no further part in the battle.

Mid-September saw the 17th Northumberland Fusiliers, once again located in the Somme, grouped with the 119th and 227th Railway Companies RE, and re-roled, appropriately, as a railway repair battalion. They were building a railway line just to the west of where they had been fighting in Thiepval. Whilst arguably less dangerous than acting as a pioneer battalion, building railways was

---

34   2nd Wiltshires, 93.

hard graft and there was no let up in the work. Throughout this time the battalion were frequently bombarded. On the 20 October, the camp was hit by artillery killing three and injuring twenty. Lance Corporal Dunn, who had been a clerk in Darlington; Private Little, an ex-freight shunter at Heaton, who came from Bard Mill, Northumberland and was one of three brothers who died within two weeks; and Private Smith, a former clerk from Tyne Dock, who was evacuated only to die in England a fortnight later. In early November, whilst completing a station and yard at Ovillers La Boiselle, a group was hit by an artillery shell which caused twelve casualties, two fatalities, Private Taplin a Newcastle carriage cleaner died and Private Johnson a loader from Middlesborough died some two months later.

The 2nd Wiltshires found themselves back in the Somme north-east of Delville Wood at Flers in early October, having spent since early August coming back to strength in the quiet area of Loos. After a period digging a new trench-line under cover of darkness and taking no casualties, despite continuous bombardment, they withdrew to the second line trenches. These were former German trenches and enemy artillery had the exact co-ordinates and the Wiltshires incurred many casualties. They were said to be pleased when ordered to re-deploy back to the front line. On 18 October in appalling rain and filthy conditions, with trenches and shell holes full of mud and water, the battalion made an unsuccessful attack and the following day fought off a determined counter attack. They suffered 364 casualties, including at least two railwaymen both from Swindon works.

| SH King | Sgt | 2nd | Wiltshires | 18 | 10 | 16 | Gt Western | Swindon | Warlencourt |
| William Spackman | Pte | 2nd | Wiltshires | 18 | 10 | 16 | Gt Western | Swindon | Thiepval |

2nd Northamptons returned to the Somme on 19 October to the area around Trones Wood. They had spent the intervening three months around Loos and Cuinchy, a relatively peaceful time, but nonetheless not too pleasant. The parapets were 'largely revetted with corpses thinly concealed by rotting sandbags through which at night rats fled'.[35] It seems likely that the Northamptons were occupying former French positions. Corrigan suggests that 'bodies left lying where they fell were not good for morale; they were never left in the trenches for longer than absolutely necessary, nor did the British follow the French practice in the early days of burying their dead in the (trench) parapet'.[36] On the subject of the dead, Corrigan makes the position clear regarding how the British at least aimed to deal with their fallen comrades: 'Bodies were always recovered whenever humanly possible and taken back to the rear for temporary burial before being given a proper and seemly funeral'.[37] Many of the Commonwealth War Graves Cemeteries of today were formed from original temporary burial grounds where men were hastily buried, often when still in close contact with the enemy. There were countless small burial plots which, after the war, were consolidated. Many of the men commemorated on memorials to the missing were buried in these small plots, but their positions were lost in subsequent fighting over the same land.

A Morgan

1st Wiltshires left the trenches on 23 October after a miserable, but uneventful, period of poor weather; but not before two railwaymen were killed, Private Joseph Bailey, a former general labourer from Westbury, and Private Alfred Morgan, an 'issuer' from Swindon.

J Bailey

35   Northamptons, 158.
36   Corrigan, 88.
37   Corrigan, 88.

The Wiltshires war diary mentioned that two officers went to witness an experiment in intensive digging by the 6th South Wales Borderers.[38]

The Battle of The Somme eventually drew to an end in November with some of the most resistant areas, such as Thiepval, which had been a 1 July objective, holding out almost to the end. The 2nd Northamptons remained in the Somme until 18 November alternating in the front line and to the rear, and was the last of the feature battalions to be involved in this battle, although some would fight over this land again before the war was over.

THIEPVAL MONUMENT

The Thiepval monument commemorates the 72,000 soldiers who fought in the Battle of The Somme who have no known grave. There are over 950 of the 12,500 railwaymen commemorated on the memorial, and when all railwaymen who died are considered that number is probably nearer to 1,500.

---

38   1 Wiltshires War Diary, 99.

Hangover after the Somme

Autumn became winter, the third of the war. The 1st Wiltshires spent six comparatively quiet months from 1 November in the Messines area south of Ypres. The routine was usually six days in front line trenches infested with rats and usually deep in wet mud; followed by six days in support trenches; then six more days in front line trenches; and finally six days in billets with the luxury of beds and a roof over their heads, although this was tempered with having to do fatigues and duties which included supplying and assisting the front line trenches. The 2nd Wiltshires were also alternating in and out of trenches at Berles-au-Bois between Arras and the Somme. The 1st Northamptons spent six weeks on the Somme at Eaucourt from mid-November fighting a battle against the elements. Atrocious weather caused the trench system to be thigh deep in frozen filthy water, mud and muck, with dead bodies partially buried or completely covered in water, built into the parapets or frozen in the ground. These insanitary conditions denuded the battalion, and despite 'only' suffering 53 killed or wounded in this period, including three railwaymen, a draft of 500 troops did not bring the battalion up to strength, such was the loss through sickness. Private Kenneth Hamilton, a former clerk from GER in Norwich died of typhoid.

The battalions found their time out of the line to be hard graft, but unlike the previous two winters there was much more morale raising activity to keep the troops motivated and in good spirit. This helped to make the winter bearable. Christmas for the 2nd Wiltshires was spent in the trenches and their celebrations were saved for New Year. Their sister battalion 1st Wiltshires, in contrast, spent Christmas in billets before trench routine continued on Boxing Day. The 17th Northumberland Fusiliers saw the year out in the Somme completing the railway from Aveluy to Mouquet farm, and building a gun siding at Mailly-Maillet.

1917

January to March 1917 was quiet for 2nd Wiltshires spent in relatively peaceful jobs like two weeks in forestry cutting wood, or supporting railway construction. The 1st Northamptons spent until May training in hutted camps near Albert on the Somme. 1st Wiltshires were engaged in trench warfare, but alternating between the trenches and training in a quiet area of Ypres. The 17th Northumberland Fusiliers were heavily engaged building a light railway workshop, engine shed and sidings at Isbergues south of Hazebrouck, which was completed at the end of March. By early March the 2nd Northamptons were fighting to the south east of the Somme battlefield. On 4 March they attacked near Bouchavesnes close to the Canal Du Nord and incurred nearly 250 casualties.

Herbert FitzJohn	Pte	2nd	Northants	4	3	17		Thiepval	GNR		Clerk
Arthur Lane	Pte	2nd	Northants	4	3	17	20	Thiepval	Midland	Kettering	Greaser
L Marlow	Cpl	2nd	Northants	4	3	17		Fins New	Midland	Rushden	Checker

The 5th Sherwood Foresters by March 1917 were, after a relatively quiet eight months around Arras, back in the Somme and back at Gommecourt. They found many Foresters unburied lying where they had fallen on 1 July 1916. In the churchyard they found the grave of their Adjutant, who the Germans had laid to rest with a cross saying 'Here lies the gallant English Captain FHM Lewes'. Frederick Lewes had been a cadet for the Midland Railway and enlisted in 1915. Seemingly very popular, the regimental history states: 'The Adjutant Captain Lewes was probably the most popular man in the battalion being himself always smart, he was a stickler for the same trait in others'.[39] Lewes's grave was subsequently lost in the continued fighting over this ground, and today he is commemorated on the Thiepval memorial.

IWM Q7797

CAPT. AND ADJT. F. H. M. LEWES.
Killed in action, July 1st, 1916.

The 17th Northumberland Fusiliers was now a unit within the Rail Construction Engineers and, in early April, had begun building a ten-kilometre broad gauge extension from Poperinghe toward Ypres. The eventual destination was dependent upon the success of the future planned Third Ypres offensive. Their work was a combination of heavy graft and technical engineering, all carried out through any weather, and frequently under fire and gas attacks. One of the companies was building a 120-foot bridge over the Poperinghe Canal, this required not only a detailed survey and engineering but a huge amount of labour in creating levels either side of the bridge. On one day, for example, this company shovelled 60,000 cubic feet of earth and yet 'it seemed to go no-where'.[40] The earthworks connected with the bridge were finally completed 14 days later. Another bridge further down the line was over the Yser Canal and within sight of enemy positions only two kilometres away and was regularly engaged with artillery fire. Nicknamed the 'Great Midland Railway' it was completed on 12 June 1917.

In early 1917, across much of the front between the River Aisne and Arras, the Germans began to withdraw towards a carefully prepared and integrated defence line known as the Hindenburg Line. Optimising reverse slopes for maximum protection for the defenders and greatest exposure for the attackers, the Hindenburg Line comprised a series of block houses and fortifications along a pair of main trench-lines and a system of lightly held forward trenches. The line was designed to be strong and survivable and to enable rapid reinforcement by reserves concentrated in key protected locations. The Germans destroyed the countryside, buildings and infrastructure as they withdrew.

---

39   de Grave, L. W., *The War History Of The Fifth Battalion The Sherwood Foresters, Notts and Derby Regiment,* 1914–1918.

40   Shakespear, J. A., *Record Of The 17th and 32nd Battalions Northumberland Fusiliers, 1914-1919.* 63.

The Battle of Arras, 9–13 April 1917

The Battle of Arras was a joint British and Canadian diversionary attack for the French Nivelle offensive. Ample warning of attack was given by a tremendous bombardment over five days of 2,879 guns. The Canadians attacked Vimy Ridge, to the north of Arras, now famous for the enormous and impressive Canadian War Memorial. The 2nd Wiltshires, part of the British attack were to the south of Arras east of the village of Mercatel. They were given the difficult, if not mad task, of clambering out of their trenches into the open, covering 2,000 yards of ground before even getting into a position to assault, something of an open invitation to the enemy. Just as the men in the front line were about to leap out of their trenches and advance, the rain came. The Tommys, laden down with heavy kit and sodden clothing, had to negotiate the strength sapping mud, where every step was an ordeal, somehow dodge the bullets, and then if they had survived thus far, have the energy for an aggressive and blood curdling fixed bayonet assault on the enemy trenches. By contrast, the Germans had all the time in the world, from the comfort of their defended location, and with the protection afforded by being dug deep into the ground, to wait until the assaulting troops entered their killing zones, and then let rip. The Wiltshires had learnt on the Somme that heavy rain favoured the defender.

Those who survived the artillery and the machine guns and the sniping, and didn't succumb to sheer exhaustion, found that the barbed wire entanglements were uncut. As one officer said 'there was nothing for it but to get as near to the objective as possible and drop at once into the nearest hole or cover to get out of the huns' murderous fire'.[41] The survivors were withdrawn to the cover of a sunken road, but the protection was only superficial since the German artillery had the range and bearing and engaged with sustained fire. The battalion fighting strength by this time had withered to three officers and about ninety men. As night fell these men were withdrawn. To make matters worse heavy snow fell during the afternoon and throughout the night and many wounded who might have survived, died through exposure before the hard pushed stretcher bearers could get to them. By the time the battalion were finally withdrawn on 11 April at least four further railwaymen, all from the Swindon works, had been killed.

William Hedges	Pte	2nd	Wiltshires	9	4	17	21	Bucquoy Rd	
AGJ Pelling	L/Sgt	2nd	Wiltshires	9	4	17	27	Bucquoy Rd	Bufferman
Arthur Topp	L/Cpl	2nd	Wiltshires	9	4	17		Arras	Machineman
George Walker	L/Cpl	2nd	Wiltshires	9	4	17	34	Wancourt	

Two other Swindon railwaymen died shortly after in casualty clearing stations to the rear.

| William Barnes | Pte | 2nd | Wiltshires | 12 | 4 | 17 | 18 | Warlincourt | Machinist |
| Fred Morgan | Pte | 2nd | Wiltshires | 12 | 4 | 17 | 21 | Gouy-en-artois | Fitter |

The attackers, including 2nd Wiltshires, punched very hard at the Hindenburg Line, but it didn't yield, and though it was a successful attack in terms of ground captured, there was no significant breakthrough. A few days later the Wiltshire survivors were back in action until withdrawn on

41 2 Wiltshires, 111.

29 April bound for green fields and escape from battle, but not before Private Sydney Jewitt, a former porter on the Hull and Barnsley Railway was killed.

To the north of Arras the 5th Sherwood Foresters arrived back in the area of Lens in April 1917 remaining for 17 months. The fighting here was characterised by alternating in trenches, sometimes fighting pitched battles, and other times just holding the line, and time to the rear recovering. Private John Spridgeon, a former messenger for the Midland Railway, was killed when the Sherwood Forester brigade unsuccessfully attacked Hill 65 and the Fosse 3 coal mine on 23 April.

1st Wiltshires in the Messines Ridge attack

Twenty tunnels up to 2,000 feet in length between 50 and 90 feet deep, and totalling over four miles were dug beneath the German held Messines Ridge to the South of Ypres. The 17th Northumberland Fusiliers spent some time tunnelling in September 1916, and 2nd Wiltshires assisted Canadian diggers in 1917. Tunnellers had to contend with the risk of cave-ins and suffocation, and of enemy diggers trying to penetrate the tunnels and kill them, or to blast them apart with explosives. Once completed, the tunnels were filled with nearly half a million kilograms of explosive. This would be detonated alongside the artillery bombardment co-ordinated for when the infantry attacked the heavily fortified positions along the dominant ridge. The mines were blown on the 7 June as the attack commenced. The 1st Wiltshires, part of the second wave, took and then held their objectives until relieved on 20 June for only 28 killed and 98 wounded. The attack was a tremendous success, a significant amount of ground was captured, probably a result of a focused aim and clear objectives. It went so well that 1st Northamptons remained unused in reserve.

To the south of Messines, near Lens, 5th Sherwood Foresters attemped to capture Hill 65. Although only having a peripheral part in this battle a further two railwaymen were killed.

| George Swain | Pte | 5th | Sherwoods | 24 | 6 | 17 | 32 | Maroc | Midland | Derby | Labourer |
| Frederick Buggins | Pte | 5th | Sherwoods | 25 | 6 | 17 | | Arras | Midland | Toton | Labourer |

On the anniversary of the first day of the battle of the Somme, on 1 July, 5th Sherwood Foresters attacked Lens again, 16 were killed, 62 wounded and 83 were missing.

| Thomas Lilley | Pte | 5th | Sherwoods | 1 | 7 | 17 | 22 | Arras | Midland | Belper | Porter |
| Thomas Taylor | Pte | 5th | Sherwoods | 1 | 7 | 17 | | Arras | Midland | Derby | Labourer |

1st Northamptons to the coast

After being unused during the attacks on Messines Ridge, the 1st Northamptons were not redeployed to support the beginning of the Third Battle of Ypres, but instead were marched to the most northerly section of trench-line in the Western Front and occupied an area of sand dunes and sandy soil isolated from reinforcements and support. After only four days in this quiet and cushy outpost, on 10 July, the Germans attacked with overwhelming force. Firstly with a shattering artillery bombardment which initially destroyed all the crossings of the canal to the rear of the trenches, thereby cutting the Northamptons off from reinforcement, then lifting onto their trench-line. This was followed in the evening by a clever ground attack by German troops who successfully exploited the boundary between the Northamptons and the neighbouring unit and were able to capture the commanding officer and his headquarters staff. With no command structure or communications and no means of reinforcement or withdrawal, it was only a matter of time before they were overwhelmed. Despite putting up a heroic fight all but nine of the 400 Northamptons in the line were killed or captured and the battalion once again ceased to exist. There are no records of any railwaymen being killed in these actions, possibly because most had already been killed. A small nucleus of soldiers had been held in reserve to the west of the canal and a new battalion with the character of the 1st Northamptons was re-invented with the return of some recycled soldiers fit from previous injury and yet another draft of conscripts which included a large draft of men from the Durham area. This probably included Private Brown who was a Freight Shunter with NER at Shildon who was killed in November.

The Third Battle of Ypres – 2nd Wiltshires and 17th Northumberland Fusiliers

An enormous artillery bombardment of over 3,000 guns signalled the start of the long awaited 'big push'. Then, after nine days of unrelenting pounding of the guns the men from 2nd Wiltshires fixed their bayonets and led their brigade in the pouring rain across the desolate landscape of churned up mud, and deep shell holes and other debris, vegetable, animal and human. Just one battalion of four in one brigade of four in one of twelve divisions beginning the attack across the eleven-mile front on 31 July. In another division the men of 2nd Northamptons were assembled facing Bellewaarde Lake, tasked with capturing Bellewaarde Ridge. 'Perfect order prevailed, the battalion keeping its formation as if on the practice trenches'.[42] In their path was Chateau Wood 'a mass of wire and fallen trees'.[43]

The men of the 17th Northumberland Fusiliers had now been joined by the 18th Northumberland Fusiliers and seven other infantry pioneer companies. Together numbering nearly 4,000 men they were ready at the oddly named 'Mission Junction' with picks, shovels and all their pioneering paraphernalia ready to exploit the gains made, by extending the railroad. By 0800 over 300 railwaymen were shovelling away extending the line. Progress was slowed by heavy rain which made digging much more difficult, as the earth became too wet to throw. This mass of labour called the '18th Corps Light Railway Advance' was split into eight hour shifts and divided up into teams such as survey, demolition, bridging, formation, plate laying and ballasting. The teams were constantly exposed to artillery fire as they pressed hard behind the advancing infantrymen. Forty men, mainly from the Gloucester pioneer battalion, were lost from one shift when a single shell fell on the cutting they were working. A few days before on the 29 July, a team of ballasters from the Northumberland Fusiliers were hit by an artillery shell which caused 47 casualties and a number of fatalities including Private J Cavanagh who had been a carriage cleaner in Newcastle, and Driver Gladwell who had been a greaser at Spennymoor.

The 2nd Wiltshires, despite very heavy shelling, were able to capture and hold their objectives until they were relieved on 3 August. At least two railwaymen, both ex-labourers at the GWR Swindon Works, were killed, Corporal Albert Newton on 31 July, and Private F H Isaacs who died on 3 August.

The 2nd Northamptons made swift progress through the weakly held German front line and fought through the mud, artillery and machine gun fire to the enemy second line trenches, fighting until relieved on 2 August having incurred 237 casualties.

The Northumberland Fusiliers were kept busy constantly repairing shell damage to the railway lines but on the whole the lines were kept open. Overnight on the 4 August some troops were hit in their bivouac and there twenty-two were injured. Because the railwaymen were operating close to

---

42   1st Northamptons, 217.
43   1st Northamptons, 217.

gun batteries, they were constantly subject to enemy counter battery artillery fire. Sergeant Teasdale, a former Hull porter, and Private Howey, an underman from Newcastle, both died of wounds at a nearby casualty clearing station.

Whilst the battle went on around them, the 1st Wiltshires were on support duties stationed inside the Ypres ramparts. They had taken over a section of the trenches straight after being withdrawn from Messines Ridge in late June. Here their tasks included some stints in the front line trenches. The Wiltshiremen spent much time on working parties resupplying the front line trenches, which involved having to pick their way through intensive and accurate artillery fire across the destroyed landscape of the front, and were engaged with general fatigue duties such as the unpleasant task of burying dead animals. By mid-August they were withdrawn for training. The 2nd Northamptons were back in the line at Bellewaarde on 17 August and although their few days was described as quiet, they still incurred another 130 casualties including Private Thomas Madelin, a clerk from L&NWR at Coventry. By the 22 August the 2nd Wiltshires who had been training, were redeployed to second line trenches to the south to Messines.

1st Northamptons become amphibious experts

Whilst the Third Battle of Ypres raged to the south, the reconstituted 1st Northamptons, and all of 1st Division, were in conditions of supreme secrecy, concentrated in a large wired off area of coastal foreshore near a small seaside town called Le Clipon. The official reason for their confinement and security was an unnamed infectious disease. However, the true reason was that they were training in beach landings and assaults. The plan was that the division would mount an amphibious operation using two large flat-bottomed warships with an enormous raft connected between them to transport the troops to the shore. Whereupon they would disembark, capture a beachhead, and advance rapidly inland forming a second front for Ypres. But despite weeks of preparation and rehearsal the plan was cancelled.

17th Northumberland Fusiliers back to pioneers

The North Eastern railwaymen, pioneers once again, spent from late August to 23 October away from the battle, travelling firstly to Ghyvelde on the Belgian border in a fleet of forty London omnibuses and September in Nieuport on pioneering tasks. They travelled over railway they had helped to lay into the Ypres Salient where they were engaged on keeping roads and track-ways open. They were frequently bombed and strafed by German aeroplanes, and bombarded by German artillery. There was little protection since the water table was so high and digging in was impractical; there were injuries and deaths. Private Addison from West Hartlepool, Private Ritchie an ex-pilot guard from Gateshead, and a Private Grey were killed and Private Robert Craggs, the C Company cook, and a former porter from Darlington was hit and later died of wounds. Work continued at Poelcappelle, Langemarck and St Julien whilst the fighting continued nearby at Passchendaele Ridge. Harold Etherington, a clerk from York, M J Frankland, a platelayer from Tynemouth and R W Ness, a loader from Hull West, all died at the St Julien dressing station on 25 October and Oliver Cook, a quarryman from Bowes on the 30 October.

Autumn and Winter and things slow down

As fierce fighting was going on around Ypres, further south conditions for 5th Sherwood Foresters were described as 'monotonous' for the six weeks they spent holding Hill 70 in the Lens coalfield. The 8th Sherwood Forester's history reports detail of the General's daily orders: 'Generals pet orders with trench routine were that all ranks as far as reasonably possible should shave every day, and that tea leaves should not be deposited in or on the sides of trenches'.[44] It might seem strange that a General should make special mention of the minutae of life in the trenches and it may seem as though he was being unnecessarily picky, but discipline and maintaining of standards impacted on health and morale. Despite the challenges to health it was important that standards were maintained. Gordon Corrigan in *Mud, Blood and Poppycock* states 'Despite the tales of rats, lice and general filth, cleanliness and hygiene in the trenches were strictly enforced'.[45]

It was pretty quiet for 1st Wiltshires too. Their war diary notes that when their Brigadier went on leave his deputy was the CO who, only two years previously had been a Corporal, high attrition of officers made for rapid promotion.

1st Northamptons met up with 2nd Northamptons when they made a return to trench warfare on the 9 November, just as the Third Battle of Ypres was drawing to a close, having been kept away for over three months due to the beach landing training. For most of the soldiers this was their first experience of trench warfare, being shot at, and being bombarded by artillery. By the end of the month they had plenty of experience and over a hundred were killed or injured. The dead included Private M Brown, an NER shunter from Shildon killed on the 8 November 1917. The 2nd Northamptons had moved from Plugstreet to Ypres on 9 November and were in the line at Passchendaele from 21 November until the end of the month.

The ever flexible and versatile 17th Northumberland Fusiliers, capable of general labouring and specialist railway tasks, became a railway construction unit in November. Changing roles wasn't simply about changing titles, as each role had a different order of battle with different equipment tables for the quartermaster to hold, issue and account for, and different manpower requirements.

By the middle of November 2nd Wiltshires found themselves situated in an unusual underground bunker near Gheluvelt which could accommodate two battalions of infantry, 2,000 or so men. Although it was said to be stuffy, it was warm and safe, and had the added luxury of bunks, officer's quarters, and the like. This was not a bad place to spend the cold nights of November. But with nothing to do, managing boredom must have been a challenge. When the battalion emerged on 30 November, destined for the trenches, many must have felt they could cope with a few more weeks of boredom. They emerged from their underground retreat to hold the same piece of line that they had held in October 1914, but the landscape was unrecognisable.

The Northumberlanders were now partnered with the 7th Battalion Canadian Railway Troops and they worked together on the railway between Poperinghe and Passchendaele until the end of March 1918. There were marked contrasts at either end of the line, at 'Pop' the living was (comparatively) easy, subject to only sporadic artillery, and for much of the time there wasn't much to do and troops may have been somewhat bored. At the Passchendaele end of the line the troops were in the thick of it and close to the fighting infantrymen. The men alternated to give all a share of the rough and the more cushy. Still the casualties mounted, on 16 November C Company were shelled and gassed at Poelcappelle causing several injuries and Private Coupland, a plumber from York, was killed. A few days later, on 19 November, Lt Maughan was killed at Langemarck. November cost the battalion 23 killed.

Christmas was again a quiet period, 2nd Wiltshires spent Christmas Day in trenches, but made the most of the New Year out of the line. 1st Wiltshires spent December in Bapaume engaged in digging-in cables. The 1st Northamptons spent Christmas in the line near Passchendaele. The 5th Sherwood Foresters were on the Cite St Elie coal mine leading into January 1918 where, on 22 January, they were withdrawn for a period of training. The Northumberland Fusiliers continued their routine throughout Christmas, but it was made sweeter by the North Eastern Railway company having sent out 100 cigarettes per man. The 2nd Northamptons were moving back into the line on Christmas Day but were able to enjoy a traditional festive meal in a hutted camp before making their way into the line on Boxing Day.

---

44 Weetman, H.C.C., History of the 1/8th Battalion Sherwood Foresters, 1914-1918, 208 – 209.
45 Corrigan, 85.

Other 17th Northumberland Fusiliers NER men who died in November include:

M Hudson	Minty Farm	Darlington	Plumber
John Dunn	Bard Cottage	Darlington	Labourer
John Seaton	Bard Cottage	Middlesborough	Freight Shunter
JB Waind	Dozinghem	Hull Goods	Clerk
Alfred Robinson	Bard Cottage	Shildon	Lamp Cleaner
Vincent Taylor	Dozinghem	Tyne Dock	Craneman
Fred Brooks	Bard Cottage	Horsea	Platelayer
George Reay	Buffs Road	Hexham	Number taker
W Richmond	Buffs Road	Barnard Castle	Signalman

1918

The final year of the war started quietly on the Western Front, but still the death toll ticked along. The 17th Northumberland Fusiliers, engaged in railway construction work, lost ten men killed in January, at least two of whom had previously been employed by the NER, Wilf Holmes, a goods porter from Leeds Wellington Street and Harry Swainson a porter from Sexhow North Yorkshire.

21 March 1918 German attack – Operation Michael

1st and 2nd Wiltshires and 2nd Northamptons all but wiped out.

The relative quietness was shattered on 21 March by a tremendous artillery bombardment before specially trained German 'shock-troops', centred on the old Somme battlefield, spearheaded the offensive across a 60-mile front. Two divisions of Germans attacked the front at St Quentin. The overwhelming superior numbers resulted in 2nd Wiltshires having little chance and the battalion were soon overrun and, from the commanding officer downwards, those who survived were captured. At least four railwaymen serving in the battalion were killed.

As the 2nd Wiltshires were being blasted apart the 1st Wiltshires, who had been out of the line training, were deployed on 22 March into hasty positions close to Fremicourt, to the east of

Frederick Heaver	Pte	21	3	18	26	Savy	Gt Western	Swindon		
Frederick Mattock	Pte	21	3	18	24	Pozieres	Gt Western	Swindon		
Thomas Perry	Pte	21	3	18	34	Roupy Road German	Gt Western	Swindon		*T H Perry*
John Ralph	Pte	21	3	18	20	Pozieres	GER	Ingatestone	Porter	

Bapaume. Over the next forty-eight hours the battalion were subject to heavy artillery, and some short falling British shells, which caused casualties. An attack was repelled and a stronger assault was being held when the commanding officer was ordered over the telephone to 'retire at once'.[46] There seems to have been no co-ordination between flanking battalions because the battalion on the right withdrew immediately exposing the flank of 1st Wiltshires to enemy machine gun fire. It was the commanding officer's assessment that the attack had failed, but the battalion 'attempted to come back as ordered but were practically exterminated by machine gun fire'.[47] The casualty rate was huge. The battalion strength at the end of February reported as 20 officers and 624 men was now down to just three officers and 54 men. What was left of the battalion was despatched to 'Plug Street' to reconstitute and rebuild. Compared to the earlier part of the war, the number of railwaymen killed in this encounter was very low; Private Sidney Scammell aged forty-one, and Private Harold Averies, both of whom had worked for GWR at Swindon. Presumably this was because the battalion was running out of railwaymen having turned over so many soldiers. It would be interesting to know whether Private Scammell had joined the army comparatively late in the war, and was an older draft, or whether he had just been very lucky to have survived for so long.

Although 2nd Wiltshires as a battalion had ceased to exist, an ad-hoc entity of 'Wiltshiremen' was formed from cooks, storemen, soldiers returning from leave or sickness; anyone who could be spared from across the brigade regardless of cap badge, they were ordered to delay the enemy. They fought at Libermont to the east of the Canal du Nord and Roye, holding their ground for four days until relieved by French soldiers, whereupon they were withdrawn and transported, eventually, to the Ypres area.

Also in the Ypres Salient were the 17th Northumberland Fusiliers, they had been repairing railway bridges which had been subsiding in the soft ground. The 21 March was described as quiet, but they were tasked with setting up one of the bridges that they had just repaired for demolition and with dismantling sidings, yards and ammunition dumps and salvaging materials. On 23 March the railway bridge across the River Steenbeck collapsed just as a train was passing, the locomotive and wagon crashed into deep water. The train carried Lieutenant A K Wardroper's 7 Platoon and Canadian Railway Troops who were travelling to St Julian. Lt Wardroper organised the rescue of 17 men who fell into the water, but the driver and fireman who were trapped in the locomotive could not be saved.

Like many battalions, the 2nd Northamptons were caught up in the disorganisation of the attack and were committed to a series of delaying battles. After a continuous ten days of battle they were withdrawn on 2 April having incurred 404 casualties, and sent south to Villers-Bretonneux to reconstitute.

Eventually the German attack petered out, having wiped out 1st and 2nd Wiltshires and 2nd Northamptons, along with many other battalions, having been fought to a standstill and outrun their supply lines which had struggled over the land ravaged by three years of war fighting.

9 April 1918 German attack again – Operation Georgette – 1st Wiltshires overrun

The 1st Wiltshires had been sent to 'Plug Street' to reconstitute, but such was the crisis that the regeneration took place in the line. On 10 April a particularly heavy bombardment signalled the start of Operation Georgette, a German attack aimed at capturing the important Hazebrouck railway junction, at cutting off Ypres and in securing the channel ports. The Wiltshiremen, who had only just been reinforced, were overrun. In total 359 were captured, 118 wounded and 22 killed, including

46   1st Wiltshires,162.
47   1st Wiltshires,162.

C S M Sheppard

Company Sergeant Major Ashley Sheppard, who had been a GWR pilot guard at Bristol, Sergeant W Blackledge who was an L&NWR clerk based at Broad Street, and Private Henry Lewis a machine-man from Swindon. Once again the battalion barely existed standing at 70 all ranks. Many of those wounded or captured were in the battalion for less than two weeks.

The 2nd Wiltshires was reformed on 5 April and was tasked with moving an ammunition dump to the rear which took five days. On 19 April they were merged with 2nd Bedfords to form one fighting strength battalion.

The 17th Northumberland Fusiliers were deployed on 13 April to the village of La Motte, in the hitherto peaceful rear area around Hazebrouck where they were to support the 1st Australian Division in establishing a defensive line. The village had been largely untouched by war, but within two days every house in the village had been destroyed by artillery. A shell hit a billet on 20 April killing four soldiers with another dying on 26 April.

William Jeffrey	Sgt	Cinqs British	Freight Guard	NER	Newcastle Forth
F Dunn	L/Sgt	Le Grand Hasard	Goods Clerk	NER	Renshaw
ED Ord	Pte	Ebblinghem	Freight Shunter	NER	Heaton Junction
CH Whitehead	Pte	Ebblinghem	Goods Clerk	NER	Marsh Lane
W Needham	Pte	Ebblinghem	Porter	NER	Sculcoates

The composite battalion from 2nd Bedfords and 2nd Wiltshires had been relocated into the Ypres Salient, near Gheluvelt, to lick their wounds and rebuild. Like 1st Wiltshires they suffered very heavy casualties, on the same ground that they had defended in 1914, trying to delay and disrupt a heavy German attack on 19 April. The next day to the east of Bethune near Givenchy, the 1st Northamptons counter-attacked fighting through heavy machine gun fire with courage and determination. They captured their objective within twenty minutes but still suffered 112 casualties, described as 'not unduly heavy'.[48] The 1st Wiltshires meanwhile, since their latest mauling ten days before, had been fully replenished up to a strength of 780. Sixteen of the 21 officers posted in came from the Durham Light Infantry. They deployed to Kemmel and contributed to the capture of the village, suffering only light casualties despite fierce fighting.

Wiltshires marching to the Front. IWM Q740

48   Northamptons, 268.

The 2nd Northamptons had three weeks to recover before on 24 April they were involved in what turned out to be the world's first tank-on-tank battle close to the village of Villers-Bretonneux near Amiens. Along with the 13th Australian Infantry Brigade they were tasked with re-capturing the village. When they were withdrawn on the 27th their strength was only 198 they had suffered 285 killed, wounded or missing.

By the 4 May operation Georgette had fizzled out as the allies had committed huge reserves in absorbing the German fighting power ensuring that their momentum was lost, but not before over 100,000 casualties were incurred on each side.

27 May German attack – Operation Blucher-Yorck – 2nd Northamptons wiped out

A number of the most battered divisions were moved into a quiet sector of the French army in an area to the north west of Reims called the Chemin des Dames Ridge. There, inexperienced troops gained a chance to learn the realities of battle. Among the 32 battalions from four divisions were 2nd Northamptons who occupied ex-German trenches close to the village of Juvincourt, to the north of the Aisne river approximately 15 miles north west of Reims. They were in the centre of the British section of the front line. The 1st Wiltshires were carrying out training in Prouilly ten miles south west of 2nd Northamptons and to the south of the river Aisne. At 8pm on 26 May the 1st Wiltshires were given orders to move five miles nearer the front and to prepare defences. A little further to south 2nd Wiltshires had been allocated a village, Vesigneul-sur-Marne, which was 'far away from the fighting, little affected by the war, and was looking at its best in May' and the battalion made excellent use of the Marne Canal for swimming.[49]

At 1am on 27th, forward troops were hit with a heavy bombardment of gas shells followed by sustained artillery fire before stormtroopers assaulted. The 2nd Northamptons held on for several hours, until they were outflanked. 1st Wiltshires were ordered to take up positions in Bouffignereux a mile away. 2nd Northamptons and the forward line had been almost entirely wiped out. By 1130 the 1st Wiltshires had made a hasty defence line but were soon experiencing bombardment. The stormtroopers having broken through the established front line defences, crossed the River Aisne and made across the open ground towards the Wiltshires rudimentary trenches. The battalion were attacked and by 1730 the sheer weight of German attackers forced them from their positions. Further south, notice to move had been given to 2nd Wiltshires who were awaiting a fleet of French omnibuses to transport them to the battle area.

What remained of 1st Wiltshires were split into two main groups who were constantly in action as they withdrew, fighting numerous rear guards actions as they fought to keep the Germans at bay. They established a temporary defence around Branscourt on 28 May by which time 2nd Wiltshires had been transported to Bligny about six miles due south of the 1st Battalion which fell back on the 29th to a line at Faverol only three miles from where the 2nd Battalion were digging in at Bouleuse. During the night 2nd Wiltshires reported confusion as disorganised groups of troops fell back through their positions, but at that stage at least there was little enemy activity. At dawn on 30 May, the 2nd Wiltshires were attacked but held their positions through the morning. The 1st Wiltshires meanwhile, who had been in constant contact with the enemy as they withdrew, had been forced from their position to the north. At 2pm 2nd Wiltshires withdrew. Both battalions fell back to the village of Sarcy where 1st Wiltshires took positions east of the River Ardre and 2nd Wiltshires on the high ground east of Sarcy. The two battalions from different brigades and divisions, but from the same county, were holding the same line almost within shouting distance.

49   2nd Wiltshires, 149.

It was along this line, some ten miles from where 2nd Northamptons had been overwhelmed four days before the defences were shored up. 2nd Wiltshires were soon ordered to attack high ground close to Chambrecy. They took their objective and dug in. On 1 June 2nd Wiltshires fell back to the Chambrecy-Bligny road and one of the two columns of 1st Wiltshires moved to the east of Chambrecy.

All the battalions had been considerably weakened in the fighting and over the following days amalgamations were carried out to create composite battalions of fighting strength. In a week the newly formed, but inexperienced, brigades comprising three battalions had been reduced to just one battalion per brigade. 1st Wiltshires formed a Company of 1/25 Composite Battalion, which continued to hold the line in the Bois D'Eclisse to the west of Chamuzy, against frequent attack. 2nd Wiltshires formed a company of 58 Composite Battalion, alongside 9th Royal Welsh Fusiliers, also in the Bois D'Eclisse, and were attacked on 5 June resulting in significant losses amongst the Welsh contingent, but the position was held until relief on 18 June when the Wiltshire contingent reformed as the 2nd battalion. The 2nd Northamptons had effectively ceased to exist on 27 May when, after the battle, they could only muster the Regimental Sergeant Major and the Adjutant and the whole brigade of only three officers and 68 other ranks. In all 38 railwaymen died on 27 May and during this short period 55. Both the Wiltshire battalions were withdrawn by the end of June.

Map 4. Around the River Aisne May 1918

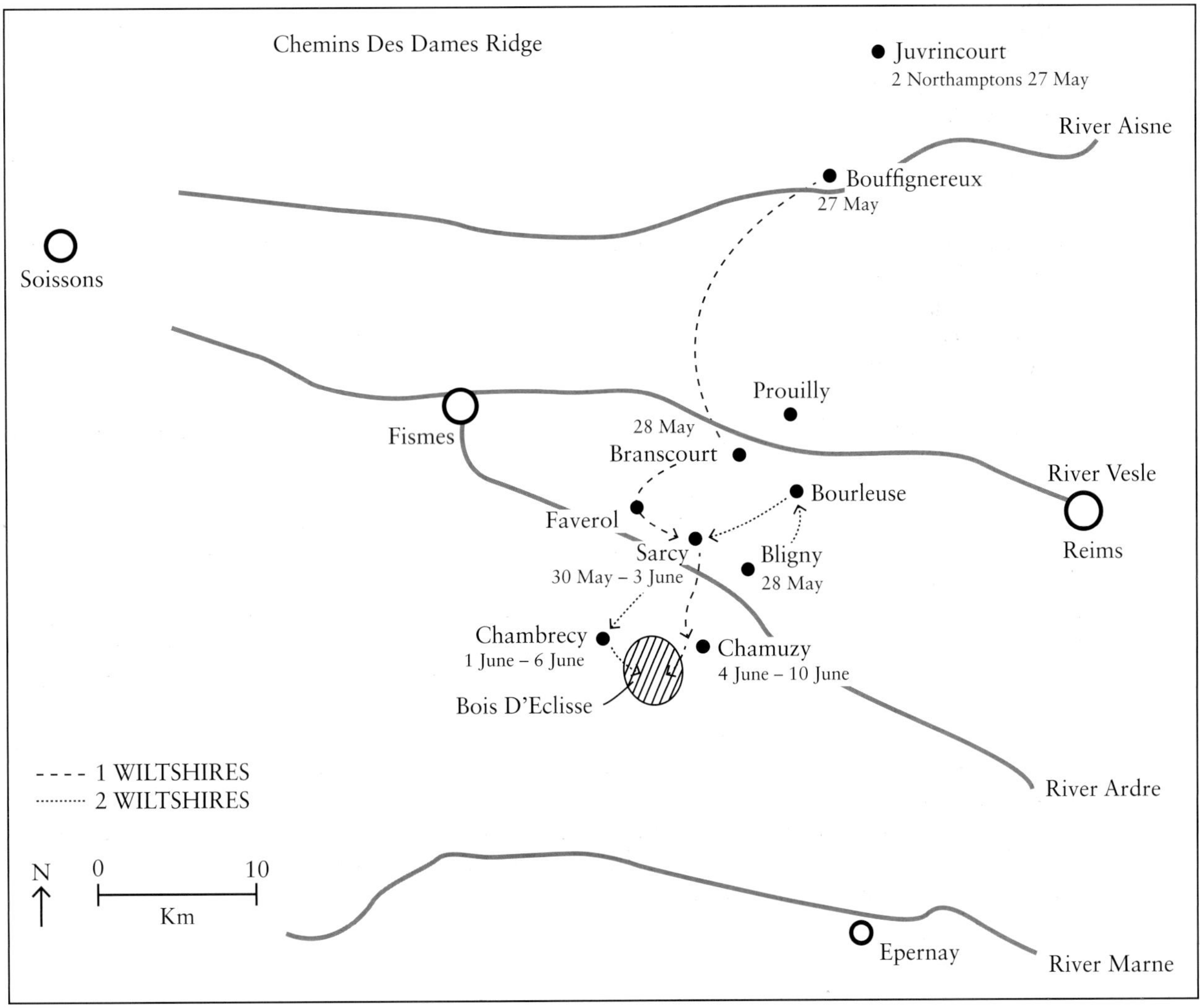

| Arthur Moreton | Pte | 1st | Wiltshires | 27 | 5 | 18 | Soissons | Gt Western | Old Hill | Booking Clerk |
| George Freer | Pte | 1st | Wiltshires | 27 | 5 | 18 | Soissons | L & NWR | Stetchford | Junior Porter |

A C Moreton

The 2nd Northamptons, which three weeks before had been virtually wiped out, were by 20 June once again up to strength. The drafts to the battalions by this stage of the war had little geographic affinity to any particular county or region. The whole division was taken out of the battle area and sent to the coast until 19 July. The battalion was then sent to the Arras area, described as 'quiet'.

Quiet in Bethune

In contrast, the 5th Sherwood Foresters, despite the carnage going on all around, found life around the mining area east of Bethune quiet as stalemate prevailed. 8th Sherwood Foresters described the position, around the villages of Gorre and Essars, as 'open warfare' since the British line was little more than a line in the ground through the ripening crops.[50] Protection was from a few slit trenches and shell holes. Movement was restricted to the limited hours of darkness and only then by moving 'over the top'.[51] The area was flat and open and the enemy had wide fields of observation from their more substantial positions. As the days got longer there was little time to improve the defences since most of the precious night-time was spent re-organising and resupplying. In any case, they couldn't dig too deep because of the high water table. The trench routine was up to twelve days in the line with six days out. 1st Northamptons moved to quiet trenches around Le Bassee to the east of Bethune on 7 April and stayed in the area until 31 August. 17th Northumberland Fusiliers were located in another quiet sector around Vimy, south of Lens, until 16 August close to where 2nd Northamptons relocated from the seaside on 19 August. The 1st Wiltshires, having rebuilt, were back in the line on 24 July at Beaumont Hamel on the Somme where they had fought in 1916.

By 6 August the 2nd Wiltshires, again rebuilt, were fighting over ground they had occupied in 1915 and 1916 to the north of Bethune and after each spell in the trenches their positions were several hundred metres further forward as the Germans were gradually pushed rearward. But resistance remained fierce.

The Last 100 days

Allied attack August 1918 and the Germans retreat.

On 8 August, a co-ordinated attack featuring 456 secretly massed tanks with infantry and air support attacked German positions near Cambrai. The tanks had been transported into position by railway troops from the Rail Operating Division (see page 127). Typically artillery increased in the days leading up to an attack but in this attack the guns were kept silent, maintaining the advantage of surprise to the attackers. The enemy were robbed of early warning to take to the deep shelters. Instead the assault commenced with co-ordinated massed attacks from aircraft, tanks, artillery and infantry. The day was a tremendous success setting conditions which gradually overcame the German defences, forcing the enemy to give ground, and marked the start of the final 100 days of the war.

The Germans fought hard, but began to withdraw, pulling back to the fortifications of the Hindenburg Line on 27 August. Construction of this sophisticated series of strong points, concrete bunkers and machine gun posts had begun in 1916. The 'line' comprised 'three old British trench

---

50   8th Sherwood Foresters, 232.
51   8th Sherwood Foresters, 233.

lines plus the ridge outpost line, the Hindenburg Line proper, the Hindenburg Support Line and finally, the Hindenburg Reserve Line', which at least in part was built alongside two unfinished canals, the Canal Du Nord and the St Quentin Canal.[52] In February 1917 the Germans had been forced back to the Hindenburg Line but had broken out in their advance of 21 March 1918, but now all of their gains were eliminated as they fell back to the positions that they had last held five months previously. The withdrawal by the Germans to this formidable fortification was completed by 11 September.

The 17th Northumberland Fusiliers meanwhile, as the divisional pioneer battalion of 52nd Division, had been following closely behind the infantry as they advanced from Thiepval. By 23 August they had advanced over ground which countless battalions had fought over in 1916 and worked north-eastwards through Gomiecourt. By the end of the month the pioneers were working across No Man's Land between Bullecourt and Queant to the south-east of Arras. They too were closing on the Hindenburg Line. Pioneering over this churned up land was hard. 'The ground was about the roughest ever experienced by us, having been fought over dozens of times. The removal of relays of rusted and tangled barbed wire was not an easy task, and all sorts of obstacles were encountered in cutting a formation in the road. The men worked like heroes and, although not even fresh when they started the job, they stuck to it for some thirteen or fourteen hours.'[53] For their labour, which was subject to regular bombardment, they had the satisfaction of seeing traffic passing their position following up the advance. 'It was an inspiring sight the following morning to see our heavy guns lumbering along where twenty-four hours before there had been nothing but desolation – shell holes, wire, gun emplacements and corpses.'[54] Having completed the task there was no rest for the pioneers, they immediately moved onto the next task, 'We spent most of the next day collecting and burying our dead, of whom there were all too many, and amongst them we discovered a battalion postman with the mail, which we collected and sent down to headquarters in the hope that it would eventually be delivered.'[55] It was clearly a long and arduous job and feeding was an issue but the 'sacred field kitchens with the equally sacred NER horses arrived'.[56] They seemed very attached to the NER horses which had survived since being mobilised in 1914 and note is made of some of the last of the railway horses being killed shortly afterwards in air bombing. At around this time they captured a German who they reportedly recognised as being a pre-war barber from Hartlepool. Although not engaged in infantry fighting the 17th Northumberland Fusiliers, rarely out of action, were constantly labouring and suffered a steady attrition of men.

Attacking the Hindenburg Line

By mid-September all six battalions, although in different brigades, divisions and armies, were assembling, along with many other battalions, across the length of the Western Front. Preparing to attack the imposing Hindenburg Line, to bludgeon their way through the interconnecting lines of defences and eventually into the open ground to the east.

Close to St Quentin, were 1st Northamptons and 5th Sherwood Foresters who would spend the rest of the war leapfrogging one another eastwards. North of them by about ten miles, having fought their way east from Beaumont Hamel across the old Somme battlefield, were 1st Wiltshires. The 17th Northumberland Fusiliers were located south-east of Arras and heading towards Cambrai. Further north to the east of Arras were 2nd Northamptons. The 2nd Wiltshires were located to the east of Bethune at Richebourg St Vaast.

---

52   Hart, P., 1918 A Very British Victory, 421.
53   17th Northumberland Fusiliers, 93.
54   17th Northumberland Fusiliers, 94.
55   17th Northumberland Fusiliers, 93.
56   17th Northumberland Fusiliers, 93.

Map 5. Final Assaults 1918

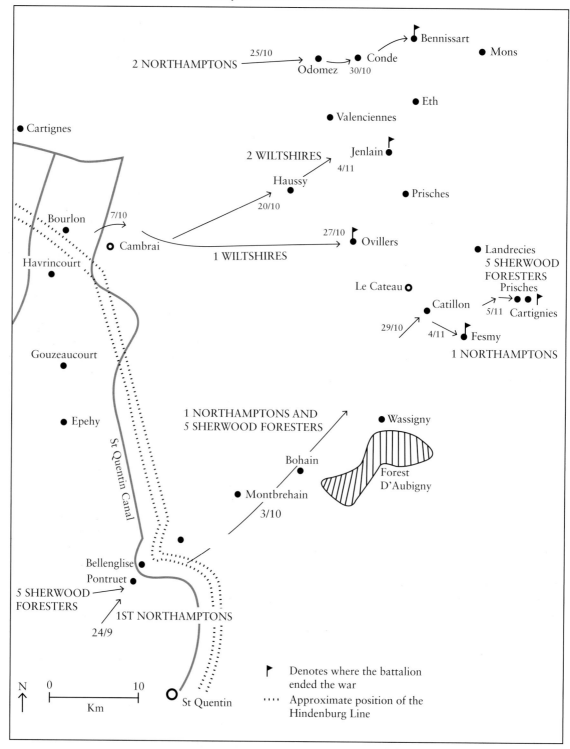

18 September – Preliminary attacks

A number of preliminary battles were fought in preparation of the assault on the Hindenburg Line. 1st Wiltshires attacked Equancourt on 18 September capturing over 220 Germans and eight field guns, but for the loss of 13 killed and 75 injured including Company Sergeant Major Arthur Loveday DCM and Bar.

Company Sergeant Major A W Loveday
1st Battalion Wiltshire Regiment

CSM Loveday died on 19 September 1918 aged thirty-one and is buried at Gouzeaucourt. He had been a frame builder's assistant in the wagon and frame shop of the locomotive and carriage department of the GWR at Swindon. He is the only one of the 12,500 railwaymen featured in this work who won two Distinguished Conduct Medals. His first was won on 19 December 1915, where he took part in a raid of the enemy trench at Ploegsteert and he delayed the enemy whilst the party was able to withdraw without sustaining a casualty. His second was for subsequent acts of conspicuous gallantry in action when he was jumped onto the parapet whilst attacking an enemy trench and forced them to surrender (See page 257).

In the hitherto quiet Bethune area of Richebourg St Vaast, nineteen-year-old Lance Corporal RG Biss who had been a goods clerk with GWR at Devizes, was killed on 19 September whilst attacking trenches with the 2nd Wiltshires. The 2nd Northamptons began advancing east on 21 September from equally quiet Arras.

The 1st Northamptons had deployed to the St Quentin area and were advancing along a river valley towards Pontruet. A well-defended spur dominated the village and the battalion, along with four tanks in support, attacked on 24 September. Infantry and tank co-ordination was still in its infancy and was a wash out. One tank got lost prior to the rendezvous, two were stopped by artillery before the advance began, and the final one suffered a map reading error and trundled off in the wrong direction. The Northamptons came under accurate and sustained machine gun fire from Pontruet and their attack petered out. It wasn't until the village had been cleared by 5th Sherwood Foresters and 5th Leicesters that the Northamptons could progress and clear the spur. For the Northamptons the costs were high with over 250 casualties, including eighteen-year-old Private George Clements an ex L&NWR boiler attendant from Euston, and having captured the hill they were withdrawn. 5th Sherwood Foresters also lost at least two railwaymen.

| R Hodgkinson | Pte | 5th | Sherwoods | 24 | 9 | 18 | 31 | Brie | Midland | Darley Dale | Labourer |
| Charles Knight | Pte | 5th | Sherwoods | 24 | 9 | 18 | 30 | Vis en Artois | Midland | Weston, Notts | Labourer |

The 17th Northumberland Fusiliers reached the Canal du Nord on 27 September and, although dry was a formidable obstacle, the pioneers were required to make three crossing points whilst in contact with the enemy. They incurred 12 casualties including five fatalities as they made their way to the tasking, but amazingly achieved the task without further loss.

J Bradley	Pte	Moeuvres British	NER	Tweedmouth	Porter
J Handley	L/Cpl	Moeuvres British	NER	Yarm	Platelayer
W E R Holdsworth	Pte	Moeuvres British	NER	Micklefield	H Clerk
S Walton	Pte	Moeuvres British	NER	Darlington	Porter
Barker	Pte	Sunken Road	NER	West Hartlepool	Capstan Lad

Assault on the St Quentin Canal and the Hindenburg Line – 28 September

The next major obstacle was the unfinished St Quentin Canal and the Hindenburg Line. One division tasked with breaching this formidable defence was 46th (Midland) Division which included 5th Sherwood Foresters, although they weren't used in the attack. The canal was a considerable obstacle to the assaulting troops. On the morning of the attack dense fog made communication difficult but effectively blinded the enemy, particularly during a steep descent to the canal. Despite the challenges, the crossing was comparatively easy and soon the attackers were on the far embankment assaulting the Hindenburg Line. Although it took two years to build, the 46th Division proved the Hindenburg Line was not impregnable. The division fought until 30 September when they were withdrawn. Only two railwaymen are known to have died.

Reginald Norwood	2/Lt	9th	Tank Corps	29	9	18	24	Bellicourt	Gt Western		Clerk
Charles Goddard	Pte	8th	Sherwoods	29	9	18	28	Vis en Artois	Midland	Derby	

The 5th Sherwood Foresters rested whilst the St Quentin Canal had been taken, rejoined the chase on 3 October attacking the final line of German prepared defences to the east of the main Hindenburg Line, known as the Beaurevoir Line, the final fortifications before Germany. They attacked the heavily defended villages of Ramicourt and Montbrehain. The 5th, 6th and 8th Sherwood Foresters were all committed to close combat street fighting in the villages. It was 'estimated that at least 25 per cent of the men engaged in the fighting actually fleshed their bayonets'.[57] Very descriptive language for what must have been a very tough fight.

By this time the Northumberland Fusiliers were engaged in the constant maintenance required in keeping the main supply routes, many of which crossed No Man's Land or recently enemy held territory, open. The ability to ensure an unimpeded flow of logistics along these routes was critical to maintaining the momentum of the attack. It would only take a short interruption caused by bombardment, congestion, or infrastructure failure, to strangle the advance. 'No rule of modern war

---

57   Priestley, R.E., Breaking the Hindenburg Line. The Story of The 46th (North Midland) Division, 116.

is more true than that which limits the speed of an army by the rate at which the railhead on which it is based can move forward.'[58]

About ten miles north of the Foresters on 7 October, around Cambrai, the 1st Wiltshires crossed the St Quentin Canal and occupied another part of the Hindenburg Line. They then mounted an attack on unfinished defences to the rear, which they captured and held despite sustaining 81 wounded and 12 killed. The 2nd Northamptons meanwhile moved eastwards from the south of Lens and 2nd Wiltshires had moved to Cambrai and were beginning to advance eastwards.

Setting up for the final attacks

Battalions were leapfrogging one another, engaged in intense fighting for a few days, having a short recovery, then returning some miles further to the east to continue battle. The 5th Sherwood Foresters next fought in the large forest of Andigny some ten miles further east. It took a week of hard fighting to finally overwhelm the defences and on 17 October captured the forest, whereupon the Sherwood Foresters were again rested.

The 1st Northamptons along with the 2nd Royal Sussex, with whom they had spent most of the war, continued the attack, firstly capturing Wassigny and then two days later moving onto Catillon two miles away and on the banks of the Sambre canal. The capture of Catillon would provide a foothold for follow-up troops, including the Sherwood Foresters, to continue the drive east. But 1st Northamptons struggled against a determined enemy, making a series of attacks around the village without success, resulting in 29 killed and 96 wounded before they were withdrawn to reorganise on the 29 October. The battalion was now close to where they had fought in 1914, although only two officers remained from those days.

| Walter Bell-Chambers | Pte | 1st | Northamptons | 23 | 10 | 18 | 19 | Highland, Le Cateau | SECR | | Apprentice |
| Edward Connor | Pte | 1st | Northamptons | 23 | 10 | 18 | 18 | Vis en Artois | Midland | Plaistow | Labourer |

The 1st Wiltshires meanwhile were running parallel to the 1st Northamptons and 5th Sherwood Foresters about ten miles further north. They had continued moving east, fighting through villages as they went. Their final battle of the war was at a village called Ovillers on 23 October, at the cost of 26 killed and 123 wounded.

The 2nd Wiltshires, a further six miles north of 1st Wiltshires, attacked the village of Haussy on 20 October. Artillery rounds dropped short nearly stopping the attack 'at times so many of our own shells among our men as to threaten disaster'.[59] 122 Wiltshiremen were killed or injured, but the village was captured, virtually unopposed. Further north still 2nd Northamptons captured Odomez on 25 October, ending the month near Mons at the village of Conde.

4 November – The last big offensive

On 4 November three armies attacked on a front of forty miles in the last big offensive of the war, aiming to capture the Sambre Canal. 1st Northamptons had a supporting role to 2nd Royal Sussex who, led by their commanding officer Lt Colonel Johnson, executed an assault crossing of the canal through murderous machine gun and artillery fire and alongside a Royal Engineers Company captured some dominating fortified lock buildings. This enabled 1st Northamptons to break out onto the high ground and capture the village of Fesmy. Lt Colonel Johnson and Major

---

58   Priestley, 128.
59   2nd Wiltshires, 168.

Findley of the RE were both awarded the VC. This was the last action of 1st Northamptons. From 18 September they had been virtually continuously in action; they had attacked the Germans seven times and withstood a counter attack three times, captured over 600 prisoners, nine artillery pieces, and around 100 machine guns. And, they ended the war pretty well where they started it.

The 2nd Wiltshires, just north of Jenlain, early on 4 November attacked and captured the village of Eth. Losses were 'light' but at least four railwaymen were killed, all from the Swindon works, three aged nineteen and one aged twenty. Given their ages, these troops were probably relatively junior conscripts who would not have fought with the railwaymen killed in the earlier years of the war.

WA Hayward	Pte	2nd	Wiltshires	4	11	18	19	Cross Roads Cemetery	Gt Western	Swindon	Apprentice Boilermaker
Reginald Lambdin	Pte	2nd	Wiltshires	4	11	18	19	Eth	Gt Western	Swindon	Machinist
Thomas Evans	Pte	2nd	Wiltshires	5	11	18	19	Cross Roads Cemetery	Gt Western	Swindon	Apprentice
G Howell	Pte	2nd	Wiltshires	5	11	18	20	Cross Roads Cemetery	Gt Western	Swindon	Apprentice

W A Hayward   R G Lambdin   T D Evans   G Howell

The 5th Sherwood Foresters crossed the Sambre Canal breaking out into the open land to the east. They cleared the village of Prisches the following day and advanced to Cartignies where they went firm until the Armistice. In the north, the 2nd Northamptons crossed the Scheldt river by pontoon bridge at Conde north of Valenciennes and by 10 November were at Bernissart just over the border in Belgium, near Mons, where they ended the war. The 17th Northumberland Fusiliers were still digging trenches and erecting barbed wire even on the 11 November and they were not told of the Armistice until the 12th.

The end of the fighting

After the Armistice, many battalions were disbanded and the troops demobilised, but the 1st Northamptons went on to advance on foot into Germany. They reported that the villages were well kept and the German people very friendly. They took the opportunity to march the Colours along the Rhine, and there must have been a lot of reflection and remembrance of the privations of the previous four years. This one battalion had experienced over 1,000 killed in action, over 600 died of wounds or sickness, and more than 3,000 wounded. Of a battalion which usually numbered slightly less than 1,000, on average the whole battalion was killed or wounded each year. In many respects it was probably a fairly typical battalion, and from this one example it is perhaps possible to appreciate the enormous carnage of human beings during this horrendous war.

Treating the injured

It was a long and slow route home for an injured soldier. At times the evacuation process was tested to breaking point, but even when it wasn't it could be slow and painful, with many dying en route. A soldier injured on the battlefront, if he was lucky, would be speedily carried by stretcher to the regimental aid post which was situated just behind the lead companies. This would comprise the doctor, perhaps a medical corporal, and little else. The RMO (Regimental Medical Officer, the doctor) had between 16 and 32 stretcher bearers so could evacuate around eight casualties at any one time. Not many, given the numbers who would typically be injured in battle. The doctor would patch up and send the casualty to the rear with stretcher bearers usually from the Field Ambulance. On a good day the injured would then pass to the Advanced Dressing Station, which might be sited in the basement of a bombed out house, a little more to the rear. Fom there they may be loaded on to carts and taken to the Ambulance Control Point, then by motor vehicle or horse drawn ambulance to the Casualty Clearing Station (CCS). This would have been the first point where any rudimentary surgical procedures would be carried out. Most of the wounds were from high explosive and shrapnel, which frequently caused complications such as shock and infection, chief of which was gas gangrene which could develop where there was inadequate blood flow. Here the injured would be triaged; the 'lightly wounded' would be kept close to the forward area and returned to their units when fit; the 'severe but survivable' would be sent along the evacuation chain, and the 'non-survivable' would be made comfortable.

Most CCSs were located on the rail network from where it was possible to load the injured onto the ambulance train for evacuation to the base hospitals in the channel ports. This wasn't a quick process. Ambulance trains averaged only around 20 mph from railhead to reception point, and the journey on the train often took twelve hours. At the base hospitals, those who were well enough, would then be evacuated via hospital ships across the Channel and the chance of recovery in Britain.

Wounded transported to the dressing station, Flers. September 1916. IWM CO811

But this was if it was a good day. There were some atrocious days when the carnage from the front completely overwhelmed the evacuation procedure, and men died where on other days they would, perhaps, have survived. In the first 60 minutes of the battle of the Somme, on 1 July 1916, there were 30,000 casualties. There were 14 casualty clearing stations along the front, each manned with 15 doctors, 15 nurses and about 70 orderlys and staff. Each CCS was capable of dealing with 150–300 casualties totalling no more than 5,000, so within one hour of the start of that battle there were seven times the number of casualties than the CCSs could cope with. Perhaps anticipating a humdinger of a battle, General Rawlinson had requested eighteen ambulance trains, but on the morning of the battle there was only one available, so the CCSs had no means of reducing their injured by passing them down the line. Even though two more arrived during the afternoon and two more overnight, only 3,200 injured were evacuated and the CCSs held over 12,000 casualties, with a further 13,800 arriving on the following day and 8,800 on the third. Numbers swelled more on 4 and 5 July and there was one soldier who finally made the CCS on 14 July having been injured on the 1st.

The 12 November 1916, wasn't a particularly bad day in the list of awful days of the battle of the Somme, but it was the day that Brigadier-General Glasfurd the commander of 12th Australian Brigade was injured near Flers; he was hit by shrapnel in the kidney. As a senior officer there would have been considerable effort put into his evacuation, but it still took ten hours to evacuate him the few miles to the CCS at Heilly Station, where, perhaps not unsurprisingly, he died. Soldiers died all along the route. Many, like the Brigadier-General, were dead by the time they arrived at the CCS.

There were 143 railwaymen who died serving in the Royal Army Medical Corps. Many are likely to have been stretcher bearers killed in carrying out their duty trying to preserve life. Privates James Tew and James Fursdon both served with 142 Field Ambulance and were killed on 23 and 24 July 1916 and are buried in Bernafay Wood Cemetery. Lance Corporal G Spendlove and Private James Neal both served with the 2/2nd North Midlands Brigade RAMC and were killed together on 25 September 1917. They all worked for the Midland Railway, Tew as a sidings foreman in Burton-on-Trent and Fursdon as a porter in Kettering, Spendlove and Neal in the Derby carriage and wagon works.

Ambulance Trains

The railway was the only efficient and effective means of conveying mass casualties from the battle zone to the hospitals and then for onward distribution across the UK to places of convalescence. At the start of the war the ambulance trains available for British injured were inadequate, converted French wagon stock. Quickly, British designed and built trains were shipped to the continent, but there was always something of a shortage. At times, such as at the start of the Battle of the Somme, temporary ambulance trains would be brought into service.

The overall casualty rate on the Western Front from battle and non-battle causes amounted to 1,139 soldiers per 1,000 of the average ration roll.[60] These statistics include the most serious to the most trivial and include the sick as well as those damaged by the fighting. Not all of those injured would require any form of evacuation, and of course many people were injured more than once. Nonetheless the total casualties was a staggering 6.2 million of which 3,443,507 were evacuated from the casualty clearing stations to the base hospitals, and a further 1,610, 672 were transported from hospitals to ports.[61] The ambulance trains on the Western Front, never more than 42 in total, moved over five million patients.

---

60   Mitchell, T.J., History of the Great War Based on Official Documents. Medical Services, Casualties And Medical Statistics, 117.

61   Mitchell, 107.

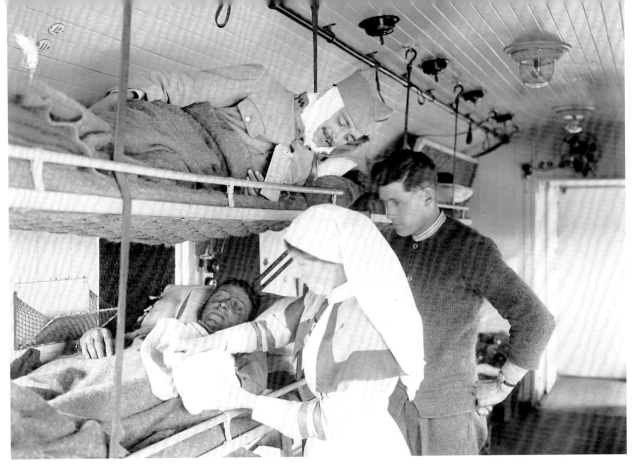

Top: IWM Q008736   Bottom: IWM Q008738

Ambulance Train 14 with personnel and French politicians, August 1915. IWM Q28853

Despite the horrific injuries of many, there were comparatively few deaths on the trains. The triage system tended not to waste precious space on a casualty who wasn't going to make it. Where the medical staff considered a patient to be too infirm to travel, they were often off-loaded at Abbeville, where many subsequently died. Records show that Private G D Banning of 17th Northumberland Fusiliers, a former fireman with NER from Hull, died at 2315 on 4 July 1916 on Number 20 ambulance train.[62] The train had been loaded at Puchevillers on the Somme at 11am and he endured over 12 hours on board with gunshot wounds to his abdomen. Banning is recorded as dying on 5 July 1916, which is when the train arrived in Rouen, where he is buried. Number 20 ambulance train is one of 30 which were in operation during the Battle of the Somme and arrived on the Western Front on 5 January 1916 having been built by GER.

Hospital Ships

Having been treated and stabilised, those deemed fit enough to make the journey home were evacuated as soon as possible across the channel to Britain. For many this would involve another long ambulance train journey, and for all, passage across the Channel by hospital ship. Fifteen allied hospital ships were sunk during the war including two former railway ships HMHS *Anglia* on 17 November 1915 and HMHS *Donegal* 17 April 1917 (see pages 197 and 204).

---

62   The National Archives WO95/4136 War Diary Number 20 Ambulance Train.

A number of RAMC men died at sea serving on hospital ships which were sunk by the enemy. Private Lawrence Edwards, who had been an ex-GWR horse loader from Oxford, is commemorated on the Hollybrook Memorial in Southampton for those lost at sea. He died on 17 April 1917 when two hospital ships were torpedoed and sank – the *Lanfranc* and the Midland-owned *Donegal* (see page 204). Private J C Snelson was killed on 10 April 1917 when the hospital ship *Salta* was sunk by a mine just outside Le Havre. Snelson of 108 Remer Street, Crewe, was one of 205 from the ship who was lost. Another railwayman recorded on the Hollybrook memorial for the same day is William Knott, a Private with the 6th Northamptons. Twenty-five-year-old Knott from Broxbourne in Hertfordshire had worked for GER for 11 years and had been a clerk in the commercial department. It seems likely that he was one of the injured who had been loaded onto the *Salta*. Two Staff Sergeants, Saul Cumber, who had worked for GNR as storekeeper, and John Ritchie, who had been a GNSR clerk based in Aberdeen, served on the hospital ship *Glenart Castle*. The *Glenart Castle* had left Newport bound for France when she was torpedoed in the Bristol Channel; 162 of the ship's company died including the two railwaymen.

British based Ambulance Trains

Nurses and ambulance train at Liverpool Lime Street station, 2 February 1916. NRM 1997–7059 HOR F 1446

The injured who arrived in the south coast ports were distributed across the United Kingdom by British ambulance trains. The sheer scale of wounded being delivered to towns and cities is hard to comprehend. For instance, 7,822 loaded ambulance trains left from Southampton and over 1.8 million casualties passed over the L&SWR lines. Over 13,000 ambulance trains transited the L&NWR network and over 6,000 across the GWR network with forty-five stations receiving ambulance trains at one time or other. The main receiving stations were Paddington (351), Bristol (395), Plymouth (239), Cardiff (207), Birmingham (200) and Birkenhead, (134). The Midland railway conveyed 3,982 trains and 339,000 injured. One hundred ambulance trains arrived at Halifax with 15,440 casualties, and 400 arrived at Aintree with a total of 72,000 injured on board.[63] Many of these trains arrived late at night or early in the morning and would be unloaded by members of the Lancashire and Yorkshire Railway ambulance volunteers, doing it in their own time and over and above their normal work.

The railway companies had, pre-war, developed a fairly sophisticated role in training for ambulance evacuation and many of the staff were qualified in first aid. This role was tested in war-time with many serving, and dying, with the RAMC, and many others volunteering for ambulance duties over and above their normal railway work.

Ambulance Train Southampton Docks, 11 April 1918. NRM 1997–7059 HOR F 2527

Right: Ambulance trains at Paddington station. NRM 1997–7059 HOR F 1783

---

63   Pratt, E.A., British Railways And The Great War. Organisation, Efforts, Difficulties and Achievements, 195 – 227.

CHAPTER 3

ARMY RAILWAYMEN IN GALLIPOLI, MESOPOTAMIA AND OTHER FRONTS

5th Battalion Wiltshire Regiment

5th Wiltshires were destined to fight the Turks throughout the war. They left England on 1 July 1915 bound for Gallipoli where they arrived on 17 July and fought until January 1916, whereupon they embarked for Mesopotamia. In Mesopotamia they took part in the attempt to relieve Kut, the taking of Baghdad and then towards the end of the war pushed into the mountains to the north east of Baghdad eventually to Kirkuk. The last survivors did not reach home until 1920.

1915

On 1 July 1915 30 officers and 946 men, many ex-GWR men from Swindon, having completed a long period of training since the battalion was raised in August 1914, boarded the SS *Franconia* at Avonmouth bound for Gallipoli. For most it would have been their first time on a ship and their first time overseas. Few would make the return trip. The Wiltshiremen would soon have got used to the routine, finding time to relax, to reflect, to anticipate the fighting to come, and to become bored. By day 14 they would all have relished getting ashore. The excitement of embarkation would have waned over the repetitive days that followed. The officers would have done what they could to keep their men fit, to keep their minds focused, and to keep them prepared for action. But inevitably lethargy would have set in.

The ship berthed in Mudros Bay on the Greek Island of Lemnos on the 15 July and all but three officers and 150 men were trans-shipped onto the SS *Osmanieh* for onward passage to Cape Helles in Gallipoli. The men who remained in Lemnos were replacements for their colleagues who were off to confront the Turks. One mile offshore the battalion was transferred into two tugs, which landed them via the grounded SS *River Clyde* which acted as a pier. So on 17 July the infantrymen were once again on land, the sand of V beach of Cape Helles.

F Baden

F Gough

A little over two weeks from leaving their barracks in Wiltshire, and barely acclimatised during their troopship confinement, they were in the searing heat of a Turkish Mediterranean summer. Almost straight off the boat the men took their place on 19 July, in the complex trench system in the steep and hilly terrain of Gallipoli. The Turks were well prepared and commanded much of the higher 'vital ground'. Privates F Baden and F Gough became the first from the battalion to die in action when they were killed by a rock fall. Both were employed by GWR at the Swindon works, Baden as a striker and Gough as a labourer.

After only nine days in Turkey, the Wiltshires were withdrawn and embarked in destroyers and minesweepers back to Mudros Bay, having had a taster of the conditions of Gallipoli. They had carried out two stints of trench duty, and many fatigues, and suffered a great number of men laid low with dysentery. Lemnos was no relief though since the transit camps were overcrowded and insanitary. But it had one significant advantage over Gallipoli, and that was at least the men were not getting shot at. Only four days later they embarked on HMS *Sarnia*, an ex-L&SWR ferry, and still crewed by former railwaymen (see page 195), and landed at Anzac Cove on the 5 August.

Map 6. 5th Wiltshires Gallipoli, July to December 1915

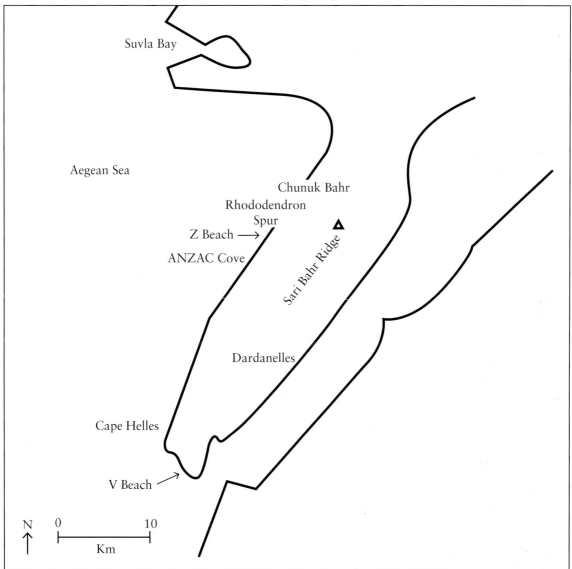

The battalion arrived to take part in what would be the last chance of a break out from Anzac Cove in 1915. A force of mainly Australian and New Zealanders carried out an attack on very difficult ground and pretty quickly their plans unravelled. Australian troops, with the support of three British battleships firing their main armament, mounted a diversionary attack on 'Lone Pine' as a prelude to the planned break out. This was an attack 140 yards wide and 130 yards in depth, but was hotly fought over for four days. The breakout force, including 5th Wiltshires, set off at night to position, to eventually attack Chunuk Bair. Any attack at night is complicated. A divisional night attack with heavily laden and inexperienced troops, untrained in night operations, across the arduous terrain of mountainous ground with sheer drops and ravines and dense and thorny vegetation, against a well prepared enemy in dream ground to defend, was doomed to failure. To make matters worse the mapping was poor and it had been impossible to carry out detailed reconnaissance. Soon the plan was terribly behind schedule, resulting in battalions being exposed during daylight and any benefit of surprise lost.

The Wiltshires were one of many battalions caught up in the confusion. Although they were involved in some skirmishing; most of the fighting was carried out by leading New Zealand battalions and casualties mounted. The unforgiving territory, Turkish dominance of high ground, and debilitating climate, made it difficult for all troops. Eventually battle weary battalions were replaced with the first reserves and 5th Wiltshires found themselves being positioned to take over defensive positions, from where the assault could continue.

In the early hours of the 10th they moved in single file along a 'steep and winding course'; they were led through the night to take up battle positions around first light towards the top of Chunuk Bair, the third highest point on the Sari Bahr ridge.[1] The night march had encountered mishaps, delays and navigational blunders. The battalion were not in a position to take over the line and so their guide took them to a place and, according to the war diary, the men were told to 'make themselves comfortable because the position is quite safe'.[2] The New Zealand officer guide may have considered that in comparison to the front line positions which they were trying to hand over to the British, this position was 'quite safe'. However, it was very close to the front line and, no matter how tired and inexperienced, infantry troops should have been aware of the implications of their position and taken steps to ensure there were adequate sentries and that the troops were prepared for action. The men were not in the peak of fitness with the war diary stating 'the men had no rest, and very little water and food since Friday evening (6th) and were consequently in a very exhausted condition'.[3] These were not battle-hardened troops. The sum of their combat experience was three weeks on Turkish soil, only two weeks of which was in contact with the enemy. According to the war diary, which was constructed after the event from accounts of the few officers that survived, the 'men removed their equipment and rifles' and after four days without sleep they slept.[4]

Ninety minutes later the Turks attacked and six battalions broke through a weak and fragmented front line. The Wiltshires' war diary explains that the men were caught without equipment or rifles and withdrew down the gully. It seems incredible that an infantry battalion so close to the enemy should on such a wholesale basis become dislocated from their kit and particularly their weapons. Soon they were cut off by Turkish heavy machine gun fire covering the gully. Having discarded their rifles, the Wiltshiremen ceased to be infantrymen and were simply targets; the enemy could, and did, engage at will. Men, the lucky ones at least, made their way back to the beach-head in small groups of fours and fives over the next four days, some carrying the bodies of their comrades. There was no cohesion, command, or control. Battalion strength had fallen from 830 when they landed on the 17 July to only 420, which included 76 who had remained at Lemnos. The battalion strength was halved in a little under three weeks. At least 19 of the dead were railwaymen. The Wiltshires, only a small part in a big attack, had failed, the division failed losing 60 per cent of its establishment and ten of the thirteen commanding officers; the allies lost 15,000 in a day and there was no breakout from Anzac Cove.

Although the rout could be considered a lack of personal and collective discipline, military discipline continued on the battlefield and the war diary notes that Private C Brooks was court martialled and sentenced to two months field punishment. Abandoning your personal weapon is a serious offence; Private Brooks must have carried out some awful misdemeanour.

The battalion and were back in the line at Rhododendron Spur only seven days after the Chunuk Bair mishap and remained at Anzac Cove until 5 September, although they were short on numbers and had to contend with many sick. They then moved to Lala Baba at Suvla Bay where they were engaged in labouring and fatigue tasks. The war diary notes the 'traces of general debility are very conspicuous

1   5th Wiltshires War Diary. 9.

2   5th Wiltshires War Diary, 9.

3   5th Wiltshires War Diary, 9.

4   5th Wiltshires War Diary, 9.

Alfred Lambourne	Pte	Helles	Swindon	Gt Western	Apprentice Boilermaker
Sydney Cornish	Pte	Helles	Stratford	GER	Clerk
Edgar Baker	Pte	Helles	Swindon	Gt Western	Machine Operator
Arthur Bunce	Pte	Helles	Swindon	Gt Western	Machinist
John Comley	Pte	Helles	Swindon	Gt Western	Labourer
Leonard Cox	Cpl	Helles	Trowbridge	Gt Western	Fireman
Thomas Farmer	Pte	Helles	Swindon	Gt Western	Fitters Helper
George Ford	Sgt	Helles	Swindon	Gt Western	Piece Work Checker
Thomas Lockley	Pte	Helles	Swindon	Gt Western	Furnaceman
Joesph Pegram	Pte	Helles	Bishospgate Goods	GER	Clerk
Robert Roberts	Pte	Helles	Euston	L & NWR	Clerk (to chief accountant)
Sidney Smith	Pte	Helles	Swindon	Gt Western	Bolt Maker
Zenas Strange	Pte	Helles	Swindon	Gt Western	Helper
William Watts	L/Cpl	Helles	Swindon	Gt Western	Labourer
Samuel Windridge	Pte	Helles	Swindon	Gt Western	
John Seager	Sgt	Helles	Swindon	Gt Western	Striker No 14 Shop
John Twyford	Pte	Helles	Swindon	Gt Western	Machinist No 16 Shop
Alan Slocombe	Pte	Chatby	Bishopsgate Goods	GER	Clerk
James Harrison	Pte	Helles	London Cartage	GER	Vanguard Committee

GWR Ford DCM MM   *Z G Strange*   *J Seager*   *J R Twyford*   *T Farmer*   *E F Baker*   *S R Smith*

A R Bunce

among our men'[5] and that it was 'very notable in the endeavours to rally men's willpower is the absence of good NCOs as there is no reserve of likely junior NCOs suitable for promotion'.[6] It seemed as though the 5th Wiltshires at that point were incapable of functioning as an infantry battalion.

During October there were three drafts of reinforcements, but by the end of the month the battalion strength only numbered 390 men and 20 officers. During this time they had lost 111 sick, five were killed and 11 were wounded. Despite the reinforcements they were only two heads up on the previous month. Dysentery was the major ailment.

---

5   5th Wiltshires War Diary, 13.
6   5th Wiltshires War Diary, 13.

By late November it was very wet and cold, on the 28th there was a heavy blizzard and the challenges to survival now included the weather. One man died of exposure. On the 29th two men awaiting removal by field ambulance were found dead on their stretchers and later three others were found dead in the trenches, one of those was Private William Jeffries who had been a labourer at Swindon. On 4 December, Private E E Caswell, who had been a porter at Swindon also died.

E E Caswell

The Wiltshires were finally evacuated from Sulva Bay on 18 December returning to Cape Helles ten days later to help facilitate the British withdrawal from the Gallipoli peninsula. The New Year started on a low ebb with the promulgation of a death sentence on Sergeant J Robins as a result of disobedience of an order given by his superior officer. Sergeant Robins was a regular soldier, he claimed he was unwell (at a time when 25 per cent of the battalion were off sick) the Medical Officer suggested he was well enough to go out on patrol, but Robins refused. The death sentence was carried out on New Years Day at 0800. All in all it hadn't been a good year for the 5th Wiltshires.

1916

The Allies surprised the Turks and withdrew from Gallipoli on 8 January, evacuating over 118,000 men, including the 5th Wiltshires, but 43,000 men remained buried in Turkish soil and 237 were men from the battalion.

In Egypt, the Wiltshires reconstituted with drafts of 700 bringing the strength to 1,100. But there was little time to relax and recover because only eighteen days later they were embarked onto HMT *Oriana* bound for Mesopotamia.

Mesopotamia

Although perhaps perceived as a sideshow to the Western Front and Gallipoli, the Mesopotamian front was expensive in manpower. The Basra memorial commemorates more than 40,000 Commonwealth soldiers who died between 1914 and 1921 and whose graves are not known. Initially troops had been in Mesopotamia to protect the oil wells around Basra, but pretty quickly an expansionist strategy developed with large columns pushing up both the great rivers Tigris and Euphrates in May 1915, supported by a navy flotilla of small river gun-boats. There were battles at Nasiriya on the Euphrates, and Amarah and then Kut along the Tigris. The advance was stopped by the Turks at Ctesiphon on the outskirts of Baghdad. The allies had overstretched their logistics and pulled back to Kut where, in December 1915, the Turks surrounded and besieged the town.

The 5th Wiltshires arrived in Mesopotamia in early March 1916 to become part of the force of some 30,000 tasked with relieving Kut. Southern Mesopotamia was a complicated network of rivers, inlets and distributaries. Communications were difficult by anything other than boat, and there were too few boats. However, after only a few days at Basra the battalion proceeded by steamer along the River Tigris arriving at Shaikh Sa'ad on 20 March. Here they found a very complicated and sophisticated trench system. For each mile of front line trench there were sixteen miles of communication trenches, indicating perhaps how static this expeditionary warfare had become and how vital entrenchment was for protection in this flat, featureless land. For much of the area, much of the time, the water table was at ground level and troops digging in soon hit water.

During the winter it was frequently wet and cold, the summer months were unbearably hot and infested with flies. In between times there were regular sandstorms which reduced visibility to zero

Map 7. Modern day Iraq showing the key towns of 5th Wiltshire's Mesopotamian campaign

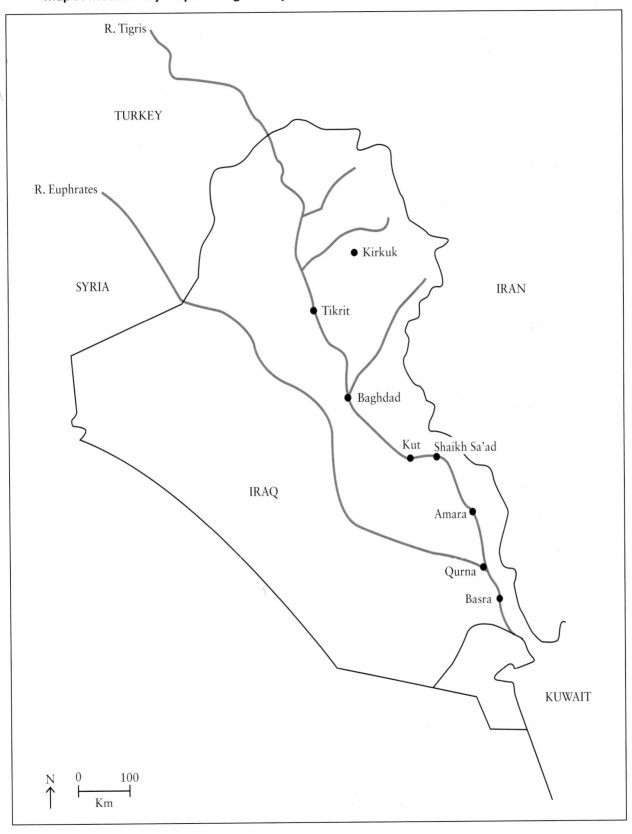

and sandblasted everything in its path. For the soldiers, their best protection was often only their uniform. If they were lucky they might shelter in trenches, if they could dig in, or in rudimentary sangars constructed above ground where they could not.

Soon after landing there was an outbreak of smallpox which resulted in one company spending eight months isolated from the rest of the battalion. The rest attacked the Turks in the cold morning of 5 April. The enemy front line trenches were captured and losses were said to be slight, but by the time the men were digging in in open countryside later in the day, 28 had been killed, three of whom were railwaymen, and 137 were injured, 17 were missing.

Willam Moody	Pte	5	4	16	31	Basra	Gt Western	Swindon	Storesman
Walter Pearce	Pte	5	4	16		Basra	Gt Western	Swindon	Machineman
Joseph Sharland	Pte	5	4	16		Basra	Gt Western	Swindon Painter	Wagon

Moody   Sharland

After several days following the lead troops, the Wiltshiremen formed part of a 7,000 men dawn attack near Sannaiyat. The 9 April started with mass confusion due to a late change in compass heading, the advance was slowed by marshy ground and then they were discovered and engaged by artillery and surprise was lost. The attack went in and some trenches were captured but could not be held and, as night fell, the attackers withdrew. The Wiltshires lost 21 killed including the commanding officer, 37 were missing and 161 wounded.

Frank Mant	L/Cpl	8	4	16		Basra	Gt Western	Swindon
AH Waldron	Pte	9	4	16	17	Amara	Gt Western	Swindon

Battle preparation immediately began for the next attack but before it could be prosecuted the Turks seized the initiative and attacked first. The Wiltshires were brought forward to bolster the defensive line and suffered 11 killed and 47 wounded, but the line was held. The progress in relieving Kut was painfully, very painfully, slow.

Edward Loveridge	L/Cpl	18	4	16	24	Basra	Gt Western	Swindon	Steam Hammerman

E Loveridge

The battalion spent the rest of April in this location digging trenches in sodden ground, the holes filling with water as they were dug. The Turks had halted the British plan to relieve Kut, and whilst the Wiltshires dug, the besieged troops were starving to death. On 29 April the Kut forced surrendered. Over 1,000 died in the siege, a further 4,000 were to die through the neglect of the Turks, and over 10,000 casualties were incurred in the failed attempts to relieve the garrison.

In this land of extremes, heat soon replaced cold, and by 7 May men were evacuated with heat injuries. The climate took the energy out of both sides and the main effort shifted to survival, and the re-integration and acclimatisation of replacements. The enemy was now heat, flies, disease and, maybe, boredom. The environment was so harsh that any injury could become a significant health problem, infection was commonplace and the medical support, mainly due to communications and environment, was poor. New troops were especially susceptible; of a draft of 66 who arrived on 19 June 41 per cent had been admitted to the medical system within two weeks.[7] Unlike the Western Front there was no half decent hospital a day or two's travel behind the lines. Decent hospitals were in India, and that was a long way away when you had your guts hanging out and flies laying eggs in them. The hospitals of Amara and Basra still suffered from the general unhealthy environment and wasn't the greatest area to convalesce. During this time, although there had been no significant fighting since April, five more railwaymen died over the hot summer months.

Thomas Yeo	Pte	1	5	16	20	Basra	Gt Western	Swindon	Chair Moulder
Ralph Crockett	Pte	29	6	16	21	Basra	Gt Western	Swindon	Machinist
Tom Hawkins	Cpl	28	7	16	25	Amara	Gt Western	Swindon	Boilermakers Helper
WW Hartwell	Pte	24	8	16	20	Basra	Gt Western	Swindon	Machinist
Daniel Bull	L/Cpl	31	8	16	27	Basra	Gt Western	Swindon	

W W Hartwell   *Tom Hawkins*   *R H Crockett*   *T D Yeo*

The battalion spent from late May to mid August static in defensive positions at Sheikh Sa'ad. For some it was too much and Lance Corporal C R Jacobs was found to have committed suicide in his tent 'while of unsound mind', an indication of the misery.[8]

New orders came instructing the battalion to march to Amarah. The higher command had decided that in order to simplify lines of communication, and especially resupply, the whole division would be withdrawn. Over nine nights they marched ninety miles and arrived in Amara in early September as the weather began to cool.

In late November, they marched back north towards future offensive operations, having rebuilt and reconstituted. The fighting force now included 'six followers'.[9] Ten days later on 8 December the men, and followers, arrived at Sinn Abtar. The men were occupied by fortifying trench lines, manning redoubts and patrolling. Christmas Day was spent in the trenches. Miserable, filthy weather returned on Boxing Day and continued for many days; the ground became very muddy and there was a biting wind. The year ended with the death of another railwayman, Corporal Heath, formerly an engine cleaner from Swindon, aged twenty, who died on 29 December at Amara.

---

7   5th Wiltshires War Diary, 47.

8   5th Wiltshires War Diary, 47.

9   5th Wiltshires War Diary, 58.

1917

The battalion set off again towards war, fighting on 11 January when they took over positions close to the banks of the Shatt Al Hai to the south of Kut. Here they dug a communication trench that they called Hai Street, which linked up with a fortified position. Digging continued throughout January in preparation for an assault on the Turkish positions and during this period of relative stalemate 19 were killed, including four railwaymen, and 49 were injured.

H Florey	Pte	17	1	17		Amara	Gt Western	Swindon	Hydraulic Forgeman
Lemuel Marsh	Pte	17	1	17		Amara	Gt Western	Swindon	Boilersmiths Apprentice
FW Rayland	Cpl	17	1	17	32	Amara	GER	Stratford	Erector
Rupert Rowe	CSM	21	1	17	32	Amara	Gt Western	Wootton Bassett	Parcel Porter

L Marsh

By 24 January the preparation was complete and the war diary stated 'spirits buoyant' and 'all appearing confident'[10] and on the 25th, after an intense artillery bombardment, the Wiltshires attacked in five waves capturing the Turkish trenches, over 100 men, and killing 234. They lost 35 killed, at least four were railwaymen, with 114 wounded.

J Sullivan

WV Axford	Pte	25	1	17		Amara	Gt Western	Swindon	Machineman
W Gee	Pte	25	1	17		Amara	Gt Western	Swindon	
HG Ruddle	Cpl	25	1	17		Amara	Gt Western	Swindon	
Joseph Sullivan	Pte	25	1	17	27	Amara	Gt Western	Swindon	Labourer

A further three railwaymen died soon afterwards.

RA Loder	Pte	28	1	17		Amara	Gt Western	Swindon	Dresser
Arthur Cooper	Pte	31	1	17	22	Amara	Gt Western	Swindon	Apprentice
FH Rawlings	Pte	31	1	17		Amara	Gt Western	Swindon	Labourer

The next attack on the 'Dahra Bend' required considerable preparation and the Wiltshires spent much of February digging trench systems, providing fatigue parties and guarding picket posts, and yet they still suffered two killed and 26 injured.

On 25 February the Wiltshires crossed the 400-metre wide River Tigris by pontoon. The crossing was much more benign than the previous day when lead battalions had to fight their way across.

---

10   5th Wiltshires War Diary, 64.

Seeing plenty of evidence of a scattered enemy with equipment, stores and artillery abandoned, the Wiltshires began a memorable march following the Tigris upstream to Baghdad. As they forged ahead, they soon began to run short of rations. On the 27th orders were given to consume half of their iron ration biscuits. The following day 'ration boats still failed to arrive and men were ordered to eat half meal issue of iron ration'.[11] The rations arrived on 2 March, and on 3 March a note is made that good grazing had been found for the animals. On the 4th 'full rations were drawn' and there is mention the following day, positively, that 'the ration question... satisfactorily settled'.[12]

The war diary contained only minimal information, a soldier getting killed would rarely command an entry, so many entries concerning rations point to their critical nature at that time.

On 11 March the Wiltshires were ordered into Baghdad, tasked with preserving law and order after the Turks had hastily left. They were greeted with 'great enthusiasm' and the friendly locals offered gifts of eggs and oranges.[13] It is doubtful whether the Wiltshiremen had eaten oranges for a while. Having occupied the city it was safe for the Royal Navy to berth river gunboats in the centre of Baghdad.

Entering Baghdad

The gunboats HMS *Moth, Tarantula, Butterfly, Firefly, Gadfly* and *Snakefly*, had experienced a tricky voyage upstream, encountering a number of heavy bombardments from Turkish gunners en route. Philip Jones was a stoker on HMS *Moth*, he had been a fireman for GWR in Wrexham but died on 19 June 1917.

Private Albert Cox, who had worked for GWR at Swindon, died on 8 March 1917 and his name is on the Baghdad memorial.

The Wiltshires were despatched along with the Hertfordshire Yeomanry towards a force of some 4,000 Turks which spotter planes had located just 14 miles north of Baghdad. The Wiltshires carried out a reconnaissance on enemy dispositions on 27 March before being ordered to attack emplacements on the Adhaim River on the 29th. The enemy could see them coming and engaged with artillery, then machine guns, but the Wiltshires continued despite mounting casualties until ordered to stop and dig in. They had lost 28 men killed, including three railwaymen, and 139 wounded. The Turks withdrew under the cover of darkness.

11   5th Wiltshires War Diary, 71.
12   5th Wiltshires War Diary, 72.
13   5th Wiltshires War Diary, 73.

William Bates	Pte	29	3	17	20	Basra	GER	Traffic Manager's Office	Clerk
Edward Gulley	Pte	29	3	17		Basra	Gt Western	Swindon	Carriage fitter
Charles Wiffen	Cpl	29	3	17	19	Basra	GER	Bishopsgate	Clerk

E Gulley

Throughout April the battalion were on the tail of the withdrawing enemy, chasing the Turks, but out of direct contact, scouting across the difficult terrain, skirmishing, fighting, attacking and digging in. In the hot and dry conditions water shortages contributed to illness and in reducing fighting power and the will to fight. On one day alone there were over 50 heat casualties. Throughout May the prospects for the Wiltshires improved, the hot weather seemed to reduce fighting and the military posture shifted from attack to defence. The troops marched to Sadiya where they were to spend the hot summer, arriving on 19 May. It was another summer of boredom, oppressive heat and flies. Moving to Abu Khamed on 12 August, they once again went into a period of static defence and routine. Sickness levels were high and sandfly fever resulted in 118 men being evacuated. Towards the end of November focus shifted from digging and road repair to pack drill and marching in preparation for future offensive operations.

On 3 December, the battalion embarked into lorries which had recently arrived in Mesopotamia, and gave significantly improved manoeuvreability and flexibility. They also had the added advantage that fuel resupply was simpler than ensuring rations for livestock. The lorries took them into the foothills around Suhaniya. This new ground was unforgiving and hard going. As winter set in, freezing temperatures at night were common. After an attack in the mountains on 5 December, the Wiltshires withdrew back to Serajik and that concluded their operations for 1917. Unlike the previous two Christmases when the Wiltshiremen had been in the trenches, this year they were able to enjoy the day out of the line, and ate turkey and goose, and on Boxing Day staged a regimental sports day.

Tuz Khurmrati 29th April 1918. IWM Q24642

1918

Early in the New Year the Wiltshires formed up with pioneers, engineers, signallers, cavalry, a section of artillery and a survey party, and were tasked to make a road fit for guns and transportation to the top of the Ain Lailah pass in the mountains, and to find a supply of water. To troops who had spent months engaged in routine and monotony this must have seemed a pretty interesting challenge. In any case it didn't take them long and the task was completed by 24 January. Thereafter, it was a return to the training routine at their encampment in Serajik which continued through the winter months until late April 1918.

It was thought that if the Turks harboured ambitions to progress to Persia and beyond, then the area between Tuz Khurmrati to Kifri to Qara Tepe was crucial because it gave them control of a vital road. So a plan was devised to clear the enemy from this area and, on 24 April, a force was despatched. After five nights of marching, the Wiltshires reached Kifri, where they rested before continuing onto Tuz Khurmrati where, along with the Royal Welsh Fusiliers, they attacked and captured the stronghold taking 1,800 prisoners, 14 field guns and much equipment.

The Wiltshires left Tuz Khurmrati on 17 October, accompanied by sections of cavalry, artillery, machine guns and field ambulance with the aim of fixing the enemy at Kirkuk. Tauq, on route, was quickly captured and working parties repaired the road and ford enabling armoured cars to cross

Map 8. Northern Mesopotamia, 5th Wiltshires 1917–1918

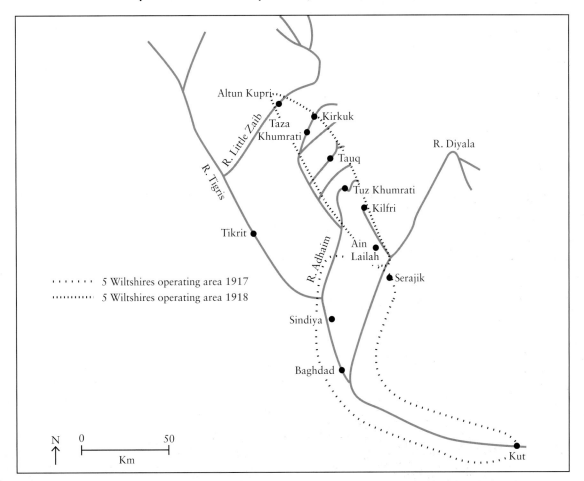

110

GREAT WAR RAILWAYMEN

the river and pursue the enemy. The battalion left Tauq along with the South Wales Borderers and continued the pursuit, attacking and clearing enemy positions along the way and eventually clearing Baziyan and then capturing the bridge at Kirkuk. They pressed on capturing Altun Kupri, their furthest position north on 31 October. The battalion were concentrated at Guk Tappah when the Armistice was declared.

The battalion had set sail on 1 July 1915 and, apart from a few days transitting through Egypt, spent the whole of the war in arduous conditions overseas. There would have been comparatively few respites, and few, if any, men would have received any home leave. It wasn't until January 1919 that troops began to be demobilised.

In May 1919, 78 Wiltshiremen in India awaiting transportation home for demobilisation were despatched to fight alongside the 1st Royal Sussex in the North West Frontier in the 3rd Afghan war.

The last Wiltshiremen returned home in 1920, but 747 never returned of whom 55 per cent were killed in action, 20 per cent died of wounds and 25 per cent died of other causes. The highest death rate was during the Gallipoli campaign.

Other Campaigns

Salonika

Troops were deployed to Salonika (now called Thessalonika), Greece, in October 1915 to join the multi-national efforts of Serbia, Russia and Italy, with numerous reinforcements arriving in mid-1916. Much of the fighting was against Bulgarians around Lake Doiran in what is now the Republic of Macedonia, but the mosquito was as big an enemy as the Bulgarians and equally hated. The First Battle of Doiran was fought in late April and early May 1917. At least 23 railwaymen were killed mainly from 7th Wiltshires, 7th Royal Berkshires and the 7th Oxfordshire and Buckinghamshire Light Infantry. Eleven were Great Western men with six from the Swindon works and nine were L&NWR men all from Wolverton works.

David Anthony	Pte	7th	Royal Berks	Doiran	Gt Western	Britton Ferry	
FJ Atkins	Pte	7th	Ox & Bucks LI	Doiran	L & NWR	Wolverhampton	Labourer
DJ Barnwell	L/Cpl	7th	Ox & Bucks LI	Doiran	L & NWR	Wolverhampton	Labourer
Herbert Churchill	Pte	7th	Royal Berks	Doiran	L & SWR		Apprentice
Spencer Harrison	Pte	7th	Ox & Bucks LI	Doiran	L & NWR	Wolverton	Carriage Cleaner
Albert Harding	L/Cpl	7th	Ox & Bucks LI	Doiran	Midland	Bourneville	Clerk
Walter Howes	Pte	9th	Glos	Doiran	Gt Western	Charlton Kings	Slip Labourer
Arthur Parish	Pte	10th	Devons	Doiran	Gt Western	Kingswear	Porter
GA Sirett	Sgt	7th	Ox & Bucks LI	Doiran	L & NWR	Wolverhampton	Labourer
John Smith	Pte	7th	Wiltshires	Doiran	Gt Western	Swindon	Timber Porter
AE Tack	Cpl	7th	Ox & Bucks LI	Doiran	L & NWR	Wolverton	Painter
WJ Tooley	Pte	7th	Ox & Bucks LI	Doiran	L & NWR	Wolverton	Trimmer
LH Tovey	Pte	7th	Royal Berks	Doiran	Gt Western	Paddington	Lad Clerk

The Second Battle of Doiran took place in September 1918. Fighting in mountainous terrain against heavily defended strongpoints favoured the defender. Reminiscent of trench-to-trench warfare of the Western Front, or of Gallipoli, the British soldier was expected to advance across open ground in a futile attempt to winkle the defenders from their sangers and trenches atop the mountain hilltops. The battalions of 66th Brigade; 12th Cheshire and 9th South Lancashires were committed and were stopped in their tracks. Private Seagrave, a former fireman with L&NWR at Birkenhead, serving with the Cheshires and Captain Alick Trotter MC, serving with 9th South Lancashires, who had been an apprentice at West Hartlepool for the NER, were both killed. As these battalions were wiped out, the 8th Kings Shropshire Light Infantry were committed and with them were Ernest Stockton an L&NWR labourer from Crewe, and E Colley an ex-GWR man from Ironbridge. Both were killed. So the 67th Brigade, comprising mainly of Welshmen and J Brassington, an ex-GCR goods porter from Connahs Quay, with the 11th Royal Welsh Fusiliers, was killed. 2nd Lieutenant Charles Davies an ex-clerk for the Cambrian Railway, and Wiliam Jacobson a former labourer with the Alexandra and Newport Docks Railway, both serving with 7th South Wales Borderers were killed. 67th Brigade fared better than 66th Brigade, but still incurred 65 per cent casualties. Soon it was the turn of the Scottish with 77th Brigade, and whilst no railwaymen have been identified, they too were cut to shreds incurring 50 per cent casualties. In all there are 52 railwaymen commemorated in the Doiran cemetery

Archangel – North Russia

After the Russian revolution, the Bolsheviks made peace with Germany and a civil war broke out between 'Red' and 'White' Russia. Britain had been providing supplies to Archangel and thousands of tons had built up which the Bolsheviks began using in the fight against the Whites. The British thought that if these supplies could be protected from the Bolsheviks, the Whites could then use them to defeat the Reds, whereupon the Whites would then take on Germany again. So an expeditionary force was despatched.

Incredibly many of the units deployed were of raw soldiers, one, the 2/10th Royal Scots had seen no overseas action and had served only as a garrison and feeder battalion, comprised mainly of those deemed unfit for active service. They arrived in Archangel in late August 1918, five months after the first British troops, and by September those unfit Scotsmen were patrolling forests and marshland along the River Dvina. As the winter set in the Dvina iced up, hampering the Royal Navy and gifting freedom of moment to the Bolsheviks. On Armistice Day the Scots were attacked by the Bolsheviks and 19 were killed and 34 wounded, including twenty-four-year-old Arthur Ralphs, a former number taker for GWR at Market Drayton. War continued in North Russia and inexperienced soldiers had to contend with the harsh conditions of a Russian winter sometimes patrolling through snow ten feet deep. Gradually they were forced back towards the northern ports. Private Charles Cruise, a former porter for GWR at Birmingham, serving with the 45th Battalion Royal Fusiliers, died on 10 August 1919 and is commemorated on the Archangel memorial.

CHAPTER 4

MILITARY RAILWAY OPERATIONS ON THE WESTERN FRONT AND PALESTINE

Beaucourt November 1916. IWM Q1573

The railway revolutionised war fighting, it enabled mass movement and concentration of force in a way hitherto impossible. Troops and supplies could be rapidly moved across huge expanses of real estate and campaigns could be sustained for long periods by railway resupply. In no small way the trench warfare carnage, and indeed European if not World War, was facilitated by the railway.

France and Germany constantly updated and revised their rail plans in the lead up to the war.

The German doctrine for rail construction in the advance, as was the situation for them in 1914, was that engineering officers of the regiments formed part of the reconnaissance with the forward elements of cavalry, so that they could gain valuable intelligence of the state of the railway. The purpose was to ensure that railway re-building and construction was not delayed since the whole tempo of advance relied upon railway construction and maintainance of the railway supply network. Without rapid construction the supply chain would be constrained and the advance would peter out.

Britain, as an island nation, required no such complex railway planning, or not in the sense of expeditionary warfare, so to a large degree the British learnt European railway operations as they went along. Much of the credit for what was subsequently learnt and delivered must go to Eric Geddes, pre-war a senior manager with NER, but called up and made a General, he ran the railway on the Western Front. He championed the professional railway interests of the 40,000 railwaymen who were mobilised into the Rail Operating Division of the Royal Engineers. These men grafted their newly acquired military skills to their knowledge and experience from the railway. Theirs was a crucial role, requiring specialist skills not easily acquired, an understanding forged over many years and probably as much to do with the corporate knowledge of each railway company as the individual. Geddes, also initiated along with Brigadier Holland (see page 237), supporting the canal logistic operations to relieve some of the pressure on the railway system.

As well as the Western Front railway troops operated in Egypt and Palestine (7,323 troops in 1918), Gallipoli, Italy (1,300 troops in 1918) and Salonika (2,680 troops in 1918). There were specialisms for railway construction, broad gauge railway operation and light railways, and there were even a number of specialist civilian railway companies manned by employees of British railway companies.

959 of the 12,500 railwaymen were Royal Engineers of whom 475 died serving within the railway specialisms of the Royal Engineers. The worst day was when RMS *Aragon* was sunk off Alexandria on 30 December 1917 when at least 67 railwaymen died (see page 209).

Railway Operations on the Western Front

By late 1914, the French railway network was stressed to breaking and the Belgian railway system had all but ceased to exist. Bridges had been blown and track destroyed in an attempt to slow the German invaders. Many of the indigenous railwaymen had been mobilised and many killed or captured. If the BEF were to be sustained, then British railwaymen were required to help rebuild the network and then to develop and operate the supply chain.

Rail Construction

The first railway troops to deploy, of what became a force of twenty-nine construction companies, on 15 August 1914, were the 8th (Railway) Construction Company RE. Each company comprised six officers, at least three of whom were commissioned railwaymen, and about 200 other ranks. Railway construction and repair, whilst on the whole a comparatively safer occupation than being an infantry soldier at the front, was definitely hard graft. The conditions were marginally better with more time spent in billets behind the line, but there were certainly many who experienced arduous conditions within range of enemy artillery and on occasion close behind the front line. Lines of communication would have been a high priority target for 'deep' artillery strikes and, as the war drew on, for enemy aircraft.

Rail construction got off to a slow start with only 1.5 miles being laid in 1914, but as things became more static this increased to 104 miles in 1915, 417 in 1916 and 814 miles by 1917 before the German advance forced a retreat with the loss of miles of track.[1] Several hundred miles of track was requisitioned from British railway companies and ripped up and transported. Some track came from as far afield as Canada.

It was established that to construct at the rate of one mile per day in ground that was described as 'good going' would require between 2–3,000 men, and where considerable digging was required this was at a rate of 10–20 unskilled labourers to one skilled worker. Whereas this balance shifted to one skilled to 2-3 unskilled if the work was technical such as the construction of bridging.[2] Often railway construction companies were supported by labour from infantry pioneer battalions such as the 17th Northumberland Fusiliers who were wholly recruited from the NER (and it was something of a mystery why they were not established into the Royal Engineers), whose usual role was to support combat troops. Wartime railway routes typically followed the most simple topography which often led to very windy tracks because it took less labour and time.

Bernafay Wood September 1916. IWM Q4319

A typical rail construction company was the 262nd (Great Western Railway) Company, comprising 200 platelaters, 18 carpenters, 12 blacksmiths, 2 fitters, 2 engine drivers, 1 clerk, 1 draughtsman, 2 cooks and an interpreter. The company was formed from railway volunteers in February 1917 and employed mainly in the Ypres Salient.

---

1   Henniker, 166 & 281.
2   Anderson, E.P. The Railway Organisation of an Army in War, Royal United Services Institute, Journal 72 (1927), 506.

Railwaymen from 262 rail construction company who died.

John Griffiths	Spr	12	5	17	34	St Woolas Newport	Gt Western	Newport	Blacksmith
Alfred Boxall	2Lt	25	10	17	31	Bedford House	Gt Western	Shrewsbury	Assistant
James Joynes	Spr	14	11	17	42	Brandhoek 3	Gt Western	Cheltenham	Packer

Such was the demand for railway construction in France that 13 civilian railway engineering companies were formed, such as the GWR manned 3rd Civilian Railway Company who served a three-month term working beyond the reach of the enemy. These companies were little more than a stop-gap and created some resentment because they enjoyed better conditions and were paid more than the railwaymen who had volunteered for the colours. In the end it was considered that 'the cost and trouble was out of proportion to their value' and although there were more civilian companies available to deploy, the War Office found other ways of delivering the capability. [3]

277 Railway Company. IWM Q47503

3   Henniker, 223.

As well as track laying, the construction companies also built railheads and yards. A typical railhead required over 6,000 tons of stone, and stone was in short supply. Labour and steamrollers needed to consolidate the stone were even scarcer. But a railhead could not function without a large area for moving supplies, which often took longer to build than the railway infrastructure.

Rail Operating Division

Rail Operating Companies (ROCs) were responsible for the logistics of the railway, for assembling and loading wagons, and shifting goods from the channel ports to one of four massive supply and distribution dumps, called supply nodes, and then onto the front.

GWR soldiers from the Rail Operating Division in France.

Each ROC comprised 3 Officers, 38 Senior Non Commissioned Officers, 36 Corporals, 72 Lance Corporals and 120 Sappers. Typically they would operate about thirty locomotives plus associated rolling stock. Every man was required to learn the French railway rules and regulations and to sign the routes before being cleared to operate on French infrastructure. Unfortunately when the first of some 18,500 professional railwaymen deployed to the Western Front there was a shortage of khaki uniform and they were issued blue uniform. They were considered by some to be conscientious objectors which caused them some grief until they were outfitted into khaki.

Ports were allocated to a supply node, which supported an army and a particular battle area and all the divisions within that area.

Army	Port	Supply node	Area	Number of Divisions
1st	Boulogne	Boulogne	Bethune	14
2nd	Calais/Dunkirk	Calais	Ypres	12
3rd	Dieppe/Le Harve	Abbeville	Arras	14
4th	Rouen	Abancourt/ Romescamps	Somme	15
Source ROD on the Western Front				

Bulk goods, which had been loaded at the ports, were then unloaded at the supply nodes from where divisional supply trains or DSTs were loaded for onward distribution to the fighting divisions. It was calculated that it would take two to three hours to load a train although four hours was usually allowed. Every two days a DST would be dispatched for each of the divisions. In this way logistics planners were able to manage the throughput of products and maintain timely and, critically, consistent delivery to the customer; an early form of 'just in time' delivery. The DSTs would trundle at the approved military line speed of 25 mph to the divisional railhead where the stores would be unloaded and trans-shipped to motor vehicles, horses and carts, or if the troops were lucky, onto the light railway network. It was calculated that 150 lorries were required to unload one supply train and the prompt unloading of trains from the railheads was essential to ensure that there was no blockage in supply.

During the last two years of the war there were over 60 divisions in the line at any one time. As each division needed a train load of supplies every other day and this required about 30 train moves per day. This sounds pretty simple, but each train comprised 40 or so wagons, each of which required loading and unloading, and the fork lift had not yet been invented. Most of the loading was done by hand and was heavy, hard and slow work. Thirty trains a day would sustain the armies on the battlefield, little more. Offensive operations would require yet more supplies.

In terms of scale it was calculated that the weekly tons distributed in 1916 to the Western Front amounted to 195,000 tons, comprising 33,700 tons of general stores and supplies, 12,250 of railway stores, 15,000 of timber and 15,000 of stone.[4] It is possible to gauge the degree to which the army was mechanised by its requirement for fuel and forage, where over three times as much forage was required than fuel, 36,000 tons of forage to 9,500 of fuel. Horses and mules provided much of the heavy lift capability from the railheads to the front. In August 1917 for example there were 368,000 horses and 82,000 mules on the books.[5] Whilst pack animals were vital in ensuring the loads reached the troops they created something of a logistics burden themselves. 'A horse ate about ten times as much as a man, and the delivery of hay and oats constituted a major burden on the army's transport services'.[6] In January 1918 horse rations were cut by two pounds per day which saved 500,000 tons of shipping, although what the horses thought about this is unclear.[7]

Over and above the logistics trains were the ammunition trains. In this war ammunition requirements were like no other. Nearly 5 million tons of ammunition was transported to the Western Front which over the course of the war would have amounted to a weekly expenditure of 18,000 tons. The supply of ammunition increased as the war progressed and the BEF grew. Expenditure varied depended upon activity. During the initial phases of the Battle of The Somme over 40,000 tons were expended per week. This amounts to nearly 500 tons of artillery falling on each mile of front every day for 13 days. This might explain why death and injury was on such an industrial scale. But the main point is that this level of ammunition expenditure required 571 ammunition loads of 10-ton wagons just to keep the railheads supplied, with further loads needed to feed the supply nodes from the ports. The ammunition requirement has been calculated as what seems like an astronomical amount of a train load per day for each quarter mile of front. Prior to the June 1918 offensive there was a requirement of eighteen trains per day in the Ypres area just to maintain a steady state in replenishing the daily ammunition expenditure, and during the build up to the offensive this rose to 21, then to 24 and finally 32 at the height of the offensive. A further four to eight trains a day were required to shuttle between advanced depots and forward dumps. So all in all up to 40 trains per day comprising up to 33 wagons were required each day just to deliver ammunition. The tonnage was dwarfed in 1918 with the break into the Hindenburg line when the rate increased to 54,000 tons per week.[8]

---

4   It was calculated that 1 ounce more in the ration packs would require 72 tons more to be distributed per day.
5   Singleton, J., Britain's Military Use Of Horses 1914-1918, Past and Present Journal Number 139, 190.
6   Singleton, 196.
7   Singleton, 198.
8   Military Statistics of the Great War, 481.

Above: 15in Shells Albert Road 28th June 1916. IWM Q4168   Below: IWM Q001766

To cope with the vast demand for ammunition, a number of main ammunition dumps were opened during 1916–1917. A ROD loco depot was co-located. The main ROD workshop and depot was Audruicq, which was midway between Calais and St Omer. A heavy repair shed was established at Borre just north of Hazebrouck in the Ypres area, with workshops outside Rouen and south of Etaples. Locomotive depots were scattered across the combat zone some quite close to the front.

Taking the Somme area as an example, ammunition trains were loaded with all types of artillery

Army	Ammunition Dump
All	Audruicq
3rd 4th	Blargies Nord (Abancourt)
1st	Dannes (Boulogne)
3rd 4th	Rouxmesnil (Dieppe)
3rd	Saigneville (Abbeville)
2nd	Zeneghem (Dunkirk)
Source – ROD on the Western Front	

ammunition. Even a small artillery shell is heavy and lifting hundreds of shells is back breaking work. In the relative comfort of the main ammunition dumps it was hard enough, but unloading at the forward dumps at Contay, Albert and Puchevillers, within contact of enemy, artillery would have been much harder, where the shells were frequently unloaded in the dark, with all the additional hazards this entailed. At the forward dumps the shells and cartridges would have been swiftly transferred for onward distribution, carried in all weathers and frequently in the dark. Often it would be by light railway, or by lorry, and failing that horse-drawn gun limber, or by pack horse which could carry between four and eight shells.

Whether you were lugging ammunition, food, fodder or fuel it would have been hard work, but dealing with vast tonnages of ammunition brought their own challenges. Shells, unless initiated with a primer and a charge, are relatively benign, but charges containing cordite are unstable. Cordite is safe so long as it is not introduced to a spark or fire. A steam locomotive creates a lot of heat, sparks and cinders, all of which bring the risk of combustion and explosion. Dealing with ammunition was always a risk. Indeed three sappers won the George Medal posthumously, for dealing with an ammunition fire (see page 254).

Second only to ammunition in terms of tonnage, was the supply of stone to the battle area. Geddes[9] calculated that 1,134 wagons of hardcore were required per day.[10] It was also calculated that 13,000 tons a day were required just to maintain the roads.[11] This was used in an attempt to maintain the roads and keep them passable in the chalky quagmires of the front, remembering that whilst the British were dropping 1,500 tons of ordnance into each mile of the enemy front line Germans were doing similarly, constantly destroying attempts to make approaches passable. The remainder was used in maintaining the railway tracks, in providing pathways and footings in the ammunition dumps, casualty clearing stations and accommodation billets.

And then there was coal, several thousand tons of which were required, and imported, each week to power the locomotives, and for a few lucky soldiers located near to the depots, to provide them with heat and warmth if they could purloin the odd chunk or two.

The railway which brought all the tonnage of ammunition, stone or coal up to the front, also then ferried many of the injured back to the base hospitals close to the point at the channel ports where the ammunition had been unloaded.

9   Eric Geddes was a railwayman who joined NER in 1911 as Deputy General Manager. He was made Director-General of Military Railways and Inspector-General of Transportation with the BEF in 1916 and made a Major-General. Geddes and his team of senior railwaymen in military uniforme, worked closely with Field Marshall Haig to ensure that the logistic support could cope with the demands of a fast growing British Army on the Western Front. Geddes was subsequently appointed the First Lord Of The Admiralty. He became an MP and was in effect if not title the first Minister of Transport. Geddes was the most senior railwayman in the British Army.
10 Aves, W. A. T., R.O.D. The Railway Operating Division on the Western Front. The Royal Engineers in France and Belgium 1915-1919, 50.
11 Henniker, 215.

The railway was the most efficient means of moving troops around the battlefield, although London buses were used to move infantrymen short distances, and battalions could march, in some cases many miles, but the train could move en masse. Hundreds of battalions and support troops were moved around by quite basic troop trains. Soldiers were crammed forty men to a wagon, with the capacity for eight horses, and the typical train comprised thirty such vans, seventeen flat bed trucks and two brake vans. The officers would occupy the one passenger coach. A single train could convey 1,200 men (or 240 horses) shifting a battalion and its equipment. Moving troops introduced an added complexity to the already complex business of logistics. Ammunition and supplies were complex enough, but when dealing with 'talking freight' it becomes infinitely more challenging. A case of rations doesn't wander off, argue back, need feeding, or require ablutions, but at least the talking freight is also walking freight, unless it is a casualty on an ambulance train. As anyone who has experienced a long air delay knows, or even those delayed by the rail network, patience can be severely tested whilst trying to travel. Add soldiers and officers to wartime railway operations then it is almost bound to become stressful. The professional railwayman may have a solution, but on the Western Front that professional railwayman was likely to be outranked many times over by those with no knowledge nor care for the operational difficulties of a foreign railway in wartime. So step in the RTO – or rail transportation officer. A man tasked with smoothing this interface, attempting to make the talking freight behave as near as possible to cargo. Interestingly an account of the RTO describes his role thus 'his most important duty is in no circumstances to interfere in the technical working of the railway. It is therefore best to appoint to this branch officers with no previous railway knowledge. In this way they only perform their proper function of liaison between railway and the army.'[12]

From 1916 there were two sets of five trains which were kept on call for moving brigades. By this means it was possible to give a foot-slogging infantry brigade mobility, and mobility was a competitive advantage in mobile warfare. Not that warfare was mobile in 1916, but the Generals wished for the breakthrough which would enable mobility, and feared an enemy breakthrough which would require mobility to plug gaps in the line and deny the enemy free passage. So, the railway had a part to play in both offensive and defence operations in being able to enable both mobility and concentration, both principles of war.

An insight into the experience of moving by rail is given in the regimental history of 5th Leicesters who were moved south in September 1918 to take part in the offensive on the Hindenburg line. 'Our journey southwards was uncomfortable and uneventful. The only remarkable feature was the acrobatic skill displayed by the mess staff, transferring meals from the kitchen cattle-truck to the officer's mess cattle-truck. Even at the usual speed of a French troop train, it is no easy task to drop off the train with a pile of plates in one hand, a dish of potatoes in the other, walk fast enough to catch up the carriage in front, and finally, in spite of signal wires, sleepers and other pitfalls, deliver all safely at the "Mess". Yet this was done not once but often.'[13]

The whole day may have been a long time to spend on the train, but that was nothing compared to the overland route established in 1917 between Cherbourg and Italy for onward passage by ship across the Mediterranean. It is hard to imagine how unpleasant the 1,450 mile trip must have been, taking about five days at an average speed of 15 mph. No wonder a key part of the line of communication was the establishment of rest camps and hospitals along the way!

War fighting required reliable sustainment, a routine based on organisation and hard physical labour. Sustaining the Somme campaign would have required enormous co-ordination, not only from the ROCs supplying the DSTs, but back through the base supply dumps, the ports, through the British railway network as far back as the shell filling stations and armament factories. The railway was integral to warfare. The volume shifted by railway is illustrated by stores lost at 20

12   Anderson, E.P., The Railway Organisation Of An Army In War, Royal United Services Institution, Journal 72, 510. Pratt, 28 and 629 takes a contrary view believing it is essential for the RTO to have railway knowledge.

13   Hills, J.D., The Fifth Leicestershire. A record of the 1/5th Battalion the Leicestershire Regiment T.F., during the War, 1914-1919. Chapter XVI.

Ordnance Depot at Saigneville, one of the main ammunition dumps, when it was bombed on the night of 22 May 1918 and over 60 million rounds of small arms ammunition exploded.[14] Small arms ammunition would only have been a small part of the total tonnage of ammunition, and all ammunition would have been moved via the railway. Surge operations such as a large frontal assault would require a build up of ammunition and the supply considerations would have received a high priority in the General Staff's planning. Attacks could fail due to logistics shortfalls, such as at Loos where there was insufficient artillery ammunition. In order to deliver this capability there were 1,398 locomotives, 50,640 wagons and 883 miles of track and for narrow gauge 1,267 locomotives, 5,665 wagons and nearly 668 miles of track in France.[15] All of which had been shipped across the Channel.

There is at least one ROD engine still in operation today number 5322 which was built in Swindon in 1917 and served with the ROD. Today the locomotive has been restored and operates out of the GWR Didcot railway centre.

Light Railway Operations

IWM Q1699

Pre-war the British, unlike the Germans, French and Russians, had no intention of using light railway. The British plan for distribution relied upon mechanised transport, lorries. The Europeans stockpiled large quantities of light railway infrastructure and were organised to rapidly lay 60 cm track behind advancing armies in order to ensure that logistics supported the advance rather than impeded it. Perhaps the British had not appreciated the conditions of stalemate and trench warfare, nor how quickly the overused road network would break down, or how bombardment and rain

---

14   Brown, I. M., British logistics On The Western Front 1914-1919, 191.
15   Great War Statistics, 607. See also Henniker, 251-258.

would churn up the tracks and roads making conveyance by lorry or horse-drawn cart slow and inefficient, if not totally impossible. As ever Tommy's initiative was to the fore since, unlike the French or Germans, there was not a highly organised system of prefabricated light railway which could be rapidly laid. Instead soldiers built wooden tramways or cannibalised existing tramways. The British tactical light railway, a Geddes initiative, was not formally adopted on the Western Front until 1916 and became known as the War Department Light Railway.

Engineers coming down the line. IWM Q8404

Twenty-seven Light Railway Operating Companies (LROCs) were established on the Western Front, mainly British, but also from South Africa, Canada and Australia. A railway background was not essential because light railway did not operate over the French network and petrol driven engines did not require the skills level of a steam loco, but nonetheless they were often manned by ex-railwaymen. The petrol tractors were typically deployed closer to the front line than steam locos, since they emitted a lower signature compared to the smoky steamers. The tractor of choice was the Simplex, but others were produced including one based on the Model T Ford, but they lacked the pulling power of the Simplex.

By September 1917 the light railway on the Western Front moved 20,000 tons of stores a day, amounting to 350 tons per week for each mile of track, and 30,000 men per day.[16] In the artillery-

---

16   Henniker, 161 and 184.

savaged land round Ypres and the Somme, an extensive light railway network transformed the ability of the army enabling provisions, especially ammunition to be brought right up to the front line. The railway engineers were able to lay and maintain light railway trackway in the most exposed and dangerous locations. By contrast the roads were exceptionally hard to maintain and were often impassable due to the combination of bomb damage, rain and massive over-usage.

Fourteen railwaymen are known to have died from just the 10th LROC. They originated from eight railway companies and covered a range of different trades and jobs from all over the country.

Edward Atkins	Spr	22	7	17	29	Canada Farm	Midland	London(City)	Clerk
Richard Collins	Spr	22	7	17	26	Canada Farm	SECR		Oil Issuer
SJ Cook	Spr	28	2	19		Theux	Gt Western	Barnstable	Packer
Charles Cooper	Spr	22	7	17	20	Canada Farm	L & NWR	Birmingham	Parcel Vanman
William Dickens	Spr	2	3	19	33	Theux	L & NWR	Bletchley	Labourer
CV Dodd	Spr	22	6	18		Terlincthun	GCR	Gorton Shed	Labourer
Alfred Flippant	Spr	1	3	19	27	Theux	L & SWR		Plate Layer
Alexander Hay	Spr	17	1	18	20	Duhallow ADS	GNSR	Kittybrewster	Cleaner
S Hayward	Spr	23	6	18		Longuenesse	Midland	Derby	Painters assistant
Charles Hounsham	Spr	14	8	18		Ligny	Midland	Pye Bridge	Signal fitters assistant
WG Morton	Spr	22	7	17	21	Canada Farm	L & NWR	Willesden	Cleaner (Loco.)
John Sears	Spr	19	7	17	33	Canada Farm	Midland	Derby	Clerk
Albert Tricker	Spr	19	7	17	24	Canada Farm	GER	Stratford	Machineman
John Walstow	Spr	21	12	15	32	Lijssenthoek	L & NWR	Longsight	Joiner

Arras 1918.
IWM Q8577

Railway Artillery and Siege Batteries

Because of the diabolical state of the road network close to the front, and the inevitable resultant congestion, it was exceptionally difficult to manoeuvre large and heavy artillery pieces over the battlefield. Some guns were towed by caterpillar tractors or traction engines, but most were hauled by horses. The horses, and frequently the men, struggled to move the guns through the quagmires which had been roads, and so railway guns came into their own being flexible, comparatively manoeuvrable, and powerful.

The first rail mounted heavy artillery was deployed in mid 1915 and was manned by Siege Batteries of the Royal Garrison Artillery. Each battery comprised two independently operated guns. They co-existed with railway troops who provided their mobility and support and each gun group included a train of at least six railway wagons. By the end of the war there were 64 railway guns deployed: 17 were 9.2in, 43 were 12in, 4 were 14in guns.

Harold Pemberton, a postman in civilian life, found his way into the Rail Operating Division via the Royal Monmouthshire Royal Engineers and in June 1916 he operated a section of track between Dernancourt and Meaulte on the route to 'Happy Valley' where many of the artillery batteries were located on the build up to the Somme attack. He and his mucker operated a junction from a comfy hut which contained their worldy goods and included two bunks. He recalled 'On 24 June it was a clear night with German artillery lighting the sky when at 2030 one big gun started the (British) bombardment. A couple of days later a big 12-inch railway gun pulled into position near our hut. We were told to keep the doors and windows open. The gun fired and that was the end of the hut, the roof fell off and the windows fell out and the gun was a good 70 yards behind us.'[17]

Two of the enormous 14-inch guns were naval guns built for a cancelled Japanese battleship and were subsequently mounted on 16 axle, 243 ton, railway gun carriages. They could fire a 1,586 lb shell 34,600 yards. The gun was conveyed by its own locomotive, the 'fighting train' and included a wagon for shells and a wagon for cartridges, a command post, a fitter's wagon and a brake van. Another train was called the 'living train' and carried stores and the gun crew of thirty. The horse wagons used by the crew were set up with bunk beds. The rear of the command post wagon was set up as an 'officers mess', and for one gun at least was complete with piano.

Typically the gun positions were on curved track sidings called gun spurs. By moving the gun along the curvature the bearing of the gun could be shifted, the gun itself only had two degrees of traverse. This meant that the gun could fire from any curved area of track. When fired the gun would recoil up to 34 inches at the maximum elevation, and the remaining recoil force was dissipated by allowing the entire vehicle to roll backwards 20–30 feet until stopped by its brakes. The gun would then be winched back into its firing position by a fixed anchor at the front.

Because the guns were built as a pair for the turret of the battleship, the breach of one, called 'Scene Shifter' opened to the left, and the other called 'Boche Buster' opened to the right.

There was pressure to get these guns to France and into action because a precise heavy weapon was needed for the attack on the Hindenburg Line. The guns were barely finished when they deployed, and each gun had a civilian fitter from Vickers Armstrong deployed as a Sergeant Artificer. The two guns, formed 471 Siege Battery, and were transported to France via the Richborough-Dunkirk ferry (see page 282) in May 1918. There was nearly a disaster disembarking Boche Buster, the stern of the ferry heeled over alarmingly as the weight shifted. Prompt action to redistribute the vessels balancing tanks saved the gun from toppling over the side. They were first in action on 8 August 1918.

Monty Cleeve commanded 'Boche Buster' and recalls that these, the largest of all the railway guns, were by far the most manoeuvrable and he struggled to get the army command to understand the utility of their employment, but he did employ the gun in 'shoot and scoot' missions where it would fire from one location, move, and then fire from another. This made it a difficult target

---

17   IWM Sound Archive, 10939, Harold Pemberton.

for enemy artillery. 'It took most railway guns three hours to come into or out of action whereas Bosch Buster was so mobile that we could be up and away within five minutes.'[18] Cleeve selected key railway triangles which would enable him to manoeuvre his gun onto different gun spur firing positions. All these positions had been previously surveyed and marked, and with careful shunting, the gun could be laid on precise azimuths for accurate predicted fire. On one occasion he fired onto the same target from three positions on the same night.

HM Gun 'Boche Buster', operated near Arras, and HM Gun 'Scene Shifter', near Bethune. Unlike most army artillery which is classed as an 'area' weapon designed for an effect over a large area, these guns were precision weapons targeted at key installations or infrastructure. A total of 235 rounds were fired by the two guns during their four months on the Western Front.

King George V fired a shot from Boche Buster, which became known as the 'Kings Shot', the first of twelve rounds fired at a railway junction at Douai on 8 August, and a direct hit. General Sir Martin Farndale states: 'It was said by Gunners to mark the turning point of the war, opening up the road to victory. Few single artillery rounds can ever have affected a battle so much in terms of destruction and improving morale.'[19] Cleeve said that the King was very knowledgeable and studied the maps carefully suggesting that key railway junctions should be the main target of this form of artillery.

Scene Shifter. IWM Q003868

18   IWM Sound Archive, 7310, Monty Cleeve.
19   Farndale, M., History of the Royal Regiment of Artillery: Western Front 1914-1918, 288.

Siege Battery	Railway Guns	Siege Battery	Railway Guns	Siege Battery	Railway Guns
18	2 x 12in	64	2 x 12in	103	2 x 12in
44	2 x 12in	82	2 x 12in	104	2 x 12in
45	2 x 9.2in	83	2 x 12in	128	2 x 12in
52	2 x 12in	86	2 x 12in	366	2 x 9.2in
53	1 x 12in, 1 x 9.2in	89	2 x 12in	444	2 x 12in
63	2 x 12in	92	1 x 12in, 1 x 9.2in	471	2 x 14in

After the war Boche Buster and Scene Shifter were stored at the Chilwell Armament depot (see page 274) where they were abandoned and forgotten until Cleeve found them again early in the Second World War.

12in railway gun firing at Mealte 1916. IWM Q916.

The guns clearly became personalities in their own rights, Harold Pemberton remembers two 12 inch howitzers called Lion and Tiger, and another called Fanny, and a 9.2 inch railway gun with the unusual name of 'Lady Constance'.

Tank transporting

The tank, whilst potentially a battle winning innovation, was very slow, cumbersome and unreliable. If it wasn't for the railway then it would never have made the battlefield. Unable to use roads tanks developed a symbiotic relationship with trains. Trains could provide a reliable and comparatively speedy transportation service, so long as they could be loaded and unloaded easily and so long as there was a railhead within an easy 'crawl' from the battle front. The first tank attack at Flers in the Somme in September 1916 involved 49 tanks, and all were brought into battle by trains. They were carefully unloaded from makeshift ramps at railheads within range of enemy artillery. The ramps were made of sleepers and it took 20 men ten hours to build, and required precise shunting, for if the train driver hit the ramp, the weight of the train would almost certainly knock the ramp down.[20] The famous tank battle of Cambrai in 1917 involved 436 tanks all of which were delivered to the battlefield by railway, and by then the makeshift wooden ramp had been replaced by a wagon which converted into a ramp, significantly reducing the time taken to load and unload.

Ex-railwayman Eric Potten took part in the Cambrai attack in a tank named *Foggy*, all tanks in F, the 6th Battalion began with F. The railway had transported the tanks to a railhead from where they had edged forward into the village of Gouzeaucourt. The crewmen drove their tanks into the remains of houses and then camouflaged them ready for the attack. They completed final battle preparation in thick fog and on 20 November edged the few hundred metres up to the front line, where they waited. At 0500 on the morning of the 21st the guns opened up, the crew took their rum ration and they advanced as fast as they could, about 6 mph. Each 'female' Mark IV tank had a crew of eight, an officer, a driver, four machine gunners, a gearman, and one other. Potten, an ex-Midland Railway clerk from Sheffield, was a machine gunner in the left hand sponson on one of the two machine guns on that side.

> 'We got to the main German lines and into the wire. It was terrific, wire great in depth and height, we reckoned about 15 feet deep and 9 foot high in places. They were taken by surprise, the Germans got down in their dugouts and we picked them off as we went along.'[21]

> 'We went over the front line and we got slightly ditched in a small communication trench which gave way. We managed to get out. The infantry were following behind us. They liked having a tank in front of them. Our objective was the bridge at Masnieres. This was five miles from the start line and represented a terrific advance. A tank got onto the partially blown bridge but toppled off into the canal. The crew got out. We patrolled up down for an hour or two firing into the German occupied houses the other side of the canal.'[22]

Potten's archive gives a sense of the claustrophobia of tank operation: 'you could see nothing except where the gun goes out. I could see their trench and just fired along their trenches.'[23] The driver and officer could see where they were going, but only had limited view.

---

20   Henniker, 311.
21   IWM Sound Archive, 11042, Eric Potten.
22   IWM Sound Archive, 11042, Eric Potten.
23   IWM Sound Archive, 11042, Eric Potten.

'We wore chainmail masks in case of richochets as there had been such a lot of casualties from bullets chipping off bits of tank... We wore our tin hats, they were the only thing to stop us getting brained when the tank went up or down... After a few hours it was very hot and stuffy... we were very glad to get out and get a breath of fresh air.'[24]

Amazingly when parallel to the enemy they got out the leeward side and got some fresh air whilst the gunners in the other sponson continued to engage. They also were able to re-supply from supply tanks, reloading the ammunition before returning to patrol the line. Eventually Potten and his crew were relieved in contact and handed *Foggy* over to another crew. *Foggy* was later knocked out having lost a track in Bourlon Wood and Potten and crew were sent forward under cover of darkness to recover the machine guns.

Private H J Taylor, a former locomotive cleaner from the L&NWR at Abergavenny, also served in F Battalion, he wasn't as lucky as Private Potten and was killed at Cambrai.

Mark IV Tank Cambrai. IWM Q46932

The 336 tanks that survived the battle were subsequently withdrawn for re-organisation at a concentration area at a small village called Erin, twenty miles west of Bethune, from where they could be forward mounted to any railhead in the Western Front. The train/tank combination introduced manoeuvre warfare, surprise and flexibility to the long static battlefield. If the concentration was shrouded in secrecy and movement was by night, then it was virtually impossible for the enemy to predict precisely where a tank attack might appear next. It is hard to overstate the effect that such

---

24 IWM Sound Archive, 11042, Eric Potten.

a terror weapon would have upon the enemy dug in, tired, worn out and frightened that at any moment the tank could attack them. The fear was probably irrational, there was a lot more front than there were tanks and tanks weren't particularly reliable, but such is the destabilising effect of a shock weapon on the psychological well-being of the combatant. This effect could not have been achieved without the railway.

Privates John Bashford and Robert Grundy both served with 8th Tanks Corps and were killed together on 8 August 1918 in the Battle of Amiens. They both had worked for NER, Bashford a lamp trimmer at Middlesborough, and Grundy an apprentice at Shildon Works. 2nd Lt George Walker was killed the following day with 10th Tank Corps, he was also an NER man, an ex-clerk from Brotton. The following day on the 10th Private Bennett Newman of 4th Tank Corps was killed; he had been a warehouseman with GWR at Swindon. Eric Potten transferred to the Whippet tank and took part in the final advances of the war and survived to return to the railway.

Railway Operations in Egypt and Palestine

Background

Egypt was important because of the strategic nature of the Suez Canal which linked Britain to the far flung reaches of the Empire. The canal needed protecting at all costs. Egypt was under British control, but the states which are now Palestine, Israel, Syria, Jordan and Lebanon all formed part of the Ottoman Empire.

Prior to war, the Turks, with German support, began construction on the 1,875 mile 'Baghdad Railway', crossing the Ottoman Empire from Constantinople to Basra with a fork at Aleppo extending down to Medina on the Saudi Peninsula with narrow gauge connections to Damascus and Beirut. At the outbreak of war, construction began through Palestine along the coastal plain southwards. The British feared that the railway meant that the Turkish could rapidly mass, concentrate and deploy force into Palestine or Mesopotamia and easily and quickly switch between the two.

The main protection of the Suez Canal was the general poor going of the ground through Palestine, which, to a large degree, enemy rail construction overcame, and the inhospitable Sinai Desert. The British suspected a Turkish intent to attack Egypt and in February 1915 a small Turkish force did cross the desert and approach the canal. The General staff in Cairo saw that the only viable defence was to create a substantial buffer beyond the Sinai and into the mountainous terrain of southern Palestine. But the Sinai was a considerable obstacle to the British and the few roads and tracks were along the flat coastal plain. Much as the railway overcame the natural obstacles for the enemy in the north, the railway could bridge the desert enabling British troops to penetrate into southern Palestine.

Railway construction began in earnest and the small village of Kantara, situated between Port Said and Ishmailia, became the centre of operations and was soon an enormous terminus and stores depot with over forty miles of sidings and vast ordnance and supply dumps. It was from here that construction began of a broad gauge railway into the desert. Railway troops became critical in the plans to protect the canal.

Pressure mounted when the allies withdrew from Gallipoli in December 1915, when it was realised that this released thousands more Turkish troops for operations in Mesopotamia or Palestine. Only months later in April 1916, several thousand Turks attacked within ten miles of Kantara, they were repelled as they were the following August, when they attacked postions in Romani on the coast some 25 miles from the canal and Kantara. One response was that all wells within range of the canal were pumped dry, something which today would probably be considered a war crime. As it was this was the last time the Turks got within range of the canal.

Capturing the buffer zone

The first piece of infrastructure to be put in place was a 5-mile stretch of narrow gauge railway along the coast, followed by a 30-mile standard gauge railway line from Kantara to an oasis in Sinai. This was an entirely different prospect to railway engineering in Britain. Engineers had to contend with stiflingly hot conditions, working in deserts and mountains, but like all soldiers they had to make the best of a bad job, and despite the adversities 'get on with it' and they did just that.

As the British troops advanced along the coast, rail construction kept close behind. Infantrymen pushed forward from the railhead at Romani capturing El Arish and whilst infantry advanced to Rafa, the railway construction teams projected the railway forward to El Arish keeping the railhead close to the battle. The advance came to a halt at Gaza with the railway at Deir el Belah. Despite determined attacks in late March 1917 and mid-April 1917 Gaza could not be cracked, and thousands of troops died trying to cross open and exposed ground, or attempting to penetrate barbed wire entanglements. Many lay where they fell for some months until Gaza was finally captured and they could be buried.

Sinai. IWM Q56155

Having failed to take Gaza, a new commander took over, General Sir Edmund Allenby, who decided to attack across the Sinai, with the first objective being Beersheba. This was precisely the ground that was thought to be a key deterrent for the enemy in attacking the canal. It was unforgiving with steep sided wadis, poor tracks and few wells making it difficult for men and animals. Allenby massed 467,000 men and 160,000 horses, mules, camels and donkeys. The biggest problem for such a force was water, particularly watering the animals. Without water an advance would fail.

Before the fighting force could advance Allenby needed his infrastructure in place. The railhead was pushed forward, protected by picquets of cavalry and yeomanry, as the line was built at a pace of up to two miles a day from Rafa to Karm, 36 kilometres north-west in the desert.

Following closely behind the railhead, were engineers laying a pipeline pumping water from the distant River Nile. Ahead of the pipeline water was loaded into rail wagons then, at the railhead, decanted via canvas watercourses into containers mounted onto camels which were then carried forward to the troops. As the railway was extended, the pipeline followed, until eventually there was no need for the railway to carry water. The pipeline became so extensive that it would eventually require 17 pumping stations. Once completed the engineers concentrated on repairing captured wells and sinking new ones. Well water was considered to be suitable for human consumption but not of sufficient quality for steam locomotives, so the pipeline was used to provide water for the locomotives.

The railway infrastructure made it possible to support sufficient troops to cross the Sinai and from the railhead mount an attack and capture Beersheba some 15 miles away. Attention then shifted back to Gaza which was bombarded by warships, attacked on 2 November and cleared by the 8th. The Turks were being pushed back as the buffer zone was established.

Chasing the Turks

As the retreating Turks were pursued by cavalry and the Royal Flying Corps (RFC), work continued at a pace on establishing the railway. The capture of Gaza facilitated the extension of the standard gauge from Deir el Belah through Gaza towards Deir Sineid. The railway task was now to re-build the Turkish network, fast enough to keep the distance between the forward edge of friendly troops and the railhead to a minimum. An army reliant on a large number of animals required a disproportionate amount of fodder and water. Soldiers required less food and water and could, in extremis, go hungry. As long as the railway could keep up with the forward troops, then the Egyptian Expeditionary Force needed to rely less on the slow and labour intensive pack animals for supply and could sustain more and more troops in the field. The men of 96th and 98th Light Railway Operating Companies were sent forward onto the captured Turkish narrow gauge network where they established operations northwards. Securing Wadi Surar Junction Station, known as Junction Station, split the Turkish army, cut off Jerusalem and also enabled light rail operation from Deir Sineid towards Jerusalem. The cavalry meanwhile pressed on capturing Ramleh and Ludd, and then Jaffa (now Tel Aviv) on the coast on the 16 November.

Deir Sineid was connected to the broad gauge on 28 November 1917, linking the light railway network and significantly improving the line of communications. It had been planned to broaden the gauge along the captured narrow gauge line so that trains could run through from Kantara, but conditions were so bad that the sappers abandoned the line and built an entirely

IWM Q50817

new route along the coastal plain and through the mountains. A narrow gauge line was built to Jaffa and the line from Junction station to Beersheba was upgraded to broad gauge. Meanwhile, from Kantara to Rafa, the track was gradually doubled creating considerable increased capacity. This was technical engineering to a demanding timescale and despite all the challenges the railwaymen delivered. Even rectifying a number of own goals such as the bridge that had to be rebuilt after it was pointlessly blown up when the enemy had long gone, or the wooden bridge that needed rebuilding having been embarrassingly burnt down by the Military Police who had been tasked to protect it, but had built a fire on it to keep warm![25]

Jerusalem, which had been cut off following the capture of Junction Station, was finally occupied after some very bitter fighting in the hills around the city, when the garrison surrendered on 9 December. Thereafter, campaigning stopped because of poor weather, but engineering continued and the railwaymen had time to improve communications before the offensive began again in February 1918. The standard gauge from Rafa was opened to Deiran 93 kilometres away on 8 January 1918. The line to Jerusalem opened on 27 January 1918 after the engineers had re-built four bridges destroyed as the Turks withdrew, of which two were over 30 metres long.

Fighting between Jerusalem and Jericho and the Jordan valley was exceptionally hard, over precipitous slopes, rocky ridges and narrow ledges. Slopes were swept with machine gun fire and the wadis were exposed killing areas. Those who survived the wadis had to tackle a succession of steep ridges, lifting each other over the steep rocks, and having reached the summits were immediately engaged in hand to hand fighting. Nevertheless they pressed on and Jericho was captured on 21 February.

Meanwhile the railway sappers were engaged in a wide range of network improvements designed to support the troops and deliver an infrastructure to enable the future policing of an extended empire. The line to Beersheba was completed in May. The route to Jerusalem was upgraded from light railway to standard gauge by June 1918.

Routing the Turks

Allenby delivered his masterstroke on 19 September 1918, which completely broke through the Turkish defences. He immediately tasked his engineers and pioneers to build crossings of the trenches to let the cavalry through who were then let loose. By the end of the day they had penetrated eighteen miles into the Turkish hinterland; they continued rapidly, captured Nablus, the railway junction at El Afule and Nazereth. By the 21st, the routed Turks had become a demoralised rabble. Amman was captured on the 26th and 10,000 enemy surrendered, and Damascus was occupied on 1 October. The cavalry rode on capturing Aleppo, and the junction with the Baghdad railway on the 26th. Meanwhile the railway construction battle was keeping up, replacing Turkish narrow gauge at a rate of about a mile and a quarter per day. The Turks knew their cause was lost and an armistice was agreed on 31 October. One of the terms of the armistice was that the Allies controlled all of the railways.

Even after the armistice, rail construction work continued and by January 1919 the network connected to Haifa. Overall the railwaymen had laid over 1,000 km of track, created 86 stations, and operated 169 locomotives, 2,500 wagons, 50 coaches and 98 hospital coaches.[26] The average daily tonnage transported by the railway system peaked in August 1918 at 2,317 tons per day. The Army Service Corps records show that the force daily requirement amounted to 900 tons of hay, 500 tons of biscuit, 120 tons of meat and 100,800 boxes of matches almost all of which had been transported over the railway line.[27] If the Royal Engineers railwaymen on the Western Front had

---

25 Loch, H.O., With The British Army in the Holy Land, 106.

26 A Brief Record Of The Advance Of The Egyptian Expeditionary Force Under The Command Of General Sir Edmund H. H. Allenby G.C.B. C.G.M.G. July 191 to October 1918, 92.

27 Egyptian Expeditionary Force, 95.

Railwaymen from 115th Company RE, from L & NWR

Arthur Preece	Spr	4	12	16	37	Kantara	L&NWR	Llangammarch	Underman
HP Griffiths	Spr	12	2	17	28	Kantara	L&NWR	Bangor	Labourer
J Patrick	Spr	16	7	17	37	Kantara	L&NWR	Tipton	Underman
David Davies	Spr	30	8	18	39	Llangammarch	L&NWR	Llandovery	Labourer
R Lawson	Spr	26	5	18		Ramleh	L&NWR	Preston	Labourer
Herbert Goodman	Sgt	28	9	18	33	Gaza	L&NWR	Newport Pagnell	Ganger

WW Smith GER

E Kiddy GER

Railwaymen from 116th Company RE, from GWR

William Meredith	Cpl	26	8	15	25	Codsall Ch	Gt Western	Codsall	Packer
Ernest Smith	Sgt	25	9	18	36	Ramleh	Gt Western	Maidenhead	Labourer
John Price	Sgt	3	11	18		Gaza	Gt Western	Llanvihangel	Ganger
AM Alexander	L/Cpl	11	11	18	29	Cairo	Gt Western	Maidenhead	Labourer
CE Simpson	Spr	12	11	18		Ramleh	Gt Western	Winchcombe	
F Proctor	Spr	5	2	19		Haifa	Gt Western	Maidenhead	

Railwaymen from 226th Company RE

T Banner	Spr	14	10	18	36	Cairo	GNR		Platelayer
A Mountain	L/Cpl	14	3	19	33	Haifa	NER	York	Guard
W Balderstone	Spr	2	1	18	35	Hadra	Midland	Skipton	Labourer
Thomas Bretherton	Spr	19	4	18	28	Ramleh	L & NWR	Standish	Sub-Ganger
Joshua Finney	Spr	12	7	18	30	Beersheba	L & NWR	St Helens	Underman
George Price	Spr	21	9	18	34	Hadra	L & NWR	Lancaster	Draughtsman
Joseph Ayres	Spr	28	7	18	41	Beersheba	L & NWR	Bedford	Sub-Ganger
Frederick Edwards	Spr	20	10	18	29	Kantara	GCR	Sheffield	

been experts in logistics and those in the Egyptian Expeditionary Force had been been experts in expeditionary engineering. There can be no doubt that Allenby's tremendous success could not have been delivered without the efforts of the railwaymen working hard in extreme conditions.

The railway troops of EEF comprised 115th, 116th, 265th and 266th Railway Construction Companies, the 299th Indian Rail Construction Company, the 272th Light Railway Construction Company, 96th and 98th Light railway operating company. 1st Bridging Company of Canadian Railway troops, 1/23, 2/23 and 3/32 Sikh Pioneers, 5,500 troops from the Rail Operating Division and 29,000 members of the Egyptian Labour corps.

Officers and SNCOs 116 (GWR) Railway Company RE

Over 370 railwaymen died in the Egypt and Palestine theatre of operations. There are 220 names on the cemeteries dotted around Palestine and the eastern fringe of Egypt in Kantara, Ishmalia, in Deir El Belah, Gaza, Beersheba, Ramleh, Haifa, Jerusalem, Beirut and Damascus.

Map 9. Palestine 1917/1918 showing the eventual extent of the railway network

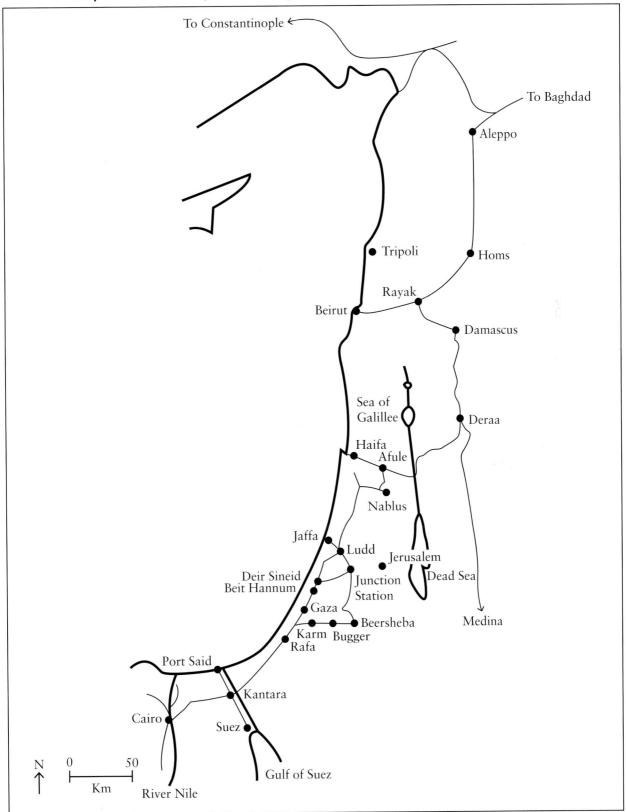

CHAPTER 5

AVIATOR RAILWAYMEN

The Royal Flying Corps, Royal Naval Air Service and the Royal Air Force

The Royal Flying Corps was established in 1912 at a time when only a very few people knew how to fly, and the flying machine had never been used in warfare. This was only three years after Louis Bleriot had flown the English Channel and nine years since the Wright brothers succeeded in the first heavier than air powered flight. Flying was a new technology and the pioneers frequently learnt as they went along. The early military aviators had to gain support from the army commanders, and from politicians for their new specialism and compete for limited resources. They had to develop a means of flying training, open a flying school, develop capable instructors and sell a vision as to how conquering the third dimension might revolutionise warfare; and, of course, build aeroplanes and recruit and train pilots. Of all the Regiments and Corps the RFC had one of the fastest and most spectacular evolutions. Only six years after the RFC had been spawned, warfare had changed forever, and in recognition of the importance of air warfare the Royal Naval Air Service and the Royal Flying Corps were merged to form the Royal Air Force.

Only two years after establishment of the RFC, airmen were sent to war. There were only 52 trained pilots. The small, largely experimental embryonic air force, needed to gain experience in flying and fighting in wartime. They needed to rapidly grow, in aircrew and flying machines. They needed to develop tactics and procedures to give the crews a chance of survival, and to gain experience to pass onto newer pilots. A flying training infrastructure was established in Britain capable of training many more aircrew. After a slow start, the training machinery eventually produced thousands of pilots. Initially the RFC attracted professional soldiers, but by 1916 many of the recruits were volunteers, most of whom had already seen action. Technically skilled railwaymen such as apprentices, managers and clerks seemed to have been attractive to the RFC.

The pilot training system needed to replace pilots killed in warfare, accidents and training, but also to enable the RFC to grow. In 1917, for example, it was decided to expand from 108 to 200 Squadrons. An average rate of 435 pilots were trained per month between 1916 and 1918, with over 1,000 completing training in March 1918 and by the end of the war there were nearly 30,000 pilots in the RAF.[1]

But despite this the losses remained huge. A survey of 283 Sopwith Camel Pilots who were trained in 1918 found that 46 were killed in action, 89 were 'missing' in action, 65 were wounded, 60 were sent home for more training, and only 23 remained to continue the fight.[2]

1   Morley, R., Earning Their Wings: British Pilot Training, 1912-1918. Downloaded from www.ecommons.usask.ca/bitstream/.../RobertMorley.
2   Morley, R, 112.

The Railway Airmen

	Rank	Name	Sqn	Type	Date	Co	Place	Job
1	Air Mech	W H Cox	13	BE2C	5/12/15	Midland	Derby	Apprentice
2	2Lt	Frederick Lucas	16	Curtis JN3	20/10/16	GER		
3	Lt	Charles MacIntosh	18	FE2B	5/4/17	Dean & Dawson	London	
4	2Lt	Frederick McLean	29		16/6/17	GNSR		Student
5	2Lt	Tom Littler	1	Nieuport 23	3/7/17	GWR	Swindon	Apprentice
6	Capt	John Manley	19		18/9/17	GWR	Swindon	Privileged Apprentice
7	Lt	Gerald Paget	1 Aus	BE2A	13/7/17	NER	Blaydon	Yard Master
8	Capt	Herbert Cleghorn	No 1 Depot		17/10/17	Caledonian		Engineer
9	Lt	John McCash	3	Sopwith Camel	22/11/17	Caledonian		Apprentice Civil Engineer
10	2Lt	George J Cooke	20	RE8	22/11/17	GWR		Lad Messenger
11	2Lt	John Orrell	57	DH4	2/12/17	GCR	Gorton	Apprentice Fitter
12	2Lt	Bertram Raggett	10	FK8	5/1/18	NER	Gateshead	Fitter
13	Flt SLt	Harold Day DSC	8	Sopwith Camel	5/2/18	GWR	Swindon	Apprentice
14	Lt	GW Croft	48	Bristol F2B	16/2/18	GCR	Grimsby	Clerk
15	2Lt	Edward Evans			19/2/18	GER	Stratford	Apprentice
16	Capt	Maurice Scott MC	91		17/3/18	Midland	Derby	Privileged Apprentice
17	Capt	EW Monk	8	AW FK8	29/3/18	GER		Clerk
18	2Lt	Clifford Hackman		Avro 508	7/4/18	Great Western	Swindon	Clerk
19	AM2	Valentine Hudson	Z 15	Airship	13/4/18	Midland	Derby	Clerk
20	Flt Lt	Joesph Taylor	G	DH4	17/4/18	GWR	Swindon	Premium Apprentice
21	2Lt	JHV Latham		D116	20/4/18	L&NWR		Junior Clerk
22	Lt	Thomas Lucas	School AG	BE2e	15/5/18	GWR	Swindon	Draughtsman
23	2Lt	Jack Benton	52	RE8	31/5/18	GER	Peterborough	Clerk
24	Lt	Thomas Simpson	65	Sopwith Camel	1/6/18	GWR	Newport	Apprentice
25	Lt	Nelson Mason	210	Sopwith Camel	11/6/18	NER	Newcastle	Clerk
26	2Lt	Henry Stephens	42	RE8	26/8/18	GWR	Newport	Clerk
27	F/Sgt	William Felton			2/7/18	GER		Clerk

	Rank	Name	Sqn	Type	Date	Co	Place	Job
28	2Lt	Jack Pagram		Short 184	18/7/18	L&SWR		Clerk
29	Lt	William Dulin		FE2B	29/7/18	GWR	Swindon	Apprentice
30	Lt	William Lee	58 training	Avro 504	19/8/18	NER	Newcastle	Clerk
31		David Duthie	2	AW FK8	23/8/18	Caledonian		
32	Lt	William Hogg	18	DH4	4/9/18	North British		Clerk
33	Flt Cadet	T Burt	41 training	SE5a	11/9/18	NER	Darlington	Clerk
34	Flt Cadet	Eric Evans	53 training	Sopwith Camel	13/9/18	GWR	Noth Sheen	Clerk
35	2Lt	Stanley Read	27	DH9	25/9/18	GWR	Reading	Clerk
36	Capt	William Scotcher MC	50		15/9/18	GER	Stratford	Draughtsman
37	Capt	James Phillips	35	AWFK8	16/9/18	Caledonian		Erector
38	Sgt	Ethelbert Purling	14	RE8	21/9/18	GER	Trowse	Clerk
39	Lt	Albert Smith	218	DH9	29/9/18	GER	Norwich	Apprentice Fitter
40	Capt	Edward Drake	209		29/9/18	GWR	Fighguard	Fitters Apprentice
41	Lt	F Hopkins	108	DH9	1/10/18	GCR	Sheffield	Clerk
42	Lt	Karl Ibison	213	Sopwith Camel	4/10/18	Lancs & Yorks		Clerk
43	2Lt	Francis Crump	21	RE8	6/10/18	Midland	Bitton	Clerk
44	2Lt	Albert Hadlow	70	Sopwith Camel	6/10/18	SECR	Dover	Fitters Apprentice
45	2Lt	William Bowler	5		2/11/18	L&NWR	Crewe	Clerk
46	2lT	Oliver Price	56	SE5a	4/11/18	GCR	Nottingham	Clerk
47	Lt	Samuel Davison DCM	112		30/11/18	GCR	Stalybridge	Clerk
48	Lt	A E Lloyd			14/12/18	GWR	Exeter	Clerk
49	2Lt	William Howett	4 Fighting School		17/12/18	Midland	Nottingham	Assistant Attendant
50	2 Lt	Sydney Wells	55 Sqn	DH4	16/3/19	L&NWR	Crewe	Junior Clerk

Air Mechanic WH Cox
13 Squadron
5 December 1915
Aged 19
Achiet Le Grand

Apprentice
Midland
Derby

W H Cox appears to have been the first railwayman killed as aircrew and at a time when the RFC was still comparatively small. It would be over two years before the next railwayman died in the air. On 5 December 1915, Cox was observing for an Australian pilot 2Lt A R H Browne. They, along with a second BE2C from 13 Squadron, were escorting an aircraft on a photographic reconnaissance mission to Bellenglise when, near Bapaume, they were attacked by German fighters. A German pilot Leutnant G Leffers subsequently claimed shooting down a BE2C around Achiet Le Grand at 1400. It is believed that Browne was able to crash land but he subsequently died of wounds. Cox was for a time at least a prisoner of war, but he too was to die from his wounds.

2Lt Frederick R Lucas
16 (Reserve) Squadron
20 October 1916
Aged 18
City of London Cemetery Manor Park

CCE*
GER

 Frederick Lucas was commissioned on 10 August 1916 and was killed in a flying accident near Littlehampton whilst flying in a Curtis JN3 on 20 October 1916. Given his age it seems likely that he was a direct entrant into the RFC and was commissioned some way through his training. He was flying a 16 (Reserve) Squadron aircraft at the time so was probably completing his training.

* a department within GER

Lt Charles Mackintosh
18 Squadron
5 April 1917
Aged 38
Vaulx Hill

Conductor
Dean & Dawson*
GCR
London

Charles Mackintosh was an observer in an FE2B on a photographic reconnaissance mission. He would have been in charge of the camera and tasked with leaning over the side of the aircraft to take the important pictures. Shot down near Bapaume, Macintosh was recorded as killed in action and the Pilot, Lt H A R Boustead died of wounds. It is conceiveable that the craft was attacked from the rear killing Macintosh and injuring Boustead, who was rescued from the wreckage only to die shortly thereafter.

* a company owned by GCR

2Lt Frederick W McLean

29 Squadron
16 June 1917
Avesnes le Comte

Student
GNSR

There is no record of Frederick McLean being killed in action, but it is known that 29 Squadron were a Fighter Squadron who deployed to France in March 1916 and at the time of McLean's death were operating Nieuport 17s around Ypres. It seems most likely that he was killed in a flying accident.

2Lt Tom Littler

1 Squadron
3 July 1917
Aged 19
Bailleul

Apprentice
Swindon
GWR

Tom Littler was flying a single seat Nieuport 23 aircraft number B3486, with 1 Squadron, the senior squadron in the Royal Flying Corps, on an offensive patrol out searching for enemy aircraft to engage. He was bounced by a friendly aircraft in what would today be called 'blue on blue' or 'friendly fire' and was shot down and killed by a 46 Squadron Sopwith Pup.

Lt Gerald Paget

1 Squadron Australian Flying Corps
13 July 1917
Jerusalem

Yard Master
Blaydon
NER

 Gerald Paget was a popular man both within the railway and latterly working with the Australian forces. The NER magazine reports that 'he had an intense enthusiasm for matters concerned to the railway and was especially interested in new ideas and inventions'.[3] He also seemed to be developing a promising career having worked for Midland Railway in Derby and with Parsons' Marine Steam Turbine Company on Tyneside before joining the NER in 1909, where he worked in a range of jobs and looked to be being groomed for greater things. An ideal recruit then to the RFC.

Paget was flying with Lt Archibald Searle in a BE2A from 1 Squadron of the Australian Flying Corps. They were shot down and killed and having no known grave are remembered on the Jerusalem memorial. His Australian commanding officer wrote: 'With his death passed away a man whom the whole squadron admired and respected. He was always ready with bright suggestions for improving and helping us with our work. Never idle he was always about the camp doing good to someone and cheering everyboy up in general. He took far more than his share of the work. We have lost the most popular member of our mess. He simply loved the Australians and we loved him.'[4]

---

3   North Eastern Railway Magazine, 1917, 198.
4   North Eastern Railway Magazine, 1917, 198

Capt John Manley

19 Squadron
18 September 1917
Aged 20
Bailleul

Premium Apprentice
Swindon
GWR

19 Squadron flew the Spad 7 and were operating from the Ypres area. It is likely he wasn't killed in action and therefore he was probably victim to a flying accident.

Captain Herbert Cleghorn

No 1 Depot
2 September 1917
Aged 26
St Omer

Civil Engineer
Caledonian

Herbert Cleghorn, along with two older brothers was commissioned into the Royal Engineers, he served at the front from January 1916. Subsequently he transferred to the RFC. On the day he was killed he was operating from the No 1 Aircraft depot at St Omer, which by this time of the war had become a huge establishment where pilots were frequently held pending allocation to other squadrons, or were undergoing training or refreshing. It seems likely that he was killed in an air accident.

He was the sixth of ten children of John and Margaret from Alyth in Perthshire. Alfred and John survived the war but his elder brother William was killed only a month after Herbert on HMS *Mary Rose* and his youngest brother Allan a subaltern in the 1st Gordon Highlanders was killed on 7 Sepetmber 1916.

Lt John McCash

3 Squadron
23 November 1917
Aged 24,
Arras Flying Services Memorial.

Apprentice Civil Engineer
Caledonian

John McCash from Perth would have known and probably worked with Herbert Cleghorn and they may had been friends. McCash joined the 6th Black Watch but transferred to the RFC. The Commonwealth War Graves Commission (CWGC) website states that he was killed serving with 35 Squadron but Henshaw states that he was was killed flying with 3 Squadron.[5]

On the day that McCash was killed, the RFC were heavily engaged attacking Bourlon Wood at low level providing close air support to the hard pushed infantrymen fighting on the ground. The aircraft were vulnerable at low level to ground fire, pilot error, and attack from above, especially as the Richthofen Circus commenced their first patrol in the

---

5   Henshaw, T., The Sky Their Battleground. Air Fighting And the Complete List of Allied Air Casualties From Enemy Action In The First War. 257.

Lt John McCash (continued)

area on the 23 November. Sixteen Sopwith Camel pilots from 3, 46 and 64 Squadrons were downed in two days.

John McCash was flying a Sopwith Camel patrolling the Bourlon Wood area with a second machine flown by a Canadian Lt F H Stephens. It is not known what caused the crash; they may have collided, been hit from ground fire, or shot down from German aircraft above.

2Lt George J Cooke

52 Squadron
23 November 1917
Aged 20
Zuydcoote

Lad Messenger
Paddington Goods
GWR

Most of the railwaymen who flew were clerks, apprentices or managers, but George Cooke was very junior in the railway and had been employed as a lad messenger. He joined the army in September 1914 aged seventeen and survived Gallipoli and France before being commissioned into the London Regiment. He served with his regiment in France and then joined the RFC where he became an observer.

On 23 November he was observing for artillery in a 52 Squadron RE8 number A4273 flown by Lt CHM Platt when they collided with another RE8 from the same squadron flown by 2Lt CM Pears. Both aircraft crashed and the crews were killed.

2Lt John T Orrell

57 Squadron
2nd December 1917
Aged 20
Hazlebeke

Apprentice Fitter
Gorton Works
GCR

John Orrell was flying a DH4 on a bombing and photo reconnaissance mission along with his observer 2Lt J G Glendinning. Lt H Bongartz of Ja 36 claimed to have shot down an English aircraft which was probably Orrell's machine. Orrell was killed and Glendinning was taken prisoner but died two weeks later.

2Lt Bertram R Raggett

10 Squadron
5 January 1918
Lijssenthoek

Fitter
Gateshead
NER

Information concerning Bertram Raggett, the son of a vicar, is a little sketchy. According to the CWGC 2Lt Raggett was serving with 10 Squadron and is buried at Lijssenthoek cemetery. This was the location of a casualty clearing station so it seems likely that Raggett died of wounds. 10 Squadron flew AW FK8s and one from the squadron was shot down in the area on the 3 January, although not flown by Raggett, but this shows that 10 Squadron were operating in the area at this time. There is no record of him being killed in action or shot down so it is likely that he suffered a flying accident.

Flight Sub Lieutenant Harold Day DSC Royal Navy

8 Squadron
5 February 1918
Aged 20
St Mary's Advanced Dressing Station

Apprentice
Swindon
Great Western

Harold Day shot down eleven aircraft (nine in 41 days) establishing himself as one of the most successful fighter pilots, until his aircraft broke up in the sky and he came crashing down to his death. Harold, who came from a tiny hamlet called Wernddu outside Abergavenny, had been an apprentice at the GWR works at Swindon, and his technical prowess served him well, gaining a commission in the Royal Navy and access into the technical and highly experimental Royal Naval Air Service. Day was originally part of 10 Squadron RNAS flying Sopwith Triplanes, and he got his first kill with them on 12 August 1917, shooting down an Albatros. He transferred to 8 Squadron flying Sopwith Camels, where he honed his skills. He shot down an enemy on 6 December, and another on 27 December which was followed by nine more until on 5 February, soon after shooting an Albatros down, he was positioning upon another target when his aircraft plummeted to the earth, killing him. Only 17 days later he was awarded a posthumous Distinguished Service Cross. His citation reads:

'In recognition of the skill and determination shown by him in aerial combats, in the course of which he has done much to stop enemy artillery machines from working. On 6 January 1918, he observed a new type of enemy aeroplane. He immediately dived to attack, and after a short combat the enemy machine went down very steeply and was seen to crash. On several other occasions he has brought down enemy machines out of control.'[6]

On 1 April 1918, with the formation of the Royal Air Force Number 8 Squadron of the Royal Naval Air Service, became number 208 Squadron Royal Air Force.

Lt GW Croft

48 Squadron
16 February 1918
Ham British

Clerk
Marine Department
Grimsby Docks
GCR

In the back half of February and early March 1918 the Allies concentrated on bombing of German aerodromes, railway networks and troop concentrations. These were usually well defended and so attrition was high. Lt Croft was the observer in a Bristol F2B from 48 Squadron flown by Sergeant ET Hardeman. Oberleutnant W Reinhard from Ja6 claims to have shot down a 'Bristol' west of St Quentin and this was probably Croft and Hardeman. The plane came down in flames, possibly the very worst way to die.

---

6   London Gazette citation, 22nd February 1918.

2Lt Edward Tilney Evans
19 February 1918
Aged 19
City of London Cemetery Manor Park

Apprentice
Stratford Works
GER

Edwards Evans, the son of a director of Tilneys Brewery in Mile End, was killed in a flying accident near Bristol on one of the final flights before he was posted overseas on operations. Killed whilst still training, but as the picture below shows, he had already been awarded his wings.

Capt Maurice DG Scott MC
17 March 1918
Ockbrook, Derbyshire

Privileged Apprentice
Midland
Derby

Maurice Scott's war record bore some similarity to Harold Day. He also shot down or captured eleven enemy aircraft and a balloon. In a later war he would have been regarded as an 'ace' but the term wasn't in widespread use during the Great War. Scott served originally with the 3rd Royal North Lancashires until transferring to the RFC in February 1916. On 3 April 1916 whilst serving with 18 Squadron he scored his first victory as an observer on a Vickers FB 5 by capturing a German reconnaissance aircraft. Scott then trained as a pilot and was posted to 54 Squadron flying the Sopwith Pup shooting three aircraft down before being posted to 46 Squadron as a flight commander. During September 1917 he shot down seven enemy aircraft, six of them with Sopwith Pup B2191.

He was posted back to 'Blighty' in October 1917, but only a few months later in March 1918, whilst serving with 91 Squadron based nearby Tangmere, he was killed in a flying accident at Shoreham. His Sopwith Pup is reported as looping, rolling and then diving into the ground. Scott survived the accident but died a day later having not regained consciousness. By some cruel twist of irony his award of an MC appeared in the *London Gazette* of the following day.

His citation read:

'For conspicuous gallantry and devotion to duty in aerial combats. On one occasion his patrol encountered seven enemy machines, two of which he drove down out of control. He has destroyed eleven enemy aeroplanes, and proved himself a very dashing patrol leader'.[7]

---

7   Supplement to the London Gazette, 18 March 1918 (30583/3431)

Capt E W Monk

8 Squadron
29 March 1918
Aged 23
Beauval

Clerk
Chief Traffic Managers Office
GER

Captain Monk was the pilot of an AW FK8 with 8 Squadron with Lieutenant C B Wilkinson as his observer. They were engaged in spotting for the artillery when they were shot down by an enemy aircraft and killed. Monk had a varied career, originally joining the Royal Field Artillery in 1914, and spent time as a signaller, before being commissioned into the London Regiment where he spent fifteen months in the trenches before transferring to the RFC flying as an observer during the Battle of the Somme before retraining as a pilot. It is thought that when he was shot down he had been attacked by five aircraft.

Corporal E C Lovelock

57 Squadron
1 April 1918
Aged 21
St Pol

Porter
Pilning
GWR

Corporal Lovelock, was an observer in a DH4 flown by 57 Squadron. It is recorded that he was killed in action in DH4 A7406 but there is no mention of the pilot being killed. If the pilot survived it is possible that Lovelock was shot in air combat or from ground fire.

2Lt Clifford Hackman

92 Squadron
7 April 1918
Aged 20
Winchcombe

Clerk
Stores Department
Swindon
GWR

Clifford Hackman was killed on 7 April 1918 when the Royal Air Force was less than a week old. It is likely that Clifford, who was flying an Avro 504 trainer, was learning to fly, and his instructor was Captain Norman England. The Avro collided with a Sopwith Pup flown by 2Lt Victor Craigie above Tangmere and all three were killed. They were from 92 Squadron, which at the time was based at London Colney but moved to France in July 1918.

Flt Lt Joseph H Taylor

G Squadron
17 April 1918
Aged 21
East Mudros

Premium Apprentice
GWR
Swindon

Joseph Taylor, who had been commissioned into the RNAS, was killed alongside his observer Lt Conrad Betts in Greece when his DH4 number B9485 nosedived on take off, crashed and burnt out.

2Lt JHV Latham
50 Training Squadron
20 April 1918
Aged 19
Grimsargh Churchyard

Junior clerk
L & NWR
Grimsargh

J H V Latham was killed whilst flying an aircraft called a D116 number A9751. He was afforded a military funeral with over thirty rifleman firing a last volley.

Lt Thomas H Lucas
School of Air Gunnery (Egypt)
15 May 1918
Aged 27, Cairo

Draughtsman
Swindon
GWR

Thomas Lucas had served Great Western for 13 years before joining up, initially with the Hampshire Regiment before he transferred into the RFC. He was killed in an accident whilst flying BE2e number 4532.

2Lt Jack W Benton
31 May 1918
52 Squadron
Aged 20, Terlincthun

Clerk
Peterborough
GER

Jack Benton had joined the GER in November 1912 aged fourteen and in February 1917 he enlisted into the Honourable Artillery Company. He subsequently transferred into the RFC.

On 29 May 1918, Jack Benton was an observer with a 52 Squadron RE8 flown by 2Lt J K Watson on a bombing sortie, although damaged they were able to return safely to their aerodrome. The following day Benton was airborne observing for Lt HP Illsley when they were hit whilst over Chambery. Benton was wounded and died the following day.

2Lt Thomas E Simpson
65 Squadron
1 June 1918
Aged 23, Vignacourt

Fitters Apprentice
Newport
GWR

Thomas became an apprentice at the GWR works where his father was divisional locomotive superintendent in 1911. He served first in the Monmouth Regiment transferring to the Army Service Corps before joining the RFC. He sailed for France on 25 May and was killed on 1 June one week later. In what must have been one of his first flights he became lost, then encountered engine trouble with his Sopwith Camel. He landed near Breteuil in soft ground and the Camel overturned but Simpson's luck held and he escaped. His luck didn't last and whilst inspecting the front of the aircraft his own machine gun fired and killed him. It must have been quite a rare combination of circumstances to have been killed by your own machine guns! The Camel was salvaged and rebuilt and was became a night fighter with 151 Squadron.

Lt Nelson Mason

210 Squadron RAF   Goods Clerk
11 June 1918   Newcastle
Ebblinghem   NER

Nelson Mason served with 210 Squadron RAF, formerly 10 Squadron RNAS, equipped with the Sopwith Camel. There are no records of him being killed in combat, it is likely that he was killed in a flying accident. He had been employed by NER as a goods clerk at Newcastle.

2Lt Henry Hill Stephens

42 Squadron   Clerk
28 June 1918   Newport
Aged 19   GWR
Aire

Little is known about what happened to Henry Stephens, he was flying in a RE8 or 'Harry Tate' as they became known, of 42 Squadron, one of thirteen planes lost on the day, shot down by machine gun fire. This may have damaged the machine and he was killed in the crash, or perhaps more likely he was hit and this caused the plane to crash. There is no mention of an enemy aircraft, so it seems likely he was shot from the ground.

Flight Sergeant William R Felton

203 Sqn   Clerk
2 July 1918   GER
Aged 25
Ilford Cemetery

Wiliam Felton, from Ilford, was killed in a flying accident when he lost control of his aircraft and crashed into a field close to Broadstairs in Kent.

2Lt Jack AH Pegram

18 July 1918   Clerk
Aged 18   L & SWR
Hollybrook Southampton

Jack Pegram was on patrol flying a Short 184 seaplane from Westgate-on-Sea in Kent, along with his observer 2Lt L A Thrower. They were accompanied by another Short 184 flown by Lt J A E Vowles, and 2 Sopwith Camels from Manston flown by Lts Vincent and Wagstaff.

2Lt Jack AH Pegram (continued)

They were bumped by seven German Brandenburg Seaplanes some miles off the north Kent coast. Both flying boats made forced landings on the sea but it seems that Pegram's machine caught fire which killed the crew. Jack Pegram is commemorated on the Hollybrook Memorial in Southampton, indicating that his body was not recovered. The crew of the other aircraft appear to have survived.

Lt William Walter Motta Dulin
Central Dispatch Pool of pilots
29 July 1918
Wimille

Apprentice
Swindon
GWR

William Dulin was killed flying an FE2B number B1878. No other details are known.

Lt William Lee
58 Training Squadron
19 August 1918
Aged 26
Hadra

Clerk
NER
Newcastle Forth

Lt William Lee was killed piloting an Avro 504J in Egypt, but is shown as serving in 5th Royal Irish Fusiliers. This indicates that he was training as a pilot and had not completed his training and so had not transferred to the RAF. The 5th Royal Irish Fusiliers had served in Gallipoli, Salonika and Palestine and had returned to Europe on 30 April 1918.

2Lt David Duthie
2 Squadron
23 August 1918
Aged 25
Arras Flying

Caledonian

David Duthie was an observer in an AW FK8 with 35 Squadron. He was wounded on 23 November 1917, during the battle of Cambrai and on the same day that Lt J W McCash was killed (see page 141), whilst on a reconnaissance patrol. His pilot was forced to land and Duthie was taken to hospital. He recovered and on 23 August 1918 flying in another AW FK8 with 2 Squadron his aircraft was hit by anti-aircraft fire and the plane fell into a dive and crashed to the south west of La Bassee killing Duthie and his pilot Lt E O Drinkwater.

Lt William Hogg

18 Squadron
4 September 1918
Aged 23
Arras Flying

Clerk
North British

The RAF were trying to exploit the German withdrawal from Lens. 18 Squadron were engaged on bombing missions and at least three DH4s were lost, including that of William Hogg and 2Lt A E Stock, which was shot down in flames. Their bodies were reported as being unrecognisable. Among the other losses were nine Sopwith Camels from 70 Squadron lost in a single action when they met with 30 Fokkers over the front line.

Flight Cadet T Burt

11 September 1918
41st Training Depot Station
Aged 19
Darlington West

Clerk
Darlington
NER

Cadet Burt, who had seen service with 69 Division in their cyclist regiment, was learning to fly and was killed in a flying accident whilst piloting SE5a number E4074.

Flight Cadet Eric H Evans

53rd Training Depot Station
13 September 1918
Aged 22
North Sheen

Accounts Clerk
London
GWR

Only two days after T Burt had been killed, Eric Evans also crashed whilst flying Sopwith Camel F4189. Evans had previous service as an artilleryman.

2Lt Stanley C Read

27 Squadron
25 September 1918
Aged 19
Grand Servacourt

Clerk
Goods Department
Reading
GWR

Stanley Read was an observer in a DH9 from 27 Squadron on a bombing mission when they were shot down in flames to the west of Bohain. Both Stanley Read and his pilot 2Lt V Cosgrove were killed. Lieutnant S Garsztka of Ja 31 claimed the kill.

Stanley's brother, who was also a goods clerk at Reading, had been killed earlier in the war on 21 May 1915, aged twenty, whilst serving with the Berkshire Yeomanry.

Capt William G Scotcher MC

50 Squadron
15 September 1918
Aged 28
Ilford Cemetery

Draughtsman
Stratford Works
GER

 William Scotcher began work as an apprentice at Stratford in 1906. He eventually qualified as a draughtsman and got a job with the Argentinian railway (see also page 238). Soon after war was declared he, along with other railwaymen expatriates in Argentina, returned home to join up. He served with the East Yorks at Gallipoli where he was one of the last to leave, and Egypt before serving in France. He was commissioned into the East Yorks and was awarded the MC on 14 November 1916, by which time he had already transferred into the RFC as an observer.

His citation reads:

'For conspicuous gallantry. He commanded his platoon with great determination, when his trench was constantly being blown in by shellfire. He exposed himself freely in order to encourage his men. Though partially buried by a shell, he carried on his work as soon as extricated.'[8]

He was killed in a flying accident on 15 September 1918 whilst serving with 50 Squadron, which was a home defence squadron based in Kent, and is buried in Ilford.

Capt James E Phillips

35 Squadron
16 September 1918
Aged 19
St Emilie

Apprentice
Erector
Caledonian

James Phillips was shot up a few times in what must have been a pretty short career as a pilot. Like others mentioned, he flew the AW FK8, a somewhat ungainly bird, not particularly attractive and not exactly a fighter. On the afternoon of 3 Apr 1918 he was flying a 35 Squadron machine on patrol around Amiens when he was engaged by an enemy aircraft; his plane was hit and he was forced to land.
A week later on the 10th he was on a morning patrol over Villers-Bretonneux and his engine was shot up during air combat. Again he was able to make a forced landing and both he and his observer were unhurt. On 20 April when flying over Villers-Brettoneux he was engaged and his observer was injured. On 16 September Phillips was on patrol with 2Lt RV Hepburn having left Moislains aerodrome at 10am. Both were killed when the aeroplane was hit by an anti-aircraft shell.

---

8   London Gazette citation 14th November 1916.

Sgt Ethelbert Purling

14 Squadron	Clerk
21 September 1918	Trowse
Aged 22	GER
Jerusalem	

Ethelbert Purling, from Thorpe Hamlet, Norwich, transferred to the RAF from the 1/4th Norfolks which he joined in November 1914. On 21 September 1918 he was flying as an observer in an RE8 with his pilot Lt Johnnie Webster MC, an Australian from Tasmania. They were flying at low level with other aircraft in the squadron supporting the ground attack on Nablus and Haifa. They attacked a large body of troops and transport but were hit by ground fire, spun, and crashed in flames. The following day when the troops had captured the ground where the crash took place, the bodies were recovered and were buried with honours at Shibleh between Nablus and the river Jordan.

Lt Albert E Smith

218 Squadron	Apprentice Fitter
29 September 1918	Norwich
Aged 19	GER
Arras Flying	

Barely four months after enlisting on 23 April 1918 Albert Smith was dead, killed whilst acting as an observer in a DH9 of 218 Squadron. By this time of the war the training must have been truncated since he was deployed to France, presumably fully trained, on 20 August. The battle for the Hindenburg Line was in full swing. Albert Smith and his pilot 2Lt JC Pritchard were jumped by five enemy aircraft, Pritchard dived away but crashed and both were killed.

Capt Edward B Drake

209 Sqn	Fitters Apprentice
29 September 1918	Marine Department
Arras	Fishguard
	GWR

On the same day Captain Edward Drake flying a Sopwith Camel from 209 Squadron on a low level patrol was shot down, believed to be by Leutnant P Baumer of Ja2, to the south of Sailly.

Lt F Hopkins

108 Squadron	Clerk
1 October 1918	Sheffield
Harlebeke	GCR

108 Squadron were unlucky enough to be caught by 33 Fokker DVIIs whilst on a bombing mission. Three DH9s were downed with two crews being killed, including Lt Hopkins and his observer Lt JW Firth.

Lt Karl G Ibison
213 Squadron   Clerk
4 October 1918   Lancashire & Yorkshire
Aged 19
St Baafs-Vijve

213 Squadron were flying missions around Roulers and Karl Ibison was lost. There is no information as to what happened, but another squadron pilot had been killed in that area earlier in the day.

2Lt Francis L D Crump
21 Squadron   Clerk
6 October 1918   Bitton
Aged 22   Midland Railway
Lapugnoy

Francis Crump was commissioned into the Worcestershire Regiment and transferred into the RAF. He flew with 21 Squadron who had a name for effective spotting for artillery. On one day during the Messines offensive in June 1917 they put 72 enemy artillery batteries out of action by spotting and co-ordinating counter battery artillery fire onto them. It is presumed that Crump was killed in an accident flying an RE8 in a reconnaissance and army co-operation role spotting for artillery

2Lt Albert Llewellyn Hadlow
70 Squadron   Fitters Apprentice
6 October 1918   Marine Department
Haringhe   Dover
                                                                SECR

Albert's squadron was formed at South Farnborough, Hampshire on 22 April 1916, and at the time of death was flying Sopwith Camels from Droglandt near Ypres.

2Lt William J Bowler
5 Squadron RAF   Clerk
2 November 1918   Crewe
Aged 19   L& NWR
Douai

William Bowler was a member of 5 Squadron which was a Corps Reconnaissance Squadron, flying an RE8. Bowler and his observer 2Lt F W Pike were killed whilst carrying out their duty of artillery observation or aerial photography.

2Lt Oliver Price
56 Squadron
4 November 1918
Aged 23, Valenciennes

Clerk
Nottingham
GCR

Oliver Price, who was from East Cottage, Ruddington, Nottinghamshire, was flying a 'close offensive patrol' in his SE5a of 56 Squadron when he was hit by anti-aircraft fire, his aircraft fell into a slow spin and crashed and Price was killed.

Lt Samuel Davison DCM
112 Squadron
30 November 1918
Manchester Gorton

Clerk
Stalybridge Goods
GCR

Samuel Davison survived the war only to be killed in a flying accident in Kent on 30 November 1918. He was a member of 112 Squadron who were a home defence squadron flying Sopwith Camels and were tasked with defending London from attack. Their airfield was located in the Kentish Downland at Throwley. Davidson had won the DCM sometime previously and since the DCM wasn't awarded to officers he must have been commissioned from the ranks.

2Lt William F Howett
4 Fighting School
17 December 1918
Carrington Notts

Assistant Attendant
Mechanical Engineers Department
Midland

William had been learning to fly at the 4th Fighting School at Frieston in Lincolnshire and was killed in a flying accident.

Lt AE Lloyd
14 December 1918
Aged 20
Newton Abbot

Goods Clerk
Exeter Highweek
GWR

A E Lloyd had enlisted into the Devonshire Regiment in 1917 and was killed in a flying accident near Chester.

2Lt Sydney Wells
55 Squadron
26 March 1919
Aged 19
Cologne South

Junior Clerk
Crewe
L& NWR

According to the CWGC, Sydney Wells, who came from 19 Nelson Street, Crewe, was serving with 48 Squadron, and therefore would have been flying in the F2B two seat Bristol Fighter. But according to other research he was with 55 Squadron observing in a DH4 which was the only aircraft to be lost on the Western Front on 5 April 1918 in the midst of the German offensive. According to this latter account Wells and his pilot 2Lt P H O'Lieff were taken prisoner. Since Wells is buried in the Cologne South cemetery he had almost certainly been a POW. Wells died in March 1919, and so it is possible that he was a victim of the influenza outbreak that swept Europe.

Most of the airmen killed during the Great War were in aircraft, but a few were killed in lighter than air-craft; balloons or airships whose great advantage was their incredible duration which made them ideal patrol or observation craft.

Air Mechanic 2nd Class Valentine Hudson
13 April 1918
Aged 18
Hollybrook, Southampton

Clerk
Minerals Dept
Derby
Midland

Valentine Hudson was part of the three-man crew of HM Airship Z15, operating from the Royal Naval Air Station Mullion, or its satellite at Toller in Dorset. The Z15 carried out long-range coastal patrols supporting naval ships, and helping to protect the British sea lanes. The Z15 was lost at sea two miles south of Exmouth, the crew were killed, and since the memorial to them is the Hollybrook memorial in Southampton it indicates that their bodies were not recovered.

Airman Albert Barnes
14 Balloon Section
16 July 1918
Berles

Parcel Porter
Manchester London Road
L & NWR

Static balloons were used to provide observation of the battlefield. The main role was in the direction of artillery. A well-sighted balloon with a capable observer meant that it was difficult for the enemy to operate artillery without it being identified and engaged, or to mass reinforcements. Balloon operation gave commanders an appreciation of the battlefield and enemy activity and often warned of enemy intentions.

W G Ostler was an ex-booking clerk at Crouch Hill, a Midland Railway station in London. He was part of 17 Balloon section, based in Salonika, and survived the war. His experiences are recorded at the Imperial War Museum.

Airman Albert Barnes (continued)

'There were 120 men in the balloon section. About eight officers, who were the observers in the balloons, directed artillery fire for the gun batteries. The remaining men managed the balloon. Some were winch controllers. There was 4,000–5,000 feet of steel winch cable to each balloon. There was a gas squad whose role was to create the gas from a combination of silicone, caustic soda and water. Producing the gas was a slow process and so once inflated, balloons would be kept inflated. If they needed to be moved then troops would manhandle the balloon with four men to each guy rope, of which there might be ten to a balloon.'[9]

So 40 men would be required to 'walk' a balloon between locations. Ostler reports the maximum distance that they walked a balloon was 18 miles overnight. There is no information available as to how Albert Barnes died or what his role was in the balloon section.

Captain Walter Warneford AFC RAF

Northsea Airship Number 11	Pupil Engineer
15 July 1919	Crewe
Hollybrook Southampton	L&NWR

Walter Warneford worked at Crewe as a pupil engineer from 1912–1914 where he was no doubt assisted by his father in gaining employment, as his father was the works manager. Warneford joined the Kite Balloon Section of the Royal Naval Air Service in 1914. He was to become quite a distinguished airship pilot engaged in patrols of the coastal waters, escort duties and hunting for submarines. The airship was an ideal platform to provide support to convoys and naval task forces. Warneford carried out deck landing trials on the new aircraft carrier HMS *Furious* in 1918, and later that year he took command of NS11, based at Longside in Aberdeenshire, establishing a number of endurance records and a world record for endurance of 2,300 miles and 100 hours 50 minutes in the air.

Warneford survived the war and continued to be in the vanguard of airship operational flying and development and was awarded the Air Force Cross (AFC) in 1919. He was killed when NS11 exploded off Sheringham in Norfolk when the airship appears to have been struck by lightning. By a strange coincidence, Warneford's cousin Reginald, also the son of a railway engineer albeit on the Indian railway, was also in the Royal Naval Air Service. By even stranger coincidence Reginald destroyed an enemy airship by dropping bombs on it. Zeppelin LZ37 exploded and Reginald's aircraft was blown upside down and the engine stopped. Forced to land in enemy territory he coolly effected repairs before flying home. He was awarded the VC. Reginald Warneford was killed in a flying accident on the day he was awarded the French Legion d'Honnour.

A drinking fountain memorial to Walter Warneford was established at the Viaduct Sports and Social Club at Earlestown, Lancashire, where his father Hayden had become the wagon superintendent.

Not all of the railwaymen who died in the RFC or RAF were aircrew, some were ground crew.

---

9   IWM Sound Archive, 39, W.G. Ostler.

Captain Fred E Mocatta
28 August 1918
Aged 29
Golders Green Jewish Cemetery

Engineering Department
Paddington
GWR

Fred Mocatta was a qualified engineer beginning his career with GWR at the start of the war. Commissioned into the Artillery he served in Gallipoli with 29th Division, also Egypt and France, where he was invalided home on health grounds. He then became attached to the Aircraft Production Supply Department and utilised his engineering skills. He was reported as having 'rendered very great and excellent service to the state' and on 1 April 1918 he was given a 'special appointment at the ministry of munitions'. His death was due to septic meningitis.

Captain Ernest S Bramham
7 November 1918

Electrical engineer
GWR

Ernest Bramham was the assistant in charge of electrical testing for GWR, but joined the RFC in July 1915 as an equipment officer. This was a non-glamorous job, but another example of how the railway staff were able to bring their specialist knowledge for the benefit of the military. He went on to Farnborough and eventually into the aircraft construction service. Although he served in France with 18 Squadron he was to die from the influenza pandemic of 1918.

Sergeant Charles Roberts
26 December 1917
Giavera Arcade, Italy

Clerk
Swindon
GWR

Charles Roberts was killed serving with 34 Squadron who were one of five RFC squadrons deployed to Italy in November 1917 and flew the RE8. It is possible that Sergeant Roberts was ground crew and certainly the airfields were bombed and an RE8 was destroyed in a bombing raid on 31 December. But the fact that so many of the aircrew were clerks, apprentices or managers, it is more likely that Sergeant Roberts was aircrew and killed in an accident.

Right: IWM Q055991

CHAPTER 6

NAVAL RAILWAYMEN

Railwaymen served and died in famous capital ships and tiny workboats, and died in some pretty unusual circumstances throughout the war.

Many railwaymen served as stokers, although only a few were locomotive firemen in their civilian employment. Some Able Seamen came from the railway ferries but many had no obvious connection to the sea. A number served as sick berth attendants (SBA), three of the four SBA who went down with HMS *Formidable* were labourers, but the railway had a very strong network of volunteer ambulance detachments and this was a source of first aid qualified personnel who were ideal for medical roles in the Navy and Army.

Amongst the first to die in the war were 35 railwaymen amongst 1,459 men killed when HMS *Aboukir*, *Hogue* and *Cressy* were sunk by a single U-Boat on 22 September 1914. Just over a month later *Good Hope* was sunk by another U-Boat in the South Atlantic with a loss of 25 railwaymen in the ships company of 1,600 who perished. At least 50 railwaymen died on various ships at the Battle of Jutland on 31 May 1916. The youngest to die was Boy 1st Class Stephen Curd aged sixteen, on *Invincible*, he had previously been employed at LB & SCR as a greaser.

Servicemen accept the risks of dying in action, but to die whilst the ship is in a safe anchorage must surely be the act of some gross incompetence. This was the fate of over 2,000 men and eighteen railwaymen, and there is little certain explanation for their demise, but it was almost certainly not enemy action. *Bulwark* exploded off Sheerness, *Natal* at Cromaty Firth and *Vanguard* anchored at Scapa Flow. Even more bizarre was the fate of *Narborough* and *Opal* lost with all but one crewman, including at least four railwaymen, when both ran aground together in bad weather off Scapa Flow on 12 January 1918.

Nearly 200 railwaymen died in the Royal Naval Division, fighting in Gallipoli and the Western Front.

BIG SHIPS

HMS *Aboukir*, HMS *Hogue* and HMS *Cressy*   22 September 1914

Aboukir, and her sisters *Hogue* and *Cressy*, were part of the Seventh Cruiser Squadron based at Harwich. They were old, obsolescent ships, which for two years prior to the war had been left to rot moored in a creek. They were hastily made ship-shape and were manned mainly by urgently called-up reservists, who at this time of the war were less well trained than their full time counterparts. The squadron were tasked with supporting destroyers in blockading German ships in the North Sea, but the cruisers were better in rough weather and so frequently patrolled without the mutual support of the destroyers who were forced into harbour. Although the ships should have zig-zagged in order to deter U-boats, since they had never seen evidence of any, they tended to maintain a straight course. Furthermore the worn out engines kept them to low speeds. No wonder then that the Grand Fleet called them 'the live bait squadron'. [1]

It is difficult to imagine the experiences of members of a ships company when warships are steaming towards one another about to engage in conflict. For most of the crew the enemy would be unsighted. They would be below decks getting on with their normal duties. An insight into life in the bowels of the ship comes from former railwayman Charles Minter who had been an engine cleaner

---

1   Massie, R.K., Castles Of Steel. Britain, Germany And The Winning Of The Great War At Sea, 129.

HMS *Aboukir*. *IWM* Q38002

and spare fireman at Margate before joining the Navy as a stoker. Minter describes working aboard the battleship HMS *Hibernia*. 'There were four stoke-holds, each with six boilers and there were eight stokers in each stoke-hold, and some stokers in the engine room. Probably about forty stokers for each four-hour watch. We were trimmers as they called it in the merchant service. We fetched the coal to the fireman in skids with no wheels but runners which slid over the steel footplates easily. The boilers were coal fired and forced draught, great big fans blowing down the whole time. There was water in the ash pit under the grates and the air going through that made it ripple. There was no dust, it was comparatively clean for what you would expect. The fires had to be cleared of clinker and ash every watch, which we dumped through the ships bottom at sea by means of the ash expeller. It was a great dish and the ash and clinker was ground up and air was blown in. Then they opened a valve to let the sea come in, the air kept it there and the ash went out to sea.'[2]

On 22 September, the squadron was spotted by Lt Otto Weddigen, the captain of *U9*, a 403 ton 188 foot elderly U-boat with a crew of 28. It was only luck, or bad luck, that put *U9* in the same part of the North Sea at the same time as the 7th Cruiser Squadron. Weddigen had been due to blockade Ostend but a gyro-compass failure delayed him leaving port. He navigated by dead reckoning across the sea, and although considerably off course, he spotted smoke on the horizon. Weddigen crash dived and despite the heavy seas successfully attacked *Aboukir* with a single torpedo. The other ships, oblivious to the submarine's presence, suspected that *Aboukir* had hit a mine. The torpedo had broken the back of *Aboukir* and she sank within 20 minutes and 527 of her ships company died.

The *Great Western Magazine* published an article by Thomas Spragg who was a naval reservist and worked for GWR in the electrical engineering department in Paddington. The language of the editor is interesting stating that 'he had a most thrilling experience'. Probably few of us today would describe it quite in those words.

---

2   IWM Sound Archive, 9420, Charles Minter.

Among the crew of HMS Aboukir, which was sunk in the North Sea on September 22, was Thomas H. Spragg, naval reservist, who was a wireman on the Great Western Railway Electrical Engineer's staff at Paddington. He had a most thrilling experience, of which the following is his account:

'I had been on duty at the guns from 2 am to 5 am. On being relieved nothing suspicious could be seen. I turned in around 0515 am and was asleep when, at 0620 am, there was a loud explosion, but being in the after turret I did not get much of it. Acting on the orders of the captain of the turret we immediately closed up around the guns at our action stations until he had ascertained the cause. We all thought that we had hit a stray mine. Then the order came to close watertight doors, and we went below to make sure that they were closed. The next order issued was to clear away the main derrick and I assisted to do this but realised that it was useless as the ship then had too much list to port to get the two big boats out. Our port lifeboat had been shattered by the explosion, so that we had only one boat left, which we lowered, and the sick men and what injured could be found were put into her and she left the ship. The captain then gave the order from the bridge for the stokers to muster on the forecastle and the marines on the quarterdeck, which was quietly and orderly done. Though an old seaman myself I was surprised by the quietness and orderliness of everyone. Then I saw the Hogue and Cressy steaming towards us and our ship seemed to steady herself. I really thought that she was going to keep afloat so, being cold, I went back to the turret and dressed; but on gaining the boat deck again I saw that she had started to settle and I heard the captain on his megaphone telling us to all to do our best for ourselves and wishing us good-bye and good luck. I took my upper clothes off and threw them into the water. I took the bearing of the Hogue's cutter, dived, and swam until I was clear, as I thought, from the suction of the ship, then turned on my back and quietly paddled, watching the ships bottom as she gradually heeled over.

When the Hogue's cutter came close to me I had just laid hold of her when I heard and felt a second and third explosion almost simultaneously, and we realised it was submarines and not mines. The coxswain of the boat then got his orders to take her back to his own ship, which was his duty, but I managed to hang on and scramble into her.

Almost immediately I saw our commander get into the boat, of which he took charge, taking men in as we pulled for the Cressy. We were put aboard and she steamed ahead firing her guns. I was given some cocoa and a blanket and went forward and out of the way and stood watching the twelve-pounder firing at the submarine some 500 yards off. I distinctly saw the conning tower blow up and three or four men come out of her as she sank. Then I heard the explosion of the torpedo that hit Cressy and turned to a man that was standing by me and said, "This is no place for us now, we are in the way." I jumped overboard and caught a mess stool and drifted away. Another man got hold of the other end, but I think he could not swim. After a time he must have given up hope as he was struggling continuously, and I talked to him, trying to get him to do as I was doing, but he would not listen I think he had gone too far and I was almost as bad myself. I did not see him go, but instinctively felt the stool relieved of its weight. Then I was picked up just as I saw destroyers appear, coming up at full speed. I was taken into the boat and put aboard Coriander of Lowestoft, a fishing smack.

I wish to put it upon record the splendid work done by those four Britishers in the smack, which I am sure could never be beaten. Some time after that I was taken on board the Legion destroyer and brought to Harwich, where we were received by the officers and boys of the Training establishment at Shotley. I cannot say enough of the kind treatment we received from all ranks. I am now ready to return to duty and am looking forward to a chance to have my own back.

I want to take the opportunity of thanking the officials and men of the Great Western Railway for their kindness to my wife and child whilst I have been away.'[3]

3   GWR Magazine, 1914, 290.

Thomas Spragg

Despite what Thomas Spragg thought he saw *U9* did not sink and within two hours she had sunk all three ships totalling 36,000 tons, killing 1,459 sailors, only 857 sailors were rescued. The torpedo and U-boat combination, having achieved the first success three weeks before with the sinking of HMS *Pathfinder*, was now established in this world first multiple warship engagement, as a significant weapon of destruction.

R Barrett

HMS *Cressy. IWM* Q38576

At least 35 railwaymen from ten different railway companies died in this first significant naval action of WWI. About half of the dead railwaymen were stokers, employed deep in the bowels of the ship, below the waterline, tending the noisy machinery and stoking the numerous coal-fed boilers. It would have been hot, noisy, unpleasant work. The duty stokers on the *Aboukir* probably knew nothing of the attack. The lucky ones would have been killed instantly in the explosion, the unlucky ones would have survived to be scalded to death by exploding boilers or drowned as the sea surged in, leaving them no escape. Since they were employed by the Navy as stokers you might assume that they had been firemen on the railway, but their range of civilian employment ranged from plate layers to telegraphist and included eight former labourers, seven porters, a carter, gas fitter, bricklayer, linesman, dining car attendent and carriage examiner.

HMS *Hogue*. IWM Q21354

It was initially believed that the sinkings were the result of five or six submarines, as it seemed that the nation could not believe that only one submarine could create such havoc.[4] As Massie in *Castles of Steel* says, 'It was the loss of life and the blow to Britain's naval prestige that stunned the nation.'[5]

HMS Cressy

A Rogers   *J Ruddick*   *J Prett*   *J Hull*

HMS Aboukir

W F Lee   *W Nicholls*

HMS Hogue

A Isaacs   *W Ingate*   *J Thurston*   *W Tems*   *J Rider*

---

4   Massie, 137.
5   Massie, 137.

Name	Rank	Ship	Memorial	Age	Company	Location	Job
William Barrett	Seaman	Aboukir	Chatham	35	NER	West Hartlepool	Mooringman
John Hogan	Seaman	Aboukir	Chatham		NER	West Hartlepool	Mooringman
William Nichols	Stoker 1st Class	Aboukir	Chatham		GER	Ipswich Lower Yard	Platelayer
Cecil Ross	Stoker	Aboukir	Chatham		GNR		Labourer
William Hall	Stoker 1st Class	Aboukir	Chatham		GNR	Gas Works	Stokers Assistant
George Lee	Stoker 1st Class	Aboukir	Chatham	33	GWR	Old Oak Common	Carriage Cleaner
William Cordwell	A/S	Aboukir	Chatham		L & SWR		Labourer
Charles Ralph	Stoker 1st Class	Aboukir	Chatham		L & SWR		Assistant Telegraphist
Thomas Adams	Able Seaman	Aboukir	Chatham	35	L & NWR	Lancaster	Loader
J Medhurst	Stoker 1st Class	Aboukir	The Hague	31	LB & SCR		Labourer
Alfred Jordan	A/S	Aboukir	Portsmouth		LB & SCR		Porter
Robert Allison	L/Carpenter	Aboukir	Chatham	40	SECR		Marine Porter
Henry Russell	Seaman	Aboukir	Chatham	36	SECR		Carriage examiner
Ernest Tupper	Stoker	Aboukir	Chatham	30	SECR		Labourer
Maurice Woods	Seaman	Aboukir	Chatham	25	SECR		Marine fireman
Alfred East	Seaman	Cressy	Chatham	33	SECR		Linesman
Arthur Rogers	Seaman	Cressy	Chatham	32	NER	Devonshire Street Goods	Porter
Edward Yates	Stoker 1st Class	Cressy	Chatham		L & NWR	Waterloo	Goods Porter
George Clemson	Stoker	Cressy	Chatham	25	Midland	St Pancras	Hotels
George Coleman	A/S	Cressy	Chatham	25	Midland	St Pancras	Dining Car Attendant
Henry Jones	Seaman	Cressy	Chatham	25	L & NWR	Garston	Seaman
Henry Rickard	Stoker 1st Class	Cressy	Chatham		L & NWR	Broad Street	Goods Porter
James Ruddick	Stoker 1st Class	Cressy	Chatham		GER		Labourer
Jesse Prett	PO Stoker	Cressy	Chatham	44	GER		Donkeyman
John Hull	Seaman	Cressy	Chatham		GER	Goodmans Yard	Porter
John Moran	Stoker	Cressy	Chatham	24	L & NWR	Edge Hill	Joint Maker
Sidney Smith	Stoker	Cressy	Chatham	25	Midland	Leicester	Labourer
Albert Isaacs	Seaman	Hogue	Chatham	40	GER	Colchester	Bricklayers labourer

Name	Rank	Ship	Memorial	Age	Company	Location	Job
Walter Ingate	Seaman	Hogue	Chatham		GER		Quay Labourer
Sidney Thurston	Seaman	Hogue	Chatham	33	GER		Labourer
Louis Statham	Seaman	Hogue	Chatham	38	GCR	Grimsby Dock	Marine Dept
Walter Tems	Stoker 1st Class	Hogue	Chatham		GER	Stratford Oil Works	Gas Stoker
Job Rider	Stoker 1st Class	Hogue	Chatham		GER	Parkstone Quay	Labourer
J Clarke	Able Seaman	Hogue	Chatham	35	L & NWR	Dunstable	Carter
William Harris	Stoker 1st Class	Hogue	Chatham	27	L & NWR	Wolverton	Loader
Alexander Begg	L/Stoker	Hogue	Portsmouth		North British		Surfaceman
J Jolliffe	A/S	Hogue	Chatham		GER	Grimsby Dock	Dock Gateman

HMS *Good Hope*   1 November 1914

HMS *Good Hope*, a 14,000 ton obsolescent Armoured Cruiser, formed part of the South Atlantic Squadron commanded by Admiral Craddock tasked with protecting the important sea lanes from South America, and with locating and attacking the German East Asiatic Squadron of Admiral Von Spee which comprised the modern and capable armoured cruisers, the *Scharnhorst* and *Gneisnau*.

There was a lot of ocean to hide in, and neither Admiral had much idea where the other side was as information was sketchy, so Craddock patrolled the vast ocean and on board the ships routine continued. The Navy was all about routine. Time was divided into five watches of four hours and two watches of two hours; the dog watches. The purpose of the dog watch was so that the men were not fixed to the same time each day. Off watch there were other duties to keep, and there was time for messing and for sleeping. Charles Minter on HMS *Hibernia* provides an insight into life on the mess decks during the Great War. He was allocated number 1 mess right in the bows of the ship, a curious place for a team of stokers to be billeted. In the mess they slept in hammocks rigged to the bulkheads, relaxed in their limited off duty time, and ate. Cooks on board ship cooked. They didn't prepare the sailors meals, that was a mess responsibility.

> '*The Navy supplied bread, tea, sugar, potatoes and meat. If you wanted anything else you bought it from the canteen. The Leading Hand was a sort of caterer and every night you would have a jolly good dinner. Depending upon how lavish it was depended on what you paid.*'[6]

On the face of it it seems a bit mean of the Navy not to prepare and produce the food, but that is only a comparatively recent innovation of the senior service. Traditionally messes were in charge of their own meals, giving them some flexibility and control in an environment where they had virtually no control of their destiny. Minter describes an occasion when he was duty mess cook. 'I was cook of the mess with another man and we had a 7-pound tin of corned beef for that day. We put it with peas and in rice and mixed it all together and the man said to me "now take it up to the galley and get it cooked". Well I stepped over a bulkhead, this big step, went into the next mess where the floor was

---

6   IWM Sound Archive, 9420, Charles Minter.

wet and I went down.' Having deposited the meal onto the mess deck he put it all back in the tray and returned to the mess whereupon his colleague said, 'get it back in that tin and into the galley. It will be brown when it is done.'[7] As the ships operated through any seas twenty-four hours a day, the routine continued, there were always men working and men resting as the shifts ruled their lives. On *Good Hope* these men were largely reservists who had little practical experience of gunnery or war fighting.

HMS Good Hope

W J Deacon

T Libou

IWM Q21297

G Harris

F Beard

As Craddock's ships continued to patrol the seas, sightings from spies ashore and the volume and strength of intercepted wireless messages made it clear to both sides of an enemy presence nearby. Early on 1 November 1914 Craddock turned his squadron towards the Germans and as they closed he prepared to engage.

Craddock knew they had little chance and their only option was to close sufficiently for his smaller inferior gunned and older ships to have the range of the enemy, which made his ships incredibly vulnerable. If he couldn't close the range, the Germans would pick them off with their superior firepower: Sixteen 8.2 inch guns versus only two 9.2-inch guns. His chance relied on getting his secondary armament: 17 6-inch guns in range. Any chance would be fleeting, when the setting sun would make it difficult for the German gunners. However, after sunset, his fleet would be silhouetted against the falling light, giving another advantage to the Germans. His gunners had not trained for night-time battle so he knew he needed to fight in the remaining daylight.

Von Spee, capitalising on his advantage, simply maintained the distance by turning his ships further away. Once the light fell enough for the Germans to have the advantage they engaged. *Scharnhorst* fired ranging shots on the *Good Hope*, hitting one of the two 9.2 inch gun turrets with the third shot,

---

7   IWM Sound Archive, 9420, Charles Minter

putting this gun out of action. Still Craddock closed with the enemy hoping against hope that he could get his 6-inch guns to bear, which was virtually impossible because of the rough sea. It simply made easy pickings for the Germans. HMS *Monmouth*, another obsolescent ship manned by reservists, was soon silent as she slipped out of the line. *Gneisenau* continued to engage, as though for gunnery practice. *Scharnhorst* meanwhile achieved no less than thirty-five direct hits as *Good Hope* continued to absorb the punishment before eventually exploding. The main action lasted less than an hour. Having polished off *Good Hope*, Von Spee located *Monmouth* as she was trying to effect emergency damage repairs, and she too was engaged and sunk.

Good Hope and *Monmouth* were lost with all hands, a total of 1,600 British sailors died, at least 27 were railwaymen, and the Germans received only six hits suffering four injured. The British had suffered their first defeat at sea in nearly 100 years at what became known as the Battle of Coronel.

Name	Rank	Memorial	Age	Company	Location	Job
Thomas Lihou	A/S	Portsmouth		Gt Western	Guernsey	Docker
William Deacon	A/S	Portsmouth	35	Gt Western	Swindon	Shedsman
F Beard		Portsmouth	35	Gt Western	Swindon	Labourer
George Harris	A/S	Portsmouth	34	Gt Western	Stourbridge Junction	Relay Packer
Albert Downs	Officers Cook 2nd class	Portsmouth	19	NER	Dairycoates	
Chapman Thornton	A/S	Portsmouth	26	NER	Gascoigne Wood	Freight Shunter
William Ford	A/S	Portsmouth	33	Midland	Birmingham	Porter
Albert Johnson	A/S	Portsmouth	25	Midland	Nottingham	Labourer
Samuel Hammond	A/S	Chatham		GCR	Immingham	Marine Dept
James Alsbury	L/S (South Africa and China Medal)	Portsmouth	34	Midland	Derby	Rope Splicer
Arthur Stephens	PO (China Medal 1900)	Portsmouth	34	Midland	Derby	Painter
James Sutton	A/S	Portsmouth	35	GCR	Grimsby Docks	Marine Dept
George Jayes	AB	Portsmouth	34	GCR	Leicester	Porter
Charles Phillips	Stoker 1st Class	Portsmouth	35	IOW Central		Coal Porter
William McCarten	AB	Portsmouth	29	Midland	Derby	Clerk
William Lawson	Stoker	Portsmouth	33	GNR		Labourer
J Bent	Stoker	Portsmouth	28	L & NWR	Dudley Port	Porter
S Cotton	A/S	Portmouth	26	L & NWR	Aston	Goods Porter
John Dudley	Stoker	Portsmouth	26	L & NWR	London Road	Tableman
George Edwards	A/S	Portsmouth	28	L & NWR	Farnley Junction	Tuber
G Hill	A/S	Portsmouth	29	L & NWR	Northampton	Scaffolder
P Lack	Stoker	Portsmouth		L & NWR	Northampton	Labourer
Edgar Lawrence	A/S	Portsmouth	34	L & SWR		Labourer
Sidney Warren	A/S	Portsmouth	32	L & NWR	Euston	Carriage dept
Thomas Tester	A/S	Chatham	34	LB & SCR		Labourer
Charles Vinall	A/S	Portsmouth	28	LB & SCR		Engine Cleaner
Thomas Kelly	Stoker	Portsmouth		LB & SCR		Machinist

HMS *Formidable*   1 January 1915

IWM Q38891

Through a tremendous gale and very difficult sea conditions HMS *Formidable* steamed down the English Channel in the early hours of 1 January 1915. The swell made for uncomfortable conditions for the sailors, but it gave just one small comfort, the chances of a U-boat attack were significantly diminished. Yet at just after 0200, whilst passing twenty miles off Start Point on the Devon coast, the *Formidable* was struck by two torpedoes. The first torpedo hit the number one boiler on the port side; a second explosion caused the ship to list heavily to starboard. The stricken ship was settling into a sea of thirty-foot waves battering the ship. There was reported to be no panic as the men waited for lifeboats to be lowered, although many were smashed as they were lowered into the water and their occupants killed. The captain and his pet dog Bruce stood firm and went down with the ship.

Only two boats survived in the pitching seas, one with 70 men aboard was found by the trawler *Provident* about 15 miles off Berry Head. The other, also with 70 men aboard, fought the gale and

Name	Rank	Memorial	Age	Company	Location	Job
James Burnell	Sen SBA	Chatham	33	L & NWR	Crewe	Tuber
Albert ED Kinlay	Sen SBA	Chatham	23	L & NWR	Crewe	Labourer
Henri V Russell	Sen SBA	Coppenhall	29	L & NWR	Crewe	Labourer
John V Russell	Sen SBA	Chatham	29	L & NWR	Crewe	Labourer
Henry Hopkins	PO	Chatham		L B & SCR		
William Howland	Stoker	Chatham		SECR		Fireman

rowed and bailed for 22 hours. One seaman sat over a hole in the boat for the entire time, before making land at Lyme Regis by which time 22 men had died.

In total 199 men were saved, but 550 were lost including at least six railwaymen, four of whom were Sick Berth Attendants who had all worked in the L&NWR works in Crewe. Two were brothers Henri and John Villiers Russell (see also page 240).

HMS *Viknor*   13 January 1915

The Royal Mail Ship *Atrato*, which carried passengers to and from the West Indies, was converted to an armed merchant cruiser and renamed HMS *Viknor*. On 13 January 1915 she was patrolling off Malin Head off the Northern coast of Ireland and was lost with all 293 hands. The cause is unknown, there was a fierce storm blowing, but she may have hit a mine as this was an area of known enemy mine-laying activity. Some bodies were washed ashore and were buried in Northern Ireland, but Able Seamen William Stokes and A Groves, both ex-L&SWR seamen, were never found.

HMS *Bayano*   11 March 1915

HMS *Bayano* was another example of a requisitioned liner turned into an armed merchant cruiser. She wasn't particularly well armed or armoured, liners were not built to withstand bombardment and explosions. Torpedoed by *U27* whilst on passage from Glasgow to Liverpool, *Bayano* sank quickly with the loss of 195 crew, including George Case, a fifty-five-year-old stoker, an ex-labourer with the SECR, most likely caught in the engine room as water gushed in drowning any trapped men. Able Seamen Arthur Knight, an ex-L&SWR crane driver and Richard Bell, an ex-L&NWR shunter, may have had more of a chance, as their jobs were not confined to the engine spaces, but they too died, and none of the bodies were recovered.

HMS *Goliath*   13 May 1915

At the outbreak of war, *Goliath* was another obsolescent warship which had lain in reserve for some time. But by April 1915 she was supporting landings at Cape Helles in Gallipoli. She was torpedoed whilst at anchor in the early hours of 13 May by a Turkish torpedo boat which fired two torpedoes causing a massive explosion. Almost immediately the ship began to capsize. Despite the close proximity of land, many of those who managed to get into the water were swept out to sea and drowned. 570 of the 700 hands aboard died including at least eleven railwaymen.

J Gulley

F A Escott   *R W Wallis*

Charles Bayley   *M Lamacroft*

Left: IWM Q21299

Name	Rank	Memorial	Age	Company	Location	Job
Charles Bayley	A/S	Plymouth	25	GER	Lowestoft	Fire Brigade
John Steel	Stoker	Plymouth		GWR	Fishguard	Marine Fireman
Richard Wallis	Seaman	Plymouth	28	GWR	Penzance	Goods Dept
Frederick Escott	RMLI	Plymouth	28	GWR	Lawrence Hill	Goods Porter
Walter Lamacroft	Stoker 1st Cl	Plymouth	33	GWR	Brent	Engineer
James Gulley	RMLI	Plymouth	27	GWR	Newton Abbot	Striker
Hugh Roberts	A/S	Plymouth	25	L & NWR	Garston Dock	Dock Gateman
Peter Beegan	Stoker 1st Cl	Plymouth	27	L & NWR	Lime Street	Carriage Dept
Tom Middleton	RMLI	Plymouth	45	L & NWR	Huddersfield	Labourer
Percy Walker	RMLI	Plymouth		L & NWR	Dewsbury	Driver
William Gilbert	L/S	Plymouth		Midland	Derby	Packer

THE BATTLE OF JUTLAND
31 May – 1 June 1916

The Battle of Jutland was the greatest confrontation of seaborne tonnage the world had ever known, when the leviathans of two of the most powerful industrial nations engaged in a short but violent battle in the North Sea. On the British side was the Grand Fleet, based at Scapa Flow in the Orkneys, and on the German side the High Seas fleet at Wilhelmshaven. The Germans were keen to engage with the Grand Fleet and hatched a number of plans to lure the British out of their safe anchorages; eventually they achieved this with Admiral Hipper's Battle-Cruiser Squadron enticing Admiral Beatty's Battle-cruiser Squadron and Admiral Jellicoe's Grand Fleet to sea. The Royal Navy at Jutland comprised 151 fighting ships, including 28 battleships, 9 battle-cruisers and 78 destroyers. The German fleet totalled 99 warships, including 22 battleships, 5 battle-cruisers and 72 other ships.

Although it will never be known how many railwaymen served at Jutland it is known that over 50 railwaymen died and it is likely that there were many more serving on the capital ships which survived the battle. On board the three Battle-cruisers lost were 23 railwaymen, if a similar number were drafted on board the remainder of the capital ships it would suggest that at least 260 other railwaymen fought at the battle and survived. HMS *Hampshire* survived the battle, only to be lost some days later taking seven railwaymen with her. The railwaymen who died were from 11 ships, 23 were Stokers, 17 Able Seamen, 3 boy sailors, a signaller, a Royal Marine, a surgeon and two stewards.

What follows attempts to focus on the ships upon which railwaymen died. It draws upon *The Fighting at Jutland* to give a sense of the experience of war at sea.[8] The action at Jutland is described in different ways, but for simplicity three phases are used here:

---

8 There is no place in this book to tell the story of the battle, for those whose interest is piqued by this work should access *The Fighting at Jutland: The Personal Experiences of Forty-five Officers and Men of the British Fleet*, edited by H W Fawcett and G W W Cooper, and available for free download on-line.

1	The battle-cruiser action	1550–1750 hours
2	The battle fleet action	1800–2100 hours
3	The night action	from 2220 hours

I   The Battle-cruiser action   1550–1750 hours

The battle-cruisers were at full speed and had made contact with the enemy, and 'at 15.48 hours had commenced action on nearly parallel southerly courses, at a range of 14,000 to 18,000 yards.'[9] Travelling at 25 knots and with 500 yards between ships in line astern steamed, *Lion, Princess Royal, Queen Mary, Tiger, New Zealand*, and *Indefatigable*. At 1600, Admiral Hipper's Battle-cruiser squadron, in the opening salvos of the battle, hit *Lion* with a 12-inch shell, destroying one of the gun turrets causing significant damage. The ship was only saved by the courageous action of an injured gun commander who sacrificed himself and his gun crew by ordering the closure of a watertight door condemning them to the inferno, but saving the ship. *Lion*, though damaged could fight on.

HMS *Indefatigable*   1604 hours

Deep below the waterline in the working bowels of the 590-foot long, 22,000 ton, battle-cruiser *Indefatigable*, Fred Comley, Harry Dean and Hubert Claridge would have been at battle stations. All three were stokers, engaged working in the hot and noisy environment of the engine room, tending dials, oiling and maintaining the turbines, or in the vital job of shovelling coal, maintaining the 31 boilers which together produced 32,000 Kw of energy to drive four huge propellers. The stokers toiled to provide the ship with the means to fight. Deep down in the hull these men had no time for strategy, tactics, or seamanship, theirs was a constant flog, a high pressurised routine, from which there was little respite save from a few hours in their hammock, slung in any spare or convenient space in their mess deck or even around their machinery. Comley was an eighteen-year-old, former GWR vanguard, Dean was ex-Midland railway repair labourer, and Claridge a former GWR packer from Fairford.

Able Seaman Williams, an ex-cleaner with L&NWR at Chester, was also aboard the *Indefatigable*. It is not clear what his role on this ship was, but as a seaman he could have been manning one of the main 12-inch guns, or a lookout, or employed in the ship's magazine preparing ammunition. Boy 1st Class George Raymond, an ex-van boy from Midland's St Pancras station, would have been engaged in errands and passing messages, in all likelihood he would be stationed to the rear of the bridge ready to pass messages in the event of a communication breakdown. He may have been alongside Ordinary Signaller Cyril Hardwick, an eighteen-year-old ex-porter from Midland's Cheadle Heath station, who would have manned signal lamp or flags. Almost certainly, unlike the stokers, he would have had an awareness of what was going on around him. He could have tasted the salt on his lips and felt the wind and smell the ship's smoke, and cordite when the guns fired. Meanwhile *Indefatigable* continued to steam steadily towards the Germans.

Aboard *Indefatigable*, the stokers, within their deafening environment, their world, dictated by the commands from the bridge, apprehensive, but confident in their ship and crew. Above deck, Hardwick and Raymond would have seen the gun flashes across the murky sea, and heard the whistling of rounds overhead, and the sickening crash and smoke of the direct hit on *Lion*.

Four minutes later *Indefatigable* was hit by three 11-inch shells. This was witnessed by the navigation officer of HMS *New Zealand* : 'she was hit by two shells, one on the foc'sle and one on the fore turret. Both shells appeared to explode on impact. Then there was an interval of about thirty seconds, during which there was absolutely no sign of fire or flame or smoke, except for the little actually formed by the burst of the two shells. At the end of the interval of about thirty seconds the ship completely blew up, commencing from for'ard. The main explosion started with sheets of flame

---

9   Fighting at Jutland, 4-10.

followed immediately afterwards by a dense, dark smoke, which obscured the ship from view. All sorts of stuff was blown high into the air, a 50-foot steam picket boat, for example, being blown up about 200 feet, apparently intact though upside down.'[10]

Deep in the bowels the stokers would have died instantaneously from the crashing pressure; it is doubtful that anyone survived long enough to go through the horror of drowning. Boy Raymond may have been aware, for a few seconds, of the impact, until he too was blown apart in the detonation of thousands of tons of ship.

Only two crew of a ship's company of 1,019 survived. One of the two survivors was Signaller C. Falmer: 'There was a terrific explosion aboard the ship, the magazines went. I saw the guns go up in the air just like matchsticks – 12 inch guns they were – bodies and everything. She was beginning to settle down. Within half a minute the ship turned right over and she was gone. I was 180 foot up and I was thrown well clear of the ship otherwise I would have been sucked under. I was practically unconscious, turning over really. At last I came on top of the water. When I came up there was another fellow named Jimmy Green and we got a piece of wood, he was on one end and I was on the other end. A couple of minutes afterwards some shells came over and Jim was minus his head so I was left on my lonesome.'[11]

Name	Rank	Ship	Memorial	Age	Company	Location	Job
Fred Comley	Stoker 2 Cl	Indefatigable	Plymouth	18	GWR	Bristol	Vanguard
Charles Hedges		Indefatigable	Chatham	21	GER		Boilermakers apprentice
Harry Dean	Stoker	Indefatigable	Plymouth		Midland	Upper Bank	Labourer
Cyril Hardwick	O/Sig	Indefatigable	Portsmouth	18	Midland	Cheadle Heath	Porter
George Raymond	Boy 1St Cl	Indefatigable	Chatham		Midland	London St Pancras	Van Boy
Hubert Claridge	Stoker	Indefatigable	Plymouth	19	GWR	Fairford	Packer
T Williams	A/S	Indefatigable	Plymouth	19	L & NWR	Chester	Cleaner

HMS *Queen Mary*   1626 hours

Some of the crew of *Queen Mary* would have witnessed the explosion of the *Indefatigable*, but there was little time for a feeling of loss for comrades and shipmates as battle was in full flow. Again, deep in the bowels, Stokers William Simpson, Robert Ford, Joseph Jones and Richard Thomas, would have been entirely unaware of what was taking place on the upper decks. Henry Tullett was an ex-LB&SCR striker and Royal Marine likely to have been stationed in or around X turret, at the rear of the ship, traditionally the preserve of the Royal Marines, and William Marriott probably somewhere above decks. Only 22 minutes later HMS *Queen Mary* had been destroyed, as reported by an officer from HMS *Tiger*:

'The Queen Mary *was next ahead of us, and I remember watching her for a little and I saw one salvo straddle her. Three shells out of four hit, and the impression one got of seeing the splinters fly and the dull red burst was as if no damage was being done, but that the armour was keeping the shell out. The next salvo that I saw straddled her and two more shells hit her. As they hit I saw a dull red glow amidships and then the ship seemed to open out... the whole ship seemed to collapse inwards. The funnels and masts fell into the middle, and the*

---

10   Fighting at Jutland, 17, Navigation Officer HMS *New Zealand*.
11   See IWM Online Exhibition http://archive.iwm.org.uk/upload/package/26/jutland/south.htm .

hull was blown outwards. The roofs of the turrets were blown 100 feet high… the Tiger just cleared the remains of the Queen Mary's *stern by a few feet.'[12]*

HMS Queen Mary. IWM Q21661

Both forward magazines exploded killing all but 21 of the 1,026 on board.

IWM SP001708

The loss of *Indefatigable* and *Queen Mary* prompted Beatty to make his now famous remark:

'There seems to be is something wrong with our bloody ships today.'[13]

All of the Battle-cruisers were being punished by the large calibre shells. The engineering officer of HMS *Tiger* describes his experience below decks as the ship is getting pummelled:

'A heavy thud, followed by a deafening report immediately overhead, intimated that a heavy shell had penetrated the side armour and burst inboard… penetrated the upper deck and the armoured deck, and punched a neat hole in the steel bracket supporting the main steam pipe… Had it struck the pipe the whole engine room staff would have been wiped out, and the ship completely disabled.'[14] Nonetheless this single shell had caused extensive damage: *'The shell bursting in the ammunition passage killed a dozen men, set fire to the ready use cordite in the passage rendering it necessary to flood the midships 6-inch magazine, cut through the fresh and salt water mains… No examination could be made to locate the trouble, as through the hole in the deck were pouring the fumes from the burning cordite, and the engine room was immediately filled with dense smoke, which rendered it impossible to see…'[15]*

---

12   Fighting at Jutland, 19.
13   Attributed to Vice-Admiral David Beatty (later Admiral Of The Fleet and First Earl Beatty).
14   Fighting at Jutland, 57.
15   Fighting at Jutland, 59.

Name	Rank	Ship	Memorial	Age	Company	Location	Job
William Simpson	Stoker 1 Cl	Queen Mary	Portsmouth	17	NER	Blaydon	Porter
Robert Ford	Stoker 1 Cl	Queen Mary	Portsmouth		NER	Newcastle	Carriage Cleaner
Joseph Jones	Stoker	Queen Mary	Chatham		NER	West Hartlepool	Plate Layer
William Marriott	OS	Queen Mary	Plymouth		L & NWR	Netherfield	Apprentice
Richard Thomas	Stoker	Queen Mary	Portsmouth		L & NWR	Holyhead	Fireman
Leonard Bridge	Steward	Queen Mary	Portsmouth	19	Railway Clearing House	London	Clerk
Henry Tulett	Pte RMLI	Queen Mary	Portsmouth		LB & SCR		Striker

HMS *Tiger* suffered over 20 hits but continued in action, 24 men were killed including one railwayman.

Name	Rank	Ship	Memorial	Age	Co	Job
William Parker	Stoker	Tiger	Chatham	20	GNR	Relayer

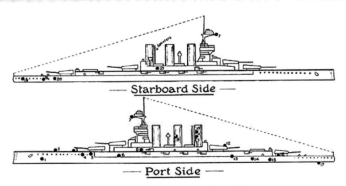

— Starboard Side —

— Port Side —

— HITS SUSTAINED BY H.M.S. "TIGER" —

1	5·9"	9. 10. 11	11"
2	11" Pitched on forecastle · burst in cable locker flat	12	11"Burst on 'Q' turret Blew in Centre sighting hood.
3	Two 11" projectiles burst in Sick Bay just before turn at 4·35 p.m.	13	11" Did more damage than any other projectile
4	11"	14. 15	11" Did not penetrate belt.
5	Hit 'A' barbette · 12"	16	11"- Burst on 'X' turret
6	Burst in flour store · 11"	17.18.19.20	5·9"
7	Carried away steaming light · 11"	21	12" Broke back of Steam pinnace & Nº 4 Derrick. Blew away battery door and part of bulkhead
8	11" bounced off without doing much damage.		

Shortly after *Queen Mary* had sunk, the German High Seas Fleet was spotted, which was a shock for Jellicoe who thought they were still in port. Beatty turned north and broke free from Hipper's Battle-cruiser squadron. In that short engagement, the British scored 17 hits, and received 44 and had lost two battle-cruisers.

2 The battle fleet action

1800–2100 hours

HMS *Defence*   1815 hours

The next stage of the battle saw the Grand Fleet deploy into battle formation, including the 1st Cruiser Squadron, which formed the advanced cover for the approaching Grand Fleet. HMS *Defence* alongside *Warrior, Duke of Edinburgh* and *Black Prince* formed the 1st Cruiser Squadron. At 1815, *Defence*, whilst attempting to position herself to finish off a crippled German ship, exposed herself to a German broadside and got finished off herself.

HMS Warrior, Defence and Black Prince. IWM *SP462*

Name	Rank	Ship	Memorial	Age	Company	Location	Job
Ernest Hastie	O/S	Defence	Plymouth	18	NER	Darlington Works	Greaser
Reginald Corser	ERA 4	Defence	Plymouth	25	GWR	Sundon Loco	Fitter
Charles Nunn	A/S	Defence	Portsmouth		NER	Keyingham	Plate Layer
Leonard Sleigh	A/S	Defence	Plymouth	19	Yorks & Lancs		Tinsmith
Norman Franklin	A/S	Defence	Portsmouth		Cardiff	Cardiff	Dock Gateman
Andrew Mellor	ERA 4	Defence	Portsmouth		Caledonian		Apprentice Fitter

According to the report from HMS *Obedient*, '*Defence* was heavily engaged and salvoes were dropping all around her. When she was on our bow three quick successive salvoes reached her, the first was over, the second short and the third all hit… the ship heeled to the blow, but quickly righted herself and steamed on again. Then almost immediately followed three more salvoes. Again the first was over, the second short and the third a hit, and again the shell of the hitting salvo could be clearly seen to strike, this time between the forecastle turret and the foremost funnel. At once the ship was lost to sight in an enormous black cloud, which rose to a height of some hundred feet, and quickly clearing, showed no signs of a ship at all.'[16]

She exploded killing all 903 crew, including at least six railwaymen. During this action HMS *Black Prince* became separated from the rest of the squadron.

At the same time, *Warrior* was also being engaged and getting severely damaged. The ship's engineering officer's report gives a feel for what the ship's company experienced trying to save their damaged ships:

'At around 1815 I heard a terrific explosion at the after end… Most of the lights went out… immediately afterwards there was a heavy roar of water and steam… Several men came running forward… one with blood pouring down his face… I had to assess the damage… I perceived what appeared to be Niagara at the after end of the engine room… A blast of steam on my face warned me that I hadn't long to deal with the quantity of water that was pouring in, and that the only thing to do was get the men out as quickly as possible… When it appeared that they had all gone I followed myself. It was pitch dark… I turned forward and felt my way by the handrails along the platform at the tops of the cylinders towards the door at the fore end… When I got there a stoker told me I could not get through there as the mess deck was on fire. At this moment, with this in front and the roar of steam behind me, I felt like a trapped rat… but just then I realised a man was calling my attention to a glimmer of light above, and the next minute I found myself climbing out through a torn rent in the deck.'[17]

Having escaped he was still trying to access the surviving engine room in order to preserve the power of the ship. Shells were still falling and the upper deck was in tatters, fires were burning and smoke was thick. 'I then endeavoured to collect my scattered wits with a view to putting out the fire, but I found that I had the greatest difficulty in getting my brain to work at all… on such occasions when it is difficult to originate anything, evolutions rehearsed at drill work automatically, and at this moment I found my subordinates readier than myself in carrying out measures that I had myself devised… It was now a little past 1830 and for the next two hours we fought and struggled to put the fire out.'[18]

He thought that nobody could be alive in the engine room. They could not get at the fire because of steam from the engine room. Eventually at about 2100, having controlled the fire, they were able to raise one of the hatches to the engine room and were amazed to find people shouting. These engineers escaped. They had been trapped for some hours in a flooded engine room with rising water and in pitch dark, 'at the start there were about eight of them, and they kept hold of each other to save their lives as long as possible, but one by one they kept dropping off and getting lost and drowned in the water, till at last there were only three left. They thought at one time that the ship had been abandoned, but the click of a valve being worked conquered their fears of that.'[19]

The *Warrior* was hit at least 15 times by 11 and 12-inch shells. There were 68 killed and 34 wounded but none were reported as railwaymen. The ex-SECR ferry HMS *Engadine* took the *Warrior* under tow, but she later sank.

---

16 Fighting at Jutland, 82.
17 Fighting at Jutland, 89.
18 Fighting at Jutland, 89.
19 Fighting at Jutland, 89.

HMS *Invincible* 1833 hours

Surgeon George Shorland, the former Medical Officer from the Railway Clearing House, would have set up his hospital in the centre of the ship, ready to triage and treat injuries caused by the impact of high explosive impacting upon metal, and metal impacting on flesh. But before Shorland could be called to action *Invincible* took a catastrophic hit which penetrated her magazine and the ship exploded in a fireball with the loss of over 1,000 killed and with only six survivors later plucked from the water.

HMS Invincible. IWM Q39269

Name	Rank	Ship	Memorial	Age	Company	Location	Job
George Shorland	Surgeon	Invincible	Portsmouth	39	Railway Clearing House	London	Medical Officer
Louis Wright	Stoker	Invincible	Portsmouth	31	Midland	Wellingborough	Porter
Leonard Worters	A/S	Invincible	Chatham	22	GWR	Kensington	
John Acton	A/S	Invincible	Portsmouth	42	L & NWR	Holyhead	Seaman
Alfred Brown	ERA 4	Invincible	Portsmouth	21	L & SWR		Carriage Cleaner
HF Hoskins	A/S	Invincible	Portsmouth	18	SECR		Loco & Carr
H Williams	Stoker	Invincible	Portsmouth	31	L & NWR	Holyhead	Fireman
Stephen Curd	Boy 1st Cl	Invincible	Portsmouth	16	LB & SCR		Greaser
Thomas Dobie	Stoker	Invincible	Portsmouth	22	G & SWR		Fireman
William Lovett	Stoker	Invincible	Portsmouth		GCR		Hand Driller

Even the mighty battleships were getting punished by the German gunnery. HMS *Warspite* was badly hit; indeed she endured over 150 hits. During the battle her executive officer was sent below to assess the damage:

> *'I crossed the cook's lobby and told ammunition supply parties that things were going on all right. Went through to foc'sle mess deck and was just going forward when 12-inch shell came through side armour on the boys' mess deck. Terrific sheet of flame, stink, impenetrable dust, and everything seemed to fall everywhere with an appalling noise. Called for No. 2 fire brigade... we got a hose on, and put out the burning refuse... The shell hole was clean, about a foot in diameter; big flakes of armour had been flung right across the mess deck wrecking everything. Many armour bolts came away... smoke was pouring up through holes in the deck, and it occurred to me that the high-angle gun magazine was very close... Water from the cut fire mains was pouring below and smoke soon stopped.'*[20]

Further aft he saw No. 5 fire brigade and helped to plug a severed fire water main before continuing rearwards. When he returned he found that a shell had hit and killed several of the No. 5 fire brigade. Water was pouring down a shell hole into trunking which led into the central engine room. He knew they needed to prevent water getting into the engine room so they plugged the trunking, cutting off ventilation to the engine room, and Royal Marines set to plugging the hole in the ship's sides with hammocks. As the Commander wandered the ship, she was continuing to be bombarded. He found time to have a cigarette and watch the main galley being taken out by a 12-inch shell. Another shell hit aft and he went rearward to search out the damage. 'A large triangular piece had been blown out of the top corner of the main (armour) belt about a foot above water. The fresh water and oil fuel tanks had been blown to pieces... men tried to plug the hole, but tons of water was coming in and washing them back all the time. As it was all oil fuel they looked like a lot of goldfish swimming about. A marine remarked, "This will mean a drop of leave"... Tried for a bit to shore up with hammocks but it was hopeless as the force of the sea was tremendous. Decided to fill the whole compartment with hammocks... it took 600 hammocks... which eventually stopped the trouble, but not till late that night.'[21]

The Commander continued around the ship chivvying crew and assessing damage as *Warspite* continued to be bombarded. He was caught in the flash and shock of a shell hitting and thought he was hit, but was fine apart from being shaken and he carried on. 'The noise was deafening and rather nerve shattering. You could not hear yourself speak, and had to shout in everybody's ear.' Although the impression of a ship in action taking continuous hits from large calibre weapons is one of chaos and carnage, the sea routine continues for those unaffected. 'Marines of port 6 inch ammunition supply were playing cards on the deck quite happily.'[22]

3   The night action   from 2220 hours

> *'It was by this time about 2130, and quite dark. Our chief anxiety was that we were unaware of the relative positions of any of our ships or squadrons except the battle fleet, and also we did not know the position of the enemy.'*[23]

The third phase of the battle was the night. The 4th Destroyer Flotilla led by HMS *Tipperary* were engaged overnight. From 2330 the flotilla were engaged in a battle that saw *Ardent*, *Fortune*, *Tipperary* and *Sparrowhawk* sunk, and *Broke* heavily damaged and limping for home.

---

20   Fighting at Jutland, 68.
21   Fighting at Jutland, 70.
22   Fighting at Jutland, 72.
23   Fighting at Jutland, 171, Navigating Officer, HMS *Broke*.

HMS *Fortune* at 2345 hours

After several hours of quietness it became clear that the flotilla were in the midst of the enemy when *Fortune* was engaged and at least four large ships were spotted. The Captain of *Ardent* reported that *Fortune* was hit hard and he increased speed and turned sharply in order to bring his torpedoes to bear. As he engaged he saw the very damaged ship sinking. Only one of the crew of 67 survived.

John Brown	ERA 4	Fortune	Portsmouth	24	NER	Darlington	Rivetter

HMS *Tipperary* at 2345 hours

An officer on board HMS *Tipperary* recalls:

> *'At around 2345 I suddenly heard a salvo of guns fired from some ships to starboard at extremely short range. They were so close that I remember the guns seemed to be firing from some appreciable height above us. At almost the same instant the Tipperary shook violently from the impact of being hit by shells. (I was told afterwards that the first salvo hit the bridge and it must have killed the Captain and almost everyone there)… The enemy's second salvo hit and burst one of our main steam pipes, and the after-part of the ship was enveloped in a cloud of steam, through which I could see nothing. Losing all their steam, the turbines were brought to a standstill, and we dropped astern out of the action… The whole thing happened so suddenly and was over so quickly that I think we were all quite dazed. Aft we had been hit by only three shells and only a few of the gun crews were wounded, but when the steam cleared away we found that the majority of the men stationed amidships were killed or wounded, including those ratings which had come up from the engine room and stoke-holds, while forward the ship was on fire with flames coming out of the forward coal bunkers, and the bridge alight and an absolute wreck.'*[24]

Henry Dodd	L/ Stoker	Tipperary	Portsmouth	25	LB & SCR	Driller
Augustus Turner	PO Stoker	Tipperary	Portsmouth	42	SECR	Labourer,
James Delderfield	Stoker 1 Cl	Tipperary	Portsmouth	31	GER	Fire Brigade
Thomas Vivash	A/S	Tipperary	Portsmouth	20	Lancs & Yorks	Porter

HMS *Ardent* at 0001 hours

Those on board HMS *Ardent* witnessed *Tipperary* getting hit and the inferno which illuminated the sky for a long time. As the *Tipperary* burned, *Ardent* came across a large German warship and attacked at once. They were 'taking on a division of battleships'.[25]

The commanding officer Lieutenant Commander Arthur Marsden said:

> *'Shell after shell hit us, and our speed diminished and then stopped; then the dynamo stopped and all the lights went out. The guns ceased firing one by one…. I could feel the ship was sinking… The leading signalman came up to me and said in the most cheerful way, "Well, the old Ardent done her bit alright, sir." The ship was nearly gone and it only remained for us to try and save as many as the crew as possible.'* [26]

---

24 Fighting at Jutland, 190.
25 Fighting at Jutland, 193.
26 Fighting at Jutland, 193.

The captain continued:

'A terrible scene of destruction and desolation was revealed to me as I walked aft (with some difficulty)... Several of my best men came up and tried to console me, and all were delighted that we had at length been in action and done our share. But many were already killed and lay around their guns and places of duty. Most of the engine room and stokehold brigade must have been killed outright... All of a sudden we were lit up again and the enemy poured four or five more salvoes at point blank range... this would be about ten minutes from the time we were first hit.'[27]

'The captain "flopped over the side into the sea".... I could see many hands in the water about forty or fifty I should think. There was no support beyond life belts, life buoys and floating waistcoats, so I was afraid that few of us could possibly survive, especially as I realised that all the destroyers had gone on, and that no big ship would dare to stop, even if they saw us in the water. I spoke to many men, and saw most of them die one by one. Not a man of them showed any fear of death... None of the men appeared to suffer at all; they just seemed to lie back and go to sleep.'[28]

Only the Captain, who was picked up around 0600, and one other survived the ship's sinking, at least three railwaymen were lost.

IWM Q020958

27 Fighting at Jutland, 195.
28 Fighting at Jutland, 196.

Edwin Foster	Stoker 1 Cl	Ardent	Portsmouth	21	NER	York	Cleaner
Albert Townley	Stoker	Ardent	Portsmouth	19	NER	York	Fireman
Thomas Cullen	OS	Ardent	Portsmouth	19	GNR		Clerk

HMS *Broke* at 0015 hours

HMS *Broke*, leading half of the 4th Destroyer Flotilla, the ships in line astern, swung around to engage a German battleship with torpedoes from very close quarters. *Broke* was battered with fire from the battleship only yards away and was severely damaged.

> 'I remember feeling the ship give a lurch to one side as a salvo hit us... At this moment I become conscious that I could get no answer from the quartermaster at the wheel, so shouting to the Captain that I was going below, I jumped down onto the lower bridge. There in the darkness I found complete chaos. The quartermaster and telegraphman were both killed, and the wheel and telegraphs were shattered and apparently useless. I found the midshipman had followed me down to assist, and we were both just starting to strike matches to make certain that communication with the engine room was gone, when I heard the Captain's voice down the pipe shouting, "full speed astern both".' [29]

An officer from the nearby HMS *Sparrowhawk* takes up the narrative:

> '*Broke* had also put her helm over to steer out to port away from the enemy, but just as we were both turning I saw *Broke* hit by a salvo forward, and, to my horror, when she should have eased her helm and steadied on a course to fire a torpedo as we were doing, I saw that she was still swinging very quickly to port as if her helm was jammed hard over, and was coming straight at us... We were only about half a cable (100 yards) apart, and I saw that a collision was absolutely inevitable; there was no time to avoid it. So in addition to the enemy's gunfire, which was straddling us with every salvo, we saw *Broke* coming straight for our bridge, absolutely end on, at twenty eight knots.' [30]

The two ships collided. The officer on *Broke* continues:

> 'On picking myself up I at once saw that we had one of our own destroyers bumping alongside, and an ugly looking rent in her side abreast of the bridge showed where we had hit her. Steam was roaring out of her fore-most boiler rooms and it was extremely difficult to see or hear anything. Our ship appeared to be settling by the bow, and at intervals gave unpleasant lurches from side to side, which for one moment made me think she might be sinking... The Captain ordered me to go aft and get the after steering gear connected... Getting aft was no easy job as all the ladders were gone, and scalding steam was hissing out of the boiler rooms from a dozen different places.' [31]

As the two ships hit, the officer from *Sparrowhawk* was one of a number of crew thrown onto the *Broke*. 'The whole of the *Broke's* foc'sle was an absolute shambles, but I crawled along until I came to a place I could stand up... I could not see *Sparrowhawk* owing to the clouds of escaping steam. As

29 Fighting at Jutland, 174.
30 Fighting at Jutland, 184.
31 Fighting at Jutland, 174.

I was getting to my feet I met a fellow who said, "Who the hell are you?" I told him I was the Sub-Lieutenant of the *Sparrowhawk*, and added that *Sparrowhawk* had sunk and that I was going to report to the Captain of the *Broke* and ask for a job... The Captain didn't realise that it was *Sparrowhawk* that he had rammed until I informed him of it. He told me to go back to my Captain and tell him that he had given orders for the crew of *Broke* to be transferred to the *Sparrowhawk* because *Broke* was sinking, and I was to ask for *Sparrowhawk's* engines to be worked so as to endeavour to get the ships apart... About this time the enemy ceased firing... I had to jump across a gap of about six feet from one ship to the other, but didn't succeed in clearing it, but luckily caught the lower rail of *Sparrowhawk* with my left arm and hung there with my body between the two ships.'[32] The Sub-Lieutenant was hauled aboard: 'I found my Captain and gave him the message from the Captain of the *Broke*. His remarks were, "but that's a pity, Sub, because I've sent across precisely the same message to him. This ship is also sinking fast!"' [33]

Some men made the hazardous passage between ships in different directions. By which time the escaping steam had been got under control and the two Captains were able to communicate by megaphone. The engines were controlled and pulled the ships apart. If *Sparrowhawk* was not in enough of a mess just after *Broke* broke free, *Garland* nearly collided with *Sparrowhawk*, but by luck and fast reactions narrowly missed, but *Contest* which had been bringing up the rear, struck *Sparrowhawk* slicing five feet off her stern. As *Broke* drifted off, the crew of *Sparrowhawk* concentrated on saving their ship, which by now could only steam slowly in circles, stern first, illuminated and exposed by the still burning *Tipperary*.

Broke was able to limp off away from the battle area, eventually making it back to port, having incurred 50 crew killed and 30 injured.

John Wilson	Stoker 1 Cl	Broke	Portsmouth	NER	Hull Docks	Dredgerman
Frank Orpet	L/ Stoker	Broke	Portsmouth	L &SWR		Holder up

HMS *Tipperary* burned for over two hours until around 0200: 'We could not cope with the fire forward, it being impossible to get along the upper deck, as the ready supply of ammunition for the forward guns was exploding box by box at short intervals. All the boats were completely smashed, but two life-saving floats were undamaged... Shortly before 2am the 1st Lieutenant noticed that the ship was going and gave the order "Everybody aft". Then the 1st Lieutenant ordered "Everyone for themselves"... By the time I got to the rails, the stern of the ship was well up in the air and the propellers were out of the water, so I slid a rope on to the port propeller, and thence into the sea.'[34]

Eventually he was picked up by the Carley float. The Sub-Lieutenant from *Sparrowhawk* reports: 'At 0610 a float with survivors was spotted, the men were singing "It's a long, long way to *Tipperary*".'[35] Compared to a float, *Sparrowhawk* must have seemed an improvement, but the ship was very badly damaged, and although they had spotted the survivors they had no means of going to their assistance. It was another hour and a half before the exhausted men were taken on board. 'Sixteen of the 23 (survivors) collapsed, five of whom died on the quarter-deck. They were all tremendously pleased to have reached something more substantial than their Carley float.'[36] There were only 12 survivors from the ship's company of 197.

Although *Sparrowhawk* was eventually taken in tow it proved an impossible task and she was scuttled.

---

32 Fighting at Jutland, 185.
33 Fighting at Jutland, 185.
34 Fighting at Jutland, 191.
35 Fighting at Jutland, 188.
36 Fighting at Jutland, 188.

HMS *Turbulent*

Around the time when the 4th Destroyer Flotilla were engaging the 13th Destroyer Flotilla were also in battle. HMS *Turbulent* was rammed by a German battleship and sunk, with the loss of 90 of the 102 crew.

Name	Rank	Ship	Memorial	Age	Company	Location	Job
Frank Blackburn	O/S	Turbulent	Portsmouth	18	Midland	Derby	Foundry boy

HMS *Black Prince*

Black Prince had become detached from her squadron some hours before. Her fate was something of a mystery and she was never seen again by the Royal Navy. It is believed that around midnight she was engaged in a very close contact battle with at least four German battleships. She was hit at least 12 times from large calibre shells and sunk with all hands within 15 minutes. At least nine railwaymen died from six different railway companies.

By daylight on 1 June the only battle between the Dreadnoughts was over. The Royal Navy had lost more ships and over 6,000 sailors to the Germans 2,500, but the German High Seas fleet rarely put to sea again.

Name	Rank	Ship	Memorial	Age	Company	Location	Job
Arthur Cole	A/S	Black Prince	Chatham		GWR	Brentford	Goods Dept
William Bacon	Stoker 1 Cl	Black Prince	Chatham		GER	Goodmans Yard	Messenger
James Dobie	Stoker 1 Cl	Black Prince	Portsmouth		NER	Newcastle	
Albert Dean	Steward	Black Prince	Portsmouth		GCR	Hyde Road	Traffic Dept
Walter Fowler	A/S	Black Prince	Chatham	19	Midland	London St Pancras	Dining Car Attendant
Frank Cudby	A/S	Black Prince	Chatham	20	Midland	Upminster	Porter
Moses Weston	Boy 1st Cl	Black Prince	Portsmouth	18	Midland	Peterborough	Tube Sweeper
William Burgoyne	Seaman	Black Prince	Plymouth	22	G & SWR		Carter
Frederick Iddon	Stoker	Black Prince	Portsmouth	19	L & Y		Train Booker

HMS *Hampshire* 5 June 1916

HMS *Hampshire*, having fought at the Battle of Jutland and returned to Orkney Islands, was ordered to transport Lord Kitchener to Archangel in Murmansk. *Hampshire* left Scapa Flow at 1640 on Monday 5 June 1916; her escorts had to make for sheltered waters and so she continued alone. She was struggling to make headway in a force nine gale and shortly after 1940 struck a mine which exploded on the port side just forward of the bridge. Power was lost and the ship quickly began to sink. No radio call for assistance was made. A little over ten minutes later *Hampshire* sunk bow first about a mile and a half off the coast.

Three rafts made it to the shore. The first had about 40 men in it when it left the sinking ship, it picked up another 30 from the water but only six were alive when it made shore, the rest had died of exposure. On the second raft, four out of 50 remained alive. On the third float four of the six on board had died. Only 12 of the crew survived, the remaining 643 died including Lord Kitchener and his staff.

IWM Q039007

H Sweetzer   *W Gibson*   *H Hills*

Name	Rank	Memorial	Age	Company	Location	Job
Herbert Sweetzer	Stoker 1 Cl	Portsmouth	24	GWR	Reading	Loco & Carriage
William Saloway	Signal Boy	Portsmouth	16	GWR	Swindon	Loco & Carriage
William Gibson	ERA 4	Portsmouth	22	NER	Darlington Works	Boilersmith
Herbert Hills	Boy 1 Cl	Chatham	17	GER	Romford Grease Factory	
Harold Hicks	RMLI	Portsmouth	24	NER	York	Engine Cleaner
Gilbert Randall	Stoker 1 Cl	Portsmouth		GWR	Trowbridge	Engineering
John Shanks	Stoker 1 Cl	Portsmouth		G & SWR		Signaller

HMS *Laurentic*   25 January 1917

Laurentic, an armed merchant cruiser and former Royal Mail Ship, tramped the seas in a wide range of missions, transporting German prisoners from Africa, cruising the Indian Ocean and the Far East, and ferrying to and from the New World. Amongst the crew of nearly 470 were two ex-L&NWR men, Petty Officer Charles Bartlett, a former loader from Curzon Street Station in Birmingham, and Albert Gamble, an ex-carriage cleaner from Euston.

Shortly after leaving the Royal Naval base in Lough Swilly, County Donegal on 25 January 1917, the *Laurentic*, bound for Halifax Nova Scotia, struck a mine and sank within an hour. Lost with the ship were 354 of her crew, and 3,211 gold bars, weighing 43 tons, being transportation to Canada to pay for war stocks. Charles Bartlett was lost with the ship but Albert Gamble's body was recovered and he was buried in the Upper Fahan Churchyard in Donegal.

Between 1917 and 1924 over 3,000 gold bars were salvaged, which was an enormous feat, but given that the ship held more than many countries' national stocks, it was probably worth the risk of recovery. Another five bars were recovered in 1932, leaving 20 which are said to remain with the ship.

HMS *Narborough* & HMS *Opal*   12 January 1918

A A Loose

Narborough was part of the 12th Destroyer Flotilla based at Scapa Flow in the Orkneys. On 12 January 1918 she was patrolling in foul weather the rough seas off the Northern Scottish coast along with the Cruiser *Boadicea* and her sister ship *Opal*. By early evening the weather was so bad that *Opal* and *Narborough* were sent back to the safer waters of Scapa Flow. Neither ship arrived. At 2127 a message was received to say that *Opal* had run aground but it was not until two days later, because of the appalling weather, that a vessel could be despatched to assist. It was discovered that both ships had run aground and were abandoned and there was only one survivor who was from the *Narborough*.

HMS *Narborough*

Name	Rank	Memorial	Age	Company	Location	Job
Lawrence Nicholson	Stoker 2nd Cl	Portsmouth	18	NER	Hull West	Porter
Arthur Loose	Stoker	Portsmouth	28	GER		Stoker
Sidney Button	O/S	Portsmouth	23	Midland	Heather Leic	Porter
George Boynton	A/S	Portsmouth	20	Hull & Barnsley		Lampman

HMS *Opal*

Name	Rank	Memorial	Age	Company	Location	Job
Herbert Christie	Stoker	Portsmouth	28	NER	Darlington	Plumber

HMS *Raglan*   20 January 1918

Raglan was a specialist ship, called a monitor, built to bombard enemy coastal defences. She had a couple of large calibre guns, a shallow draught to get close inshore, and was wide and tubby for stability. Her top speed was an unimpressive 7.6 knots. It seems that whilst en route to the Mediterranean she suffered a machinery breakdown in the Atlantic off the coast of Spain and was found by the cruiser *Diana* which took her in tow, finally arriving in the Dardanelles on 22 July 1915. During the Gallipoli campaign she built a bit of a reputation as a poor shot, despite having an RNAS float plane to aid with artillery spotting for ground troops ashore. The *Raglan* was at anchor (possibly her engines were still unreliable), when she was attacked by the German battlecruiser *Goeben* and the light cruiser *Breslau*. Despite being at anchor, *Raglan* came into action and began ranging with salvoes from her big 14-inch guns. The ship had not been designed for engaging enemy ships, her role was to fire in support of troops on land. But the gun crew engaged until the turret was

HMS Narborough IWM Q74270 IWM (above).   HMS Raglan IWM SP599 (below)

hit and was so badly damaged that the ship was abandoned. 127 men were killed and 93 survived.

Amongst those killed were three railwaymen, Able Seamen George Anness, a former L&NWR junior carman from Broad Street, William Olley, a former GER labourer from Stratford works, and eighteen-year-old Fred Hunt, a signaller and former labourer at the Midland Railway in Derby.

Zeebruggle Raid and HMS *Vindictive*   23 April 1918

The Zeebrugge raid was a daring attempt to cut off the harbour at Zeebrugge by scuttling specially prepared ships at key points within the narrow harbour approaches and so denying the port to the enemy. Crucial to the mission success was the successful landing of 4th Battalion of the Royal Marine Light Infantry on the harbour mole from the cruiser *Vindictive* which aimed to divert the enemy, capture the German blockhouses, and soak up resistance so that the blocking ships could get into position.

Militarily the raid wasn't a great success, but is celebrated as a heroic if tragic action. Private Stanley Jackson, aged twenty-four, formerly a fireman with the NER at York, served with the 4th Royal Marine Light Infantry (RMLI) and was injured and died as the survivors withdrew. He was one of 227 killed and is buried in Dover.

STRANGE SINKINGS

HMS *Bulwark*   26 January 1914

Bulwark exploded whilst at anchor early on the morning of 26 November 1914 on the River Medway at Sheerness. Only 12 of her crew of 750 survived. A court of enquiry established the likely cause as overheating of cordite charges which, contrary to regulations, had been stored in passageways between magazines. It was speculated that a damaged shell could have become live and was dropped thus igniting a chain reaction sufficient to detonate the ship's magazine.

Name	Rank	Memorial	Age	Company	Location	Job
Rowland Hill	A/S	Portsmouth	24	NER	Hull	Freight Shunter
Alex Maitland	Stoker	Portsmouth		Caledonian		Signalman
R Pritchard	Stoker	Portsmouth	35	LNWR	Holyhead	Labourer
John Wathen	Stoker	Portsmouth		LNWR	Holyhead	Fireman

HMS *Natal*   30 December 1915

Natal was at anchor in Cromarty Firth in Scotland. At 1520, without warning, the ship exploded and within five minutes capsized. Around 400 of the ship's company died either in the explosions or were drowned in the ship, or in the freezing waters of the Firth. It was never discovered why *Natal* exploded. There was a lot of sensational speculation about spies and sabotage, but in reality it was probably due to cordite igniting in a magazine. At least four railwaymen died.

Name	Rank	Memorial	Age	Company	Location	Job
Thomas Davidson	Pte RMLI	Chatham		Lancs & Yorks		Train booker
Frank Clark	O/S	Chatham	21	NER	West Harlepool	Porter
Reginald Harvey	Stoker 1 Cl	Chatham	25	GER	Lowestoft	Labourer
Mark Tippey	Stoker	Chatham	21	NER	Stockton	Fireman

HMS Natal. IWM Q74935

R Harvey

M Tippey

HMS *Vanguard*   9 July 1917

History was to repeat itself, this time at Scapa Flow, at around midnight on 9 July 1917 when the battleship *Vanguard* seemingly spontaneously exploded. As with *Bulwark* and *Natal* the *Vanguard* was at anchor in a safe anchorage. A catastrophic explosion blew the ship apart with the loss of 800 lives, including at least 11 railwaymen and two Australian stokers who had been sent aboard the battleship to spend some time in her cells. There was much speculation again about the cause, but it was subsequently thought to have been a deterioration in cordite or a result of a smouldering fire somewhere within the ship.

Name	Rank	Memorial	Age	Company	Location	Job
Bertie Watson		Chatham		GER	Oulton Broad	Porter
James Gapes	Pte RMLI	Chatham	39	GER	Bishopsgate	Goods Porter
Joseph Mason	O/S	Portsmouth	19	NER	Newcastle	Assistant Toll Collecter
Leonard Ashford	Stoker 1 Cl	Chatham		Midland	Tilbury	Carriage Cleaner
William Braidley	A/S	Chatham	18	Midland	Derby	Labourer
George Smail	Smith	Chatham		SECR		Locomotive Depot
Albert Ball	Stoker	Plymouth	26	Gt Western	St Germans	Engineering
Gilbert Jones	A/S	Chatham	32	L &NWR	Birkenhead	Clerk
Richard Tetlock	Signalman	Plymouth		L & NWR	London Road	Clerk
Owen Williams	Officers Steward	Chatham	22	L & NWR	Holyhead	Cabin Boy
John McLellan	O/S	Chatham	19		Caledonian	Ticket Collector

SMALL SHIPS

HMS *Lord Airedale*   18 March 1915 and 29 November 1916

Lord Airedale was a converted Grimsby trawler, one of many pressed into minesweeping service with the Royal Navy and manned with Reservist crews, and had the unlucky record of being sunk twice. On 18 March 1915 a number of minesweepers, including Lord Airedale, sought shelter in Bridlington Bay to ride out a severe gale. The minesweeper attempted to take to deeper and safer water but got into difficulty. The Bridlington lifeboat crew were summoned. Today the heroes of the RNLI can launch their powerful highly equipped rescue boats into almost any sea, but still it can be a very dangerous business. A hundred years ago the prospect facing the Bridlington Lifeboat crew must have been stark indeed. Despite the rough sea and the obvious risks the crew of ten oarsmen and three officers made their preparations. The preparations took time, they had to get the local council to bring the launching horses, and by this time the Lord Airedale appeared to have grounded on rocks. Coastguards attempted to get a line to the vessel from the shore but were unable to secure it.

Launching the lifeboat in the conditions was extremely hazardous, time consuming and difficult even with the eventual assistance of 250 soldiers from the Norfolk Regiment who were billeted locally. The launching horses dragged the lifeboat into the sea, encouraged by the soldiers, until some of the horses were virtually submerged by the waves, and the lifeboat oarsmen were able to tackle the thrashing sea and make towards the stricken vessel; two of the horses and one of the launching crew had drowned. The crew rowed through the towering seas and tried three times to reach the minesweeper, but it was impossible and all twelve of the crew of the *Lord Airedale*, including twenty-four-year-old Albert Mayson, who had been a seaman with the Lancashire and Yorkshire railway based at Fleetwood, were lost.

After the storm blew out, the *Lord Airedale* was salvaged, repaired and returned to service. There was another ex-railwayman in the crew, Albert Boobyer, a former signal porter with GWR at Swimbridge. He is certain not to have known that already a railwayman had perished with the boat, and may not have even known the ship had previously sunk with all hands. Seamen are a superstitious lot, and you have to wonder whether anyone would have crossed the gangplank of such a ship if they had known. Things didn't get any better and the *Lord Airedale* hit a mine on 29 November 1916 and sank, taking twenty-one-year-old Albert and six of the crew of fourteen with it. The *Lord Airedale* was probably unique in sinking twice and taking a railwayman with it each time.

MV *Star of Freedom*   19 April 1917

The *Star of Freedom*, another trawler conscripted into the Royal Navy for minesweeping duties in coastal waters was lost with all her crew whilst minesweeping, unsuccessfully, off Padstow on 19 April 1917. Joesph Remphry a thirty-seven-year-old former GWR carriage cleaner from Penzance was among those lost.

HMS *Recruit*   9 August 1917

Recruit was a small and agile destroyer, one of many patrolling the North Sea. On 9 August 1917, she was torpedoed and sunk, there were 54 casualties. Three railwaymen died – Stokers Harry Marshall, a former GER wagon greaser, Edward Parsonage, a former GWR fireman from Slough, and Alexander McInnes, a former seaman with the Caledonian Railway.

HMS *Tornado* and HMS *Surprise*   23 December 1917

Three destroyers *Tornado*, *Surprise* and *Torrent* were sunk when they sailed into a German minefield set to protect the approaches to Rotterdam. Over 350 lives were lost including Able Seaman Walter Potter, a former porter with GER at Hatfield, on *Surprise*, and officers mess steward Reginald Ewart, a former L&NWR dining car page from Euston, on *Tornado*.

SS *Daybreak*   24 December 1917

Frank Sumner, from Fenny Compton, Warwickshire, had been employed as a porter with GWR at Leamington Spa and by 1917 was a signaller on *SS Daybreak*, a 3,200 ton, 'defensively armed', merchant vessel. On Christmas Eve 1917 the ship was one mile East of South Rock light vessel, off the coast of County Down in Northern Ireland. She was hit by a single torpedo and sank rapidly, all 21 crew on board perished. *U87*, who was believed to have torpedoed the *Daybreak*, was rammed and sunk by HMS *Buttercup* whilst trying to attack a convoy the following day.

HM *Trawler Gambri*   18 January 1918

HM Trawler *Gambri* was sunk by a mine off Eastbourne with the loss of all her crew of 21. Three ex-railwaymen died – Charles Bloomfield, a twenty-three-year-old former booking clerk from the LB&SCR from Croydon, George Blanshard, an ex-NER trimmer from Hull, and Ernest Speight, a twenty-four-year-old ex-Midland railway porter from Cononley, in North Yorkshire.

E Speight
(CPGW.Org)

HMS *Bittern*   4 April 1918

Bittern was a small torpedo boat destroyer and was sailing in thick fog off Portland when she was in collision with the *SS Kenilworth*, which was considerably off course. The *Bittern* quickly sunk and all 63 hands were lost. At least three of the crew were railwaymen, Stokers William Follett, aged nineteen, ex-SECR, Harold Thompson, a former labourer with GWR at Haverfordwest, and twenty-two-year-old Able Seaman James Cloke, a former packer with GWR at Porthcawl.

HM *Submarine L10*   4 October 1918

The 230ft long submarine *L10* was commissioned in June 1918, and amongst her small and close knit crew of 38 were two railwaymen, twenty-two-year-old Frank Hutchings, an ex-GWR labourer from West Ealing and twenty-six-year-old John Stewart an ex-SECR assistant electrical examiner from Dover. On 4 October, the *L10* intercepted four German destroyers one of which was partially disabled having struck a mine. *L10's* captain, Alfred Whithouse, engaged and sank the damaged craft, but in so doing made herself easy prey for the other destroyers, who did what destroyers do, and destroyed the submarine which was lost with all hands.

HM *Submarine J6*   15 October 1918

HMS *Cymric* was an old 'top sail schooner', and a so called 'Q-ship', disguised as a harmless civilian vessel, but with concealed armaments. She had already sighted two submarines seemingly basking on a flat calm sea during the course of the day and had taken offensive action. In late afternoon the crew of *Cymric* spotted another submarine on the surface and, judging the submarine's actions to be hostile, went to actions stations and engaged. The warship was engaging the friendly submarine *J6* by mistake. Unfortunately the attacking crew had mis-identified the submarine as U6 because at the crucial moment some sort of rope or cable was hanging down the side of the conning tower and from a distance turned the friend *J6* into an enemy U6. The captain of the *Cymric* not realising in the heat of the moment that U6 had been sunk some three years previously. The submarine crew attempted to fire off a recognition signal with a rifle but this was interpreted as hostile intent and the signalman was killed in the initial engagement. A shell exploded in the control room wrecking it completely and *J6* sank whilst trying to escape and it was only when picking up survivors that *Cyrmic's* error became clear.[37] Ernest Armstrong was an Engine Room Artificer on board *J6*. He had been employed by the NER at Gateshead.

---

37   See Evans, A.S., Beneath The Waves. A History of HM Submarine Losses 1904-1971.

THE ROYAL NAVAL DIVISION

It is highly likely that the majority of railwaymen who volunteered for service in the Royal Navy did so because they were marginally more attracted to life on the ocean wave than they were to living in a hole in the ground. If you had the opportunity to choose you might weigh up the misery of life in the trenches – wet, dirty, muddy, cold, confronting instant death from shrapnel or high velocity bullet, or an agonising slow death with your guts hanging out whilst sliding into a flooded shell hole, alone and deep in No Man's Land – against the extreme noise, heat and filth of a battleship boiler room tackling the fear of a torpedo or mine attack blowing a hole into the ship, where mercilessly you hope that you are instantly killed by the pressure wave, rather than a slower death of drowning as the water pours in and the ship sinks. When it comes down to it people avoid the option they fear the most. Depending upon their preference would dictate at which recruiting office they paraded. Those chosing the Royal Navy had made a decision, presumably, to avoid all that army hole in the ground stuff. Imagine the shock then when Winston Churchill decided to re-deploy surplus matelots to overnight become infantrymen. So became the Royal Naval Division (RND) with battalions named after glorious Admirals of the past including, Drake, Anson, Howe, Hood and of course Nelson. At least 234 railwaymen died whilst serving on board RN warships, but 189 died fighting on land with the RND or Royal Marines.

The RND was formed in September 1914 and by early October had been deployed to Belgium. Almost all units were lacking in the most basic of equipment and of the support troops considered vital to support a division in the field such as artillery and a field ambulance. When you consider the amount of time it takes to work up and prepare a division for operations today, their preparation must have been woeful. The division were tasked with defending Antwerp, but quickly this was realised to be a hopeless task and were withdrawn. The Benbow battalion, having been cut off, did not receive the instruction to withdraw before it was too late, and their only realistic option was to make for the Netherlands where they were interned for the rest of the war.

The RND then spent most of 1915 training before being deployed to Egypt for Gallipoli, where they were in action throughout the campaign. Thereafter the RND was transported across the Mediterranean to France and took part in the latter stages of the battle of Ancre, one of the final battles of the Somme campaign in 1916. The division were fiercely proud of their naval lineage and even though by 1916 there were many army units forming part of the division, the naval traditions lived on despite some senior officers trying to snuff them out. General Shute had an unpopular four months in command, which might be summed up by a poem by Lieutenant A P Herbert:

The General inspecting the trenches exclaimed with a horrified shout
I refuse to command a division which leaves its excreta about.
But nobody took any notice no one was prepared to refute,
That the presence of shit was congenial compared to the presence of Shute.
And certain responsible critics made haste to reply to his words
Observing that his staff advisors consisted entirely of turds.
For shit may be shot at odd corners and paper supplied there to suit,
But a shit would be shot without mourners if somebody shot that shit Shute.

The division fought on throughout the remaining campaigns in the Western Front, at Ypres and Passchendaele in 1917, countering the German offensive in 1918, and through the final push to the war's end.

Thirty-two-year-old Stoker First Class Alfred Matthews, a former platelater from GER and serving with the Collingwood battalion was captured at Antwerp and became the first railwayman from the RND to die succumbing whilst in captivity in Berlin on 24 November 1914.

Eight railwaymen were killed serving with the RND in Gallipoli on 4 June 1915. Nineteen-year-olds Able Seamen George Dalton, an ex-loco cleaner from the North British Railway and Frederick Elliot an ex-NER number taker from Newcastle, were both killed serving with the Collingwood battalion. Killed alongside five men from the Hood battalion, Stokers Walter Hornsby and John Turner worked for the NER as fireman and engineman. Stoker Lionel Lilley had been a GER labourer at the Stratford Works Iron Foundry. Stoker William Male had been a porter with SECR and Able Seaman Sidney Brookman a GWR telephonist from Swansea. Two other railwaymen died, P O Robert White an ex-clerk from the Railway Clearing House and Stoker Beatie an ex-L&NWR porter from Wigan.

Private Alfred Berridge, who was awarded the Military Medal and served wth the Portsmouth battalion of the Royal Marines Light Infantry, died aged twenty-one on 9 July 1915 in Gallipoli and is buried at Pink Farm Cemetery Helles. He had lived at 28 Radford Street, Mansfield, and had been a number taker for the Midland Railway at Mansfield.

Able Seaman George Spencer MM was killed serving with 188 Trench Mortar Battery, part of the RND, fighting in the final days of the Battle of the Somme on 13 November 1916. The former GCR shunter from Rotherham has no known grave, and is commemorated on the Thiepval memorial to the missing. Nine other railwaymen from the RND were killed on the day, six of whom also appear on the Thiepval memorial, Ernest Burnip, an ex-NER carriage cleaner from Newcastle, Herbert Hardcastle and ex-NER lamp lad from Bishop Auckland, Stewart Malcolm an ex-Caledonian fireman, Gilbert Shelton an ex-GWR apprentice from Wolverhampton, all serving with the Hawke battalion, and Harry Hunt an ex-GNR clerk serving with the Hood battalion and William Davis an ex-porter with the Midland Railway at Kettering. Three former railwaymen serving with the RND are buried in the Ancre CWGC – George Perry an ex-labourer with GWR in Neath, Jack Bramley an ex-GNR trimmer and John Errington an ex-parcels porter with L&NWR in Carlisle, who served with the Drake, Hawke and Hood battalions.

Able Seaman Jabez Staples and Petty Officer James Purves were both MM holders and were killed in consecutive days towards the end of the war as the allies broke through the last defences of the Germans, the Hindenburg line. Jabez Staples, aged twenty, who served with the Hood battalion, had been a frame builder's assistant with Great Western at Swindon, died on 29 September 1918. James Purves, aged thirty-seven and a former North British Railway labourer from Ayton, Berwickshire, died the following day.

CHAPTER 7

RAILWAY MARITIME

Prior to the outbreak of war the railway companies were significant owners of ports and ships. Operating 216 ships, the Lancashire and Yorkshire Railway maintained the largest fleet, along with some of the largest and most modern dock and port complexes. The government requisitioned 64 railway vessels by October 1914 and in total 126 were called up, along with most of the railway companies port facilities, many of which had recently been the subject of considerable private investment which the government then nationalised.

Railway ships could be divided into three main types: passenger ferries operating on the main routes such as Folkestone-Boulogne or Heysham-Dublin; freighters which operated on longer routes such as Hull-Hook of Holland; and pleasure vessels which were predominately paddle steamers. The paddle steamers were particularly attractive to the Royal Navy because their low draught made them ideal for the hazardous task of minesweeping.

Railway ships served in a wide range of roles, some were retained by their railway owners and continued to fly the red duster and plied their peacetime routes supplying essential services such as mail and foodstuffs to the Channel Islands and Ireland. Others continued to mainland Europe until occupation of the ports made this impractical, and some ships and crews had been interned. The L&SWR had operated routes across the South Coast pre-war, to the Channel Islands, Le Havre, St Malo and continued to operate cross-Channel services throughout the war with often four or five operating every night. This route was the only route open to mainland Europe for civilians. Some ships remained in a civilian capacity but were utilised as part of the logistics supply chain to the Western Front. The SECR ships *Victoria, Invicta, Onward* and *The Queen*, for example, continued on cross-Channel operations and conveyed 6,500,000 people and 450,000 tons of freight without a single casualty. The *Duchess of Argyll* conveyed 326,608 passengers across the Channel in 655 trips, mainly at night. Others were requisitioned, flew the White Ensign and were crewed by the Royal Navy. Although some requisitioned ships remained crewed by their civilian ships company who signed on with the Royal Naval Reserve.

The SECR provided HMS *Empress, Riviera* and *Engadine*, the GCR owned *Killingholme, Broklesby* and *Cleethorpes* were converted into seaplane carriers so becoming the first real aircraft carriers. *Engadine* had a role to play at the Battle of Jutland by launching the aircraft which spotted the German fleet, flown by Lieutenant Rutland, to be ever then known as Rutland of Jutland. The *Manxman* of Midland railway was also converted into a seaplane carrier, but unusually continued to be manned and run by the company.

The requisitioned ships and crews provided workhorses to the fleet and the military in familiar waters and much further afield, and the crews had to acquire many new skills. Some vessels served as transports, such as the *Sarnia* from SECR, while others were fitted as minesweepers, such as SECR's *Hythe* and *Folkestone* which, having been converted, were dispatched to Malta and thence the Dardanelles where amongst other things they were used as landing vessels and crucially helped evacuate troops from Suvla Bay. Ironically the *Hythe* and *Sarnia* were involved in a collision and *Hythe* sank with the loss of 155 lives; the *Sarnia* was lost off Port Said in 1918. HMS *Duchess of Rothesay* was employed as a minesweeper and successfully swept over 500 mines but not without incident, in 1917 two mines exploded 70 feet off each beam which lifted the ship completely out of the water, without substantial damage.

Another L & Y ship working in Gallipoli ferrying troops, became involved in a salvage operation of a sunken freighter saving a valuable cargo of mules. A number of ships, such as the *Anglia* from

L&NWR's fleet, served as hospital ships, but in reality they were more akin to ambulance ships ferrying injured across the Channel from the base hospitals around the French ports.

In some cases, all ships in a fleet were requisitioned. For example, all the Caledonian company's ferries were requisitioned, and apart from the three ships interned in occupied ports, all of the GCR and Lancashire and Yorkshire fleets were taken. It wasn't only ocean-going ferries which were requisitioned, NER committed its fleet of six tugs, of which one, the *Char*, was lost with all hands, and GCR similarly provided two tugs which became the primary Admiralty tug boats for Immingham and Grimsby. They were moored every night for two years off Spurn Head in dangerous, darkened conditions ready to render support if needed.

Thirty-six of the requisitioned ships were lost; 17 were either torpedoed or sunk by U-boats; seven were mined; and three were captured. The first and the last railway ships to be lost were involved in collisions, as were two others, indicating that the hazards to mariners in wartime were not just the enemy. GER were probably the most unfortunate in losing six ships.

Company	Requisitioned	Lost
Caledonian	8	2
Glasgow & SW	9	2
GCR	16	4
GER	8	6
GWR	12	1
L&Y	31	5
L&NWR	4	3

Company	Requisitioned	Lost
L&SWR	5	3
LB&SCR	4	3
LB&SCR & L&SW Joint	4	1
Midland	7	1
North British	5	0
SECR	13	4

It is possible that the railway companies recorded the war dead from their merchant fleets differently. In some companies, for example, GER individuals lost at sea from the merchant marine were recorded in the railway roll of honour and included in the list of the St Paul's memorial service (held on 14 May 1919).[1] But not all railway companies recorded their merchant dead in the same way, and indeed even GER is inconsistent in that Captain Fryett (see page 199) does not appear in the main body of the St Paul's list, although he does have a specific mention on the second page.

1915

HMS *Roedean*   GWR   13 January 1915
The former GWR ship SS *Roebuck* renamed HMS *Roedean* had already experienced a few mishaps before being requisitioned. She caught fire in 1905 and sank under the weight of the hose water, and she ran aground near St Helier in the Channel Islands in 1911. She was converted to a minesweeper in 1914, but in January 1915 she broke her moorings in a gale in Hoy, Orkney, and drifted onto the bow of the depot ship HMS *Imperieuse* and sank. Fortunately there was no loss of life.

---

1   Cathedral Service, Wednesday, May 14th 1919, In Memory of the Railwaymen of Great Britain and Ireland who have died in the service of their country during the War 1914-1918.

HMS *Tug Char*   NER   16 January 1915

Stranton was one of the most powerful and modern tugs operating out of Hartlepool at the outbreak of war. She was requisitioned and given the name *Char*, and although she operated with her original NER crew she was supplemented with RN personnel and in January 1915 was based at Ramsgate.

On the night of 15 January during a terrible storm, perhaps the same one which had seen the end to *Roedean*, the *Char* was preparing to tow the Belgian ship *Frivan*, and whilst attempting to manoeuvre in very strong winds and a rough sea the *Char* ran into the bows of the other ship and was holed under the waterline. The *Frivan's* Captain reported that the tug drifted away and he was unable to assist since 'walls of water swept over their vessel' and so he could not lower any boats. Although cries for help could be heard from the *Char's* crew she had soon drifted away in the mountainous seas. It is believed that the force of the hurricane-strength winds blew the *Char* onto the Goodwin Sands, and despite the Deal Lifeboat being launched, no trace of tug or the 18-man crew was found.

All the crew had a long association with the *Char*. William Booth had been employed by the NER tug department for forty-four years; his son William died with him. The youngest was Matthew Hastings who, although only twenty, had been on the tug for seven years.

W Booth   R Fergus   G Nossiter   E Booth   J E Hunter   M Hastings

W Hatch

J P Whale

Edward Booth	Deck hand	22	Plymouth	Deck Hand
William Booth	1st Engr	58	Plymouth	Engineer Artificer
Ralph Fergus	Mate	36	Plymouth	Mate Tugboat
Matthew Hastings	Deck hand	20	Plymouth	Deck Hand
William Hatch	Deck hand/ Fireman	24	Plymouth	Fireman
John E Hunter	Deck hand/Fireman	25	Plymouth	Fireman
George Nossiter	2nd Eng	48	Plymouth	Second Engineer
John Whale	Lt		Portsmouth	Master of Tug

SS *Guernsey*   L&WSR   9 April 1915

SS *Guernsey* struck rocks on the French coast. The nearby lighthouse was not operational because of the war.

SS *Duke of Lancaster*   Lancashire & Yorkshire   8 May 1915

The SS *Duke of Lancaster* was torpedoed in the North Sea.

SS *Don*   Lancashire & Yorkshire   8 May 1915

The SS *Don* was captured seven miles east of Coquet Island, Northumberland, by a U-boat and then scuttled.

HMS *Immingham*   GCR   12 June 1915
The *Immingham* was requisitioned as a stores carrier and worked between Gallipoli and Mudros; she collided off Lemnos Island with the minesweeper *Reindeer*, herself a former GWR ferry, which hit *Immingham* amidships. The crew escaped onto the *Reindeer*, which was ferrying two companies of 4th Royal Scots, before the ship sunk.

HMS *Hythe* (and HMS *Sarnia*)   SECR   28 October 1915
HMS *Hythe*, a former SECR cross-Channel ferry was requisitioned and converted to a minesweeper in 1914, but was employed to ferry troops because it was hoped that the shallow draught would help protect her from the enemy torpedo threat. Not designed for troop carrying and with no passenger accommodation, the troops were crowded on the deck, making the ship top heavy. There were over 250 on board when the *Hythe* left Mudros for the 50-mile trip to Cape Helles.

As the *Hythe* approached the beachhead a larger ship was spotted on the opposite course bearing down on them. Several attempts at a change of course by both ships failed to avoid a collision. *Hythe* was struck 25 feet from the bow on her port side, leaving a gaping hole. The force stopped her dead in the water and her foremast fell causing many casualties. The force of the impact caused the *Hythe* to swing around by the stern and break free. *Hythe* had struck the larger ex-L&NWR ship HMS *Sarnia*. The Captain of the *Hythe* ordered 'everyman for himself'. *Sarnia* was holed and limped back to port steaming stern first to avoid taking on water.

155 died, mainly from 1/3rd Kent Field Company Royal Engineers of which six were ex-railwaymen and Fitter Staff Sergeant George Smith from 91st Heavy Battery RGA was a former erector with NER at Gateshead.

Frank Harmer	Sapper	LB & SCR	Engine Cleaner
Henry Heasman	Sapper	LB & SCR	Engine Cleaner
Stanley Kimber	Sapper	LB & SCR	Engine Cleaner
Frank Funnell	Corporal	LB & SCR	Engine Cleaner
Horace Pemberton	Sapper	L & NWR	Draughtsman
William Salter	2nd Corporal	LB & SCR	Engine Cleaner
George Smith	Fitter Staff Sergeant	NER	Erector

The ships company who died were: P O Charles Potter, Trimmers Joseph Paisley, William Hand, James Donald, Albert Burrows, Seaman John McDonald and Robert Brebner, Stoker John Boyle, Assistant Engineer Percy Webb and Cook Arthur Clark. It is unclear whether any of these men were former railway employees.

The disaster was compounded by the lack of life jackets and emergency lifeboats and could have been avoided entirely if shipping followed a set route inward and outward bound from Cape Helles. The Court of enquiry recommended that no soldier should travel on a ship without having a life jacket with him.

HMS *Tara*   L & NWR   5 November 1915
Seamen are superstitious and when the Royal Navy changed the name of the SS *Hibernia*, orginally an express passenger steamer owned by the L&NWR and operated between Holyhead and Ireland, to HMS *Tara*, many of her ship's company considered this to be unlucky. They had more cause to be

more worried when the 'lucky' ship's cat leapt overboard in an attempt for freedom whilst moored in a Mediterranean port and a boat was launched to 'rescue' the cat.

On 5 November 1915 off the coast of Cyrenaica, whilst patrolling a quiet area of coastline, *Tara* was torpedoed by *U35*. The torpedo killed everyone in the engine room and the ship rapidly took on water. Ninety-three of the crew of 104 took to lifeboats. The ship's dog was rescued from the water, but the 'lucky' cat was never seen again. William Thomas, the sixty-five-year-old quartermaster realised that his friend was not in the boats, and went back into the sinking ship to find his mate who was asleep below deck! Awakened, he was hustled into a boat, but as *Tara* settled in the water the quartermaster became caught between the ship and the lifeboat and had his leg crushed and broken. *U35* surfaced and towed the lifeboats away from a British garrison to land on the North African coast where they were taken prisoner by Senussi tribesmen. *U35* had a successful career and sunk over 220 ships accounting for over 500,000 tons, the *Tara* was her 28th sinking.

So began an epic and trying journey on foot and living rough, which was to last for 135 days. The crew were marched, many barefoot, through the desert and across mountains. Conditions were harsh. Exposure to heat, lack of food and water, and crucially lack of first aid equipment, meant that soon many of the men were suffering, none worse than William Thomas, who had gangrene and needed surgery. An amputation was performed using only a pair of scissors but he died a few days later. By 15 November they were joined by the survivors of another victim of *U35*, the crew of HMS *Moorina*.

Throughout the days the crew were marched, finding little respite and shelter, and minimal food. On 26 November, they arrived at Bir el Hakim an incredible 250 miles from where they landed. Here they established a rudimentary encampment. They were told that they would be stuck here until the end of the war. The Captain, in an act of desperation, wrote a letter to the nearest Turkish garrison commander pleading for help from the inhumane conditions. By Christmas Day many men were ill with dysentery but those that could sang carols around the camp fire. On Boxing Day heavy artillery was heard in the distance and hopes were raised, and then dashed, as this signalled the advance of the British and that relief would soon arrive.

Unbeknown to the 'Tarans' armoured cars nicknamed the 'Petrol Hussars' were operating in the difficult terrain of the mountains.[2] An armoured car lost a tyre at the exact place where there was an abandoned enemy vehicle. A soldier mooching about in the debris of the wrecked vehicle whilst the new tyre was fitted, by chance picked up a piece of paper. This, by extraordinary good luck, turned out to be the Captain's letter. The army knew that the *Tara* had been lost, and suspected the men were in captivity, but had no idea that they had been so mistreated and were so near death. The Duke of Westminster, who commanded one of the armoured car companies, volunteered to mount a rescue mission.

The supremely confident Duke set out leading 43 vehicles, but with no mapping, no idea where Bir el Hakim was, and with an Arab guide who had not been to the spot in 30 years. They had no idea whether the sailors would still be there, and weren't even sure they were going in the right direction. After very many hours and something near to 100 miles, a lot further than they had anticipated, their guide had recognised no landmarks. There was some worry about petrol, and water, but the Duke urged them to press on. Amazingly, eventually the guide is said to have recognised a fig tree as a point where he had tended his father's sheep as a child. From there they travelled the remaining 20 miles and found the encampment.

The armoured cars had, astonishingly, negotiated 120 miles of desert No Man's Land without a map and had found the imprisoned sailors. The sailors thought they were hallucinating when vehicles appeared from nowhere. Soon the sailors were gorging on the army supplies, and chain smoking the welcome cigarettes. For some of the sailors the Duke had arrived just in time. The sailors were returned to Egypt and were repatriated eventually home to Wales.

---

2   Buchan, J., The Long Road to Victory, 34.

F Barber	Steward	5.11.15		Plymouth	Holyhead
Griffiths Roberts	Eng Sub Lt	5.11.15	26	Portsmouth	Holyhead
Richard Phillips	Eng Sub Lt	5.11.15	38	Portsmouth	Holyhead
John Parry	Fireman	5.11.15	56	Plymouth	Holyhead
Thomas Jones	Head Stoker	5.11.15	56	Plymouth	Holyhead
William Jones	Head Stoker	5.11.15	58	Plymouth	Holyhead
George Cox	Artificer	5.1.16	54	Hadra	Holyhead
John Hodgson	Seaman	10.1.16	49	Hadra	Holyhead
Robert Williams	Eng Lt	28.1.16	52	Hadra	Holyhead
Thomas Pritchard	Seaman	4.4.16		Chatby	Holyhead
William Thomas	QM	13.11.15	65	Chatby	
Walter Jackson	Cook	5.11.15		Chatby	

The Duke received a DSO for his exploits.

In total, 11 crew were lost with the ship, a further four railwaymen died during the captivity. Thomas Pritchard seems to have survived the sinking, the captivity and the rescue only to die in safety on 4 April 1916. Neither William Thomas nor Walter Jackson are shown on the L&NWR roll of honour, but there were errors on all the rolls, and it doesn't mean that they were not railwaymen. They have been included in this list on the basis that they probably were.

HMHS *Anglia*   L & NWR   17 November 1915

IWM Q22775

Twelve days after *Tara* sunk, her sister, the auxiliary hospital ship HMHS *Anglia*, struck a mine and sunk within 15 minutes one mile east of Folkestone. The *Anglia* was returning to Dover from Calais, and was loaded with 390 injured soldiers plus doctors, nurses and 56 crew. There were many ships in the area but first on the scene was a collier called *Lusitania*. As the *Lusitania* picked survivors out of the water she struck a mine and sank. The *Anglia* began to sink bow first and her stern lifted completely out of the water. A destroyer, possibly HMS *Ure*, passed below the stern enabling about 40 survivors to jump to safety onto the warship. *Ure* and submarine depot ship HMS *Hazard* took on some of the 300 survivors, but around 150 including 25 crew died, many of these were caught in the hospital wards forward of the bridge where the mine struck.

The L&NWR crew were all from Holyhead and are commemorated on the Tower Hill Memorial. His Majesty King George V sent messages of condolence as he had a particular interest in the ship for only days before he had been aboard the *Anglia* being evacuated after being thrown from his horse whilst reviewing the troops on the Western Front.

Name	Age	Rank	Name	Age	Rank
N J Campbell	37	Purser	George Williams	57	Chief Engineer
William Lewis		Quartermaster	Joseph Williams	32	3rd Engineer
William Bassett	50	Seaman	O Thomas		Head Stoker
Richard Thomas	16	Deck Boy	R Stuart	29	Fireman
R Roberts		Chief Steward	James Redmond	29	Fireman
Meredith Williams	28	2nd Steward	J Lewis	41	Fireman
W H Calloway		Steward	Owen Jones	45	Fireman
J Hughes	16	Cook	Owen Jones	28	Fireman
TH Owen		Galley Boy	J Jones	60	Fireman
Robert Williams	20	Cabin Boy	R Evans	43	Fireman
Albert Ashton		Cabin Boy	John Jones	60	Fireman
Lewis Hughes		Engineers Boy	R Pritchard	20	Coal Trimmer
Albert Ashton		Cabin Boy	John Jones	60	Fireman
Lewis Hughes		Engineers Boy	R Pritchard	20	Coal Trimmer

Duchess of Hamilton   Caledonian   29 November 1915

HMS *Duchess of Hamilton* was a paddle steamer requisitioned in 1914 first as a troop transporter and then as a minesweeper. On 29 November 1915 she was sunk off Harwich by a mine from the German submarine *UC-3*. Although nine men went down with the ship only 2nd Engineer J Stark is known to have been a railway employee. The other men were Naval Reservists and may not have been railwaymen. Deck Hands James Green, Angus O'Henley, Burton Verill, William Yorker and Trimmers Joseph Johnson, Edward Manning, Thomas Matthews and Leading Seaman Laurence Hutchinson.

SS Dearne   Lancashire and Yorkshire   22 December 1915

Little is known about the fate of the SS *Dearne* other than it was detained at Hamburg at the outbreak of the war and lost whilst in enemy hands.

1916

SS Leicester   GCR   21 February 1916

The *Leicester* was a GCR-requisitioned store carrier on passage from Portsmouth to Cromarty with 600 tons of general cargo when she detonated a mine on 21 February 1916 and sank two and a half miles south east of Folkestone. A minefield had been laid in that location by the German submarine *U6*. The captain and six hands were saved by trawlers but the remaining 17 hands were lost.

Name	Age	Rank
F Barker		Fireman
Gerhard Brummond	41	Cook
Robert Charlton	44	First Engineer
Ernest Cosman	41	Second Engineer
J Cumblidge		Steward
Edward Goodey	32	Fireman
Ernest Hague	39	2nd Officer
George Harrington	26	Seaman
Arthur Hollingsworth	22	Second Donkeyman
Albert Hudson	52	First Donkeyman
Charles Larson	15	Mess Room Boy
Arthur Parker	43	Fireman
Edward Shepherd	31	Fireman
Harry Smith	53	Fireman
Arthur Wringe	51	Fireman
A Dales		Seaman
George Edmonds	58	Seaman

SS *Brussels* and Captain Fryett   GER   23 June 1916

Captain Charles Fryett was employed by the NER as a Master, captaining their vessels on passage between Hook of Holland and Tilbury. Fryett commanded a succession of vessels as he and ships were rostered. On 2 March 1915, Fryett was commanding the *Wrexham* which was a Grand Central Steamer. Ferries were then operated in a pool and at this time it was in use by the Great Eastern. A surfaced submarine was encountered about a mile away, and the *Wrexham* was ordered to stop. Fryett was aware of a German threat that every merchant vessel found in British waters would be destroyed, and so he ordered full speed ahead. He was able to dodge the submarine, shoals and mines and the *Wrexham* survived to sail another day.

On 28 March 1915, Fryett, now commanding the SS *Brussels* on route to Rotterdam, sighted a German submarine four miles away. The submarine signaled *Brussels* to stop but as Germans had now sunk 22 British Merchant ships without warning, Fryett decided to attempt to save his ship by either forcing the U-boat to submerge or ram it. The submarine submerged and it wasn't certain whether the *Brussels* had hit it, but the ship escaped. Subsequently the Admiralty awarded Fryett a gold watch with an inscription stating that it was awarded for attacking a submarine on 28 March 1915.

Fryett was again in command of the SS *Brussels* on 22–23 June 1916 sailing from the Hook of Holland bound for Tilbury. She was apprehended by five German Destroyers and the ship and crew were captured. Fryett and his First Officer were taken away and interrogated about the submarine incident for which Fryett had been awarded his gold watch. He was subsequently charged with the sinking of *U33*, despite the fact that *U33* had survived the incident and was at that time patrolling the Mediterranean. The basis of the charge was the inscription on his watch. He was sentenced to death by firing squad. [3]

3   Great Eastern Railway Magazine, volume 6, number 69, September 1916, 218-226.

After the execution a notice was put up in Bruges:

> NOTICE. The English captain of the Mercantile Marine, Charles Fryatt, of Southampton, though he did not belong to the armed forces of the enemy, attempted on 28 March 1915, to destroy a German submarine by running it down. This is the reason why he has been condemned to death by judgement this day of the War Council of the Marine Corps and has been executed. A perverse action has thus received its punishment, tardy but just. Signed VON SCHRODER, Admiral Commandant of the Corps de Marine, Bruges, 27 July 1916.[4]

The plight of Fryett was of huge national interest, within days of his execution the matter was raised in parliament, and questions were asked on at least seven occasions throughout August 1916.[5] Such was the outcry that the King wrote a letter to Fryett's wife.

Far from being forgotten and abandoned in a foreign graveyard after the war, the body of Captain Fryett was exhumed and with tremendous pomp and ceremony returned home for reburial. He was transported by the destroyer HMS *Orpheus* from Antwerp to within sight of the white cliffs where two further destroyers *Taurus* and *Teaser* escorted the hero into Dover harbour. His coffin was met by Admirals, Generals and Lords and led by the Royal Marines band. A military procession marched to the railway where the coffin was loaded onto a wagon to London. This wagon was also used to convey Edith Cavell, a nurse who assisted over 200 allied soldiers to escape from German-occupied Belgium, who was also executed by the Germans, and later, the unknown warrior. The Edith Cavell wagon has been preserved and can be found on the Kent and East Sussex railway.

In London there was another procession to St Paul's Cathedral where a service was held, attended by representatives of the King and Prime Minister and many hundreds of worthy folk. The streets were lined with thousands paying their respects. After the service the procession marched to Liverpool Street Station where the massed band of the GER played whilst his coffin was loaded onto a GER train to Dovercourt. Two carriages on the train were required just to carry the wreaths from London. School children lined every station along the route. At Dovercourt he was met by an Admiral where there was a further parade to the churchyard overlooking the harbour where the Bishop of Chelmsford officiated the service and finally the last post was played as Captain Fryett was finally laid to rest.

There is a memorial to Captain Fryett at Liverpool Street Station, probably passed by thousands every day, yet seen by few, and understood by even less. Money raised from a public collection funded the Fryatt memorial hospital in Harwich. It is amazing to think that a ferry captain managed to capture the public imagination to such a degree.

Some time later the SS *Brussels*, which had been scuttled, was salvaged. Although she was in a poor state she was handed over to the British by the Belgian Government and accepted by the British Ambassador before being towed back to the Tyne where there was yet another civic reception. The ship was refitted and converted into a sheep and cattle carrier and plied between Dublin and Preston.

The Wreck of SS Brussels. IWM Q15044

4 Pratt, 911.
5 See Hansard 31 July 1916, vol 84 cc2080-1, 1 August 1916, vol 85, c44, 2 August 1916, vol 22, cc1070-4, 2 August 1916, vol 85, cc281-2, 2 August 1916, vol 85, cc278-9, 3 August 1916, vol 85, c512, 3 August 1916, vol85, c498, 7 August 1916, vol 85, c648, 9 August 1916, vol 85, c1048, 16 August 1916, vol 85, c1853.

IWM Q66269

IWM Q023358

Below: IWM Q004101

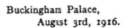

Buckingham Palace,
August 3rd, 1916.

Madam,

In the sorrow which has so cruelly stricken you, the King joins with his people in offering you his heartfelt sympathy.

Since the outbreak of the war, His Majesty has followed with admiration the splendid services of the Mercantile Marine.

The action of Captain Fryatt in defending his ship against the attack of an enemy submarine was a noble instance of the resource and self-reliance so characteristic of that profession.

It is, therefore, with feelings of the deepest indignation that the King learnt of your husband's fate, and in conveying to you the expression of his condolence, I am commanded to assure you of the abhorrence with which His Majesty regards this outrage.

Yours very faithfully
STAMFORDHAM.

HMS *Clacton*　　GER　3 August 1916

The *Clacton* was sunk by *U73* on 3 August 1916 while she was going going alongside HMS *Grafton* off Kavalla Bay in the Aegean Sea. Five men were lost in the sinking.

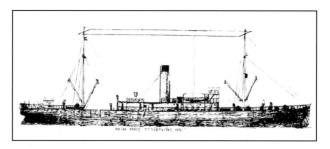

	Robert Clarke	22	10	15		Plymouth	GER	A/S	
	Francis Mortimore	3	8	16	44	Chatham	GER	Lt (Engr)	

R Clarke　　　　　　　　　　　　　　　　　　　　　　　　　　　　　　　　*L T Mortimore*

HMS *Duke of Albany*　　Lancs & Yorks　25 August 1916

Having set off patrolling from Orkney along with her sister ship, on 24 August 1916, she was struck by a torpedo from *U27*. Two men were killed instantly as the torpedo penetrated the port engine room. The Captain gave the order to abandon ship and as men took to the boats some capsized. As she sunk, within six minutes of being hit, depth charges which had been left armed detonated killing a number of people in the sea.

　HMS *Duke of Clarence* attempted to ram the U-boat and then came to the rescue saving 17 crewmen. Twenty-five crew of the 106 on board perished. The Captain went down with the ship.

John Birnie	39	Greaser	Fleetwood	Lancs & Yorks	Fireman
Herbert Beardoe	28	Donkeyman	Plymouth	Lancs & Yorks	Donkeyman
Ralph Carey	22	A/S	Portsmouth	LB & SCR	Eng Cleaner
Thomas Carson		Greaser	Plymouth	Lancs & Yorks	Fireman
Sam Glass	28	Fireman	Plymouth	Lancs & Yorks	Fireman
Albert Maskell	45	Lt	Plymouth	Lancs & Yorks	Second Engineer

SS *Colchester*　　GER　21 September 1916

SS *Colchester* was captured by the enemy in the North Sea and the crew of 29 were interned including her master who the GER magazine reports: 'had only recently been promoted and had no connection with submarine encounters, so that it cannot be conceived that the Germans will find an excuse for serving him as Captain Fryatt was served'.[6] Clearly at the time they were worried that he would meet a grizzly end. The *Colchester* was subsequently sunk whilst in enemy service.

GER Magazine Nov 1916

SS *The Queen*   SECR   26 October 1916

SS *The Queen* was involved in evacuating refugees from Ostend in 1914. On 26 October 1914 she rescued over 2,000 Belgian refugees in very difficult conditions from the French ship *Admiral Ganteaume* which had been torpedoed. In September 1916 she rescued the disabled *Queen Empress* and towed her to safety. On 26 October *The Queen* was one of a number of transport and hospital ships plying the Channel when she got caught up in a German torpedo boat raid on the Dover barrage and allied shipping. The Royal Navy dispatched a destroyer squadron, but not before the Germans had sunk HMS *Flint* and a number of fishing boats and captured *The Queen*. The Germans allowed the crew to take to their boats before they torpedoed and sank *The Queen*. Somehow, in the confusion, the ship's cook, twenty-year-old Lewis Dilnot, was killed and his body was not recovered. This short sea skirmish was subsequently named the Battle of Dover Strait.

1917

SS *Copenhagen*   GER   5 March 1917

SS *Copenhagen* was on route from Harwich to Hook of Holland and was torpedoed in the North Sea. At least five of the crew were lost at sea: Arthur Atkins, Charles Brundle, William Chaplin, Arthur Hammond, firemen, and Harry Barney, donkeyman, but it is not known whether any were railwaymen.

HMS *Duchess of Montrose*   Caledonian   18 March 1917

HMS *Duchess of Montrose* was a paddle steamer requisitioned as a minesweeper. She was lost near Dunkirk on 18 March 1917 after striking a mine. At least 12 were killed but only three are known to have been railway employees.

William Brown	36	Plymouth	Sec Engineer
Robert Houston		Plymouth	Steward
Archibald MacElwee	50	Portsmouth	Eng Lt

Other crew who died were: Deck Hands N McDonald, D J MacLennan, C Warden, 3rd Engineer W Fair, Trimmer T E Gibbon, Telegraphist C H Panther, Assistant Steward A MacPherson, PO A R Tuffin and Sub Lt GL Lesmond.

SS *Achille Adam*   SECR   23 March 1917

The SECR ship *Achille Adam* was bound for Newhaven from France and was attacked by gunfire from a U-Boat. Two crew were killed and the ship captured. The U-boat forced the crew into a damaged and leaking lifeboat and sank the ship. After 28 hours the crew were picked up, but not before four more men had died of exposure.

William Arnold	27	Tower Hill	Seaman
James Clift	30	Tower Hill	Fireman
Albert Gillham	15	Tower Hill	Telegraph Boy
Albert Port	29	Tower Hill	Seaman
Harry Wright	25	Tower Hill	Second Engineer
Daniel Wyborn	63	Tower Hill	Fireman

HMHS *Donegal*   Midland   17 April 1917

The *Donegal* was used as a hospital ship ferrying wounded across the Channel. On 17 April 1917 she was in passage between Le Havre and Southampton steaming with a larger hospital ship the *Lanfranc* when they were both torpedoed by *U21*. Eleven crew and 29 wounded soldiers on board *Donegal* died. There were two members of crew who had survived the sinking of the *Titanic* and the *Britannic*. Archie Jewell, an Able Seaman, who had been a lookout on the *Titanic,* and John Priest, stoker. Jewell went down with the *Donegal*, but Priest survived! William Clifford, Andrew Cowley, Charles Dawkins, Thomas Hammond, Nelson Hill, Robert Hughes, Samuel Richards and Peter MacFadyen died. It isn't clear whether any of the crew who died had been railwaymen. Private William Knott an ex-GER clerk from London, and injured serving with the 6th Northants, was lost in the sinking of one of these ships.

HMS *Nepaulin (ex Neptune)*   Glasgow & South West Railway   20 April 1917

HMS *Nepaulin* was a Clyde paddlesteamer converted into a minesweeper and operated off Dover. Ultimately she was unsuccessful as a sweeper, being sunk by a mine off the Dutch coast. *UB12* laid the mines which also sunk HMS *Duchess of Montrose* a few weeks previously and HMS *Laforey* where railwayman George Day, who had been a GWR packer from Aynho was one of the 59 ship's company who died. Eighteen crewmen went down with the *Nepaulin*, but it is not known whether any had been employees of G&SWR, but the wireless operator Ernest Hilton had been a telegraphist with the Midland Railway at Heysham before joining the Royal Navy and being posted to this former railway ship.

SS *Hebble*   Lancashire & Yorkshire   6 May 1917

SS *Hebble* was a freighter re-quisitioned as an ammunition carrier. The ship was on passage from Scapa Flow to Sunderland when she struck a mine laid by *U42*, on the approach to Sunderland. The Chief Engineer Emanuel Laycock aged sixty-two and four seamen were killed in the explosion and the other 11 crewmen were rescued. *U42* struck one of her own mines off Tynemouth and was sunk with all hands.

Thomas Cutter	49	A/S
Charles Ford	59	A/S
Archibald Howard	36	Fireman
Abraham Jackson	41	Stoker

HMS *Newmarket*   GER   16 July 1917

The *Newmarket* was requisitioned as a mine-sweeper in 1914 and was sunk by *UC38* in the Aegean Sea on 17 July 1917. At least 60 of the crew were killed of which at least eight were known to have been railwaymen.

P Robinson

Some of the crew from Newmarket GER magazine 1915

Name	Age	Memorial	Rank
William Barber	22	Plymouth	Steward
William Chittock		Portsmouth	Eng Sub Lt
Henry Cunningham	31	Chatham	A/S
Fred Garrard		Plymouth	3rd Eng
William James	52	Plymouth	Bosun
Oscar Randall	29	Plymouth	Steward
Percival Robinson	45	Portsmouth	Eng Lt
Herbert Widocks		Plymouth	Chief Steward

Anjou   LB & SCR   18 July 1917
Mined in the Bay of Biscay.

Maine   LB & SCR   21 November 1917
Torpedoed between Newhaven and Dieppe whilst loaded with ammunition.

1918

HMS *Louvain*   GER   21 January 1918
Louvain, was the former SS *Dresden*, which in peaceful times had plied the Harwich to Antwerp route as a ferry for GER, but was taken over by the Admiralty in 1915 and converted into an Armed Steamer. Bound for Mudros in Greece, she was sunk by *UC22* in the Aegean Sea. Around 224 died and there were fewer than 20 survivors.

Also believed to be amongst the crew was nineteen-year-old Ordinary Seaman Harry Wood who had been a greaser for GCR at Dunford Bridge.

Kent & Chapman & Watson

Name	Age	Rank
William Chapman		Fireman
George Hales		Greaser
Henry Kent		Donkeyman
Walter Leeks		Greaser
Alfred Smy	30	Ch Cook
Harold Watson		Eng Lt

SS *Normandy*   L & SWR   25 January 1918

The SS *Normandy*, carrying general cargo and mail, steaming between Southampton and Cherbourg was torpedoed and sunk by *U90*. Twenty-seven died, 14 crew and 13 passengers and 13 survived. It is not clear whether the ship was crewed by railwaymen but since at least eight of those who died were from around Southampton it seems fair to assume these were probably L&SWR men. Indeed Able Seamen Batrick and Ingram appeared to share a house. Five of the passengers who died were Sappers, at least three of whom worked for the Rail Operating Division (ROD) and may have been railwaymen including Sapper George Cannell who had been a clerk for the Cheshire Lines Committee but had been serving with the 13th Reinforcement Company of the ROD.

P Battrick	22	A/S	Sidney Page	36	Fireman
Frederick Budden	40	Chief Eng	Thomas Pleace	48	Chief Officer
Alexander Glouskofsky	39	A/S	Wallace Waugh	45	Steward
Bertie Holloway	35	Fireman	Walter Young	44	Fireman
Ingram	33	A/S	William Cloy	26	
Mulgrave	16	Assistant Steward	Gilbert Dawson	20	L/S
Oliver Thomas	56	Fireman	Patrick English	24	A/S

SS *South Western*   L & SWR   16 March 1918

The *South Western* was sunk by *U59* nine miles south of the Isle of Wight, whilst on passage from Southampton to St Malo carrying general cargo. There were 24 killed and six survivors including the Captain. It isn't clear whether there were any railwaymen amongst the dead.

Frederick Miller	49	Ch Steward	BWJ McCarthy	18	Steward
Charles Hartley	20	A/S	Horace Newton	15	Deck Boy
Maxwell Frame		L/S	George Parsons	62	Carpenter
Owen Aldis	25	2nd Engr	John Platt	57	A/S
WSS Burton	61	Stewardess	JP Short	60	Steward
EB Cochrane	46	Stewardess	Harry Strange	60	Steward
Frederick Coles	46	Fireman	J Sweetingham	67	Cook
William Day	23	Fireman	Robert White	31	A/S
R Deathe		Steward	William Williamson	29	Fireman
William Fielding	34	A/S	Albert Welsh	39	A/S
Joseph Gomes	25	Fireman	Yves Le Gac		Pilot
Edward Le Page	41	A/S			

SS *Slieve Bloom*   L & NWR   30 March 1918

The SS *Slieve Bloom* was a freighter lost in a collision with *USS Stockton*. The ship was carrying a mixed cargo including railway rolling stock and 370 cattle.

SS *Rye*   Lancs & Yorks   7 April 1918

SS *Rye* was torpedoed by German submarine *UB-74* whilst on passage from Newhaven for Rouen. Two railwaymen were known to have been killed – Joseph Chilvers a fifty-six year-old cook and steward, and Thomas Pettinger a twenty-eight-year-old fireman.

SS *Unity*   Lancs & Yorks   2 May 1918
The SS *Unity* was torpedoed by *U57* on 2 May 1918 whilst sailing from Newhaven to Calais with a cargo of ammunition. Twelve crew were killed of which at least nine were railwaymen.

Fred Heterick		Chief Officer
A Thompson	39	Chief Eng
Frederick Whitehead	46	Fireman
Ernest Appleyard	37	Fireman
William Bateman	24	Fireman
Edward Creaser	32	A/S
Charles Hansome	18	Fireman
John Jones	34	Fireman
John Rockett	65	A/S
John Gibson		Fireman
Thomas Walsh		L/S

Chesterfield   GCR   18 May 1918
The *Chesterfield* was requisitioned immediately upon completion and so would never have been crewed by GCR. She was torpedoed in the Mediterranean by *U52* and at least four crew died, but they were not thought to be railwaymen.

Wrexham   GCR   19 June 1918
The *Wrexham* was requisitioned in 1916 and was lost having run aground off the mouth of the Yugina river in the White Sea on passage from Murmansk.

HMS *Sarnia*   L & NWR   12 September 1918
Sarnia survived the collision with HMS *Hythe* (see page 195), only to be sunk by torpedo in the Mediterranean on 12 September 1918.

Frank Deeley	OS	12	9	18		Plymouth	L & NWR	Clerk
George Hodgen	Asst Eng	12	9	18		Plymouth	L & SWR	Assistant Engineer
John Le Huquet	Steward	8	9	16	40	East Mudros	L & SWR	Chief Steward
Albert Unwin	Steward	12	9	18		Plymouth	L & SWR	Steward

SS *Onward*   SECR   24 September 1918
SS *Onward* caught fire whilst alongside at Folkestone. The fire was so fierce that the wooden columns of the dock side ignited and to save the jetty the ship was scuttled.

HMS *Marsa*   G & SWR   18 November 1918
Marsa, formerly the paddle steamer *Mars*, collided with a British destroyer off Harwich. The quick action of the crew resulted in them being able to beach her but she broke in two.

Duchess of Richmond   28 June 1919

Whilst operating in the Aegean after the war, the *Duchess of Richmond* (right) met her end when she contacted a mine, indicating, even after hostilities had ceased, the ongoing hazards to shipping of this indiscriminate weapon.

Above: Duchess of Richmond.   Below: RMS Aragon IWM Q045682

RMS *Aragon* 30 December 1917

The former Royal Mail Ship *Aragon* was in December 1917 transporting troops. There were 2,700 on board which included 160 nursing sisters On 30 December, whilst entering Alexandria Harbour, *Aragon* was turned away due to a submarine threat. Whilst turning sharply she was hit by a torpedo and quickly began to sink.

A number of destroyers close by came to assist, including HMS *Attack,* which struck a mine and sank. It was women first to the boats and the nursing sisters were evacuated, but 610 passengers and crew were to die including at least 60 railwaymen most of whom served with the 96th and 98th Light Railway Operating Companies RE.

A survivors report from an unknown officer in a letter to Mr John Hannay: [7]

'The troops were ordered to get "off" and they managed to do so by attaching ropes from the ship to the destroyer. On other parts of the ship troops were ordered to "take the water" and rafts were let loose. In a few minutes the sea was full of struggling men. On the boat deck where I was performing duty, the ship's boat crews were working in vain to get off the remainder of the boats, which had become jammed by the list. One could feel her going fast, and the list was rendering it impossible to stand upon the deck. About fifteen minutes had elapsed from the time of the explosion, when the Commander gave the order – "Every man for himself".

IWM SP 002054

Then there was a rush to get over the side, but nowhere was there any sign of panic. The discipline throughout was astounding, and troops clung on to each other, singing and cheering until they reached the water level, and then broke up into struggling masses...

---

7   Source Mr Adrian Rowe, Kloof, South Africa.

The Aragon was disappearing rapidly amid a roar of rushing water, and the smashing of internal fittings. Scores of poor fellows still clung to the decks, and now at the last moment were attempting to throw themselves into the sea, rather than be "sucked under", but from the great height to which the bow had raised, they were being killed outright as they touched the water...

With one great surge, a roar of inrushing water, and the explosion of the ship's boilers, she went beneath the surface. Once out of sight, a grim silence seemed to settle on all, and I shall never forget the expression written upon mens' faces, as I saw it then. The spot over which she sank seemed enormous, and all around were struggling men and wreckage, upturned boats and rafts, to which they were clinging...

On the destroyer, all hands were busy helping unfortunate ones, and preparing to clear a way for her to move ahead, when a shout rang out and the next instant there was a terrific explosion. The middle of the destroyer had been smashed and men blown into the air. Oil, fumes, splinters of wood and steel flew in every direction, and she broke in halves and commenced to sink at once: the two ends, bow and stern – rising into the air and the middle sinking rapidly, where the torpedo had hit. There was no chance to do anything but "jump for it" which I did, as did also everybody else who could do so. It is impossible to describe the "mess" there was around those severed remains of that fine destroyer as they sank, and there was little hope to be entertained for those who could not swim, as the only means of rescue remaining were the two trawlers, who were near at hand, and upon which the Sisters were: besides these, only the Aragon's boats were available for rescue work; everything else, excepting rafts and wreckage, had disappeared. However, these boats did wonderful work, and took hundreds of rescued fellows back to the trawlers, where the Sisters worked unceasingly and with great heroism. Other trawlers soon became visible on the horizon, and were rushing at top speed to the scene, but as the port was at least eight miles from the ship, they took quite a while to arrive, and many went down in the interval.'

Surname	Rank	Age	Unit	Company	Location	Job
W Archibald	Pnr		96 LROC	NBR		Loco Cleaner
E Ashby	Spr		96 LROC	L & NWR	Willesden	Fitter
GO Baines	Spr	22	98 LROC	GWR	Chirk	Under Shunter
H Beamiss	Pte	19	5th Bedfords	GER	Cambridge	Acting Fireman
FJ Bowder	Spr	26	98 LROC	L & NWR	Buxton	Fireman
GE Brown	Spr	39	98 LROC	NER	Driffield	Clerk
W Burgess	Pnr	35	96 LROC	GCR	Altrincham	Goods Porter
HG Chequer	Gnr		RGA	GWR	Swindon	
J Cowin	Spr		96 LROC	L & NWR	Patricroft	Fireman
VC Cox	Spr		RE	L & NWR	Watford	Guard
J Dennis	Spr		RE	L & NWR	Nuneaton	Cleaner
GA Douglass	Spr	22	98 LROC	NER	Gateshead	Number Taker
J Dyas	Spr		96 LROC	Cambrian		Checker
WG Finden	Spr	25	96 LROC	Midland	Leigh on Sea	Porter
FW Gray	Pnr	36		Midland	Bristol	Porter
H Hesk	Spr		98 LROC	NER	Hull	Fireman
LFJ Howes	Spr	22	98 LROC	L & NWR	Wolverton	Fireman
W Hudson	Spr	42	98 LROC	Railway Clearing House	London	Clerk
F Hunneysett	Spr	26	98 LROC	LB & SCR		Pass Guard
FC Hyson	Spr		98 LROC	LB & SCR		Engine Cleaner & Passed fireman
A Johnson	Spr		98 LROC	NER	Starbeck	Fireman
A Kitchen	Spr		98 LROC	Midland	Burton	Porter
TC Lovejoy	Spr	26	98 LROC	L & NWR	Euston	Clerk
PH Lowe	Spr	25	96 LROC	GNR	Netherfield	
HJ Minns	Spr	28	96 LROC	SECR		Painter
WJA Paddock	Spr		96 LROC	Midland	Walsall	Goods Porter
OJ Payne	Spr	20	98 LROC	GER	Middleton	Porter
J Stavridi	Spr	20	98 LROC	GER		Clerk
SH Taylor	Spr		96 LROC	L& NWR	Northampton	Fireman
A Thurston	Spr		98 LROC	GER	Cambridge	Porter
FG Unwin	L/Cpl	23	96 LROC	GER	Middle Grove	Signalman
W Vine	Spr	36	RE	Midland	Stroud	Clerk
HW Walker	Spr	22	96 LROC	NER	Selby	Cleaner
RF Ward	Spr		98 LROC	NER	York	Cleaner

O J Payne

PART TWO

STORY OF THE RAILWAYMEN WHO DIED

The first part of this book has told of railwaymen who fought on the sea, land and in the air, this part considers the story of where those railwaymen who died came from and their roles in the railway. The tables on pages 33 and 34 show that 75 per cent of railwaymen came from just 40 roles and 33 per cent from 30 locations. Although 1,943 railwaymen who died were clerks, (15 per cent of the total), there were very many trades, occupations and professions represented by those who served and died. Similarly, locations ranged from the massive railway works in places like Derby and Swindon, down to tiny stations and signal boxes. The aim is to consider some of the range of jobs from across the railway, by looking at two of the massive works, Derby and Swindon, to look at a number of middle sized to small stations, from Reading and Cambridge to Wellingborough, Beccles, Attenborough and Southam & Harbury.

In the first part of the book many of the higher quantity job roles would have been mentioned, so focus turns to some more unusual railway roles such as, creosoter, draughtsman, fish porter, telegraphist/telephonist, platelayer, crane lad and policeman. Although the vast majority of railwaymen who served and died were private soldiers, there were some senior managers and consideration should be had of their contribution.

Although this book is about British Railways, a number of Argentinian railways were British owned and so there will be a brief consideration of the contribution by British employees in Argentina. The railway has always been something of a family, sadly demonstrated by the number of brothers and fathers and sons who died for the cause. No consideration of the railway family would be complete without some focus on the paternalistic and family nature of the railway and how people stuck together throughout the war.

CHAPTER 8

THE RAILWAY WORKS

Railwaymen who fought and died came from every corner of the nation. From the large city stations to the tiny rural halts. But the largest concentrations came from where the railway companies had their engineering works, the big railway towns, where it seemed almost everyone was touched by the railway.

The top 31 locations by number killed (see page 34) amounted to 4,070 of the 12,500, a third of the total. The table below shows the main locomotive and carriage works by company and the ranking by number of the 12,500. Ten of the top 31 locations were engineering works.

Company	Engineering Works	Ranking
GER	Stratford	12
GCR	Gorton	22
GNR	Doncaster	
GWR	Swindon, Wolverhampton	2, 31
LB&SCR	Ashford	
LNWR	Crewe, Wolverton	7
L&SWR	Eastleigh, Nine Elms	
L&Y	Horwich	
Midland	Derby	1
NER	York, Shildon, Gateshead, Darlington	4, 24, 19, 6

The individual railway companies engendered strong family traditions and, although the work was hard and often dirty and for some quite dangerous, there were strong paternal and social traditions. Many of the owners, shareholders and senior managers tried to create reasonable conditions for a family life. Often this was out of necessity as many of the then new railway towns were located far from existing conurbations. Infrastructure was built to support the workers, this included houses, churches and sometimes pubs, or clubs. Support extended to encouraging welfare, charity and societies for activities as diverse as pigeon keeping, allotments, to self-improvement and first aid. Railway life was often holistic, self-contained, and constrained by rules and rosters, and arguably somewhat controlling, not too unlike the armed forces.

To gain a better understanding of the contribution of the railway towns it is appropriate to look at the contribution of two, where the highest number of railwaymen were killed – Derby the home to the Midland Railway, and Swindon the Great Western engineering works.

The locomotive and carriage works in Swindon employed 14,000 people in 1914. It is known that over 450 men from Swindon lost their lives serving in the armed forces during the war. Although it is unclear how many served it is possible to extrapolate from the total GWR figures: 22,955 men served and 2,524 died.[1] For GWR as a whole 10.9 per cent of those who served died and nine times as many as died served. On this basis between 4,000–4,500 men from Swindon served which

---

1   *Great Western Railway Magazine*, December 1922, 538.

would be between 27 per cent and 31per cent of the 1914 headcount. It is known that 18 men from A Erecting workshop died and that 217 returned to the works. So 18 per cent from this workshop died, 12 times as many who died served. If this was replicated across the works then the number who served could have been higher than 4,500. In Derby, 441 men died and in the absence of other evidence around 4,000 from the works may have served.

Throughout the war the works continued to contribute to both the railway, itself hard pressed by losing so many to uniformed employment, and directly to the war effort.

The Midland Railway Works at Derby

Derby Works 1910 NRM 1997-7397_DY_2920

Centred around the railway station there were a number of discrete areas which together formed the Derby railway complex. Immediately opposite the station was the locomotive works, long since closed, which led onto the coach works at Etches Park. To the south of the locomotive works and bisected by the railway lines to Nottingham was the carriage and wagon works, now known as Litchurch Lane, and still the home of some railway operations, notably the Canadian firm Bombardier's train building factory, currently the only such facility remaining in the UK. To the south of the station on what is now the station car park, was the former St Andrew's goods yard, which had been a L&NWR operation, and to the south of St Andrew's, the other side of London Road and opposite the carriage and wagon works, was Midland's own goods yard. A mile north of the station was another large goods yard called St Mary's most of which has since been built upon.

Locomotive Works

Most of the expanse of workshops was completed by 1882; the oldest part of the loco works dates back to before 1844. Much of the heavy industry took part on this site which included foundries, blacksmiths shops, boilerworks, machine shops, fitting shops and assembly plants. There were four engine sheds, three of them traditional 'round houses', circular buildings with a turntable in the centre and numerous railway spurs on which were parked locomotives. No 1 shed, the first roundhouse, which sits behind the first works buildings, still exists and has been converted into Derby College.

The original building of the locomotive works. The roundhouse is at the rear.

Engine Shed. NRM 1997-7397_DY_2743

In the loco works there were a number of discrete workshops.

Number 9 Workshop

At least thirteen men died who had worked in the Number 9 workshop. On the evidence of those killed there appears to be a less 'heavy' bias to this workshop and more to teaching. There were four apprentices, four privileged apprentices; usually middle class professionals who had paid to gain experience, and only one labourer; a moulder's boy; two machine boys and a machine man. Three served in the air force, two privileged apprentices, Maurice Scott MC (see page 144) and C W Jones, and apprentice W H Cox. The average age, where it is known was twenty. You have to wonder whether the men from Derby Number 9 workshop who continued to labour within those familiar walls, were aware of any of the exploits of their colleagues who went to war, many of whom were to die. Did they recall Maurice Scott and know that he had been one of the first air aces the world had known.

Number 18 Workshop

Machine shop at Derby Works, 11 November 1921. This shop was fitted with a variety of drilling, milling and planing machines. NRM 1997-7397_DY_12243

At least 23 Derby men died who had worked in the Number 18 workshop. By the roles of those killed there was a wide range of engineering tasks performed in this workshop; five were labourers; four strikers; four apprentices; two riveters; a machine boy; a plater's helper; a tuber and holder up, a springmaker's improver. By contrast to Number 9 shop, the average age of those where known, was twenty-nine. The first to die was Rifleman Joseph Ramsdell who had been a plater's helper, killed within days of the war, serving with the 2nd Kings Royal Rifle Corps on 14 September 1914. He was thirty-five and would have been a reservist. So very early in the war the men of 18 shop would have felt the loss. A particularly bad period for the shop was November 1917. On the 7th, J P Regan, a former striker, was killed serving as a driver for the Royal Field Artillery. Three weeks later P McQuone, who had been an apprentice, died serving with the Medical Corps. It probably took weeks for notification to reach the former railwaymen's workplace, but you can believe that the men, in a comparatively small close-knit workshop, would have felt the loss. Worse was to come when three of their former number died on 1 December fighting in the battle of Cambrai. Trooper Thomas Gorbell had been a machine boy and the son of Thomas and Louisa from 7 Railway Terrace, and two men from the same workshop, who joined the same regiment 2nd Grenadier Guards and died together in the Cambrai battle – Thomas Price from 77 Graham Street and Albert Murfin from 1 Eagle Street.

Not all the men from 18 workshop were young, Charles Thornley an ex-riveter who lived at 80 Rivett Street was forty when he died, serving with the 2/5th Sherwood Foresters. Thomas Winfield from 45 Peach Street, was over twice the age of the young apprentices and had probably served for many years in the works as a striker, he would not have been conscripted and despite his age volunteered to serve his King and Country and served in the Royal Defence Corps and died in 1917 aged forty-six. He is buried in the Nottingham Road Cemetery, Derby, along with at least three other colleagues from number 18 shop; the last of whom was thirty-eight-year-old A Mee, a former striker from 37 Westbury Road who died in February 1919. Even after the war had ended and men were beginning to return demobilised back to the railway and back to number 18 shop after life changing and horrific experiences, still men were dying who had been called to serve.

Carriage & Wagon Works

Situated to the south of the locomotive works were the carriage and wagon works, capable of a wide array of engineering tasks. There was a foundry and blacksmith but also a sawmill and timber bending and timber drying shops used in building the wooden coaches. This land was extensively redeveloped in the 1970s into the BR engineering research centre and occupiers of the site today remain largely connected to the railway.

St Andrew's Goods Yard

Situated at the extreme south end of the station, this former goods yard is now the station car park.

St Mary's Goods Yard

St Mary's Goods Yard which adjoined Mansfield Road to the north of the city was the arrival and departure point of much of the goods into the city, and where produce was unloaded and transhipped onto horse-drawn drays. This was the centre of railway commerce rather than engineering. Around the plethora of sidings were bonded warehouses, stables and stores.

Twenty employees from the bustling yard were killed in the war. Indicating the different mix of employees there were eight porters; four clerks; two were invoice sorters; there was a delivery sheet registry man; a drayman; a dray shunter; and a gateman. The gateman was Henry Sharpe who died aged twenty-three in 1917 serving with 8th Lincolns; because of his job he would probably have been known to everyone. The first man from St Mary's to die was twenty-three-year-old former invoice sorter Lawrence Massey who served with 1st Coldsteam Guards and was killed in January 1915. Two St Mary's men died together serving with the 8th Seaforth Highlanders on 22 August 1917 in the push at Passchendaele, twenty-one-year-old Francis Blyth and ex-messenger twenty-year-old Reginald Thompson who had been a clerk, are both commemorated at Tyne Cot CWGC memorial.

The railway works employed an enormous range of jobs and trades to keep the specialised industry of the railway functioning. The works were amongst the most complicated integrated engineering facilities in the country. In the case of Derby, the 441 who were killed during the Great War were employed in 101 different jobs and trades. The most numerous being labourer and clerk, which together numbered 171, amounting to nearly 40 per cent of the total. This is indicative of the sorts of job roles the railway felt it could afford to lose without any significant detriment to industrial capacity, and if the roles could not be dispensed with they were more readily accessible to female labour.

THE 101 JOBS OF THE 441 DERBY RAILWAYMEN

Apprentice	Demurrageman	Machine Boy	Stampers Boy Stay
Assistant Fitter	Draughtsman	Mechanics Improver	Tapper
Assistant Sawyer	Dray Shunter	Messenger	Steam Raiser
Assistant Tuber	Drayman	Motor Attendent	Storage Batteryman
Attendent (Power Station)	Electric Lab Attendent	Moulder	Storesman
Bottle Washer	Erector	Moulders Boy	Striker
Box Fitter	Fettler	Office Porter	Surveyor
Bridge repairers assistant	Fitter	Packer	Telegraphist
Caller up	Flatter	Painter	Ticket Printer
Carriage washer	Foreman Cleaner	Painters assistant	Tinman
Cellar Man	Foundry Boy	Passed Cleaner	Tinsmith
Chair Caster	French Polishers Boy	Photographers Assistant	Tinsmiths Assistant
Cleaner	Furnaceman	Platers helper	Tube Drawer
Clerk	Gangman	Plumber	Tuber
Coach Body Maker	Gateman	Point Oiler	Turners Boy
Coach Body Makers Boy	Grinder	Porter	Viceman
Coach Finisher	Hammer Driver	Privileged Apprentice	Wagon Makers Boy
Coach Finishers Boy	Hammerman	Rivetter	Wagon Painter
Coach Painter	Holder Up	Rope Splicer	Wagon Repairer
Coach Painters Boy	Improver	Sawyer Boy	Waiter
Coal Trimmer	Inspector	Scotcher	Wheel Turner
Constable	Income sorter	Shop Clerk	Wheel Maker
Crane Man	Joiner	Slotter	Wheelwrights Boy
Cupolaman	Labourer	Springmakers Improver	Wireman
Delivery Sheet Registrar	Lifter	Springmakers Assistant	Wood Machine Boy
			Writer

Dray drivers, foremen, clerks and officials at St Mary's. 20 August 1911. NRM 1997-7397_DY_9639

Regiments of Derby men who fell

The 441 railwaymen served in over 60 regiments and corps as well as the Royal Navy and Royal Marines.

In total, 99 of the 441 railwaymen served in just one regiment, the Sherwood Foresters (Notts & Derbyshire). Of which 33 were in the 5th Battalion, of whom 17 died in July 1916 on the Somme. Seventeen were in the 10th Battalion, 16 in the 2nd Battalion and 12 in the 1st. The Foresters are perhaps a typical example of an English County Infantry Regiment whose numbers swelled enormously as a result of the war, to a number of battalions which will hopefully never be surpassed. The memorial in Derby is a commemoration to the 140,000 who served in this one regiment and the 11,409 who died. Although the railway numbers look huge when considered in isolation and serve as an example of the sacrifice, they are tiny in comparison to the numbers who died from all walks of life.

REGIMENTS WITHIN WHICH THE 441 DERBY RAILWAYMEN SERVED

Cavalry	Infantry	Infantry	Corps
5th Lancers	Border Regiment	Middlesex Regiment	Machine Gun Corps
6th Inniskilling Dragoon Guards	Cameron Highlanders	North Staffords	Royal Army Medical Corps
8th Hussars	Cheshire Regiment	Northamptonshires	Royal Army Ordnance Corps
16th Lancers	Coldstream Guards	Northumbrian Fusiliers	Royal Army Service Corps
19th Hussars	DCLI	Notts & Derbyshire	Royal Engineers
Derbyshire Yeomanry	Devonshire Regiment	Royal Fusiliers	Royal Field Artillery
Royal Horse Guards	Durham LI	Rifle Brigade	Royal Garrison Artillery
South Nottinghamshire Hussars	Dorset Regiment	Royal Berkshires	Royal Horse Artillery
Worcestershire Yeomanry	East Lancs Regiment	Royal Irish	Royal Flying Corps
	East Yorks Regiment	Royal Irish Fusiliers	Tank Corps
	Essex Regiment	Royal Irish Rifles	
	Gloucestershire Regiment	Royal Warwicks	Royal Navy
	Grenadier Guards	Royal Scots	Royal Marines
	Hertfordshire Regiment	Royal Scots Fusiliers	
	Highland LI	Royal Welsh Fusiliers	
	Irish Fusiliers	Seaforth Highlanders	
	Kings Own Scottish Borderers	Somerset LI	
	Kings Own Yorkshire LI	South Staffords	
	Kings Royal Rifle Corps	South Wales Borderers	
	Lancashire Fusiliers	West Yorks (PWO)	
	Leicestershire Regiment	Wiltshire Regiment	
	Loyal North Lancs	York and Lancs Regiment	
	Manchester Regiment	Yorkshire Regiment	

Regiments shown in alpha-numeric order not by precedent.

The Fallen

The railwaymen of Derby, served in all campaigns of the war, and now rest in cemeteries large and small, and many in the fields where they fell. They are buried or commemorated in 186 cemeteries. The top six amounting to 30 per cent being Thiepval (38), Derby (Nottingham Road) (21), Tyne Cot (21), Arras (20), Menin Gate (19) and Loos (10). Interestingly, with the exception of Derby, all the others are memorials for soldiers with no known grave, a quarter of the Derby men have no known grave. For others their final resting place was further afield, from Berlin and Cologne, for prisoners of war, to Suvla and Helles in Gallipoli, Baghdad and Basra in Mesopotamia, Damascus, Malta and Genoa. The 25 buried at Derby (Nottingham Road) were men who, having been injured, were evacuated to England and subsequently died of wounds, or killed in training accidents before even getting into the war zone, or died from disease or illnesses such as the 1918 influenza epidemic.

The first railwayman to die from the Derby works was twenty-seven year old former labourer, Gunner George Brindley, from 27 Princes Street, Pear Tree, who died on 24 August 1914, closely followed by labourers William Beavis and Arthur Noon and porter Charles Lester who all died on the 26th serving with 1st Rifle Brigade, 2nd Kings Own Yorkshire Light Infantry and 1st Somerset Light Infantry. Since they were killed so early in the war it is likely that they were all ex-regular soldiers, mobilised at the start of hostilities.

The worst day for the Derby works was, as for many places across the country, 1 July 1916, the first day of the Battle of the Somme. On that day 20 railwaymen from Derby died and 16 have no known grave. Thirteen were from the 5th Sherwood Foresters, the Derby City battalion. They ranged in age from nineteen-year-old James J Smith who had been a machine boy at number 6 workshop and lived at 32 Lynton Street, to forty-four-year-old Edward Spencer a former ganger. The other men from the 5th Sherwood Foresters were F A Alldred, Ernest Derbyshire, William Dumelow, Frank Frost, Victor Harrison, F Poyser, George and William Webster, Antony Wilcox and Company Sergeant Major Thomas Goodwin. All with no known graves, lost in the attack at Gommecourt. A Bickerton and R E Rose were also killed and are buried, along with JJ Smith, in Gommecourt Wood Cemetery.

Twenty-year-old James Draper, who lived at 8 Arboretum Street and had been an apprentice in Number 9 workshop, fought with the 8th Somerset Light Infantry from 1 July on the Somme. When the battalion were relieved on the 4th they had suffered 443 casualties. James Draper is buried in Derby having died on 18 July presumably injured at the Somme, and evacuated home.

Another bad day for Derby was the 28 March 1918, with nine men killed including 2Lt John Hay from the 2/7th Sherwood Foresters, an ex-clerk, and Sergeant Ernest Boot, another clerk who died with the 2/1st North Midlands Field Ambulance of the Royal Army Medical Corps.

Twenty-four-year-old, Battery Sergeant Major B Bowring, of A Battery 232 Brigade of the Royal Field Artillery and former apprentice also fell. He had been mentioned in dispatches and awarded the Distinguished Conduct Medal.

2Lt Eric Tomblings RE

Eric Tomblings had been an assistant engineer in the 'New Works' department at Derby. Commissioned into the Royal Engineers he served in Gallipoli where, like thousands of others, he suffered a severe attack of dysentery, the effects led to him having a breakdown. He was eventually invalided home. He died by his own hand 'whilst temporarily insane... from wounds on the neck and arms inflicted with a razor' on 21 January 1916.[2] Was he insane or was he suffering from post-traumatic stress or stress from a perception of failure of being invalided home? Whatever the cause, he was one more added to the statistics of loss, and one more for the roll of honour.

Private Peberdy, a twenty-seven-year-old former coach body builder, from 108 Russell Street and who had served in the Royal Army Medical Corps, was probably the last Derby railwayman to die in the Great War as late as 30 April 1919. However, it is certain that servicemen including railwaymen continued to die from injuries into the 1920s, but since these men weren't deemed to have died in the war many of them did not feature on their company rolls of honour, or were treated as war casualties by the CWGC.

Derby community

The tightly packed railway terraces around Derby created close knit communities, families used to the hard graft and tough life of heavy physical labour but not attuned to dealing with death and injury and the emotional tumoil of loss at this wholesale scale. Time and again families would have experienced grief, in one of the small artisan houses the drapes would be closed in respect for a father, son, or brother who died. Yet just down the road there could be celebrations as a loved son returned on leave, or apprehension as another son completed training and was engaged, motivated and heading to the front. Elsewhere familes had to deal with the father convalescing from wounds and the son discharged 'services no longer required' who was found not up to the job. The community would have experienced it all.

The Railway Mechanics Institution was a social club for the workers at Derby works. It was also a place where classes took place for the workers, and there was a library.

Liversage Street and Canal Street, only a few hundred metres from the station and works, were touched by the war early with the sinking of HMS *Good Hope* on 1 November 1914. Arthur Green of 40 Liversage Street, and James Alsbury of 36 Canal Street were lost with the ship. Arthur, aged thirty-four had been a painter at the carriage works, and James a rope splicer at number one shop. They were both old hands with the RN having been awarded the China Medal in 1900, and had settled down to a railway career before being re-mobilised for

Derby Mechanics Institution about 1910.
NRM 1997-7397_DY_1785

war service. Arthur's wife Hannah and James's wife Beatrice would have been united in grief, but were no doubt supported by the many friends and neighbours. Perhaps Hannah was supported by Charles Nall who lived up the street at number 20 with his father Abraham, or John Green who lived next door at 22 with his mother Anna Maria. Charles, who worked as a grinder in number 7 shop, and John an apprentice in number 22 shop, later joined the local regiment 2nd Battalion Sherwood Foresters, both were killed. A couple of houses up from James Alsbury lived Thomas Longden at 29 Canal Street. A former apprentice at number 9 shop, he was the son of Mr & Mrs William Longden and he died serving with the 2nd Grenadier Guards in 1915. Further up Canal Street at number 82 lived eighteen-year-old Frank Blackburn with his Mum and Dad, Joseph and Mary. Frank had worked as a foundry boy in number 7 shop along with Charles Nall and was killed at the Battle of Jutland when HMS *Turbulent* was sunk. William and Mary Danks next door at number 84 were able to support their neighbours after Frank was killed, but within a couple of years their son William, who had been a wagon repairer boy but joined up to serve in the Seaforth Highlanders, was dead just 11 days before the armistice. Unlike the others in Liversage Street and Canal Street it seems likely that William was nursed by his parents in their tiny railway cottage until the bitter end and is buried in Derby.

This concerns just eight men, on two streets, employed by one employer, in only one town. These men never returned, but for their friends and families lives had to go on. You have to wonder about the effect the sacrifice had on these close knit communities over many years, probably over complete lifetimes. A ten-year-old in 1918 who had no involvement in the war, could have carried with them the mental scars of their community's loss through another war only 22 years later, and for the rest of their lives.

The Great Western Railway Works at Swindon

Swindon, like all railway towns, was close knit, and to lose 427 men from the same works, most of whom were under thirty, must have had not only a long term impact on families and the community, but also on the industrial output of GWR for many years to come. A twenty-year-old killed in 1916 could have been expected to be in productive labour until their retirement aged sixty-five in 1961. An enormous gap was left by those who failed to return.

MAIN OCCUPATIONS OF THE SWINDON (427)	
Labourer	67
Apprentice	51
Machinist	20
Machine man	17
Framebuilders assistant	16
Clerk	15
Helper	17
Wagon painter	14
	217 (51%)

As with Derby, the highest number killed by railway job role were labourers and apprentices, but there were far fewer clerks killed in Swindon (15) compared to Derby (72).

The works
Unlike in Derby where different railway companies competed for access to the town, Swindon was solely a GWR affair. Selected originally because it was equidistant from Bristol and Reading, and operationally it made sense as a place to maintain locomotives. In time this became the GWR locomotive carriage and wagon shops which, similar to Derby, contained all the facilities required to build locomotives and carriages and indeed marine engines for the GWR ferry fleet from scratch. In 1892, it was claimed to be 'the largest establishment in the world for the manufacture and repair of railway engines, carriages and wagons', employing almost 10,000 men. Erecting Shop 'A' covered nearly 6 acres which was nearly doubled in size in 1919 which made it the largest permanent workshop in Europe. [3]

L2 boilermaking workshop

William Gillman who served with the London Regiment survived the war and his sound archive is in the Imperial War Museum. Prior to the war he was a boiler-maker's mate with the GER at their Stratford works in East London. He describes some of the activity in the Stratford boiler workshop.

3   Maggs, C.G., Rail Centres: Swindon, 45 and ,51.

SWINDON – JOB ROLES 85

Apprentice	Crane driver	Hammer driver	Rivetter
Assistant Examiner	Draughtsman	Helper	Shop clerk
Assistant Works Manager	Dresser	Horseman	Shunter
Assistant Wheelwright	Dressers Foundry	Horse box builder	Staff clerk
Boilermaker	Driller	Hydraulic forgeman	Stampers assistant
Boilermakers assistant	Electrical fitter	Hydraulic forgemans	Stationary engine
Boilermakers Helper	Engine cleaner	assistant	driver
Bolt Maker	Erector	Issuer	Steam hammerman
Brass Finisher	Fitters turner	Labourer	Storeman
Bricklayer	Finisher	Lampman	Striker
Buffer man	Fitter	Machine Operator	Telegraphist
Carpenter	Fitters helper	Machineman	Timber porter
Carriage fitter	Fitters labourer	Machinist	Tinsmith
Carriage frame builder	Forgemans assistant	Motor attendant	Telephonist
Chair moulder	Forgemans helper	Moulder	Turner
Checker	Framebuilder	Pad maker	Wagon builder
Clerk	Framebuilders	Painter	Wagon painter
Coach body maker	assistant	Patcher	Wagon smith
Coach finisher	Furnaceman	Piece work checker	Wagon writer
Coach builder	Gas fitter	Plumber	Warehouse clerk
Coach painter	Greasemaker	Porter	Warehouse man
	Grinder	Premium apprentice	Wheelwright
			Woodwagon builder

'My main job was knocking down rivets 7/8th inch thick some of them in the the steel frame of the engine. You had to hit them with enough to split out and rivet the two plates together. You had to be hefty. I had muscles standing out like melons. I was fit as a fiddle. When engines came in with copper stays leaking in the fire box we used to go to them with a sack, knock the stays down to stop the leak in the fire box, and then go onto another job or back to the engine repair shed. It was a heavy job; I learnt how to use a hammer. Sometimes I would have to cut a piece out of a fire box and repair it, I helped the platers too and cut out covers for boilers'.[4]

No less than 26 boiler makers or apprentice boiler makers were lost from the Swindon workshop. John Edwards from 1st Hampshires died on 7 November 1914. Corporal Walter Shakespeare, Lance Corporal Tim O'Keefe and Privates Harry Walton and G Gill all died serving with 1st Wiltshires. In the sister 2nd Battalion, Privates Stevens, Hayward and Marchant died, and from the 5th Battalion Lance Corporal F C Haylock, Private March and Alfred Lambourne.

---

4   IWM Sound Archive, 9420, Charles Minter.

Number 13 Frame builders shop

At least 17 frame builders assistants and one frame builder died. The frame builder was Lance Corporal Thomas Gray who died with 2nd Wiltshires. The most decorated soldier to die from Swindon, Arthur Loveday (see page 257), was a frame builder's assistant, who died serving with 1st Wiltshires along with Fred Maslen, J Carey and Dave Robbins. From the 2nd Battalion there was Bertrand Manners, Francis Wilkins, neither of whom outlasted Thomas Gray for long. Three frame builders nearly made it through the war, Jabez Staples MM from Hood battalion RND, Frederick Leonard from RFA and Company Sergeant Major Herbert Staples from 7th Wiltshires.

Swindon Junction station

J & C Rigby built many of the GWR stations including Swindon Junction Station. Rigbys entrepreneurially capitalised on an opportunity, knowing that all trains would be stopped for at least ten minutes at the station as locomotives were changed, they did a deal with GWR to build the station and gift it to GWR on the condition that trains did indeed stop for at least ten minutes. Rigbys built an elaborate station with lavish rooms and a hotel, becoming the first refreshment rooms on the railway. At least four porters from the station died, Sapper Leed from 205 Field Company RE, Frederick Weeks and Harold Averies from 1st Wiltshires and E E Caswell from 5th Wiltshires.

REGIMENTS WITHIN WHICH THE 427 SWINDON RAILWAYMEN SERVED			
Cavalry/Other	Infantry	Infantry	Corps
Royal Glos Hussars	Bedfords	London	ASC
Royal Wiltshires	Border	Middlesex	RAMC
Hussars	Coldstream Guards	Ox & Bucks LI	RAOC
	DCLI	Royal Fusiliers	RE
RN	Devons	Rifle Brigade	RFA
RMLI	East Kent	Royal Berks	RGA
	East Lancs	Royal Dublin Fusiliers	MGC
	East Surrey	Royal Munster Fus	Tank Corps
	Gloucestershire	Royal Warwicks	RFC/RAF
	Grenadier Guards	Royal Welsh Fus	
	Hampshire	KSLI	
	KOYLI	Somerset LI	
	Lancs Fus	Welsh	
	Leinster	Wiltshires	
		Worcesters	

It seems likely that the recruiting sergeant who turned up at the Swindon works was from the Infantry and more particularly the Wiltshire Regiment. Over 150 of the 427 who died served in the Wiltshires.

The Fallen

The first man to fall was Private Charles Kibblewhite of 1st Wiltshires who died, aged twenty-nine on 24 August 1914. George Sawyer and George Tompkins, stationary engine driver and machineman in number 16 shop were killed on 13 October 1914 serving with 1st Wiltshires (see pages 43–46). On 12 March 1915 four Swindon men serving with the Wiltshires fell in Ypres – Ernest Moulden, clerk, Walter Shakespeare, apprentice boiler maker, Maynard Summers, labourer and Edward Townsend, forgeman's helper.

Perhaps the saddest day for Swindon was on 10 August 1915 when ten railwaymen died from 5th Wiltshires fighting in Gallipoli. Eighteen-year-olds Zenas Strange, a former helper, and Sidney Smith, a boltmaker, twenty-one-year-old Arthur Bunce, machinist, twenty-two-year-old Samuel Windridge and Edgar Baker, a machine operator, Thomas Farmer, a fitter's helper, George Ford, a piece work checker, John Comley and William Watts, labourers, and Thomas Lockley a furnaceman. Although the Swindon works was an enormous industrial conglomerate thus far in the war they had lost 77 men killed, losing ten in a day was punishing.

The end of the war didn't bring an end to the dying. The last from the works to die were Air Mechanic H G M King who died in June 1920 in Egypt and Private F C Anstey serving with 3rd Royal Berkshires who died in Exeter in October 1920.

Some of the fallen Swindon men were awarded gallantry medals, the most highly honoured was Company Sergeant Major Loveday a double DCM holder. Sergeant Frederick Lewis, an ex-electrical fitter who served with 15th Signal Company RE; Sergeant George Ford from 5th Wiltshires, an ex-piece work checker; Corporal Charles Coles from the RFA, an ex-labourer; Gunner John Henry, an ex-boilersmith's helper; and Able Seaman Jabez Staples from Hood Battalion of the Royal Naval Division, an ex-frame builders assistant, were all awarded the MM. Corporal Thomas Lewis of 6th Siege Company Royal Engineers who had been an apprentice fitter at the works and lived at 12 Brunel Street, Swindon, died on 2 November 1918, had been awarded the Belgian Croix de Guerre.

At least 19 of the Swindon railway fallen are buried in the town's Radnor Street Cemetery. These are men who died in training, or from wounds or illness. At least five died serving with the Air Force in 1918. Aircraftmen George Birks and Horace Golby, an ex-carpenter in the works, Air Mechanic Frederick Whatley, an ex-coach builder, who had been serving at Number 1 School of Navigation and Bombing, Air Mechanic John Minett, an ex-wagon builder at Kidderminster, and Air Mechanic Frederick Loveday, who had been a carpenter.

565 (Wiltshire) Fortress Company RE

This company of the Royal Engineers recruited mainly from the Swindon works was originally established to provide reinforcement to strong points but took on more general engineering tasks. Having embarked for France in 1915 they were engaged around Ypres specialising in bridging. During the Battle of the Somme they concentrated in laying water supplies.

The company took part in building the biggest bridge of the Great War crossing the Canal Du Nord at Havrincourt. The canal was a major obstacle to advancing and attacking the Hindenburg Line. The Company, working with a New Zealand Engineering Company who specialised in tunnelling, built the bridge across the 180-foot wide chasm in only 104 hours.

Sappers George Hatcher, ex-premium apprentice, Albert Johnson, ex-apprentice boilermaker, SA Sinnett, ex-apprentice fitter, Bertram Spreadbury, ex-coach painter, and Norman Dixon, ex-apprentice, were killed around this time working slightly to the south of the Havrincourt bridge. For Walter and Ada Dixon, from

Canal du Nord – Inglis Bridge

14 Park Lane, Swindon, losing twenty-two-year-old Norman would have been devastating just one week after losing their younger son, nineteen-year-old Edgar who had been serving in 2/4th Ox and Bucks Light Infantry and had been a former clerk at the works.

For much of the war Major Cyril Wilson MC MID was an officer with 565 Company RE which he joined in 1908. He started with GWR at Swindon in 1902 and by the beginning of the war was a draughtsman. He was awarded the MC in June 1917 and in September left having been promoted to Major, took over command of No 4 Workshop Company RE. He was evacuated suffering from dysentery and died from pneumonia seemingly brought on by influenza on 27 October 1918.

Some Railway Stations

If a third of the 12,500 came from only 31 locations, the remaining two thirds came from stations large and small across the whole of the British Isles. It is appropriate to look at a number of stations across the country, starting with Reading, the 30th largest by number who died. Then at smaller stations such as Cambridge and Beccles in Suffolk, both GER stations, Harbury and Southam Road, a GWR station in Warwickshire, Attenborough a Midlands railway station in Nottinghamshire and Wellingborough a Midland railway station, engine shed and yard in Northamptonshire.

Reading, GWR

There are 59 Reading railwaymen in the 12,500 including; 4 clerks; 6 porters; 12 labourers; 9 machinists; and a range of more specialist engineering roles such as; 2 bricklayers; 2 strikers; 2 brass finishers; a tinsmiths mate; bolt maker; rivetters mate; call boy, limewasher; draughtsman and an instrument maker. The instrument maker, Walter Treacher, and the draughtsman, Harold Louth both served in the 4th Seaforth Highlanders, an unusual regiment for Berkshire residents, and they died together on 9 May 1915 and are named on the Le Touret memorial.

NRM 1995-7233_GWR_B 603

Amongst the 59 were a father and son Charles and Alfred Povey (see page 240) and two sets of brothers the Reads, and Sweetzers (see page 242). On 21 May 1915, two Berkshire Yeomen were killed in Gallipoli, former clerk Walter Read (see page 243) and former tracer James Berry. Nine men died serving with the 1/4th Royal Berkshires, three on 23 July 1916 on the Somme; Privates William Mitcham, an ex-porter; Reginald Pratt, and ex-machinist; and Ernest Saunders, and ex-tracer.

Beccles, GER

The small Suffolk town of Beccles lost 11 railwaymen from a wide range of roles, 3 labourers, 2 clerks, a gateman, porter-signalman, carman, bricklayer, horse truck driver and a fireman. Some of the men had a good few years of service, but on the whole these were young men, the oldest was only thirty-two, and the maximum length of GER service was 12 years. The average service was three and a half years with four of the 12 having served a year or less. Of these three joined GER in early 1914 and joined the army at the first opportunity after war broke out, indicating that they were either reservists, or eager.

Private Henry Chilvers from 15 Old Market, Beccles, had been employed for only a few months as a labourer when he joined the 5th Suffolks in 1914. He almost saw the war out but died in Egypt on 17 September 1918. In the same graveyard in Egypt is commemorated Sergeant Frederick Thorpe of Waveney Cottages, an ex-gateman who enlisted in May 1915 into the Rail Operating Division. He survived the war but died, aged twenty-two in May 1919. Sergeant Joseph Bellward, an ex-clerk and enthusiastic sportsman who was keen on swimming, water polo and boxing, enlisted on 31 August 1914 and was injured whilst serving with 8th Suffolks at Delville Wood on the Somme, on 19 July 1916. Evacuated to England he died at Wharncliffe hospital in Sheffield in August 1917. He

H J Roe *F Smith* *V J J Bellward* *L E Turner* *F L Balls* *F Thorpe* *H Chilvers*

R W Parr	Rfn	ASC	25	11	17	Mendinghem	Clerk
Frederick Balls	Pte	7th East Kents	3	7	16	Daours	Labourer
Frederick Crisp	Pte	8th Kings	11	9	18	Moeuvres	Fireman
Charles George	Pte	1st Norfolk	23	4	17	Arras	Horse Truck Driver
Frank Smith	Pte	5th Norfolk	12	8	15	Helles	Porter Signalman
W H Wiggett	Rfn	106 Field Company RE	22	3	18	Grevillers	Bricklayer
Frederick Thorpe	Sgt	ROD RE	8	5	19	Ramleh	Gateman
Henry Chilvers	Pte	5th Suffolk	17	9	18	Ramleh	Labourer
Harold Roe	Pte	5th Suffolk	31	8	15	Gibraltar	Labourer
Ernest Turner	Sgt	7th Suffolk	9	8	17	Arras	Carman
Joseph Bellward	Sgt	8th Suffolk	10	8	17	Geldeston	Clerk

was one of many thousands who struggled on in countless hospitals across the country, succumbing to infection or dying a slow death as their bodies slowly gave up the fight.

Five of the 11 joined the colours in 1914, Privates Balls, Turner, Chilvers, Smith and Roe. Smith was killed in Gallipoli and Roe of 22 Ballygate Street, died of dysentry in Egypt and was, somewhat mysteriously, buried in Gibraltar. Private Balls who served with 7th East Kents died on 3 July 1916. Private Frederick Crisp, the son of Mr & Mrs Crisp of 30 Peddars Lane, Beccles, was aged fifteen when he joined the railway. He could have anticipated a long future serving the railway but he signed up and was killed serving with 8th Kings in the last months of the war aged twenty.

Wellingborough, Midland Railway

NRM 774_93

Although Wellingborough station was quite small there was a thriving goods yard and locomotive shed and the railway would have been a sizeable employer in this small Northamptonshire town.

The 25 who died were largely from the engineering and operational departments at Wellingborough. Few of these men would have interacted with the public. Their roles were typically hard graft and dirty. Five men were labourers; four were cleaners who would have been responsible for cleaning out the boilers of the locomotive, a particularly dirty job. One was a boiler washer; another a steam raiser responsible for being up very early and getting the fire in the locomotive going such that when the locomotive engineers turned up they would soon be able to get the engine productive. Some men worked with freight wagons; one was a drayman, another a shunter; one a loader; another a wagon repairer; and one was a demurragemen whose job was to collate freight wagon holdings since a fee was levied by the railway clearing house if 'foreign' stock from other companies was detained for too long. From the track, or permanent way, side of the business there was a lampman, whose task it was to light and replenish the paraffin reservoirs in the lamps at the head of the signals.

The first of the Wellingborough men to die were Arthur Neville and Ernest Sawford. They both joined the 1st Northamptons and were likely to have been reservists who had been called back to the colours. Neville, a former boiler washer from nearby Finedon, died on 14 September 1914 and is commemorated on the La Ferte Memorial. Sawford, an ex-wagon lifter was probably injured in the same battle that killed Neville and died in November. He is buried in the nearby town of Earls Barton. George Dangerfield, steam raiser; Ralph Murby, labourer; and A B Creighton, cleaner, all served with the 2nd Northamptons and died in the early part of 1915.

Private Dennis Tall, a former cleaner and Company Sergeant Major John Turland, a former drayman, were killed on the same day on 2 November 1917 serving with the 4th Northamptons in the attack of Gaza in Palestine. Leonard Cartwright, a former loader, died on 30 December 1917, serving with 96th Light Railway Operating Company, in the sinking of the RMS *Aragon* (see page 209) where many of his railway colleagues drowned.

Southam and Harbury Road, GWR

Harbury and Southam Road was a small rural station on the Great Western line, a few miles to the south of Leamington Spa, but now long gone. Even a tiny station like this had its own engine shed and small goods yard which was built to service a nearby brickworks. Despite its small size there were still three victims in the Great War: Sapper Marlow who had been a packer and lived in Mill Street in Harbury, who served with the 110th Rail Operating Company Royal Engineers and died aged twenty on 31 July 1916 on the Somme; Frederick Tasker was a carman and he died in June 1917 serving with the 10th Royal West Surreys in Ypres and he is commemorated on the Menin Gate; the third person was Raymond Brooks, son of John and Elizabeth Brooks of 5 Springfield Terrace, Harbury, a former porter he served with the 2nd Coldstream Guards and and died on 30 November 1917 aged twenty-two. He was awarded the Military Medal (MM) and is buried at Gouzeaucourt.

Attenborough, Midland Railway.

Attenborough station today is a tiny two platform affair serving a fairly upmarket suburb of Nottingham. In 1914, this was where the ammunition trains from the Chilwell shell filling station (see page 274) joined the main line. Then it was a very busy place and six of their number died in the Great War. Three were number takers, their job was to record the numbers of goods wagons leaving the yards, essentially a similar job to the demurragemen. The scale of the operation at Chilwell would have meant that the yard required a good number of number takers. The other three to die were all described as porters at Attenborough. It is likely that these roles were also related to the freight side since the railway station itself was very small. Unlike many of the railway locations, those who died were all towards the end of the war with the earliest in August 1917 and the remainder in 1918 with one dying in captivity in Berlin after the war ended.

Attenborough Munitions train, 17/9/16.
NRM 1997-7397_DY_10552

Attenborough Station. IWM HU096429

Horace Randle	Pte	1st	Coldstream Guards	16	10	18	20	Vis en artois	Number taker
A Richards	Pte	2/5th	East Lancs	24	11	18		Berlin	Number taker
E Watson	Gnr	334 Siege Bty	RGA	14	10	18		Ramleh	Number taker
Gordon Smedley	Pte	2/5th	East Lancs	30	4	18	20	St Sever	Porter
JW Huckell	Pte	2nd	Notts & Derby	19	9	18		Vis en Artois	Porter
John Herrett	Pte	7th	Royal West Kent	2	8	17	20	Menin Gate	Porter

Cambridge, GER

Twenty-three men died who served at the station or sheds around Cambridge. There were 3 firemen; 3 engine cleaners; 3 shunters; a signal fitters labourer; 4 porters; 2 porter guards; a parcels clerk; and a coalman.

Five men joined up at the outbreak of war. Alfred Kelly, who had been an 'extra porter' enlisted in 1914, joined the Suffolks and was killed in October 1916 serving with the 2nd West Yorks on the Somme. He has no known grave and is commemorated on the Thiepval memorial. Percy Chanter had been a shunter and survived for four years until he was killed with B Battery 152 Brigade of the Royal Field Artillery in July 1918. Fred Clark had been a permanent way labourer who joined the 1st Bedfords and was killed in October 1917 fighting around Passchendaele and is commemorated at Tyne Cot. Leonard Benton had been an engine cleaner and was one of the first to join up on 4 September 1914 having worked for GER for only six months before war was declared. John Searle, another engine cleaner, joined the railway at about the same time and together with Leonard Benton they joined 1st Cambridgeshire's together. Leonard Benton died in October 1915, but John Searle survived until July 1917 and was awarded the MM. A third man joined the 1st Cambridgeshires, Henry Saunders, who had been in the pre-war Territorial Army and would have been mobilised at the start of the conflict. In the railway he had been an under shunter, but by the time he was killed in September 1917 he was a Sergeant, and a holder of the MM.

There are 715 cleaners who died in the 12,500, many of whom would have cleaned locomotives like Leonard Benton and John Searle. Engine cleaner was a means of gaining entry into the railway and a stepping stone to a footplate career. Harry Sharratt, a former cleaner at Stoke who survived the war having served in the Rail Operating Division, described locomotive cleaning: '*You started on the railway as a cleaner and after two to three months initiation you began to move up the seniority. Everything was based on seniority. You were allocated an engine and you checked that engine. Your rota followed the rota of the engine. If the locomotive worked days then you worked nights and when it was on nights you worked days. You spent seven or eight hours of the ten and a half cleaning your engine. Using clean water and tallow on the boiler if it was hot, and mineral oil on wheels.*'[5] In Sharratt's case, in any spare time on the night shifts, he would be sent out 'knocking up', a thankless job waking up the drivers for their turn of duty. He recalls that this would often involve hanging around in doorways waiting between one call and the next. Like everything in the railway promotion was on seniority and every role had a hierarchy. As a locomotive cleaner you began cleaning the shunters and local goods trains, progressing eventually to the prestigious passenger engines. 'After about three years of seniority you might take the odd turn at firing, if a fireman hadn't turned up. Generally it was on the shunter and that man moved up, but eventually your turn came for regular fireman work.'[6] There was a hierarchy of locomotives and so a hierarchy of cleaners, but operating around the same locomotives there were hierarchies of firemen and drivers each man perfectly attuned to their level of seniority. Boys, often following in their father's footsteps, would covet a role as a cleaner, because cleaner could lead eventually to driving the greatest express trains of the day.

Two men from Cambridge died with the sinking of the RMS *Aragon* Arthur Thurston a former porter who was only with GER a few months before enlisting in December 1916 and joining 98th Light Railway Operating Company, and Herbert Beamiss, who joined GER in April 1916 and had been an acting fireman and had joined 5th Bedfords in April 1917. It is unlikely that they would have worked together as railwaymen but the men from Cambridge died together on the same ship.

Bombardment of stations

On 16 December 1914, four Battle-cruisers, five cruisers and 18 destroyers of the German fleet bombarded the East coast towns of Whitby, Scarborough, Hartlepool and West Hartlepool. During the short bombardment lasting 80 minutes, 1,150 shells were fired into the towns causing 137 fatalities and over 400 injured including women and children. The railway stations at Scarborough and West Hartlepool were amongst those hit. At Scarborough 'a number of shells fell within the vicinity including one within the yard, and a porter picked up a shell on the platform! Many people at once rushed to the station and boarded a train, the engine driver of which is reported to have sent the sensational telegram to his wife: "shells falling thickly around me. I am alright".'[7] West Hartlepool was also hit and sustained damage.

Some Railway Roles

Many of the hundreds of railway trades feature amongst the railway dead, but 74 per cent came from just 40 roles, the most numerous being clerk at 1,943, followed by porter, 1,750, and labourer, 1,240. Today many of these job roles have changed; the computer has pretty well made the clerk role redundant; there are few if any porters left. The fireman can only be found on preserved railways, although the last few from the steam age may still be found driving locomotives. The messenger too was eliminated, along with the horsekeeper, telegraphist and telephonist. Platelayers still exist in the

---

5   IWM Sound Archive, 12850, Harry Sharratt.
6   IWM Sound Archive, 12850, Harry Sharratt.
7   GER Magazine Volume 5, Number 50, February 1915, 45.

form of Network Rail track workers as do ticket examiners, and policemen are now no longer from individual companies but under the aegis of the British Transport Police. Whether the role is long extinct, substantially changed or not, it is timely to consider and recognise the contribution made by just a few railwaymen in those roles.

Creosoter
Three men died from the Great Western creosoting works at Hayes. Those who have creosoted fences in the open air can only imagine the strength of the fumes in an enclosed factory. Whilst the conditions on the Western Front must have been unimaginable working in a creosoting works in the early 20th century must come a close second. Arthur Poole, Mark Shadwell and Charles Smith were all creosoters and served and died with 1st Loyal North Lancs, 1st Middlesex and 76th Field Ambulance RAMC.

Dining Saloon Attendants
Thirteen dining saloon attendants died, these men were mainly from St Pancras on the Midland and Euston on the L&NWR. Sergeant Frederick Pywell of the 21st Middlesex and Private A Shorney from 13th Londons died on 10 April 1917, they both had worked at Euston.

Draughtsman
Of the 38 draughtsmen who died, 15 were officers which, given the greater requirement for educational qualification, is not surprising. What does seem surprising is that 23 were not officers. Of the officers five served with the Royal Engineers and seven with the infantry, with two in the artillery and one the RAF. Given their professional qualifications it is surprising more weren't in the engineers.

Walter Reed was a Captain with 10th Siege Battery RGA and died on 27 October 1916 and had worked for NER in Hull. He was awarded the MC (see page 256). Captain William Scotcher was also awarded the MC, and was killed in an air accident (see pages 150 and 238).

Fish Porters
railway companies were such vast and integrated businesses that they even employed fish checkers and porters on the docks of Grimsby, Lowestoft and Great Yarmouth. Eleven died including four serving with 10th Lincolns, Company Sergeant Major J England, Sergeant Joe Oxley, Private Christopher Marshall and Private John Russell. Marshall and Russell were both killed on the first day of the Battle of the Somme and have no known grave and are commemorated on the Thiepval memorial.

Crane Lad
The GER owned Hull Docks lost ten crane lads, two of whom were awarded the MM. Sergeant Harry Butler of 150th Company MGC and Private Fred Petty of 5th KOYLI. Private Reginald Dunn serving with 1/3rd Northumbrian Field Ambulance was captured and died whilst a POW.

Telegraphist / Telephonist
There were 44 telegraphists / telephonists in the 12,500, 13 of whom served in the signals section of the RE which eventually was to become the Royal Corps of Signals. Four, all from the Midland Railway, died far away from the main theatres of war in Africa. John Hopewell from Trent Lock and Matthew Atkinson from Derby in Mombasa, Alfred Sheard from Morecombe, in Dar Es Salaam and C E Higgins from Normanton in Tanzania. Ernest Hilton from Midland Railway at Heysham was the wireless operator on HMS *Nepaulin* an ex-Glasgow and South West Railway ship, and went down with the ship when she was sunk in April 1917.

Platelayer

Of the 230 platelayers who died 27 died serving with the Rail Operating Division and five with the 17th Northumberland Fusiliers, who would have continued working in railway type roles. Many of the remaining 198 were infantrymen.

Policemen

It is likely that few people are aware that the Police on the British railway network are one of the world's oldest constabularies and that railway policeman is one of the earliest roles on the railway. Sir Robert Peel passed an act in 1829 which paved the way for the formation of the Metropolitan Police, the oldest police force in the world. In 1830, the Liverpool and Manchester Railway had a number of 'policemen'. Initially the job was as much to do with the safe passage of trains as it was fighting crime, and as such railway police were the first signalmen. Indeed railway signallers are still often termed 'Bobbies'. In order to ensure safe passage along the railway line, the early routes had a Police 'house' or refuge every mile or so where the policeman was stationed. This is thought to have given the name to the now ubiquitous Police Station and may have been the origin for the word now used to describe a place where a customer boards a train, a railway station. As the railway expanded so thousands of construction workers were employed digging the cuttings and making the tunnels and embankments. The men were called navigators, or navvies for short. These fairly wild individuals needed to be controlled and the peace of the rural environments maintained; an early role for the railway policeman.

Every company had a police force, and once mechanical signalling was invented they could concentrate on fighting crime and keeping peace. At least 65 railway policemen were killed in the war and 18, over a quarter, served in the Guards. Five continued their policework with the Military Police. One, A Grant from Derby, served as a Trooper in the Royal Horse Guards.

Railway policing remains a specialist preserve and is now vested in British Transport Police, funded by the railway and for the railway and was formed in 1949.

1st Grenadier Guards	2nd Grenadier Guards
Sgt Alfred Gundry, Parkestone & Stratford	Pte John Beddis, Sheffield
L/Sgt Henry Carnall, Birmingham	Pte Edward Jordan, Liverpool
Pte SJ Cannell, Birmingham	
Pte Arthur Hind, London	
Pte HE Miller (GWR)	
Pte James Shepley (GNR)	
1st Coldstream Guards	**3rd Coldstream Guards**
Sgt Alfred Scott, Sunderland	Cpl Archibald Summers, Sheffield
Pte Harold Voyce	Pte Albert Walker, Leicester
	Pte PF Bartle, Grimsby
	L/Cpl Alexander Carr, Middlesborough

Right: IWM Q004005

CHAPTER 9

RAILWAY PEOPLE

Some senior railwaymen

The vast majority of railwaymen who served were private soldiers but some came from the higher echelons of the railway companies. The highest-ranking railwayman who died was Brigadier Holland from L&NWR. Another senior officer was Lt Colonel Feversham, Tory MP, Lord and director of NER. There was also Lt Colonel Carus-Wilson who had a rich and interesting career as both soldier and railwayman.

Lt Colonel Lord Feversham
15 September 1916

Director

AIF Burial Ground Flers

NER

Charles Duncombe, 2nd Lord Feversham was born into opulence and a 14,000 acre estate in North Yorkshire. Aged twenty-seven he became a Conservative MP and subsequently a director of NER. Commissioned into his local Territorial Yeomanry regiment, the Yorkshire Hussars, which he went on to command before forming his own Battalion, 21st (Yeomanry Rifles) Kings Royal Rifle Corps in 1915.

The 21st KRRC entered the line with 18th KRRC at Courcelette on the Somme on 15 September 1916. Lord Feversham was killed in action leading from the front in what had been the longest advance so far on the Somme battlefield. All objectives were taken, but 28 officers and 726 men from the two battalions were killed or injured. Lord Feversham was buried alongside his deerhound, also killed in action, and other railwaymen from his battalion. F R Cook, who worked for NER at York, and T Benson, a Midland railwayman from Langley Mill. Four others were also killed.

A fellow officer was Antony Eden who would go on to become Prime Minister in the 1950s. At the time the aristocrat from the north-east was the adjutant of the 21st KRRC, and the youngest in the army at only nineteen. He went on to win an MC and to become a Brigade-Major by the time he was twenty-one. Eden's father Sir William Eden, the 10th Baronet, subsequently became a director of LNER and had a railway station built on the main London to Edinburgh line at Windestone Hall near Bishop Auckland.

Cecil Sidley	Thiepval	15.9.16	NER	Darlington
Oliver Grieveson	Thiepval	16.9.16	NER	Selby
AC Kilding	Guards Cemy	17.9.16	NER	Middlesborough
Bertie Witt	Thiepval	17.9.16	Midland	Brent

It was Eden who led a small party to find and bury Lord Feversham: 'Sadly we set about our task. I read a few lines from the burial service which someone had lent me at headquarters. Dale set up the wooden cross, we gave our commanding officer a last salute and turned away, leaving him to Picardy and the shells.'[1]

---

1   Anthony Eden, 'Another World', 177. Quoted by John Lewis-Stempel in *Six Weeks*, 296.

Brigadier General Gerald Holland DSO CB CMG CIE
(Companion of the Indian Empire) MID

26 June 1917	Dock and Marine Superintendent
Aged 56	Holyhead
St Sever	L & NWR

Gerald Holland was the highest ranking and most decorated railwayman to die in the Great War. He worked for L&NWR but was a mariner by profession and at the time of his mobilisation was the dock and marine superintendent at Holyhead.

Prior to joining L&NWR he worked for Royal Indian Marine and served with the Burma Expeditionary Force from 1887 to 1889, and in 1890 was awarded the DSO. He commanded the Royal Indian Marine troopship, the *Warren Hastings*, which, on the 6 January 1897 left Cape Town for Mauritius with nearly a thousand passengers including the 1st Kings Royal Rifle Corps. Early on 14 January, eight miles off course and steaming at full speed in pitch darkness and pouring rain, she ran straight into rocks on the coast of Reunion. Holland averted almost certain disaster and loss of life by keeping the engines at full ahead fixing the ship in the rocks and giving him sufficient time, and a steady enough platform, to organise a controlled evacuation of passengers and crew. He achieved this for the loss of only two lives.

Warren Hastings (Courtesy of the RGJ museum)

He received a court martial and a reprimand for his troubles, perhaps not for the recovery, but for being so off course in the first place. He also received an exemplary order from the Governor of India for his fine conduct and saving of life.

On three occasions he was mentioned in Despatches and was also awarded the Companion of the Indian Empire. After retiring from the RIM, he was Marine Superintendent firstly in Fleetwood and then Holyhead before joining the Royal Engineers as a Lt Colonel to become the assistant director, then director, of Inland Water Transportation department in France. He died on sick leave from illness contracted whilst on active service in France.

Lt Colonel Trevor Carus-Wilson DSO TD

23 March 1918   Engineering Department
Aged 48   Paddington
St Sever   GWR

Lt. Colonel Carus-Wilson was a Territorial, and served with the Composite Cyclist Corps in South Africa during the Boer War. He joined GWR Engineering Department in 1899 and spent some time working in Swindon, and at the time of mobilisation in August 1914 was an assistant to the New Works engineer. After mobilisation he was at first engaged in guarding the wireless station at Poldhu, and later was sent to India and served on the Viceroy's Guard of Honour, which couldn't have been considered too onerous. This somewhat cushy lifestyle didn't last and by December 1915 he formed and commanded the 5th Duke of Cornwall's Light Infantry, with whom he embarked for France in May 1916.

In March 1918, he ushered his battalion forward attempting to plug a hole in the line where the Germans had broken through in the village of Verlaines. The Cornishmen deployed from a railway cutting, with no time for planning, briefing or reconnaissance, and advanced 4,000 yards to their objective. As they advanced the band played the regimental march, which shows a degree of dash and spirit, although you have to wonder how a band found themselves in the thick of what was quite a desperate battle. In the attack Carus-Wilson, who had been mentioned in despatches three times and awarded the DSO, was injured, and evacuated to hospital in Rouen, almost certainly by a British ambulance train, where he died a few days later.

Lt Colonel Samuel Sheppard DSO

21 August 1915   Director
Aged 50   Mersey Railway and
Green Hill, Gallipoli   Brecon and Merthyr Railway

Samuel Sheppard was a stockbroker and director of two railway companies. He served in the Imperial Yeomanry in the Boer War and was awarded the DSO for leading a party which swam a river capturing some enemy held islands and rescuing a drowning man. During the Great War he served with the Hertfordshire Yeomanry and was killed in action leading his cavalrymen in a dismounted attack at Chocolate Hill in Gallipoli. Eye witnesses report that despite being terribly wounded by shrapnel whilst leading his regiment, his last command was 'Go on, the Herts! Go on the Herts!'[2]

Railwaymen from Argentina

Much of the Argentine railway was built by Britons. The two largest companies were the Central Argentine Railway and the Buenos Aires Great Southern Railway. Both had their company headquarters in London. No wonder then that British railwaymen sought their fortunes in South America. Outbreak of war led to many returning and signing up and at least 161 lost their life.

William Scotcher trained as a draughtsman in Ilford with GER before joining the Central Argentine Railway. He joined the East Yorkshires but was killed in a flying accident in 1918. Wilfred Hicks was an employee of the Buenos Aires and Pacific Railway in London and lived at 49 St Helens Gardens, North Kensington, he was commissioned into the RAF and killed aged nineteen on 27 October 1918. Cyril Smethurst was another head office employee, killed on 31 March 1917 with the HAC. Victor MacMullen, a Lance Corporal in the South Irish Horse and who originated

2   See www.roll-of-honour.com/Hertfordshire/Stalbansabbey/Hertsyeoww1rollofhonour.html

from Cork, had been employed with the Buenos Aires Western Railway in Argentina. Lieutenant James Fairbairn was a Central Argentine Railway employee who served with the Sheffield City Battalion of the Yorkshire and Lancashire Regiment on the North West Frontier. He was injured in both feet but eventually returned to Argentina in March 1920 only to die within the month. He does not appear on the Commonwealth War Graves Commmission database, but is named on the memorial originally erected at Retiro station in 1925, but which now resides at the Charcarita British Cemetery.[3]

Railway Families

The railway was built upon teamwork and selfless endeavour. As soldiers, railwaymen would have fitted in and got on with whatever fate brought them. In conflict they had their buddies to draw on, they knew the dangers and when the risk was high or low. But for those who remained at home it felt high risk all the time, dreading the message that their friend, son, father or lover had been injured or killed. Many families took a hammering throughout the war. If it is hard to imagine the impact on the parent of a loss of a son fighting in war, it is unimaginable to contemplate the grief of the mother who loses two sons, or the wife who loses her husband and son, or to imagine the parents who find their seventeen, sixteen or even fifteen-year-old son lost to the war.

Fathers and Sons

From her house at 10 Dover Street, West Hartlepool, on 15 January 1915, Margaret Booth may have been kept awake by the unprecedented storm raging through the night. She no doubt would have worried about her fifty-eight-year-old husband William and her twenty-two-year-old son Edward, both crew on the NER tug *Char* (See page 194). She could not have known as she worried that the tug had been holed under the waterline whilst trying to secure a ship in the ferocious seas, and William Booth, the 1st Engineer, drowned immediately as he tended the engines below the waterline. Edward, a deck hand, may have survived a little longer, but the crew and ship were lost somewhere on the Goodwin Sands. It must be the nightmare of the mother or wife of any mariner that their loved one should be lost at sea, but especially so if father and son are killed on the same day.

1st Engineer William Booth HM *Tug Char* 16/1/15, Aged 58 Plymouth NER, Tyne Dock	Deck Hand Edward Booth HM *Tug Char* 16/1/15. Aged 22 Plymouth NER, Tyne Dock

Margaret Thomas lived at 75 London Road, in the close-knit Anglesey port of Holyhead. Her husband was a stoker on HMS *Queen Mary* and her son a deck boy on the L&NWR vessel SS *Anglia* [see page 197]. The *Anglia*, a hospital ship, struck a mine just off the coast of Folkestone, and sunk killing 150 injured soldiers and 25 crew. Amongst them was her sixteen-year-old son Richard, twenty-year-old cabin boy Robert Williams, whose mother lived further along London Road, and fifteen-year-old Holyhead born ship's cook, J Hughes. Only six months later Margaret lost her husband when *Queen Mary* was sunk at the battle of Jutland (See page 171).

3   Sylvester Damus http://www.diaagency.ca/railways/Casualties.htm

Deck Boy Richard Thomas SS *Anglia* 17/11/15 Aged 16 Tower Hill L & NWR, Holyhead	Stoker Richard Thomas HMS *Queen Mary* 31/5/16 Portsmouth L & NWR, Holyhead, fireman

Charlotte Povey lived just outside of Reading at 4 Queen Street, Caversham. She too lost her husband who had worked for GWR at Reading as a blacksmith, and less than 18 months later her seventeen-year-old son, Alfred, a machinist, was killed.

Cpl Charles Povey 2/1st Berks Battery RA 16/4/15 Aged 47 Buxton Great Western, Reading, blacksmith	Pte Alfred Povey 6th Royal Berkshires 23/9/15 Aged 17 Beaucourt Great Western, Reading, machinist

Maria Sawyer of 7 Gifford St, Caledonian Rd, Islington, lost her forty-two-year-old husband in the fighting around Arras in March 1918 and just over six months later her nineteen-year-old son. They were both called Cherry!

Pte Cherry Sawyer 2nd Essex 28/3/18 Aged 42 Arras L & NWR, Maiden Lane, loader	Pte Cherry Sawyer 9th Norfolks 8/10/18 Aged 19 Busigny L & NWR, Maiden Lane, number taker

Twins

Having her twin boys on the same ship must have been a worry to Isabelina Villiers Russell of 17 Audley Street, Crewe, a source of many sleepless nights. John and Henri were sick berth attendents on HMS *Formidable* [See page 168].

On 1 January 1915, *Formidable* struck a mine and sunk and only 199 of the 750 crew were saved. John is commemorated on the Chatham Naval Memorial indicating he was lost at sea. Henri is buried in Crewe, suggesting that he may have survived the sinking only to perish from the ordeal. The death of the twins is said to have resulted in a change of Naval policy to prevent close family members from serving on the same ship, although no firm proof of this has been located.

Sick Berth Attendent Henri Villiers Russell 1/1/15 Aged 29 HMS *Formidable* Coppenhall L&NWR, Crewe, labourer	Sick Berth Attendent John Villiers Russell 1/1/15 Aged 29 HMS *Formidable* Chatham L&NWR, Crewe, labourer

Twin brothers John and Henry Villiers Russell who died as a result of the loss of the Formidable

Harry and George Revell, ex-GWR firemen, were twins who served in different battalions of the Devonshire regiment in different parts of the globe.

Pte Harry Revell 9th Devons 30/9/15 Aged 23 Loos Great Western, Llanelly, fireman	Pte George Revell 6th Devons 1/7/17 Basra Great Western, Newton Abbot, fireman

Brothers

At least 25 mothers lost at least two railwaymen sons in the Great War.

Brothers, Privates Reginald and Gerald Wilkinson were clerks with NER, Reginald at Ulleskelf and Gerald at nearby Leeds, they served in the same battalion, the 15th West Yorkshires, the so called 'Leeds Pals' and they were both killed, along with 250 of their battalion, on the first day of the Battle of the Somme on 1 July 1916. Many of the bodies were never recovered and today the ground around the village of Serre must still contain a lot of Yorkshire. Reginald and Gerald Wilkinson are just two of the 72,000 commemorated on the Thiepval memorial to the missing, alongside them are at least three other railwaymen from the Leeds Pals – Percy Bond and George Gurmin both clerks, and Thomas Swindells, a train recorder, all three worked for the Midland Railway in Leeds.

Pte Reginald Wilkinson 15th (Leeds Pals) West Yorks 1/7/16 Thiepval NER, Ulleskelf, clerk	L/Cpl Gerald Wilkinson 15th (Leeds Pals) West Yorks 1/7/16 Thiepval NER, Leeds, clerk

Mr and Mrs Leggett of 282 Ferndale Road, Swindon, lost two of their sons, both of whom had been employed in the GWR workshops. William who had been a coach body maker was serving with the 1st Wiltshires when on 16 June 1915 the battalion, having marched from Ypres along the Menin Road attacked German positions at Hooge. Initial gains were soon lost when the Wiltshires were forced to withdraw through lack of ammunition. As they withdrew, partially over open ground, they sustained many casualties, including twenty-two-year-old William.

Mr & Mrs Leggett, can barely have got over the death of their son, before news filtered through that their younger son Ernest, aged twenty-one, a former fitter at number 3 shop, had been killed serving with the same battalion. Ernest had been defending trenches around Hooge and many were killed and injured as sustained and heavy artillery bombardment gradually destroyed the trenches. Trenches that looked out onto ground where William's body had been lost. Ernest's body would become lost in the same ground.

L/Cpl William Leggett 1st Wiltshires 16/6/15 Aged 22 Menin Gate Great Western, Swindon, coach body maker number 19 shop	L/Cpl Ernest Leggett 1st Wiltshires 2/9/15 Aged 21 Menin Gate Great Western, Swindon fitter number 3 shop

It is probable that Ernest fought in the same battle in which William had been killed, and it is unlikely that Mr & Mrs Leggett set eyes on Ernest after William's death. It is doubtful whether the parents would have been aware that both boys were killed on the same small piece of ground. They are commemorated on the Menin Gate memorial to the missing.

It cannot have been a much better experience at 65 Edinburgh Street in Hull, home to Margaret Turner, she lost two sons within two weeks in 1917. Sergeant George Turner had been a fireman for NER in Hull, and was killed aged twenty-one serving with the 5th East Yorks. She may not have even received notification of his death before brother James, aged nineteen, serving with the 11th East Yorks, and a former cleaner with NER at Hull, was killed. Her sons are commemorated at Arras memorial to the missing.

Sgt George Turner 5th East Yorks 23/4/17 Aged 21 Arras NER Hull, fireman	Pte James Turner 11th (Hull Tradesmen) East Yorks 3/5/17 Aged 19 Arras NER, Hull, cleaner

Joseph Robinson, an NER railwayman, and his wife Mary, who lived at Station Yard, Kirkby Stephen, near Penrith, had to contend with the loss of their son George, who had been an NER clerk at Cockfield, and was killed aged eighteen in Gallipoli in 1915 serving with the 6th Yorkshires.

George's younger brother Frank joined the West Yorks and nearly survived the war, but was killed aged nineteen at the beginning of September 1918. It is impossible to imagine the strains, worries and grief of Joesph and Mary, and millions of others like them.

Pte George Robinson 6th Yorks 22/8/15 Aged 18 Helles Memorial NER Cockfield, clerk	Rfn Frank Robinson 8th West Yorks 1/9/18 Aged 19 Vaulx Hill NER, Pickton Junction, clerk

Emma and Henry Read lived about a mile from Charlotte Povey at 179 Caversham Road, Reading. Their son Walter had been a clerk for GWR and was killed serving with the Berkshire Yeomanry in Gallipoli. Similarly to Frank Robinson, Walter's younger brother, Stanley, would have had to cope with his elder brother's sacrifice, whilst still turning up at work as a clerk at Reading. Probably many of the folk around would have known Walter, and as soon as he could Stanley joined up. Stanley became one of the first aircrew of the Royal Air Force (see page 149) and a commissioned officer. He was killed in September 1918 when on a bombing mission in the closing days of the war.

Pte Walter Read Berkshire Yeomanry 21/8/15 Aged 20 Green Hill Great Western, Reading, Clerk	2Lt Stanley Read 27th Sqn RAF 25/9/18 Aged 19 Grand Servacourt Great Western, Reading, Clerk

Also in Reading were David and Flora Sweetzer. The Sweetzers lived at 73 Catherine Street. Two of their sons were railwaymen working for GWR at Reading. Herbert was a fireman, and Lewis a call boy. Their elder brother Jesse, not believed to be a railwayman, died serving with the 1st Royal Berkshires at Neuve Chapelle. Just over a year later Herbert was lost at sea with HMS *Hampshire*, which was on passage to Russia with Lord Kitchener aboard when it was sunk by a mine off the Orkneys. Having lost two sons to the campaign David and Flora must have prayed that Lewis would survive. He didn't, serving with the 7th Berkshires he was killed just six weeks before the Armistice.

Pte Jesse Sweetzer 1st Royal Berks 28/4/15 Aged 31 Vielle-Chapelle (not believed to be a railwayman)	Stoker 1st Class Herbert Sweetzer HMS Hampshire 5/6/16 Aged 24 Portsmouth Great Western, Reading, fireman	Pte Lewis Sweetzer 7th Royal Berks 25/9/18 Aged 20 Doiran Great Western, Reading, call boy

Eliza Sissen, of 3 York Street, Manningtree in Essex, probably had reason to think that her son William would survive the war; unlike his younger brother Julian who had been a cellarman for GER in the hotels department, who was killed in March 1918 aged twenty-three. But only three days before the Armistice William Sissen, a stoker in the Royal Navy, died at Hasler Royal Naval Hospital from influenza. One of millions across the globe who died in the 1918 epidemic.

L/Cpl Julian Sissen 9th Squadron Machine Gun Corps 22/3/18 Aged 23 Pozieres GER, Hotel Department, cellarman	Stoker 1st Class William Sissen HM P31 8/11/18 Aged 28 Hasler RN GER, Steamers, fireman.

Mary and John Robbie, from Manse Cottage, Drumoak, Aberdeenshire, had also lost a son in the early part of the war. William, a former ticket inspector for the Great North of Scotland Railway was killed aged eighteen on one of the last days of the Battle of the Somme in November 1916. Mary and John may have assumed, having passed armistice without receiving the dreaded telegram informing of death or injury, that William's elder brother Francis was safe. The twenty-two-year-old former GNSR ticket inspector, died on 26 November two weeks after armistice. It is unlikely that he was injured in battle since his unit was a static hospital. More likely he too died of influenza. Whatever the cause, John and Mary lost two sons to the war.

Pte William Robbie 7th Gordon Highlanders 13/11/16 Aged 18 Hunters Cemetery GNSR, Banchory, ticket inspector	L/Cpl Francis Robbie 41st Static Hospital RAMC 26/11/18 Aged 22 Villers Bretonneux GNSR, School Hill, assistant ticket inspector

Frederick and Hettie Garwood of Claris, Rectory Road, Stanford Le Hope, also lost a second son after the war. Gunner Albert Garwood, aged nineteen, died on 4 December 1918 in hospital in Le Havre. They had lost their twenty-one-year-old son, Ernest, in April in bitter fighting around Arras. Both sons had been porters for the Midland Railway at Stanford Le Hope.

Pte Ernest Garwood	Gunner Albert Garwood
1st East Surrey	315 Siege Battery RGA
27/4/18 Aged 21	4/12/18 Aged 19
Aire	Ste Marie, Le Havre
Midland, Stanford Le Hope, porter	Midland, Stanford Le Hope, porter

Charlotte Jones, of 3 Knoll Avenue, Neath, lost her two sons, both former clerks for Great Western. Henry, a Second Lieutenant with 10th Royal Welsh Fusiliers, had been mentioned in Despatches and died on one of the last days of the Somme. Her younger son died less than a year later close to Ypres. When Henry was killed, she would have been able to draw support from her husband, also called Henry, but he died before William was killed in action. Poor Charlotte lost her two sons and husband in eight months.

2Lt Henry Jones MID	Pte William Jones
10th Royal Welsh Fusiliers	13th Royal Welsh Fusiliers
13/11/16 Aged 25	21/7/17, Aged 28
Euston Road	Artillery Wood
Great Western, Swansea, clerk	Great Western, Britton Ferry, clerk

It was the same for Hannah Hill of 113a Edinburgh Street, Hull, who lost her younger son Rowland who went down with HMS *Bulwark* in 1914. She then lost her husband Joseph, and then her elder son George who was killed with the 1st Northumberland Fusiliers around Ypres in 1916. Both boys had been freight shunters with the NER in Hull. She may have been able to draw strength from George's wife Beatrice, however not too long afterwards Beatrice remarried!

Able Seaman Rowland Hill	L/Cpl George Hill
HMS Bulwark	1st Northumberland Fusiliers
26/11/14 Aged 24	16/6/16 Aged 28
Portsmouth	Menin Gate
NER, Hull, freight shunter	NER Hull West, freight shunter

David and Thomas Allister lived at 28 Belper Street, Garston and worked at Garston Dock station, David as a labeller and Thomas a messenger. They joined local battalions. Thomas the 18th Kings while David joined the 8th East Lancs. Both battalions were committed to the fighting on 31 July 1917 on the first day of the Third Battle of Ypres, later known as Passchendaele, and Tom was killed. David was killed barely two months later whilst still fighting around Ypres on 11 September 1917. David, a Lance Corporal, was awarded the Military Medal. David is commemerated at Tyne Cot cemetery and Thomas at Menin Gate in Ypres; both have no known grave.

Pte Thomas Allister 18th Btn Kings (Liverpool) 31st July 1917 Tyne Cot, messenger	L/Cpl David Allister MM 8th Btn East Lancs. 11th September 1917 Menin Gate, labeller

Youngest

The vast majority of those killed were aged between their late teens and mid-twenties, but some were even younger. At least 255 railwaymen died aged only eighteen, and 52 were only seventeen, and some were younger still.

Private Ernest Plane, son of Margaret Plane of 80 Cambrian Road, Neyland, Pembrokeshire, formerly a machinist at GWR's locomotive and carriage section in Neath, served with the 6th Welsh and died aged sixteen on 30 November 1915 and is buried at Dud Corner Loos. Private Thomas Eady, son of Frederick and Minnie Eady of 26 Trefield Road, Bristol, of 7th Gloucesters died on 2 January 1916 aged sixteen in Gallipoli. He had been a note collector at the Midland Railways goods yard in Bristol. Fred Kitchener, the sixteen-year-old son of Beth Kitchener of 115 Gladstone Avenue, Wood Green, was a drummer boy with the 7th Middlesex but had been employed as a lad messenger for GNR, he died on 22 June 1915 in France. Sixteen year old Steven Curd, son of Frederick and Charlotte of 2 De Montfort Road, Brighton, had been a greaser for the LB&SCR but volunteered for the Navy and was serving on HMS *Invincible* at the Battle of Jutland.

http://www.mkheritage.co.uk/la/

Albert French does not feature either on his company's roll of honour nor in the St Paul's remembrance book to railwaymen who died in the Great War. It is known that he had been employed as an apprentice fitter between July 1913 and October 1915, at the L&NWR works at Wolverton. His work card explains that he 'left without notice' and this might explain why he wasn't included in the list of railwaymen who served. Presumably, eager to sign up and do his bit, when the offer came he left work without serving his notice period. You do have to wonder how many other volunteers have been airbrushed out of railway memorials as a result of their eagerness to enlist overcoming their contractual obligation to their employer. Since he doesn't appear on any railway memorial or role of honour he doesn't feature in the 12,500, but since we know from his railway records that he was definitely a railwayman it has been decided to include him. Albert French went on to join 18th Kings Royal Rifle Corps, who embarked for France on 2 May 1916. Forty-four days later on 15 June, just a week before his 17th birthday he was killed.

On the reverse of his employment record someone had written that he was 'killed whilst sandbagging a parapet of a trench... by four machine gun bullets in the chest'.[4] It is interesting that someone was diligent enough to record this but he was accorded no place on the roll of honour. If this is because of petty bureaucracy on the part of railway administrators since he didn't give notice then that is very sad.

The detail of his death must have come from an eye witness and somehow this message must have got back to Wolverton; possibly from others who joined from the works.

http://www.mkheritage.co.uk/la/

Some died as young as fifteen. Charles Larson, a 'mess room boy' who lived with his mother Eva at 32 Levington Street, Grimsby, was one of 17 crew of the GCR owned SS *Leicester*, who were killed on 21 January 1916 when the ship struck a mine just off Folkestone whilst the former ferry was on passage from Portsmouth to Cromaty. Albert Gilham, son of Annie Gilham from 4 Wood Street, Dover, was another fifteen-year-old boy serving on a railway ship, the SECR owned SS *Achille Adam*, which was sunk by U31 off Beachy Head on 23 March 1917, killing Albert and five other crew. George Sanderson, from 38 Dodds Street, Darlington, who had been employed by NER at Darlington, also fifteen, was serving as a bugler with the 2/5th Yorkshire Regiment. It is recorded that he died at home and is buried at Newcastle Byker Cemetery and it seems unlikely that he would have served at the front.

Oldest
At the other end of the scale the eldest to die in the field was CQMS Thomas Doyne of 10th Duke of Wellingtons who died at the casualty clearing station at Heilly Station on the Somme aged fifty-six. He had been employed as a labourer at L&NWR's Dublin North Wall. The oldest recorded death was of Private Walter Simmonds, who had worked in the GWR loco and carriage depot at Oxford and died, aged sixty-seven serving with the 258th Protection Company Royal Defence Corps. He didn't die in action overseas and it is possible that he died of old age! The oldest known to have died due to enemy action, like the youngest, were non-combatants with the Merchantile Marine. Fireman John Jones was sixty when he died in the sinking of SS *Anglia*, Emanuel Laycock, Chief Engineer on SS *Hebble*, was sixty-two when the ship sank taking him with it. Daniel Wyborn also sixty-two and a fireman on the SECR SS *Achille Adam*. The oldest to die due to enemy action was Able Seaman John Rockett who was sixty-five when SS *Unity* sank on 2 May 1918.

4 http://www.mkheritage.co.uk/la

The Railway Family Through the Railway Magazine

By the outbreak of the Great War the railway had consolidated from several hundred small lines to something over a hundred with around 20 major companies, each with its own identity, and shortly after the war in 1923 this reduced further to the big four of LNER, LMS, GWR and Southern. Proud of their individuality, manifested in locomotive design, preferred architectural style down to colour schemes and the cut of uniforms, they were nonetheless similar in their culture and that of an all-embracing inclusive and holistic nature.

A hint of the culture of a typical company, GER, comes from their magazine giving a feel for the nature of the organisation. Produced monthly it provided something for everyone. Content included contemporary and historic information of British and foreign railway companies, updates from the athletics association, music society, ambulance corps, gardening notes, 'notes from the tea room' and a woman's page. Even included were a number of articles written totally in French. A section was dedicated to births, deaths and marriages, and during the war letters from the troops, and a growing roll of honour was included. A scan through any particular month gives the impression of an organisation which encouraged total participation whether at work or at rest.

The February 1915 edition devoted its cover to bones found on Red Hill at Goldhanger, Essex, and six pages concerning pre-historic and Roman remains. The bombardment of West Hartlepool railway station is mentioned in the article on 'War and the Railway'. The report on the GER annual general meeting held at the Liverpool Street Hotel on 12 February 1915 illustrates in detail information that the company obviously feel it was important to share with the workforce. Explaining that the railway had been in effect nationalised for the war, but going on to explain the basis for the financial deal that the company had with the government, namely that if the net receipts for 1914 were less than the net receipts for 1913 then the government would compensate. By flicking through the magazine you get an impression of the effort expended to produce such a varied and detailed production each month and the high quality of the output. GER, and the other railway companies who produced similar publications, must have seen a value in commitment and motivation of their workforce as a result of the information shared. However, there are tell-tale snippets of the hierarchy involved within the companies. In the annual general meeting report again 'No praise could be too high for those men of humbler grades who, sometimes day and night laboured for the good of the State without any desire to think of their own comfort' and 'everyone from the highest to the lowest has done his best'.[5] Railway organisations were built upon grades and status where everyone knew their position within the hierarchy and the next step for advancement. It has been said before in this book, but that is not too dissimilar to the approach of the armed forces.

For those men who were on the Western Front, and by the annual general meeting there had been 3,600 who had signed up out of their total workforce of 33,000, a 'War Relief Fund' had been set up in August 1914 at the outbreak of war. The GER magazine reported 'It was early realised that the absence of the menfolk would seriously affect the well being of the wives and mothers and "the lots of little things they'd left behind them". It was felt that most of the staff remaining on railway duty would wish to help in this emergency.'[6] 'In the case of soldiers' wives, the amounts paid through the fund added to the money received from the War Office, and should total a weekly sum equal to the husband's standard wage, provided such wage was no more than 20s, if more the income would be brought up to 4/5th of the standard wage, minimum £1/'[7] It goes on to say, 'as far as possible no home should suffer for the practical patriotism displayed by a member of the family.'[8] As early as February 1915 there were 50 widows created as a result of the war.

---

5   GER magazine, Volume 5, Number 51, March 1915, 91.
6   GER magazine, Volume 5, Number 50, February 1915, 52.
7   GER magazine, Volume 5, Number 50, February 1915, 52.
8   GER magazine, Volume 5, Number 50, February 1915, 52.

One hundred dolls dressed as nurses for sale at Liverpool Lime Street station.
NRM 1997-7059_HOR_F_1772

Railway companies recognised the volunteers and later conscripts who left their employment, and most recorded those who were killed. The first 'Toll for the Brave' of GER published in November 1914 is shown.

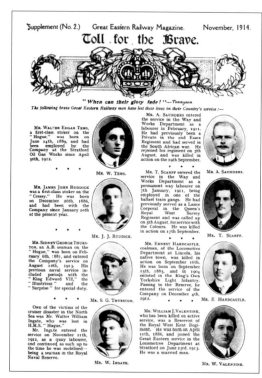

Throughout the war the magazines included letters, usually heavily censored, sketches, poems and increasingly, obituaries.

The railway companies and the families supported the soldiers in many ways, the men of the 17th Northumberland Fusiliers, for example, were sent cigarettes by NER at Christmas. The Lancashire and Yorkshire Railway raised money for railway troops in France with a sale of dolls dressed as nurses.

The GER magazine hints at what it must have been like in post-war employment. The content was largely unaltered with the 'Toll for the Brave' continuing to record war deaths into 1919. But there was scant mention of the demobilisation of soldiers back to railwaymen. Demobilisation is only mentioned on three occasions in the 1919, 1920 and 1921 magazines and in one of these cases it was referring to the demobilisation of War Department locomotives. Post-war articles included the odd piece on wartime reminiscences, an article on being a prisoner of war, and numerous mentions of 'welcome home' funds and parties such as:

> **'The King's Lynn G.E.R. Soldiers Welcome Home Fund'**
> The above fund has been formed at King's Lynn for the purpose of giving the returned soldiers a welcome home. Mr. J. E. Coston, J.P. (C.M.E.'s) is chairman, Mr. G. A. Wright (Parcels) secretary and Mr. R. Woodbine (station inspector) treasurer. The committee, as follows, represent the various departments: Mr. E. Wright (Clerical Coaching), M. Paige (Clerical Goods), Mr. Futter (Operating), Mr. Gibson (C.M.E's), Mr. Banyard (Electrical), Mr. Williamson (Goods) and Mr. Willmot (Coaching). It was arranged to have a social evening on July 3rd, but when the Mayor was approached for the use of the Town Hall and the purpose was stated, he and the Mayoress kindly offered to entertain all the returned railwayman to a tea and Concert at his own expense. This included men from the M. & G.N. railway. Besides the discharged men, the officers of the fund and a few others were invited to the tea'.[9]

There was overall no significant mention of the cessation of hostilities, or the return of soldiers, suggesting that it was not considered newsworthy, driven by the enormous numbers of those returning. In fact the only substantial mention of demobilisation was by Sir Henry Thornton the General Manager of GER meeting 200 staff and trades union officials and recorded in the 1921 magazine where he mentions that between 1913 and 1921 staff had increased by a third partially brought about by demobilisation.[10]

A more substantial article about demobilisation concerned the return of army great coats. 'As is well known, a soldier on demobilisation may hand in his overcoat, with a voucher, to any railway station and receive for it £1. The coats are forwarded by the railway to an Army Ordnance Depot and the railway subsequently receives credit. A very simple business, but some of our stations have been at times very hard pressed in handling it and as much as £120,000 has been paid out by the Great Eastern Railway stations alone, although the arrangement has been in operation for less than six months.'[11]

The GER magazine continues as per pre-war, in 1921 the first article concerning war memorials is included. There is no mention of how men who returned integrated back into their work, nor of how those who couldn't return to their previous occupation coped or were supported.

9   GER Magazine 9 Number 99, March 1919, 181.

10   GER Magazine 11 Number 123, March 1921, 216.

11   GER Magazine 9 Number 99, March 1919, 124.

CHAPTER 10

GALLANTRY AWARDS AND DECORATIONS

Reflecting nearly 100 years after the Great War it seems that everyone who fought experienced huge privation, discomfort, personal risk and deserved recognition. Everyone who fixed bayonets and marched into No Mans Land was worthy of a gallantry award. So should there be any special mention of those who were awarded gallantry awards? Railwaymen were awarded many medals and it is only fitting that a flavour of their deeds are recorded here.

Overall 5,357 decorations were awarded to railwaymen during the Great War including seven Victoria Crosses. Two of the recipients, Jacob Rivers from Midland Railway and John Miekle from Glasgow Barrhead and Kilmanock Railway, were awarded the VC posthumously, four others, all from L&NWR survived the war. The seventh VC was awarded to a former railwayman who moved on to other employment before the beginning of the war and is therefore not usually recognised as having been a railwayman.

HONOURS AWARDED TO RAILWAYMEN		
VC	Victoria Cross	7
KBE	Knight Batchelor	6
DSO	Distinguished Service Order – Senior Officers	30
MC	Military Cross – Officers	283
DFC	Distinguished Flying Cross – Officer	9
DSC	Distingished Service Cross – RN Officers	8
DCM	Distinguished Conduct Medal –Soldiers only	610
DSM	Distinguished Service Medal – Soldiers only	36
MM	Military Medal – Soldiers only	2517
AM	Albert Medal – Gallantry award (not in the contact with the enemy)	2

The KBEs and DSOs would have gone to senior officers, and almost certainly high-ranking managers within the railway companies, the MCs to junior officers from 2nd Lieutenant to Captain in recognition of 'an act or acts of exemplary gallantry during active operations against the enemy on land…' [1] The DCM was only awarded to Private Soldiers and Non-Commissioned Officers and was awarded for acts of exteme bravery and was seen as a 'near miss for the VC'. The army introduced the Military Medal in March 1916 for significant bravery, and over 2,500 were awarded to railwaymen, with the DCM being retained for exceptional acts of bravery. The Albert Medal, which was subsequently re-designated the George Medal, was made for gallantry 'not in the face of the enemy'. This was the award that could be earned by civilians and was won by railwaymen, firemen, policemen and others during the First and Second World Wars. At least two Albert Medals were awarded to railwaymen who were killed in the Great War.

---

1   www.Gov.uk/medals-campaigns-descriptions-and-eligibility.

Victoria Cross

Private Jacob Rivers VC
1st Sherwood Foresters
12 March 1915
Aged 33
Le Touret

Ballast train labourer
Midland Railway
Derby

Jacob Rivers was born in 1881 in Derby where his father George was a railway labourer. George died aged forty-one and Jacob aged eighteen joined the army. Having served in India Jacob was discharged in 1907 and joined the Midland Railway as a ballast train labourer. At the start of the war he re-enlisted and joined the Sherwood Foresters. On 12 March 1915, the battalion were engaged at Ducks Bill Salient, Neuve Chapelle, and:

'Private Rivers, on his own initiative, crept to within a few yards of a very large number of the enemy who were massed on the flank of an advanced company of his battalion. He hurled bombs at them, and his action caused the enemy to retire, and thus relieved the situation. Private Rivers performed a second similar act of great bravery on the same day, again causing the enemy to withdraw. He was, however, killed on this occasion.'[2]

He was buried where he fell, and his grave has never been found and is commemorated on the Le Touret Memorial.

Sergeant John Meikle VC MM
4th Seaforth Highlanders

Clerk
Nitshill
GBK Joint Railway

John Meikle was employed by the Glasgow, Barrhead and Kilmarnock Joint Railway Company as a clerk at Nitshill Station, Renfrewshire, on the outskirts of Glasgow. He joined the Seaforths aged just sixteen in 1915, and was posted to France in February 1916. On 20 September 1917, he was awarded the MM for his part in fighting around Menin Bridge Road at Ypres. He was soon promoted to Sergeant and was posthumously awarded the VC for conspicuous gallentry in at the Ardre Valley in France on 20 July 1918.

'For most conspicuous bravery and initiative near Marfaux, France, on 20 July 1918, when his company having been held up by machine gun fire, he rushed single handed a machine gun nest. He emptied his revolver into the crews of the two guns and put the remainder out of action with a heavy stick. Then standing up he waved his comrades on. Very shortly afterwards another hostile machine gun checked progress and threatened also the success of the company on the right. Most of his platoon having become casualties, Sergeant Meikle seized the rifle and bayonet of a fallen comrade and again rushed forward against the gun crew, and was killed almost on the gun position. His bravery allowed two other men, who had followed him, to put the gun out of action. This gallant NCO's valour, devotion to duty, and utter disregard for his personal safety, were an inspiring example to all.'[3]

---

2   London Gazette VC Citation 28th April 1915.
3   London Gazette VC Citation 13th September 1918. London Gazette MM citation 12th December 1917.

Harry Cator MM VC CDG
7th East Surrey

Porter
Thursford
M & GN Railway

Harry Cator, aged fourteen, worked as a porter at Thursford in Norfolk for the Midland and Great Northern Joint Railway before leaving the railway and becoming a labourer. He joined the army in 1914 and by June 1915 was in France with the 7th East Surreys. He fought through the Battle of the Somme as a sergeant where he rescued 36 of his men from No Man's Land where they had been held up in German barbed wire, and for this action was awarded the Military Medal.

It was during the Battle of Arras in April 1917 that he won the VC on 9 April during the battle of the Scarpe:

'*For most conspicuous bravery and devotion to duty. Whilst consolidating the first line captured system his platoon suffered severe casualties from hostile machine-gun and rifle fire. In full view of the enemy and under heavy fire Sergeant Cator, with one man, advanced to cross the open to attack the hostile machine gun. The man accompanying him was killed after going a short distance, but Sergeant Cator continued on and picking up a Lewis gun and some drums on his way succeeded in reaching the northern end of the hostile trench. Meanwhile, one of our bombing parties was seen to be held up by a machine gun. Sergeant Cator took up a position from which he sighted this gun and killed the entire team and the officer whose papers he brought in. He continued to hold that end of the trench with the Lewis gun and with such effect that the bombing squad was enabled to work along, the result being that one hundred prisoners and five machine guns were captured.*' [4]

Three days later, on 12 April, he was severely wounded by a piece of shrapnel.

Harry Cator survived the war and served in the Home Guard in the Second World War, and commanded a prisoner of war camp near Mundford in Norfolk. It is said that after this war some of the former prisoners arranged a reunion with him!

The Four VCs of the L&NWR

L/Cpl JA Christie VC
1/11th London Regiment (Finsbury Rifles)

Parcels porter
L & NWR
Euston

John Christie worked as a parcels clerk in the traffic department of L&NWR at Euston until he joined the army. In August 1915, in Gallipoli, he was wounded in the head and evacuated for specialist treatment at St Bartholemews in London. He recovered and rejoined his battalion, by then in Palestine, and in December 1917, aged twenty-two, he won the VC for conspicuous gallantry. His battalion were involved in an attack near Jerusalem. The position was captured but the enemy launched a counter attack and Lance Corporal Christie fought across fifty yards of open territory and then attacked the strong enemy force with bombs, and his prompt action successfully cleared the position and so saved many lives. John Christie survived the war but did not return to the railway. He died in 1967.

---

4   London Gazette VC Citation 8th June 1917.

Private Ernest Sykes VC
27th Northumberland Fusiliers (Tyneside Irish)

Platelayer
Micklehurst
L & NWR

Ernest Sykes was born in Saddleworth, Yorkshire in 1885, and joined the L&NWR as a platelayer (track maintenance man) at Micklehurst. Like John Christie, Ernest Sykes saw service in Gallipoli, and like Christie he was injured, evacuated to Egypt, and then sent home to England for treatment.

His foot was so badly damaged that doctors wanted to amputate but Sykes refused consent. Eventually he was considered fit enough for home service. Keen for further action he volunteered for overseas duty and was posted to the 27th Northumberland Fusiliers serving on the Western Front.

On 19 April 1917, near Arras, his battalion incurred many casualties by a machine gun firing from a flank. The gun pinned down the infantrymen. Private Sykes, seemingly impervious to the perils, braved the machine gun fire in an almost suicidal disregard for the German bullet and carried back four of his wounded colleagues. Risking almost certain death in the continuous fire he went back a fifth time and did not return to the safety of the trenches until he had bandaged all of those who were too badly wounded to be moved. For this action he was awarded the VC. He returned to the railway eventually becoming a guard and died in 1949 aged sixty-four.

L/Cpl Charles Graham Robertson VC MM
10th Royal Fusiliers

Booking Hall Clerk,
L&NWR

Charles Robertson was born in Penrith in 1879 and was employed as a booking hall clerk initially with GER at Ware, and then Bishopsgate, although L&NWR also claim that he was an employee, possibly post war. He had served in South Africa as part of the Imperial Yeomanry with 34th (Middlesex Yeomanry) Company and enlisted into the 10th (Stockbrokers) Battalion the Royal Fusiliers in 1914, and arrived in France in November 1915. He was awarded the MM on 2 November 1917 and, aged thirty-eight in 1918, and probably considered pretty old by many in the trenches, he won the VC.

'On 8/9 March 1918 west of Polderhoek Chateau, Belgium, Lance-Corporal Robertson having repelled a strong attack by the enemy, realised that he was being cut off and sent for reinforcements, while remaining at his post with only one man, firing his Lewis gun killing large numbers of the enemy. No reinforcements arrived, so he withdrew, and then was forced to withdraw again to a defended post where he got on top of the parapet with a comrade, mounted his gun and continued firing. His comrade was almost immediately killed and he was severely wounded, but managed to crawl back with his gun, having exhausted his ammunition. Lance-Corporal Robertson was alone throughout these operations except for the presence of one other man who later was killed, and the most determined resistance and fine fight which he put up undoubtedly prevented the enemy from making a more rapid advance. His initiative and resource, and the magnificent fighting spirit are worthy of the highest praise.'[5]

L/Cpl Robertson survived the war and returned to the railway. He was a Sergeant in the Home Guard in the Second World War and died in 1954. His VC is displayed in the Royal Fusiliers Museum in the Tower of London.

---

5   London Gazette VC Citation 5th April 1918.

Private Wilfred Wood VC
10th Northumberland Fusiliers

Engine Cleaner
L & NWR

Wilfred Wood joined L&NWR as an engine cleaner aged seventeen in 1914. He enlisted in early in 1916, firstly into the Cheshire Regiment but was soon transferred into the 10th Northumberland Fusiliers. He earned his VC for outstanding bravery and initiative on 28 October 1918 near Casa Van in Italy.

Private Wood captured an enemy machine gun position which had held up a flanking unit, and caused 140 men to surrender. Later his advance was held up by a hidden machine gun returning fire at close range. He then charged the gun position firing his Lewis gun from the hip, killing the enemy gun crew. Without further orders he continued to advance capturing an enemy trench from which three officers and about 160 men surrendered. 'The conspicuous valour and initiative of this gallant soldier in the face of intense rifle and machine-gun fire was beyond all praise.' [6]

Private Wood won one of the last VCs of the Great War and one of the few awarded in Italy. He returned to the railway as a fireman at Edgeley and retired in 1960 as a supervisor at Longsight Depot, Manchester. He died in 1982.

It is a fitting tribute to these brave men that locomotives bearing their names ran up and down the West Coast line until 1962 (except Christie which was withdrawn in 1934) covering more than six million miles between them. It is known that Wood and Sykes worked together on the same train on at least one occasion. Two VCs going about their normal business with customers unaware of their gallant exploits.

VC Railwaymen

Sgt J Meikle   *Pte J Rivers*   *Harry Cator*   *L/Cpl J Christie*   *Pte W Wood*

Pte E Sykes   *L/Cpl G Robertson*

Albert Medal

Joseph Farren 12th Light Railway Operating Company.   Aged 23
George Johnson 21st Light Railway Operating Company.   Aged 25
Died on 30 April 1918

Sapper Joseph Farren from Carlton near Market Bosworth was a goods porter for L&NWR at Nuneaton. He was awarded a posthumous Albert Medal along with Sapper George Johnson of 4 Oak Villas, Colwick Vale, Nottingham, a former GNR cleaner and CSM A H Furlonger DCM. They were working on an ammunition train which was being loaded at Krombeke near Poperinge.

---

6   London Gazette VC Citation 26th November 1918.

The locomotive had been detached when the second wagon in the train burst into flames. CSM Furlonger, who was in charge, ordered Sapper Woodman to uncouple the burning wagon from the remainder of the train and for the driver, Sapper Bigland, to reattach the loco and move the burning vehicle away from the rest of the train and the ammunition dump. Their prompt action saved the whole ammunition dump from going up and so preserved many lives, but as Furlonger and Farren were uncoupling the blazing wagon from the loco it exploded killing Furlonger, Farren and Johnson. The locomotive was blasted off the tracks and Sapper Bigland was badly injured. Sapper Woodman escaped without injury.

Military Cross

Twenty-seven officers were awarded the MC within the 12,500, and six are examined below.

Major Harold R Turner, MC & Bar   Clerk
297 Siege Battery RGA   LB & SCR
19 May 1918, Aged 27, Duisans

Harold Turner was awarded the bar to his MC in June 1918 and his rank was recorded as Lieutenant, Acting Captain. His second MC was awarded posthumously as he was killed on 19 May 1918. The Commonwealth War Graves Commission records his rank as Major.

> 'For conspicuous gallantry and devotion to duty. While in command of the battery which was heavily shelled for a period of six hours and intermittently throughout the day, he kept the guns in action all day and never failed to engage any target given to him. Thanks chiefly to his own splendid example of courage and coolness the whole battery acquitted itself magnificently.'[7]

297th Siege Battery consisted of six 6-inch Howitzers and by the end of the war was part of 19th Howitzer Brigade of the Royal Garrison Artillery.

2nd Lt. John Cowherd MC   Parcel Clerk
5th Worcesters   Bristol
29 September 1918, Aged 22   GWR
Hooge Crater

 2nd Lt John Cowherd from 6 Greenmore Road, Knowle, Bristol, was killed on 29 September 1918 aged twenty-two and is buried at Hooge Crater cemetery. His MC was Gazetted on 4th February 1918 and appears to have been awarded as a result of the Cambrai battle.
His citation reads:

> 'For conspicuous gallantry and devotion to duty. He attempted to force a bridge, and was driven back by machine-gun fire. He advanced again behind a tank, and when the bridge collapsed he remained, holding the bridge-head until the evening.'[8]

If this was a solo effort then it sounds worthy of a VC.

---

7   London Gazette June 1918, MC Citation. H. R. Turner.
8   London Gazette MC Citation 4th February 1918.

Lt Walter Nelson Reed MC
10th Siege Battery RGA
27 October 1916
Aged 24
Flat Iron Copse

District Engineer
Hull
NER

Walter Reed had enlisted into the 10th East Yorkshire Regiment in September 1914, and was commissioned into the Royal Garrison Artillery. He was posted to France in September 1915 and won the MC at the Battle of the Somme where he was killed by shellfire on 27 October 1916 and is buried at Flat Iron Copse Cemetery.

Captain Alick Dunbar Trotter MC
9th South Lancashire Regiment
18 September 1918
Aged 23
Doiran

Apprentice
West Hartlepool
NER

Alick Trotter of 23 The Mount, Malton, was commissioned on 8 July 1915 into 11th Yorks and Lancs and by May 1916 was serving with the 9th South Lancs in Salonika. He contracted malaria and spent late 1916 and early 1917 recovering serving as an instructor. He was gazetted with the MC in the 1918 New Years Honours list. The *London Gazette* stating that he was promoted to temporary Captain and Adjutant in February 1918 and, interestingly, ceased to be adjutant, and reverted to Lieutenant on 19 September 1918, which was one day after he was dead! An odd entry!

Trotter was killed leading from the front alongside his commanding officer Lt Colonel B F Bishop MC, in the attack, 'the orderly who was with him was blown back into a shell hole by a Heavy Trench Mortar round and when he got up there was nothing to be seen of Captain Trotter, he has little doubt that he was instantaneously killed.'[9]

Captain Roger Beverley Walker MC
Yorkshire Hussars (Attached to 9th West Yorks)
13 November 1918
Aged 32
Terlincthun

Assistant Foreman
Hull CME
NER

Roger Walker served throughout the war. He had joined the Yorkshire Hussars in 1908 and was a subaltern when war broke out. He arrived in France in early 1915. The Yorkshire Hussars merged with the 9th West Yorkshires in 1917. Captain Walker is known to have led 250 men in a successful attack on the Norman Brickstacks near Lens on 10th November 1917. He was awaded the MC at around this time, possibly for this action. Injured a year later he was evacuated to Boulogne where, two days after the armistice, he died. Two of his brothers were killed in the Great War and another was killed whilst taking part in a steeplechase.

Captain William Salter MC
17th Middlesex
9 August 1916
Aged 32
Thiepval

Surveyor
GER

---

9   The National Archives WO339/32460 c/o The Great War Forum .

William Salter died on the Somme.

The GER magazine article right is written in words typical of the time.

H. J. FENWICK, Colonel.

An Appreciation.

CAPTAIN WILLIAM SALTER, M.C., Middlesex Regiment, has died fighting for his country. So we, the staff of the Land Agent's Department, have lost a brilliant colleague and a true comrade, and Britain's Army a most promising officer and gallant gentleman. His motto was "thorough" whether in work or in friendship. Man and boy he was unswerving in his duty and unstinting in his loyalty, and we who are the poorer for his loss shall never forget the little Norfolk boy or the strong resourceful man, to whom no difficulties appeared insurmountable. Given ordinary opportunities he would have gone far, but it has been decreed otherwise, and he has died fighting for those principles which he worthily upheld in his lifetime.

The thoughts of us all go out in deepest sympathy to his loving parents, whose sorrow we trust may be mitigated by the reflection that whilst time will soften the blow, the glory of their son's last achievement will never fade. A COLLEAGUE.

CAPT. W. SALTER, M.C.

Distinguished Conduct Medal & Bar

Forty-four of the 12,500 were awarded the DCM, of which only one, A W Loveday was awarded a Bar to the medal.

Company Sergeant Major A W Loveday DCM & Bar

1st Wiltshires	Frame Builders Assistant
9 September 1918	Swindon
Aged 31, Gouzeaucourt	GWR

A W Loveday, had been a frame builder's assistant in the wagon and frame shop of the locomotive and carriage department of the Great Western Railway at Swindon (see also pages 87 and 225). Only 490 bars to DCMs were awarded in the Great War and Loveday was the only railwayman to be so honoured. Often those with DCMs were commissioned, and it seems unusual that he seems to have fought through the war and yet was never commissioned.

His citation of his first DCM was:

'*For conspicuous gallantry north-east of Ploegsteert Wood on the night of 18/19 December 1915. He was one of a party of nine, under 2nd Lieutenant Cordon, which successfully raided the enemy's trench, causing them several casualties. He held up the counter-attack by bombing, thus enabling the party to withdraw without a casualty.*'[10]

On the face of it this doesn't seem particularly heroic in the context of what was going on in every section, platoon, company and battalion across the front every day. Possibly the citation was written from a report by a tired or inexperienced officer trying to keep up with the enormous administration burden whilst still putting their life on the line every day, and conscious that the sausage machine needed more citations because the country needed more heroes. He may have been truly heroic but it never made it into paper, but the officers of the day put him forward and that was enough.

The citation for his second DCM Medal stated:

10 London Gazette DCM Citation A.W. Loveday

'On reaching the enemy trench he was mainly instrumental in gaining touch with the battalion on his right. By his determination and pluck in jumping on to the parapet with a small party of men, he successfully attacked the enemy and forced them to surrender.' [11]

Again, you have to wonder whether this incident was any different from any other. On the other hand if he had managed to survive throughout the war years through all that the 1st Wiltshires had been through, he must have been a talismanic figure, and the battalion must have felt his loss severely when he was killed on 19 September 1918.

Distinguished Conduct Medal & Military Medal

Corporal Frederick Pollard DCM, MM & Bar   Signal Porter
B Battery 40 Brigade Royal Field Artillery   Lewes
20 October 1918   LB & SCR
Carnieres

Fred Pollard, who lived at 40B High Street, Southover, Lewes, must have been exceptionally brave, or just pretty unlucky to find himself in such precarious positions so frequently that he managed to get awarded the DCM, and the MM twice. His DCM citation said:

'He accompanied the battery field observation officer in a reconnaissance. The officer was killed and another fatally wounded by shell fire. With another man he at once went to assist the wounded man and conveyed him to a place of safety. They then returned to the dead officer, collected his effects, completed the reconnaissance, and returned with information which proved correct. He showed a gallantry under close shell fire deserving of the highest praise.' [12]

L/Sgt Daniel Greene DCM MM   Porter
10th Northumberland Fusiliers   Newcastle Forth
4 August 1916   NER
Pozieres

 L/Sgt Greene, who originated from County Limerick, had been employed as a casual porter at Newcastle Forth and was awarded the DCM and the MM and promoted to Lance Sergeant in the field. His gallantry was recorded in 'Deeds that thrill the Empire' Number 13 recording that he and Private J W Scott voluntarily left their trench and took out a Bangalore torpedo (an explosive charge) and laid it by the enemy trench.[13] The torpedo failed to detonate and the pair dared No Man's Land to collect the unexploded ordnance. This was no doubt exceptionally brave, but you have to wonder whether it was totally necessary. Was the recovery of one piece of unexploded ordnance worth risking the lives of two individuals?

---

11   London Gazette DCM Citation A.W. Loveday
12   London Gazette DCM Citation. F. Pollard.
13   Deeds that thrill the Empire 13.

Sergeant Charles W Roe DCM MM   Porter
1st Royal Inniskilling Fusiliers   Wroxham
22 October 1918   GER
Aged 23
Duhallow ADS

Charles Roe from Carlton Colville near Lowestoft joined GER in 1912 initially as a lad porter at Barnby Siding, Carlton Colville before becoming a porter at Gorleston-on-Sea, Reedham, and Wroxham. He enlisted in February 1915. Sergeant Roe was awarded the Military Medal for conspicuous gallantry on 23 March 1918 for commanding an outpost at Flavy whilst under heavy rifle and machine gun fire.

Roe died on 22 October 1918 from wounds incurred on the night of 20-21 October. He was posthumously awared the DCM for this action. His citation read:

> 'When his platoon officer became a casualty in the early stages of an attack near Ledegem, on the 14 October 1918, he assumed command and led his men most gallantly through the hostile barrage under heavy machine gun fire to their objective, capturing prisoners and several machine guns. On the night of 20/21 October, during an attack on Straate, his company commander and remaining platoon officer both became casualties. He assumed command of his company and completed the capture of the village. He consolidated under heavy fire and beat off a counter attack before dawn. He did fine work.'[14]

This citation appears more colourful than the previous ones and captures some of the initiative which Charles Roe demonstrated in ensuring that the attack continued when in the absence of any other leader it could have all fallen apart.

Charles Roe was mortally injured and died, aged twenty-three, the following day at the Duhallow Advanced Dressing station and is buried in that cemetery. His brother was also killed in the war.

Sergeant Albert Morris DCM MM   Blacksmith
9th Battalion Machine Gun Corps   Stratford
23 May 1918   GER
Aged 19, Caestre

> 'For conspicuous gallantry and devotion to duty. During an attack he, as section sergeant, supervised the working of his gun for five hours, firing 15,000 rounds on enemy masses at close range, pouring water on the gun to keep it cool. He also collected stragglers and organised them as a Lewis gun team in a good position. Thanks to his coolness and example the position was held for three days against persistent enemy attacks.'[15]

Distinguished Conduct Medal

Private Henry J C Eades DCM   Policeman
1st Devonshires   Plymouth
1 September 1918   GWR
Aged 20
Varennes

---

14 London Gazette DCM Citation
15 London Gazette DCM Citation

Henry Eades was one of 65 railway policemen or detectives who gave their lives to the cause. At this time each railway company was responsible for raising and operating its own police force. He must have been pretty young for a policeman. The citation for his action clearly portrays this young soldier's courage and the effect it had on the enemy. It doesn't seem too different from those who were awarded the VC.

'In company with a non-commissioned officer he was endeavouring to get in touch with the battalion on the flank, when they met the enemy advancing to retake the positions lost the day before. Private Eades immediately opened rapid fire on the enemy, who became quite demoralised, and 200 of them surrendered. The courage displayed by this man in the face of overwhelming numbers was of the finest description.'[16]

Private Leonard A Dinwiddy DCM

Porter

3rd Coldstream Guards

Exeter St Thomas

8 October 1915

GWR

Aged 20, Loos

'For conspicuous gallantry on 25 and 26 April 1915, at Givenchy, in assisting to rescue officers and men from a deep mine full of poison gas The courage and devotion to duty displayed were very pronounced, the risk of death through asphyxiation being very great.'[17]

This citation is interesting as it specifically mentions the risks he took and his chances of getting killed. It feels particularly heroic to go underground with all the risks associated with rock falls and cave-ins in the knowledge that the mine is full of poison gas. That takes a particular sort of courage; possibly worthy of the VC, however Dinwiddy was not in contact with the enemy at the time. Six months later Dinwiddy was killed at Loos.

Corporal Richard Rossall DCM

Labourer

9th (Duke of Wellingtons)

Skipton

7 July 1916

Midland

Thiepval

'For conspicuous gallantry on the night of 2 November 1915, near Hooge. When a Lance-Corporal of their battalion on bombing patrol had been mortally wounded about ten yards from the German trenches, Serjeant Pearson and Lance-Corporal Rossall promptly went out, although a German patrol was advancing towards them. Lance-Corporal Rossall drove the patrol off with bombs, and then he and the Serjeant went forward and brought in the wounded Lance Corporal.'[18]

The motivation in this action is clear, to preserve life, no doubt a deep instinct for many. Richard Rossall, together with another soldier, risked their own lives to attempt to save one of their colleagues. Classic bravery. Richard Rossall was killed in the early days of the Battle of the Somme.

Private Lawrence Kossak DCM

Carriage Washer

12th Middlesex

Stratford

14 July 1916

GER

Thiepval

16   London Gazette DCM Citation
17   London Gazette DCM Citation
18   London Gazette DCM Citation

Lawrence Kossak enlisted at the outbreak of hostilities having worked for GER for twelve years. At thirty-eight he was significantly older than the majority of railwaymen who died. The citation for his action is interesting, as it makes clear that his bravery was not a one off but that he regularly undertook such risky raiding.

'For conspicuous gallantry on the night of 14/15 December 1915, at Bois Francais. When with a raiding party under Lieutenant Keith Trevor, Privates Kossak and Alma showed great dash and courage, and the former drove back single-handed with his bombs a hostile attack inside the German trenches. Both men had been with Lieutenant Trevor on many reconnaissances.'[19]

Kossak had clearly developed a partnership and an understanding with Lieutenant Trevor which made them effective and increased their life chances. Lawrence Kossak was badly injured at Trones Wood in the Somme (see page 68) and died on 14 July 1916.

Sgt Herbert Gollins DCM
Lancashire & Yorkshire Railway

6th Kings Shropshire Light Infantry
22 March 1918
Pozieres

The citation for Herbert Gollins stresses the fact that despite being injured he continued the attack on 26 November 1917, and over a considerable period led by example.

'For conspicuous gallantry and devotion to duty. At the beginning of the attack he was wounded but gallantly led his party forward into the enemy's lines. On seeing some of the enemy counter-attacking, he led a rush over the open, killed some of the enemy, and captured six prisoners. He continued to press forward until he established himself on his objective, where he held on for two days, though he was twice buried by shell-fire. His courage and determination were a magnificent example to all.'[20]

Private G Peacock DCM
Sheet Dresser
Peterborough
GNR

2nd Bedfords
22 August 1918, Albert

'For conspicuous gallantry and devotion to duty. During a counter attack on a village, which resulted in its recapture, our advance down the main street was being checked by the fire of a heavy machine gun. Private Peacock, handling his Lewis gun with great skill, put the enemy gun out of action, and our troops were able to push forward through the village with few casualties. On another occasion he took command of the Lewis gun section after the NCO had become a casualty and though subsequently wounded, he remained at his post and by skilful handling of the gun greatly assisted the advance of his platoon by directing covering fire on the enemy positions. He was wounded a second time, but refused to leave his Lewis gun section until ordered to do so by his platoon commander.'[21]

Peacock was posthumously awarded the DCM.

19   London Gazette DCM Citation
20   London Gazette DCM Citation
21   London Gazette DCM Citation

Sergeant William Ellingham DCM   Gas Lighter
1st Northumberland Fusiliers
18 August 1916   NER
Thiepval

William Ellingham was a Private when the citation was completed. There isn't a lot to the citation in words, but the true story is the reality behind those words.

'For conspicuous devotion to duty, as a linesman, notably near Ypres, between 23 February and 4 March 1915. His unvarying cheerfulness and readiness to go up the line, under any conditions of weather and however heavy the sniping, has set a fine example to the other signallers.'[22]

Signallers had a lonely and miserable existence forever being sent out tasked with repairing broken telephone cables. Telephony was the primary means of communication across the battlefield. Then, and now, effective communications were critical. So when the cables broke the signallers were sent out, over the top, alone with their tools searching through the carnage for the break or breaks in the line. Frequently, as soon as they returned to the comparative safety of the trenches, they were sent out again. During attacks the signaller would drag telephone cable behind him. Cumbersome, slow and exposed. This citation demonstrates the commitment and the character of the man. Those reviewing the citations in the chateaus of the headquarters to the rear would readily understand the importance of the signaller, and the perils of their daily existence. No more words were required.

Ellingham survived a further 18 months and was killed on the Somme.

Lance Sergeant John W Gray DCM   Clerk
1st Northumbrian Field Ambulance RAMC   Newcastle Quayside
2 January 1916   NER
Aged 40, Etaples

The life of a stretcher bearer or orderly was every bit as risky as the line repairing signallers.

According to NER magazine 'Sergeant Gray was wounded in the lower part of the chest on 31 December 1915, whilst on active service. For nearly a fortnight he appeared to progress towards recovery and on 11 January, in a cheerful letter to his home at Cullercoats, Northumberland, he expressed his expectation of being removed to the base and thence to England in a few days. Fate, alas, willed otherwise for news was received on 13 January that he had died of wounds in the 1st Canadian Hospital, Etaples on 12 January 1916.'[23]

The *London Gazette* recorded the award of his DCM on 14 January 1916 just two days after his death.

'For conspicuous gallantry when he left the dressing station and advanced over open country, under heavy shell fire, carrying a medical pannier, reaching the trenches and rendering first aid to many wounded. Later he took charge of a dressing station and assisted to remove many wounded men to hospital. Part of the station was destroyed by shell fire during that time.'[24]

---

22   London Gazette DCM Citation
23   North Eastern Railway Magazine, March 1916, 35.
24   London Gazette DCM Citation

There were 143 members of the Medical Corps in the 12,500 killed as they struggled with stretchers across the destroyed ground trying to save the life of injured colleagues.

Sergeant R H Hart DCM	Signal Porter
1st Royal Berks	Blaenavon
23 June 1915	GWR
Aged 29, Vielle Chappelle	

> 'For conspicuous gallantry and devotion to duty at Cuinchy on the night of 21 June 1915, in going down a mine and assisting in the rescue of four men under circumstances of great risk. On the morning of 22 June, the enemy exploded a mine, entombing about nine of our men, and this non-commissioned officer went down the mine time after time with the greatest of courage and assisted in bringing out all the men. He was badly affected by poison gas.'[25]

The deeds of Sergeant Hart seem remarkably similar to those of Leonard Dinwiddy. His battalion was involved in the digging of mines and on two occasions he rescued his comrades. The second occasion seems to have poisoned him and injured him mortally.

Lance Sergeant Francis Hocking DCM	Clerk
1/7th Middlesex	Railway Clearing House
14 May 1915	
Highgate Cemetery	

> 'For gallant conduct and resource on the night of 7 May 1915, when with a party covering important new works between our own and the German lines. The enemy stalked the party and rushed on them from flank and rear. Lance Sergeant Hocking continued to act with the greatest courage and coolness, although severely wounded, and gave a fine example to his men of steadiness and devotion to duty.'[26]

Francis Hocking joined the Territorial Army in early 1910 and when war was declared was mobilised and, along with his battalion, was sent to Gibraltar until deploying to France in March 1915. He was severely injured in the incident above and was successfully evacuated to Camberwell hospital where he died on 14 May and is buried in Highgate cemetery.

2nd Lieutenant Herbert Q Howard DCM	Gate Lad Messenger
1/2nd London	March
8 August 1918	NER
Aged 21, Vis en Artois	

Herbert Howard from March in Cambridgeshire enlisted at the outbreak of war and was awarded the DCM in January 1917.

> 'For conspicuous gallantry in action. With a few men he rushed an enemy machine gun, captured the gun and several prisoners. He set a fine example of coolness and courage.'[27]

He was commissioned into the 2nd London Regiment on 18 December 1917 and was killed on 8 August 1918 and is buried at Vis en Artois cemetery.

25　London Gazette DCM Citation
26　London Gazette DCM Citation
27　London Gazette DCM Citation

It would have been interesting to have seen how Howard's career would have progressed had he survived the war and returned to the railway. Having originally been employed as a gate lad messenger would he have gone back to that role having been a commissioned officer, or would his experiences as an officer have stood him in good stead for higher office within the railway? Would the social structures of the railway have limited his future options?

Sergeant H B Parkin DCM

2/6th West Yorks
18 September 1917
Grevillers

Clerk
York
NER

Reading Sergeant Parkin's citation you have to wonder how he wasn't awarded the VC.

'For conspicuous gallantry and devotion to duty during a very heavy bombardment of the line, followed by a raid of storm troops. Though wounded during the bombardment he refused to leave his post, and though all his men were eventually killed or wounded he succeeded in holding out single-handed and in killing an officer and two men who penetrated the post. He was again severely wounded, and on arrival of reinforcements was found propped against the trench in a pool of blood. But for his courage the enemy would have succeeded in effecting a lodgement in our line.'[28]

The DCM was awarded posthumously in 1918 and so it seems likely that he was killed in the action mentioned, given he was seriously injured.

RSM Alfred K Scott DCM

7th Cameron Highlanders
30 October 1916
Aged 25
Adanac

Clerk
Maidenhead
GWR

Alfred Scott from Maidenhead joined the Cameron Highlanders and by 1916 he was their Regimental Sergeant Major, at twenty-five, believed to be the youngest in the army. The regimental history states: 'He joined the battalion in early 1914 and has been with it ever since. He was an exceptionally good RSM, a strict disciplinarian, handling those under him with tact, a splendid organiser for whom no amount of work seemed too much. A brave man, a born soldier, he was respected and beloved by all who came into contact with him.'[29] It is interesting that someone who had been one of thousands of clerks in the railway integrated with a regiment so closely that they regarded him as a 'born soldier'. You have to wonder to what degree the 'strict disciplinarian' was 'beloved' when he was dealing with the Private soldiers in the battalion.

Alfred Scott from 14 Kings Grove, Maidenhead, came from a railway family. His father J T Scott was a permanent way inspector and his brother Douglas a clerk at the chief manager's office in London and served as a Sergeant in the 2/14th London Regiment (The London Scottish) and was killed on 30 April 1918. Another brother, G G Scott, worked in the divisional engineer's office at Gloucester and served with 275th Railway Troops of the Royal Engineers and survived the war. A fourth brother, Henry J Scott, who worked at Somerset House was a Sergeant in the Civil Service Rifles and was killed on 16 January 1916.

28   London Gazette DCM Citation
29   The History of the 7th Battalion Queens Own Cameron Highlanders, 51.

Boy Scouts 'guarding' a bridge. NRM Q30604

PART THREE

THE STORY OF THE RAILWAY COMPANIES AT WAR

OPERATIONS AND ENGINEERING

CHAPTER 11

THE RAILWAY COMPANIES

Detail of the North Staffordshire Railway Memorial (Courtesy of NRM York)

During the Great War the UK railway network consisted of a number of independent companies, the big four of LMS, LNER, GWR and Southern were not formed until 1 January 1923. However, the government in effect nationalised the railway companies throughout the war forming a special rail ministry because the network was so strategically important to the successful resolution of a war. Amongst the most important elements of the British railway system was the ability to (1) move and concentrate masses of soldiers at points across the country, (2) mobilise labour to support war industries and (3) move large quantities of freight.

The different railway companies contributed in many different ways depending upon their size and distribution and the geographical footprint in relation to the materials to be conveyed. The companies in the South East bore a massive burden, but each company had a substantial part to play. This chapter can only scratch the surface of what was achieved, but the seminal work *Railways in the Great War* by E A Pratt, a two-volume tome published in 1922, can add considerable detail of running a railway in wartime and the contribution each company made.[30]

The railway companies were some of the largest none governmental organisations in the country during the Great War, and they released over 180,000 of their employees to the war effort serving in the armed forces. For the remainder, as no doubt for everyone, more was expected from less. There was still a full passenger and freight railway to run, requiring specialist repair and maintenance of rolling stock, track and signalling equipment. But in addition the railway served the ministry of munitions railway transport branch and in particular the mechanical warfare, gun ammunition filling, trench warfare supply and explosive supply sections.

---

30   Pratt

To wage a European war, Britain needed a large army, and that army needed to be moved. Almost everything to do with that army was moved by rail – millions of soldiers from mobilisation; to and from training locations; on leave; on embarkation; those returning wounded; and those, when war was won, being demobilised. Millions of foreign soldiers staged through Britain, not least those from Canada and America, and they were moved as well. Armies required thousands of horses to move across the battlefield, for cavalry, artillery, and logistics, and horses needed feed, thousands of tons of feed. Soldiers too needed feeding and the railway shifted the logistics to sustain them.

But to fight, soldiers needed munitions, and munitions were large and heavy. The railway shifted millions of tons of munitions, from enormous naval shells to bullets for rifles. British industry was not geared up to produce such a volume of munitions and many industrial factories switched to producing munitions and many new factories sprung up. Some of the new factories were enormous and required large labour forces. The growing number of workers required in the war-related industries needed to be moved from home to work and back, to strict timetables in mass numbers to some very remote locations every day. And the railway had to cope with this whilst reducing its maintenance programme, losing many of its workers, and some of its locomotives, rolling stock, and indeed track and sleepers. The railway coped admirably.

During the Great War over 25 million tons of materials were shipped to France, much of this would have come from across Britain by railway. One of the lasting impressions of this war fought a century ago is of artillery and ammunition and yet in tonnage moved oats and hay topped the list, indicating the unmechanised nature of much of the army.

A typical horse drawn wagon owned by Lancashire and Yorkshire Railway, of the type used extensively during the Great War to transport from the railhead to the battlefront. NRM 091997-7059_HOR_F_3227

Tonnage shipped to France during the Great War.[31]

Item	Tonnage
Oats & Hay	5,438,602
Ammunition	5,253,338
Coal	3,922,391
Food	3,240,948
Ordnance stores & clothing	1,761,777
Engineering stores	1,369,894
Railway materials	988,354
Timber	842,759
Roadstone	761,540
Petrol & Sundries	758, 614
Miscellaneous	539,398
Expeditionary Forces Institute Canteen stores	269,517
Mechanised Transport	158,482
RAF Stores	123,570
Tanks	68,167
Total	**25,497,351**

Gun loaded onto railway wagons at Toton sidings, Nottinghamshire,
9 December 1916. NRM 1997-7397_DY_2896

---

31   Forbes, A., A History Of The Army Ordnance Services, 339.

Raw Materials

The railways had an important role in conveying not only the finished war products, but also many of the raw materials and constituent parts that made up the finished product. If it were possible to map the distribution networks they would criss-cross the country as cordite married up with brass cartridge cases, possibly having been refurbished at a railway workshop, with a cast shell from a foundry, with explosive to fill it, and a precisely engineered brass fuse system all then assembled to produce a finished artillery shell and cartridge system, which would then be packed into a wooden box from another factory, and sent to the front.

Coal

As an island nation with an Empire to protect and interests across the globe, Britain needed a strong navy and for over 200 years that navy had been built on 'hearts of oak' and the power of sail, but industrialisation created a naval arms race, and increasingly radical innovations transformed the navy in terms of firepower, defence and propulsion, and the modern navy relied on coal.

To sustain the greatest navy in the world required thousands of tons of the highest grade Welsh steam coal. Naval outposts were situated in locations as dispersed as Plymouth, Portsmouth, Chatham, Hull, Edinburgh, and as far north as Scapa Flow in the Orkneys. Most of the coal was distributed by the railway since passage by sea was subject to German U-boat attack. The Admiralty relied upon coal. Without coal Britain didn't have a Navy and without a Navy Britain wouldn't have an Empire.

Most of the Admiralty coal originated in the valleys of South Wales and from here it was transported along small railway companies of the Welsh valleys such as the Rhondda and Swansea Bay Railway, the Taff Vale Railway and Barry Railway onto the Great Western routes and was distributed to the coaling stations of the fleet. In the case of Plymouth and the south this was exclusively over the GWR network, but coal was also sent over key inter-company interchanges at Crewe, Bushbury, Bordesley and Banbury connecting with the north, or via Basingstoke and Reading connecting to the southern rail networks direct to the south. At Banbury, for example, the GWR connected to the Great Central Railway via a small branch line at Culworth joining up with the main GCR to the north. This was a main conduit for coal heading north, ultimately onto the GER and thence the GNR to the east coast ports. Up to 20 trains per day of coal were despatched from South Wales to Admiralty destinations.

The Culworth branch was also an important north to south route for goods, munitions, supplies and troops. This nine-mile section became one of a number of key connections in the avoidance of the congested infrastructure of London, and was linked to the ports of Southampton, Newhaven, Dover, Folkstone and latterly Richborough.

Munitions

The consumption of artillery shells throughout the war was enormous. In May 1915, when there was a particular shortage of shells, the Germans were turning out 250,000 a day compared to Britains 16,000.[32] Artillery fired a projectile, the shell, and each shell required a fuse and a cartridge. The shell was usually cast from steel and filled with high explosive. A separate fuse would be fitted to the end of the shell which would initiate detonation on impact. The cartridge was often a brass case packed with bags of cordite, and when fired would ignite providing the means of propelling the projectile. On the guns the projectile would be loaded, with the fuse having been fitted and preset, followed by a cartridge containing the correct number of bags of cordite. The gun would then be fired sending the projectile on a precise bearing and trajectory. The spent brass cartridge case would be ejected, and the next shell loaded. Artillery rarely rested and consumed an enormous amount of ammunition. The manufacture of artillery shells, fuses and cartridges therefore was of high strategic importance.

Artillery fired 170,385,295 shells in France and Belgium during the war.[33] This averages at 327,664 per month, or 10,500 shells per day. The number of artillery pieces increased throughout the war culminating in 6,437, each requiring a guaranteed supply of shells.

Averages don't tell the true story since there were periods of huge artillery bombardments. From August 1918 to the armistice some 700,000 tons of artillery ammunition was expended on the Western Front.[34] This amounts to 6,796 tons per day. On one day alone in a comparatively small area north of Arras, 300,000 rounds were fired in 24 hours weighing 4,435 tons.[35] Positioning this volume would require nearly 300 large railway wagons and if it required further transportation, 4,000 wagons each pulled by six horses which would amount to 24,000 horses purely to deliver one day's artillery allocation to one part of the front. This sort of statistic gives you the impression of the capability of the railway and that the railway truly enabled the horrific destruction of the war, and without the railway the scale of death and desolation would have almost certainly been smaller.

The life cycle of ammunition began in the assembly plants where all the ingredients came together by railway from dispersed factories across the country. Primarily the filling stations of the Royal Arsenal at Woolwich, Leeds, Liverpool, Hereford, Renfrewshire, Gloucestershire and Nottinghamshire, Hayes, Banbury, Coventry, Cardonald and Morecombe. Here high explosives and cordite conveyed in special rail vehicles and originating at the national explosives factories at Gretna or Pembrey would be packed into the forged steel shell and brass cartridge cases. The precisely milled brass fuse mechanism, many engineered by women workers in railway works, would be fitted. Shell and cartridge would be packed in wooden boxes and transported by rail to the ports, across the Channel and to the ammunition dumps where they would be brought forward to the railhead and then carried forward by light railway, or more likely horse and cart onto the gun positions.

---

32   See Dewar, G. A. B., The Great Munition Feat 1914-1918, available as a free download online, for more detail on the supply elements of logistics.

33   Statistics Of The Military Effort Of The British Empire During The Great War. 1914-1920. The War Office March, 1922.485.

34   Statistics During the Great War, see 480-464.

35   Statistics During the Great War, see 481, between 8 August 1918 and 6 September 1918 a total of 9,807,000 rounds were fired. That amounts to a staggering 426,391 artillery rounds per day. This compares to 3,526,000 rounds fired in the initial stages of the Battle of the Somme from 26 June to 9 July 1916 which totals 235,066 rounds per day.

A Lancashire and Yorkshire Railway gunpowder van. NRM 1997–7059 HOR F 1485

The sheer scale of the factories required to feed the millions of artillery shells was enormous, and necessitated the building of huge facilities on green field sites. In Scotland, the Caledonian Railway connected with the Georgetown filling station site, three miles from Paisley in Renfrewshire. Before Georgetown produced a single shell, the railway transported over 9 million bricks, 10 acres of glass, 12 acres of linoleum, 76 acres of roofing felt, 9, 500 tons of cement, 10 miles of drain pipes, 12 miles of water pipes, 80 miles of central heating pipes, 1.5 million ft^3 of timber, and 5 miles of barbed wire, to the 540-acre site and that was just to build the place.[36] To operate from it, the Caledonian laid over 18 miles of sidings. Once it was up and running there were over 20 million shells, 26 million cartridges and 30 million other components produced and conveyed in a little over two and a half years. The workforce of 15,000 were ferried out of Glasgow by the Caledonian. Just down the road the National Projectile factory in Mile End, Glasgow, produced another 2 million artillery shells.[37]

In the Scottish border town of Gretna, construction began in September 1915 of an even bigger explosives factory, an industrial city which extended for over nine miles. The main factory comprised 9,200 acres and its primary purpose was to supply cordite, essential as a propellant for artillery and contained in the cartridge. Prior to the war, much of the UK's needs for cordite was supplied by Germany, and without an adequate supply it was felt that the war would be lost. The construction project was even greater than Georgetown. Gretna was too remote for the number of workers required and a 620-acre village was built, and a complete infrastructure created including amenities such as shops, bakery and even a power station. Again most of the building materials were transported by train. To facilitate the onward distribution of cordite, 80 miles of sidings were constructed, and the site contained 17 railway platforms.[38]

Further south in Garston near St Helens, there was one of the country's largest shell inspection facilities which could cope with 200 to 300 wagons of shells per day, delivered by L&NWR from the forges casting the shells.[39] Overall over 6,000,000 shells were delivered weighing over 1,500,000 tons. At Rainhill, on the outskirts of St Helens, a new munitions depot was established where over 7 million shells were stored and maintained awaiting onward transportation.[40] Set side by side the shells would have stretched 1,326 miles. At Queensway in Chester there was a TNT factory which produced over 1.5 million tons of the high explosive.

36   Pratt, 847.
37   Pratt, 852.
38   Pratt, 850.
39   Pratt, 985.
40   Pratt, 985.

A large shell filling station was established at Chilwell in Nottinghamshire (indeed it remains an army establishment from where reserves mobilise for service overseas). Two and a half miles of sidings were laid by the Midland Railway and linked to the mainline at Attenborough from where up to 11 trains per day left full of shells for the front. The greatest number of wagons of shells in any one day was 539, and the maximum tonnage in a single year from this one location exceeded a million tons.[41] This would amount to nearly 26 million 95-pound shells as used by current artillery systems such as the AS90. If every artillery piece from the current regiments of the Royal Artillery were to fire at the expected rate of the Cold War, then it would take 330 continuous days of continual fire to expend the ammunition created by Chilwell and freighted by the Midland Railway. Of course there were many more batteries then with an enormous need for shells and many more shell filling stations feeding them, all relying upon a somewhat manpower depleted railway to deliver. Compared to the shells from Chilwell, the 9 million hand grenades produced at Warmley seems trivial, but whether hand grenade or 16-inch naval shell, they all needed transportation, and the machine of war had a habit of swallowing them up in great number.

Chilwell produced ammunition, the smaller three shells were the mosts commonly used. IWM Q030017

On 1 July 1918 there was a massive explosion in the Chilwell factory and 137 were killed and 250 injured and yet the factory was open and in production the following day and beat production records the following month.[42] In total, Chilwell filled over 19 million shells.

---

41 Pratt, 1043.
42 Haslam, M. J., *The Chilwell Story: VC Factory and Ordnance Depot.*

Chilwell After explosion. IWM HU 096428A

There were other shell filling stations such as at Quedgeley in rural Gloucestershire and at Hayes to the west of London, both on the GWR network. In Pembrey in South Wales, highly dangerous cordite, which formed the propellent in cartridges, was produced. Cordite was transported by GWR with extreme care to other works in Faversham, Kent and Chilworth, Surrey. From the shell filling stations, shells were despatched every day for ports such as Southampton or from the military port at Richborough in Kent.

Chilwell sidings. IWM HU 096418

Shells produced at Chillwell munitions factory, Nottinghamshire. IWM Q030018

If cordite was considered a dangerous commodity and needed to be handled sensitively, then the transportation of hazardous chemicals required even greater care and attention. Much of the transit of these goods was down to L&NWR from the chemical plants of the north west to the depots and ports down south. L&NWR transported 384,000 cylinders of compressed hydrogen from Runcorn for the inflation of balloons and airships, but also carried a much more sinister and dangerous cargo of 630,000 vessels of poisonous gas.[43]

At stations across the country, wagons were loaded with munitions from smaller factories and armouries. At Lepton near Huddersfield, one small station dealt with 11 million hand grenades, and 15 other stations transported 10 million more hand grenades and 50 million fuses. A firm in Warrington produced 1,980 tons of bullet rod, that was subsequently transported by LNWR and this was sufficient for 425 million bullets.[44] L&NWR even surrendered part of the great Crewe Works to become the Number 9 munitions store and 44,000 wagon loads of munitions, amounting to 330,000 tons, were moved and stored here.

Conveying munitions workers to purpose built complexes

Enormous purpose-built munitions complexes were distributed around the country typically in remote and sparsely populated locations. GWR ran 103 trains a day to convey the 33,000 work force to the Hayes shell filling station. Over the course of the war this amounted to 25 million passengers and in Quedgeley a further 4,500 daily were transported to and from work.[45] The Caledonian railway transported 15,000 workers a day, 14,000 being women, using 34 trains each

43 Pratt, 991.
44 Pratt, 991.
45 Pratt, 924, 1043.

IWM Q030050

way, to Georgetown shell filling factory from Glasgow. [46] The railway companies had to run a punctual and reliable railway service every single day of the war, and in the industrial heart of the country every service mattered because so much of the country's industry was engaged in war work, and all required what was becoming a very scarce commodity, manpower.

The SECR transported workers to the Woolwich Arsenal. Because of shift changes this meant that 64,000 passengers passed through the small station in only four hours, two in the morning and two in the evening. This required 100 people per minute to transit through the ticket barrier, probably quicker than today's ticket barriers and shows that railway companies remained focused upon revenue protection, engaging ticket checkers despite the manpower shortage. This indicates the degree to which the railway companies remained commercial despite the privations of the war. Servicing Woolwich Arsenal and a trench warfare works at Slade Green required 45 trains per day. On top of all the workers travelling to and from the Woolwich Arsenal, there was also the output of their toils to be dealt with, and during the war years over 3.5 million wagon loads of munitions were transported over the network, and towards the Front.

The Midland Railway, which covered the heart of the industrial manufacturing regions of the Midlands and South Yorkshire, and L&NWR, were both critical in transporting labour. At Longbridge, for example, Midland Railway conveyed 12,000 people each way each day to the former motor works which had switched to producing aeroplane engines and re-lining artillery barrels. But whether it was the firm that produced the ration jam, the one which made the soldier's boots, the bandages or indeed the gas that was to poison the enemy, unless the workforce lived on the doorstep they were probably delivered by train.

---

46   Pratt, 847.

Logistics

The winner in any prolonged war is evidently the side that can keep going the longest, the side that can re-constitute the quickest, the side that has an endless source of men, munitions and supplies. In short, the winner is probably the one with the most organised and efficient logistics. Strategists will argue this no doubt, but the point is that winning a war is not just about the best soldiers and war fighting skills. If you can't feed them or keep them in bullets even the best side will lose.

To keep platoons, companies, battalions, brigades, divisions, corps and armies in the field required amazingly sophisticated logistics chains, capable systems and reliable transportation. In an age before computers, just in time delivery, containerisation, roll-on roll-off, the British army beat its enemies in part because of its logistics. A key factor in the logistics was the capability of the British railway network to absorb a tremendous increase in demand, and to deliver huge quantities of product from all across the country into just a few concentrated locations.

Logistics wasn't only about the provision of the military hardware; that was not sufficient to prosecute war, soldiers needed to be clothed, shod and fed (and so did the horses, and that was another enormous requirement). There was a mass of varied products which needed to be sustained. From the Number 2 Army Main Supply Depot at Northampton, 32 million pairs of boots were stored and distributed, with the L&NWR transporting nearly 12 million with most of the remainder being transported by other operators.[47] The GCR central goods warehouse at Marylebone was utilised as an army clothing store and over 60 million pairs of boots and 36 million articles of clothing passed through the building.[48] The L&NWR from six stations in the north-west, transported 154 million yards of uniform cloth.[49] From Preston 1.5 million lbs of army biscuits were transported and two firms provided 6 million tins of jam.[50] In order to eat the rations, 2,000 tons of cutlery were transported from Sheffield, and to control usage, 1,600 tons of ration books were produced and transported from Harrow.[51] The Midland transported 40,000 motorbikes, 50,000 bicycles and 12,000 tons of saddlery from Birmingham.[52]

On the subject of food, one of the most critical food products was not for human consumption at all, but for horses. Throughout the Great War horses remained the engine room of the army. From the mounted cavalrymen and the gun teams of the Royal Horse Artillery, towing large heavy artillery pieces, to those hauling the field kitchens, the divisional supplies or ammo trains, or the quartermaster's wagon, horses quite literally provided the horse power for an army. Whether an army was static or in defence it relied upon its horses. If, for whatever reason, horses couldn't move it, then far more men were required to carry, heave, lugg or haul the heavy loads. Feed for the horses was more precious than petrol in this war, and a number of large hay depots were set up in order to guarantee a constant and ready supply of feed. Men could miss a meal, men could cope, animals could not. So, there was a real priority on both oats and hay. Thousands of tons per day of hay were sent from the Newbury Hay Depot, one of a number which constantly dispatched to France. Such was the importance of hay that soldier's rations were reduced for a time in order to make more space in the transport for the conveyance of hay. Oats and hay together amounted to over 5 million tons, more than any other product conveyed to the Western Front.

Whilst feeding the troops and horses was essential, it was also critical to ensure that the workers and families at home could eat and the transportation of foodstuffs was highly important. In the spring of 1918 the movement of seed potatoes and seed grain from Scotland was given priority over all other traffic such was its strategic importance.[53]

---

47   Pratt, 990.
48   Pratt, 876.
49   Pratt, 991.
50   Pratt, 991.
51   Pratt, 986, 990.
52   Pratt, 1044.
53   Pratt, 723-854.

A lack of shipping due to the requisition of freighters by the Admiralty alongside the risk of U-boat attack, drove much more bulk products traffic such as minerals, iron ore, and staple foods to be carried by rail. So much extra traffic was forced onto the railway that towards the end of the war there was a concerted effort to move short distance freight, deemed to be less than 15 miles onto the roads. In Liverpool in 1918, for example, 23,000 tons of munitions were switched from rail to road. [54]

In terms of supplies there are two further products worthy of mention, the railway transported 324,000 miles of barbed wire from a firm in Warrington and another firm in the north-west provided 8 million yards of surgical dressing.

Troop Movement

Resupply also included the replacement and reinforcement of manpower, much of this concerned the dispatch of troops to the front and the ongoing passage of troops on leave, and of those wounded in action. The railway also had a big part to play in the ability to surge mass reinforcements, and there is no greater example than when the Americans joined the war. Once the tap was switched, troop ships and convoys were dispatched from the United States every few days mainly for Liverpool.

Liverpool Docks stretched for eight miles and a typical convoy of 12 ships would deposit 22,000 troops in short order and the L&NWR was required to transfer them with the minimum of disruption and delay. Often it wasn't known until less than 24 hours before arrival where each ship would dock, making train planning complicated and somewhat last minute. A clever plan was devised around a datum time for the departure of the first train from Liverpool. Each subsequent train would leave a fixed time after the datum. This ensured good regulation of train services out of Liverpool and beyond and contributed in a significant way to the smooth operation of the port. Without the successful operation of the railway in distributing troops and freight it is doubtful that the port could have coped with the shipping that it did. The largest convoy of troops from America was on 31 May 1918 when 64 trains were required to transport the 33,000 troops who arrived (each train conveying 20 Officers and 620 Men). Nearly 800,000 American troops landed at Liverpool in 1918. Overall 1.3 million soldiers, 235,000 horses and 900,000 tons of stores passed through Liverpool. There were also 31,000 prisoners of war transported from Liverpool to camps in the Isle of Man. [55]

Overall during the war, the railway conveyed in the region of 100 million servicemen on 216,000 special troop trains, the L&SWR alone transported nearly 21 million and L&NWR 15 million on 38,500 trains. [56] Many more were carried on leave trains, the L&NWR for example ran 18,000 leave trains conveying over 7.3 million soldiers. The GER carried 4.2 million servicemen on leave on ordinary scheduled trains.

Movement

Like water flowing downhill and taking the easiest route so, with the exception of Admiralty coal, the railway network was feeding the wartime machine from the extremities of the country to the south and south-east and then to Europe, the Middle East and beyond. Amazing co-operation and co-ordination between the railway companies ensured that the munitions from Georgetown and Gretna travelled via the Caledonian and over the L&NWR or the Midland joining the factory products of the Midlands and north-west and transferring onto the L&SWR for Southampton, or the SECR to the Channel Ports. Similarly GWR fed the same systems with goods from the 230 facilities with sidings and the 47 munitions and government storage yards along their network, to and from Wales and the south-west, and serviced the huge Naval Dockyards and the ports of Avonmouth, Newport and Cardiff.

54   Pratt, 332.
55   Pratt, 975 – 982.
56   Pratt, 974.

The use of the London termini

London was avoided by freight traffic where possible. There was a desire to try and keep dangerous cargos away from centres of population. Also London could be something of a choke point because the conurbation's own industrial output kept the martialling yards full of wagons and the network full of trains. The L&SWR goods yards at Nine Elms in South London, for example, worked hard throughout the war years and dealt with 56,000 goods trains of over 2.4 million wagons and conveying 4.2 million tons of a wide range of military goods and stores.[57] From completed aircraft to shells, to entrenching material, rations and other resupplies, Nine Elms was perhaps typical for a yard in the capital. Another reason to keep freight out of London was that the network was crowded with passenger trains as it was one of the main hubs for the passage of people, civilians going about their work and soldiers and sailors in formed groups or as individuals in leave or on embarkation.

The great London railway termini were effective in bringing passengers to the capital, but were not ideally structured or located for onward transit, and considerable thought was put to the optimum organisation of some quite conflicting demands. At the time these stations dealt not only with passengers but also with mail and some freight, and wartime usage put heavy pressure on their capacity to cope. War did not diminish the primary function of these stations which was to service the huge commuter travel.

The commuter terminals of south London were those which experienced the greatest pressure, many of them owned by the South East and Chatham Railway. The SECR had to manage the challenges of a commuter railway where demand remained constant, with a big shift to female workers but with significantly less stock. So trains were incredibly overcrowded until January 1917 when fares were increased by 50 per cent in an attempt to reduce demand.

The challenges of troop and military logistics movements led to the specialisation of the London stations. Victoria dealt with soldiers coming on leave or returning to France and with all military post for France. This amounted to 14,871 trains carrying 6.5 million soldiers, and 10.5 million sacks of post weighing 324,000 tons.[58] Victoria also had the morbid, but essential, role of receiving the kit of dead officers which was then forwarded to Holborn Viaduct.

Because of the enormous number of troops arriving from the Front, many no doubt emotionally disturbed, exhausted, dirty and probably somewhat disorientated by the transformation from total horrific war to peace in a short period of time, special support was essential at the station. There evolved a whole range of different charities helping to ease the burden of the returning heroes. This included the Soldiers and Sailors Free Buffet, the Motor Transport Volunteers, the London District Rest Houses, the YMCA, the Overseas Reception Committee, Green Cross Woman's Guard, National Guard, Knights of St Columbus, Church Army, Salvation Army, Motor Transport Volunteers, Ladies Vigilance Society, and many more. They all had needs on the station's infrastructure and staff and a South Eastern and Chatham Railway (SECR) post-war report states: '… a considerable amount of tact has been required to be displayed by those in control of the station to meet the different requirements.'[59]

Railwaymen, and it was men and not women, had a very special task in supporting the returning soldiers, who were paid in French Francs, and so an immediate need was to change money. There were up to 14 money exchange booths along the platform operated by clerks, on 'higher grade' pay, tasked with speedily changing money for the 800 or so soldiers who would arrive on any one train.[60] The flow of soldiers on leave was fast, as often the complete train load would want to exchange money. Speed was of the essence before the next train arrived some 15 minutes later, where the

---

57 Pratt, 1015.
58 Pratt, 1088.
59 South Eastern & Chatham Railway London District –War period 4th August 1914 to 11th November 1918. Issued from London Bridge Station 12th November 1918. NRM. 42. (SECR report).
60 SECR report, 43.

whole performance would be repeated until the next train arrived 15 minutes after that. Women were not considered capable of managing these complex tasks.[61]

Cannon Street, as well as managing its daily dose of commuters, was a hub for dealing with petrol and aeroplane parts. From May 1918 an ingenious idea was implemented where after the rush hour 'peak' the station was closed to the public and was then used exclusively as a point for crew and locomotive changes between the companies for trains coming from the north heading south. At 4 pm these activities ceased, ready for the afternoon commuter traffic.

Charing Cross, on top of coping with its commuter traffic, had the role of providing an on-call taxi service for VIPs. This was called the 'Imperial A' comprising an engine, saloon and brake van, which was crewed with steam up to 24 hours a day in case a VIP, usually a senior general or government minister, needed speedy transport to France. It was used on 283 occasions, so for 82 per cent of the time the train went nowhere and presumably the crew sat about waiting.[62] Charing Cross also dealt with ambulance train traffic normally from Dover and then for onward distribution to the network of military hospitals across the country.

Waterloo was the prime terminal station of the L&SWR routes and the recipient of hundreds of thousands of servicemen travelling on leave. The other major London terminals distributed the military passengers across the nation.

Transport to the ports

From the shell filling stations, factories and warehouses of the north, the railway delivered the war supplies into the depots in the south, or direct to the ports. At Didcot, for example, a large ordnance depot was established, just one of a network of many such depots supplied by GWR. It had over 32 miles of sidings and became an important node on the GWR system, with stores being distributed on a daily basis to the ports of Newhaven, Littlehampton, Southampton, London Docks and Avonmouth.

Southampton

Southampton was probably the single most important element of the London and South Western Railway network during the war, as the gateway for the flow of troops in formed units to and from the Western and other Fronts. Southampton Docks were purchased by L&SWR, in a fairly dilapidated condition in 1892. The new owners embarked on a long and expensive modernisation which was finished just in time for the government to requisition the dockyard at the start of the war. Apart from a small corner of the docks retained for civilian operation, the remainder became Number 1 Military Embarkation Port. The L&SWR though had much occasion to utilise the 37 miles of railway and siding within the port over the coming years. Through the docks passed 7.2 million people during the war, 4.8 million for foreign shores and 2.3 million arriving or returning. 799,287 horses were embarked, but only 22,873 returned. 2.7 million tons of supplies were exported and this included 572,000 tons of hay and straw, 110,311 tons of oats, 1,839,396 tons of ammunition and a comparatively small amount, 38,876 tons, of food.[63]

The L&SWR fed the Southampton docks operation with trains and troops. On one day in September 1914 no fewer than 100 loaded trains were run to Southampton conveying 31,000 troops, 4,626 horses, 701 vehicles, 377 cycles and 502 tons of stores.[64] The company also connected over 175 military camps and also conveyed millions of troops around on leave. Typically there were 21 special leave trains to London Waterloo every Friday and Saturday night.

---

61   SECR report, 52 & 53. '.. The clerks appointed to this particular work are, of necessity, highly experienced in the handling of money..... a special experienced staff had to be found to carry out exchange duties....it has not been considered practicable to obtain provision from the female clerical grade..'.

62   Pratt, 1086.

63   Pratt, 1017 – 1018.

64   Pratt, 1010.

Newhaven

Newhaven, on the LB&SCR network, became a key military location when on 22 September 1916 it was declared a military zone and no passenger was able to leave the train at Newhaven station without a permit. Newhaven became a specialist port in the despatch of munitions and stores. The aim of the railway was to keep the docks as topped up as possible so that goods could be exported at a steady and constant rate. By keeping the sidings full it was ensured that there should be no delay or even pause in the continual loading of the war-winning supplies. On average, a train of 40 to 45 wagons was received and dealt with every hour over 24 hours every day. There were nearly 20,000 special trains to Newhaven conveying over 865,000 wagons, over 40 per cent contained ammunition amounting to 2.6 million in the total of over 6 million tons.

Dover/Folkestone

To the east of Newhaven, the twin ports of Dover and Folkestone were primarily engaged in ferrying soldiers to and from France. Mainly this was soldiers travelling on leave, or injured returning home. Many were conveyed on former railway ships. Indeed the SECR ships *Victoria*, *Invicta*, *Onward* and *The Queen* conveyed over 7 million people and over 100,000 tons of government stores and 350,000 tons of rails requisitioned for rail operations in France.[65] The majority of troops using Dover and Folkstone were transported to and from the south London terminals. On top of the ferry traffic of soldiers, Dover received over 4,000 ambulance ships which required 7,781 ambulance trains which despatched 1.2 million wounded to London via Charing Cross and to other parts of the country (See ambulance trains page 95).[66] Dover was primarily the port used for moving soldiers on leave, whereas Folkestone was the preferred port for the movement of bulk drafts of soldiers.

Richborough

Southampton, Newhaven, Dover and Folkestone, each with their specialisations, were working at or close to capacity and it was determined that another port was required to increase capacity and ensure that sufficient stocks were maintained in France, especially of artillery which was heavy and large and therefore took much railway and shipping capacity to convey.

A site was found in a marshy area of Pegwell Bay in Kent between Sandwich and Ramsgate where a purpose-built military port could be created. Richborough Port was the brainchild of the Inland Transportation Department of the Royal Engineers (with whom many railwaymen served) and the idea was to load and ship barges from Kent directly into the European river and canal network to 'canal-heads'. Over 65 miles of track were laid from Minster Junction and into the port complex. The first barge was despatched on 1 December 1916 and in total 9,644 barges carried 1.2 million tons. Over 700,000 tons of ammunition was exported via this route, and barges returned carried salvage, particularly used cartridges many of which were recycled at railway workshops across the country.[67]

Richborough, was further developed in early 1918, into an early 'roll-on roll-off' facility. The railway line connected directly to train ferries through complicated tidal rail dock gates. The ferries plied between Calais and Dunkirk where they linked with another rail dock gate and the train 'rolled off' the other end. Each train ferry had four parallel sets of railway lines totalling 1,080 feet. The main advantages were the speed of loading and unloading which could be completed in only 30 minutes and that train loads of bulk goods could be assembled far away, and transported directly to the customer overseas, in the same way as containers transport goods today. This system was used to deliver 734 tanks to the front and the 243-ton railway guns 'Scene Shifter' and 'Boche Buster' (see page 124). Without this system it would have been doubtful whether tanks could have been exported without considerable ingenuity.

---

65   Pratt, 1102.
66   Pratt, 1096 – 1097.
67   Pratt, 1106 – 1114.

The SECR delivered 8,073 wagons on 309 trains in 1916. This increased in 1917 to 95,316 wagons by 1,839 trains, and in 1918 when the improved facilities came on line this rocketed to 185,605 wagons in 3,308 trains. At its height the facility housed 18,000 soldiers engaged in keeping this vital supply line working to capacity.

Other Ports

Hull, Grimsby and Immingham were all railway-owned docks taken over during the war. The biggest dock owning railway was NER with docks in Hull, and the country's largest single dock opened by the King and christened the Kings Dock. Grimsby and Immingham, both requisitioned by the Admiralty were owned by GCR. Grimsby was converted to house Royal Naval Reserve minesweepers and Immingham became a base for submarines and torpedo boats.

Although Portsmouth, Chatham and Sheerness were Royal Naval ports, a limitation was their exposure to attack from marauding German warships and their vulnerability to mines and submarines in the confined waters of the Channel area. So the Grand Fleet decamped to Scotland, using locations at Rosyth on the River Forth, Inverurie near Inverness and Scapa Flow in the Orkney Islands. Supplying the fleet was another challenge for the railway, especially the North British Railway who supplied Thurso and the ferry link to the Orkneys. The NBR were most severely tested just after the war ended in December 1918 when the Grand Fleet was granted 12 days Christmas leave. The matelots left in parties of 14,000 at a time and on some days this required 32 special trains and put significant pressure on Edinburgh Waverley, which also coped with an average of 4,000 soldiers a day on leave from the various training centres in the area. Interestingly, the GNR also carried over half a million German POWs to the camp at Stobs near Hawick.

Requisition of equipment

The railway companies also had a great deal of equipment requisitioned for military use overseas including over 500 locomotives and 28,000 wagons and coaches. The Midland Railway provided 78 locos and 6,000 coaches and 27 miles of track. L&NWR supplied 111 locos, 6,370 coaches, 56 miles of track and 30,000 sleepers. Between the Midland and L&NWR, nearly 800 horses were also compulsorily mobilised! The provision of track, nearly 200 miles, and over 100,000 sleepers resulted in railway infrastructure being torn up. In the case of the L&SWR the 12 miles they committed came from removing the whole line between Basingstoke and Alton. The Midland Railway reduced 25 miles of double track to single, and removed a small section of railway entirely between Watnall and Kimberley and closed the stations.

The threat of invasion

Early in the war some railway companies shouldered another big burden, since military authorities were concerned about the threat of invasion along the east coast. In this event the railway would be called upon to provide the means for rapid troop reinforcement to counter any invasion. Plans were also made to deny the railway from falling into the hands of the enemy. The railway provided flexibility to the military command, rather than garrisoning a vast number of troops across the whole of the exposed UK coastline, troops could be situated in discrete locations where they could be rapidly re-positioned by the railway in the event of attack. This would have given the managers of the GNR, GER and NBR something of a headache. The three companies together formed the east coast line from London to Aberdeen. These companies were subject to well prepared and tested contingency plans requiring train sets to be available at very short notice to carry counter invasion troops across the network. They also had in place plans for the deliberate and strategic destruction of key junctions, tunnels, embankments and stations. The GNR contingency meant that they had to be prepared to deal with 500 troop trains, and a similar number of supply trains, at only a few hours notice. Such was the initial fear of invasion, that infrastructure works were carried out on the network designed to enable the faster concentration of troops. This involved the lengthening of some platforms to accommodate longer troop trains, additional ramps being provided for the speedier loading and unloading of freight trains and stagings provided at important junctions and places where troops could be unloaded. New junctions and crossovers were built and some key bridges were strengthened. Certain places featured extra lighting or additional water supplies. Trains were kept available in some locations day and night, just in case. There was on the NBR network for some years an armoured train. Since there was no invasion the plans never had to be delivered.

Man Power

The railway committed something like 180,000 staff of its 480,000 employees (in 1907) directly to the armed forces at a time when demand soared for passenger and freight services. This would have put significant strain on the individual railway companies.

SECR had 27 per cent of its 1907 workforce join the armed services, 106 were immediately called up on the commencement of hostilities, many later volunteered and more still were conscripted. [68] SECR also lost significant manpower through economic migration as workers were attracted by higher wages, particularly in munitions works which needed to attract pools of additional and capable labour. The loss was offset by recalling pensioners and to some extent by external recruitment made possible by residual levels of unemployment, but this pool diminished fast. SECR could cope with a shortage of station staff or clerks, much as it was regrettable, by taking some risks with customer service delivery, but they couldn't reduce staff in roles like shunting without putting operational capacity at risk. Consequently, the shortage of shunters was made up by redeploying guards, ticket collectors, lampmen and porters; the shortage of signalmen was mitigated by closing signal boxes and fixing points.

The shortage of labour affected different departments in different ways. Comparatively few locomotive drivers or firemen were mobilised, shunting shortages were made up by redeploying from elsewhere, station staff were expected to work longer hours (with overtime) and with fewer people on shift. There was though a severe shortage of clerks because so many had been released for war service (nearly 50 per cent of all those who served were clerks) even as early as 1915. Then to make matters even worse, in March 1915, the government issued an order stating 'that no men of military age were to be given employment unless such men were in possession of Army rejection papers' which was to further exacerbate the problem.[69]

Those remaining in the railway had to work harder and longer and they also got less time off. From the outbreak of hostilities until the end of 1915 all holiday was suspended. In 1916 'outdoor staff' were given full holiday entitlements, but clerks and stations teams had one week only. In 1917 guards and station masters were granted leave, but for other grades 'only if their duties could be covered'.[70] But still there was a labour shortfall.

Women Power

An obvious solution to the manpower shortage was to employ more women. But this wasn't such an obvious choice then as it would be today. The prevailing attitude early in the war seems to have been that women were simply incapable of many jobs. Prior to the war, women were employed in a number of roles, such as stewardesses on the railway ferries and some were interned as their ships were impounded in European ports at the start of the war. The crew of the SS *Brussels* (see page 199) saw the war out from what were in effect prison camps.

68　Jeremy, 93-111 and SECR report, 49.
69　SECR report, 49.
70　SECR report, 63.

Prejudices changed slowly and where women were employed they were often in physically arduous, but low paid work, such as engine and coach cleaning, lamp lighting, and in some administrative tasks behind the scenes.

The SECR eventually decided to employ females as clerks and yet 'The first results were not encouraging'.[71] Those women employed as clerks were only employed in the most simple and basic of duties. Looking at job specifications from a modern perspective it would seem that the role of clerk would be ideal for women. However, it wasn't considered so at the time. It was felt that women lacked the education required of a clerk. It is amazing to think this now, but it was 'with great

Fuse Making Horwich [NRM]

reluctance' that female labour was considered for roles 'hitherto considered unsuitable'.[72] During the early part of the war women were kept away from the higher grade jobs such as porter. The SECR considered the role of porter to be a struggle for women, conceding to employ women only when there was no real alternative. So many porters joined the colours that the railway companies had little choice but to employ women. Women did struggle to deal with large parcels and milk churns, though eventually this problem was resolved by the introduction of an innovative solution 'milk slides', helping to make the job one which women could reasonably undertake.

The change of heart of the railway companies was driven in part by necessity and part by government direction. The War Office published a book in 1916 about the employment of women.[73] The aim was what they called substitution: 'Thus wives have taken up their husbands' work, sisters their brothers', daughters their fathers', even mothers their sons'. Substitution of this kind has much to recommend it.'[74] It went on to state that: 'No man who is eligible for Military Service should be retained... if his place can be temporarily filled by a woman or by a man who is ineligible for Military Service...' and 'The necessity of replacing wastage in our armies will eventually compel the release of all men who can be replaced by women...'.[75] The fact that the War Department felt the need to publish a book on the subject indicates that the employment of women was controversial and since it was published comparatively early in the war, and probably at a point when both military manpower and military supply was most hard pressed, of national strategic importance. Contextually the implication is that it wasn't just the railway that was grappling with the implications of employing women.

Furthermore the document, which clearly tries to champion women employment in a whole range of previously exclusive male preserves, in what is probably blatant propaganda, goes on to say that employers 'readily admit that the results achieved by the temporary employment of women far exceed their original estimates'.[76] This too is a telling statement of the time, it is incredible that having demonstrated the belief that women can operate in sophisticated employment on equal terms to men, that at the end of hostilities they believe that women can simply be packed away again, yet they specifically mention temporary employment. You have to wonder though whether this document might actually be highly attuned political spin designed for the moment. It may have been recognised that once women had been employed in masses in many tasks that there was no going back. But it

---

71   SECR report, 53.
72   SECR report, 55.
73   Women's War Work in Maintaining the Industries and Export trade of the United Kingdom. War Office, September 1916.
74   Women's War Work, 6.
75   Women's War Work, 5.
76   Women's War Work, 5.

would serve no political purpose to mention that, better to calm the fears of the men, using discourse acceptable to the time. Women achieving far more than the original estimates was probably more to do with prejudice concerning what women could achieve, indeed the document then goes onto mention there was 'Scope for such substitution by those employers who have not attempted it for reasons of apprehension or possibly prejudice'.[77] Again turning the screw on employers suggesting that if they didn't support women workers then they were prejudiced. You have to wonder whether this document was influential in railway thinking, or whether decisions regarding the employment of women were driven purely by operational necessity. But things did slowly change and women began to permeate into some of the higher grade roles.

The government didn't only have to get their point across to the employers, then as now, the unions had a part to play, and early in the war there were many industrial disputes. One concern for the unions was the 'dilution' of labour which had come about by demarcation of trades and union specific roles. The government persuaded the unions to relax these rules so that non-union employees, mainly women, could be employed.

Against this backdrop, it is pretty amazing that women got anywhere within the railway, but gradually they broke down some of the glass ceilings into semi-skilled roles, then immensely skilled precision engineering tasks such as milling and assembly of highly complicated fuses. The evidence spoke for itself that women could perform as adequately as men in demanding roles. The barriers were not completely broken even at the end of the war only 43 per cent of LB&SCR ticket collectors were female, and only a third of porters.

Women working in the railway made a considerable contribution to the nation's ability to win the war and proved without doubt that women could successfully be employed in complicated tasks generally reserved, by union restricted practices or dogmatic management principles, for men. However, rail companies shed women with undue haste at the end of hostilities, which was perhaps to be expected as demobilised men returned to their jobs. Significant inroads had been made in the psychological positioning of women in employment, and probably none greater than the contribution of the image of women in worker's uniform, including trousers which was considered 'truly revolutionary'.[78]

The fact that so many women worked in a range of complex roles in munitions industries and the rail industry amongst others, directly led to the end of women's suffrage and the grant of the vote to women in 1918. Albeit those women needed to be over 30 years old and who were: householders, the wives of householders, occupiers of property with an annual rent of £5, or graduates of British universities. This excluded many of the women who had worked during the war. Women finally obtained equal voting rights in 1928.

British society during the Great War was stratified and women who would consider shovelling coal or cleaning trains were probably those whose husbands shovelled coal and cleaned trains, not the wives of the managers, directors or clerks. These ladies, and others of similar standing, who may have considered themselves to be of higher status and maybe a little more wealthy, were able to work for charities and volunteer organisations. Pioneering women from all backgrounds helped as auxiliary nurses, many assisting ambulance trains at stations across the country. Others formed the Green Cross Society (Womens Reserve Ambulance Corps), the Overseas Reception Committee, or the popular Soldiers and Sailors Free Buffet which served over 8 million servicemen at the London termini with 2.9 million being served at Victoria station alone.

---

77   Women's War Work, 5.

78   See Female Patriotism in the Great War. Nicoletta F. Gullage. http://www.gale.cengage.com/pdf/whitepapers/gdc/
FemalePatriotism.pdf

Top left: IWM Q2801
Top right: IWM Q10986

Bottom left: GCR Birmingham 1918. IWM Q28150
Bottom right: IWM Q28014

Above: 1908 Workers in Blacksmiths Gateshead Works NRM 10322452

Below: Fitting shop Crewe Works 1913. NRM 1997-7409_LMS_2959

Precision Engineering – The Railway Works

Having considered the contribution of the railway companies in supplying manpower to the war effort, we should now consider the important contribution of the workers who remained.

As early as August 1914 spare capacity in the railway works was utilised to support the war effort with initial orders for ambulance trains, and in early September came the first, ominous, order for 12,250 stretchers, which had been doubled by the end of the year.[79] From this small and tentative start the railway workshops became major suppliers to the War Department across a range of engineering tasks. In particular the railway came to specialise in cartridge repairs.

Cartridge repair

It was Josef Stalin who was to say that artillery is the god of war, and it has been seen how important the railway was in supplying ammunition to the front. It has also been seen that over 170 million shells were fired by the British on the Western Front. Vast piles of used cartridge cases from the thousands of shells fired every day posed something of a problem, they littered the gun positions, but more important they used up scarce resources. That was until a way was devised at a railway works, according to Pratt, to repair and re-prove the dented and damaged cartridges.[80] Only minute tolerances were acceptable because any variance would affect the ballistic properties of the shell and so reducing the predictability of where it would land. So manufacturing errors would increase the chances of shells missing their target, and landing on their own troops, 'drop shorts', to which all artillery was prone. The railway was one of few industries which could mill to such fine tolerances and so it was a railway engineer who devised the means to repair and recycle and to do it on the industrial scale required. There is some debate whether this occurred in the Horwich works of the Lancashire and Yorkshire, or the Derby works of the Midland, but from proving the engineering the processes were soon mechanised.

Spent cartridges for repair at Doncaster, NRM

---

79   Pratt, 583.
80   Pratt, 604–605

L & Y workers manufacturing ammunition at Horwich works, 1916. NRM 1997-7059_HOR_F_2047

Horwich Works 1916. NRM 1997-7059-HOR_F_1964

NRM 1997-7059-HOR_F_2776

Boston Lodge Shell Factory (Courtesy of Ffestiniog Railway)

Each cartridge case had to undergo 13 processing operations, the first of which involved being boiled in a solution of caustic soda to remove dirt and grease. This was followed by hardness testing and those that passed would go through the remaining operations. It is testament to how important cartridge re-cycling was to the war effort and the scale of the skills shortages in the works that 2,650 skilled machinists were released from their uniformed roles to return to work with their civilian railway employers. Eventually this exclusively male preserve was taken over by females. By the end of the war in the Midland Works at Derby all 13 tasks were carried out by women. In total, the railway re-machined and re-used 32 million cartridges. GWR at Swindon, for instance, processed 5.3 million and the Midland at Derby 7.4 million at a rate of up to 136,000 per week.[81] Even today artillerymen return the spent cartridges as 'salvage' something made possible by the railway.

Castings and other engineering

As well as cartridges, the railway works produced high explosive shell castings from their forges, GWR at Swindon produced 265,000 tons of 6-inch shells at a rate of 2,500 per week. The NER at Darlington forged up to 1.5 million shells with calibres up to 13.5 inch. GER produced 2.2 million shells. From June 1915 around 2,200 shells were made every week at the Lancashire and Yorkshire works at Horwich.[82] Such was the demand for shell production that even small railway locations were converted. One such being a building called Boston Lodge on the Ffestiniog railway which, during the war, made shells.

The technical skills and capacity of the workshops were in demand for other precision engineering tasks, for example, the production of fuses. The fuse function as part of the shell was to initiate the explosion. Without a fully functioning fuse the shell would not operate. L&NWR established three eight-hour shifts of skilled labour, mainly female, who milled cast brass to 100 different gauges and to minute tolerances of 3/1000's of an inch using drill bits as small as 1/16th of an inch and by precise and accurate drilling produced over 250,000 fuses. [83]

A number of the workshops were engaged in the construction of gun carriages and ammunition wagons for artillery pieces. GWR in Swindon built 338 gun carriages for the 4.5-inch howitzers, each one consisting of over 27,000 parts. They also built 1,078 ammunition wagons for the same howitzer and these comprised over 126,000 parts, along with 1,078 limbers.[84] The Midland, Lancashire and Yorkshire, L&SWR and GER all built a small number of gun carriages and limbers. Some companies built wagons for overseas deployment, for example, the Midland built 2,450 and NER 1,396 wagons.[85]

The fact that there was a skilled workforce, although somewhat depleted by the mobilisation of labour for the services, and precision equipment, meant that some railway workshops were engaged in mass-producing critical components for the ministry of munitions. The Midland Railway engineered 2.5 million fuses and 1.3 million copper driving bands for shells (each shell had one which helped to form a seal in the barrel; so ensuring that the explosive gases propelling the shell did not leak; which in turn helped to minimise variation in where the shell landed) and at one time 70–80 per cent of the whole production of copper bands for 8-inch and 9.2-inch shells were manufactured in the Midland workshops.[86] The Lancashire and Yorkshire also produced 142,000 fuses.[87] The NER workshops produced 820,000 primers for cartridges.[88] The GNR produced 150,000 nose cones for

81   Pratt, 604, 931, 1052.
82   Pratt, 1069, 890, 964.
83   Darroch, G. R. S., Deeds Of A Great Railway. A Record Of The Enterprise And Achievements Of The London And North-Western Railway Company During The Great War, 78.
84   Pratt, 931.
85   Pratt, 1069, 1051.
86   Pratt, 1051.
87   Pratt, 964.
88   Pratt, 1069.

6-inch shells. The GCR manufactured a wide range of items large and small and and cast 80,000 shells and bombs.[89]

The Lancashire and Yorkshire railway built 5,318 lorries for the Leyland Motor Company.[90] The L&SWR Eastleigh Works carried out precision engineering of many component parts for complicated machinery, shells for artillery pieces, and a range of bespoke specialist ship fittings. The L&NWR Wolverton works even built a Mobile Advanced Headquarters train for the personal use of the Commander in Chief, Field Marshall Sir Douglas Haig, which he used particularly during the latter days of the war when the coalition forces were most mobile.

It seems as though railwaymen could turn their hands to almost anything from traditional railway roles such as the Lancashire and Yorkshire forging much of the 60 cm light railway track, to forging shells, precision engineering of cartridges or fuses, building vehicles, wagons, ambulance trains, howiter carriages, gun mountings, to more unsual items such as GWR's Swindon & L&NWR's Crewe works which produced a range of false limb prosthetics. Crewe, for example, had developed this skill to provide for their own injured staff, there was no NHS in those days. And this was all despite the shortages of labour, and the fact that the ongoing maintenance of the railway vehicles and infrastructure had to continue.

Women workers using turret lathes at the Lancashire & Yorkshire Railway's Horwich works, May 1917.
NRM 1997-7059_HOR_F_2228

Right: Making Components and fittings – 1908 Gateshead works NRM 10322451

---

89   Pratt, 876.
90   Pratt, 963 – 964.

CHAPTER 12

REFLECTIONS

This book has told the story of the railwaymen who died during the Great War, and of the deeds that the railway achieved in supporting the war effort in transportation and in heavy engineering. In total some 186,475 railwaymen served representing between 30 to 40 per cent of the declared 1907 company head counts.[1] This figure overstates the percentages since some workers were replaced by workers who were themselves mobilised and were replaced again, but it does indicate the haemorrhaging of manpower of the companies to the war effort. They served in just about every regiment and corps and in almost every battle and campaign, with the largest group of 40,000 serving in the Royal Engineers in professional railway jobs.

Rank Size	Company	Abbreviation	Employees	Served	%	Died	%
2	London & North Western Railway	L & NWR	77,662	31,744	41	3,719	12
3	Great Western Railway	GWR	70,014	25,460	36	2,575	10
4	Midland Railway	Midland	66,839	22,441	34	2,833	13
5	North Eastern Railway	NER	47,980	18,339	38	1,994	11
6	Lancashire & Yorkshire Railway	L & Y	34,900	10,453	30	1,465	14
7	Great Northern Railway	GNR	32,422	9,691	30	938	10
9	Great Eastern Railway	GER	29,289	9,734	33	1,155	12
11	Great Central Railway	GCR	25,469	10,135	40	1,310	13
13	North British Railway	NBR	24,063	4,554	19	775	17
16	Caledonian Railway	Caledonian	21,545	5,229	24	706	14
19	South East & Chatham Railway	SECR	18,837	5,074	27	556	11
24	London, Brighton & South Coast Railway	LB & SCR	15,095	5,207	34	626	12
37	Glasgow & South West Railway	G & SWR	8,775	2,458	28	302	12

---

1   Jeremy

Other railway companies included in the 12,500 are, Great North of Scotland, North British, Hull and Barnsley, North Staffordshire, Highland, Taff Vale, Cambrian, Alexandra (Newport and South Wales Docks), railway companies and the Railway Clearing House.

The railway contribution of some 180,000 pales into comparative insignificance, at only 3 per cent. But it is unlikely that any organisations contributed more people to uniformed war effort. Only the Post Office employed more people than the railway companies and contributed 75,000 men, which was probably the greatest number from any single employer, but significantly less than the railway as a whole.

According to The National Archives approximately nine million men served in the British Army during the Great War. This number includes soldiers from across the Empire, the number from the British Isles amounted to 5.7 million.[2]

	Statistics of the Great War[3]	% of those who served
Served	9,000,000	
Killed	702,401	7.8%
Sick and injured	1,662,265	18.4%
Killed, sick and injured	2,364,666	26.2%

Using the official statistics of the Great War it can be seen that 7.8 percent of those who served died, and 18.4 percent were injured. Taking the wounded and injured together amounts to 26.2 percent. Or put another way over ¼ were killed or injured.

The number killed represents 29.7% of those killed, sick or injured. Suggesting that nearly 1/3 who became unwell/injured died. Or put another way your chances of dying after an injury were one in three.

This might be slightly misleading because many soldiers were injured and recovered and who were later killed. For each man killed a further 2.3 were wounded.

There is no certain number of railwaymen who were killed, adding the individual rolls of honour gives a total of 20,792 railwaymen killed. This would amount to 11 per cent of those who served compared to the overall average of 7.8 per cent. Although the death rate varied by campaign with 12 per cent of soldiers in France being killed and 38 per cent wounded.[4] The vast majority of railwaymen served in France and thus their casualty rate was consistent with the Western Front. By applying the same multiplier of 2.3 men wounded for each man killed, this would equate to 47,821 railwaymen injured. At a rate of 38 per cent wounded, the total would be 68,400. The true figure will never be known, but it would make sense to assume that between 50 and 60 thousand railwaymen were injured.

When peace returned, many men were too injured or traumatised to return to work, and this must have been the case for some of the injured railwaymen. For these men, there is no memorial to their commitment. After the war some of these men died from their wounds, and although the rolls of honour do include some who died after the Armistice others are not included. Equally, anyone who died after about 1921 would not have been included since the rolls of honour were completed before then. Their contribution is lost, but hopefully the deeds of all those who contributed are not

2   See http://www.1914-1918.net/faq.htm but also Statistics of the Military Effort.
3   Statistics of the Military Effort, 237.
4   Statistics of the Military Effort, 248.

forgotten. Their contribution recorded in this book based on just some of those who died. Although this book is about those who made the supreme sacrifice, it is important to remember that probably every single soldier was in some way scarred, mentally and or physically, by their experience.

As this book draws to a close there are a number of dimensions which should be mentioned: the loss of several hundred soldiers in a preventable railway accident in 1915, consideration of those who died as prisoners of war, a thought for the railwaymen from the opposing side, railwaymen who were executed, and finally how the railway companies and state remembered the railway dead.

Quintinshill Rail Disaster 22 May 1915[5]

The railway achieved a huge amount during the Great War, but the Quintinshill accident was something of an own goal. Shortly after 6 am on 22 May 1915, just across the Scottish border near to Gretna, was Britain's worst rail disaster when three trains collided resulting in 473 casualties of which 227 were killed. Many of the casualties were from the 1/7th Royal Scots and 42 per cent of this battalion's total casualties during the war were incurred without them even leaving Scottish soil.

As frequently happened, the north bound express was running late from Carlisle, and so, as was normal practice, the local passenger train was despatched on time and this four coach stopping service would be put into the loop at Quintinshill to let the 13 coach express come by. The west coast main line at Quintinshill consisted of an up (south bound) and down (north bound) line, a signal box, and two loops one on either side of the main lines.

Signalman Meakin had a deal with his mate, signalman Tinsley, that when the express was running late Tinsley could have a lie in, and travel to work from Carlisle by getting on the stopper service from which he could leap off when the train made its unscheduled stop in the loop. It meant that Meakin worked an extra half an hour or so, but he didn't mind.

There was more and more traffic loaded onto this part of the railway, partially as a result of the German U-boat threat and the sheer number of ships taken over for Admiralty work and partially catering for war demand. The line was over 40 per cent busier than the previous year. On the 22 May both the north and south bound loops were occupied by goods trains and so Meakin could not drop the stopper into the loop. He decided to switch the stopper across to the south bound, up line, going 'bang road' as it is sometimes descriptively termed, to let the express pass, he would then switch the stopper back across. No problem.

Because Tinsley was booking on late, Meakin needed to note the passing times, signal calls and actions occuring within the signal box so that Tinsley could write them up in his own handwriting in the auditable signaller's log later. As was standard practice, the freight guards from the two trains in the loop visited the signal box to obtain information about the next moves. Operationally this should have only taken a few minutes, but they hung around for nearer 30 minutes. It is speculation, but there was probably a brew in the offing, and a warm fire to keep the early morning chill off. Tinsley arrived, bringing with him the morning paper, which, when the train was on time, was thown out to the signallers by the passing crew. Meakin handed over to Tinsley and soon settled down to read the paper and share with his colleagues updates about the war. Tinsley, meanwhile, was concentrating on getting the signalman's log up to date. The guard of the stopper service, when being put across onto the south bound, or 'up' running line should have personally visited the signal box to ensure that the advance southbound signal was put to danger thus protecting the train. But he assumed that he didn't need to inform the signaller as the signaller had travelled on the train and was entirely clear where it was, and therefore what signal protection was required.[6]

---

5   The official report into the Quintinshill disaster is; Druitt, E. Lieutenant-Colonel, Assistant Secretary, Railway Department, Board of Trade. 17th September 1915. Downloaded from www.railwaysarchive.co.uk/Documents/BOT_ Quin1915.pdf . A recent book on the disaster is Richards, J. and Searle, A., The Quintinshill Conspiracy. The Shocking True Story Behind Britain's Worst Rail Disaster.

6   Signal protection being changing the aspect of the signal to alert locomotive drivers that the track was obstructed. A red traffic light in effect.

The failure to protect the train need not have been critical since there was no scheduled south-bound train, and in any case the manoeuvre was brief with the express only minutes behind. However, there was an unscheduled 21 coach troop train being driven by driver F Scott and fireman J Hannah heading towards the parked up stopper service. Meakin and Tinsley had taken no action, and took no further action to protect the train, and the troop train collided with the local service.

The engine and first 15 coaches of the troop train were derailed, and the locomotive and tender fouled the northbound line. The remaining six coaches became uncoupled and rolled gently down the incline away from the carnage. Fifty-three seconds later the express service ploughed into the troop train locomotive and tender killing a number of soldiers who were escaping from their mangled coaches. The upturned locomotives and the scattered coal soon ignited and fire spread through the oak-framed, derailed coaches which had been crushed from their 213 yards to a mere 67 by the impact of the crash. Anyone surviving the almighty collision impact was now subject to fire. The two engines of the express train and four coaches also caught fire, but driver Johnstone and his fireman J Graham were able to free the trapped driver of their lead engine, Driver Cowper. Surviving soldiers, plus a few sailors travelling on the express, attempted rescue and immediate first aid on those not killed by the impact and fire.

Quintinshill IWM Q65577

The district superintendent, Mr Blackstock, was swiftly alerted to the accident and by 0743 had set off from Carlisle in a special train with four doctors, 15 ambulance men and, given the size of the disaster, a totally insufficient 12 stretchers, arriving at 0810 which was about an hour and a half after the accident. The Carlisle fire brigade, probably operating a horse drawn fire appliance, arrived on the scene at 10 am, over three hours after the accident and with little to do than put out the burnt remains and begin the clean up operation.

Of the 227 killed, most were from the troop train including driver Scott and fireman Hannah and three other railway staff. The fire was so severe that 82 bodies were not recognisable and it was never entirely certain quite how many people were killed because the battalion records were destroyed in the fire. Of the 500 troops on the train, only 53 answered the roll call after the accident.

Months later in court it took a jury only eight minutes to find the two signalmen guilty and Tinsley was jailed for three years and Meakin for 18 months. Interestingly, documents recently released by the government and kept secret for 100 years (they were released four years early), indicate that Lloyd George was informed that there were suspicions that Meakin was a German sympathiser and that the accident was sabotage. There (currently) appears to be no evidence to back this up.

Although A & D companies of the 1/7th Royal Scots were wiped out, the remainder of the battalion embarked on a second train successfully arrived in Liverpool to embark for Gallipoli. There was no concession for the trauma of losing so many friends and colleagues in such a tragedy and B and C companies landed in Gallipoli on 12 June, less than three weeks after the event, and were in the front line a week later. A week after that, alongside the 4th Royal Scots, they attacked the Turks at Fir Tree Spur and a further 73 from the battalion died, with a further 14 dying on the following days. It is reported that the battalion suffered 239 casualties on the day, which must have been pretty close to the total serving at that time. One of those killed was Private, nineteen-year-old, James Fairnie, he had been a storeman for the North British Railway and had lived at 10 Bush Street, Musselburgh.

The memorial to the Quintinshill victims, Rosebank cemetery, Edinburgh.

Survivors of Quintinshill. IWM Q70009

It is recorded that the Quintinshill disaster was the result of the neglect of the two signalmen, but this probably isn't entirely true, as in many accidents fate, or luck, took a hand. If the trains had been on time then the accident would not have happened; perhaps if there wasn't such an unprecedented increase in traffic and the loops having been occupied, then the accident would not have happened; if the signalmen had done their job the accident would not have happened. But if the accident did not happen, would any more of the men have survived the attack of Fir Tree Spur, or the remainder of the war? Through the culpable negligence of two railway workers hundreds died. Was that the only negligence during the war years which resulted in many hundreds dying?

The memorial in Rosebank Cemetery in Edinburgh to the Scotsmen from Edinburgh and Leith is a tangible, if rarely visited, reminder of this disaster. But nearly 100 years ago it would have been a focus for the united grief of a city, for the loss of their sons and fathers. At least these families had a place where they could pay their last respects.

Prisoners

Simplistically it is easy to think that those who were captured on both sides were the lucky ones; their war ended and they were able, eventually, to return home. Things were never so clear cut in the fog of war, particularly in the crucial few minutes after capture. Many soldiers were killed by artillery fire, from both sides, immediately after capture in the confusion of the battle zone and beyond, as the captured troops were processed and moved rearwards. Capture was not an easy option, and at the point of capitulation there was a high chance that they could be exterminated either by an over-zealous adversary or indiscriminate artillery.

Many of the captured were injured requiring treatment, frequently dying in the casualty clearing stations to be buried alongside fighters from the opposing side. Those who made it into incarceration were not immune, and many died in the prison camps, some from the prolonged effect of battle injury or from disease.

Those at home bore the hardest burden; for some they would hear that their son or husband was missing, and months later information would indicate that they had been captured and were a prisoner. They would be able, through circuitous means, to make contact by letter or postcard, and in some cases they had to go through grieving again when their loved one died in captivity.

The earliest example of a railwayman from the Cologne South CWGC cemetery was Gunner Shurmer from the Royal Field Artillery, a former labourer with the Midland Railway in Gloucester who died on 2 December 1914. There are 23 railwaymen buried in the Berlin South West CWGC, Stoker Alfred Matthews of Collingwood battalion, who had worked for GER as a platelayer and died on 27 November 1914 was the first. This thirty-two-year-old, a reservist, was captured at Antwerp in September 1914. Stoker First Class George Sharman from the Collingwood battalion, also buried in the Berlin cemetery, died on 31 May 1915. This former L&NWR carter from London Road would have been captured in the same battle as Stoker Matthews. The last railwayman to die buried in the Cologne South CWGC cemetery was Private J Statin from 2nd Sherwood Foresters and a former L&NWR porter/goods guard from Curzon Street. Private Statin survived the war and may have had cause to look forward to his return to railway employment, when nearly a year after armistice on 2 November 1919, he died. It isn't clear whether Private Statin was a prisoner of war still locked up so long after the war ended, or more likely he was a member of the army of occupation. Of the 42 railwaymen who are buried in the Cologne South CWGC cemetery, 17 died in 1918 and five in 1919 and like Private Statin it isn't clear whether they died in captivity or as forces of occupation.

Eventually prisoners of war would have been repatriated and it must be presumed, returned to their civilian employment, where they were expected to integrate fully and continue where they left off, working alongside colleagues who by exemption had not been called and those who had fought through their war and returned upon demobilisation, and alongside the ghosts of those who didn't.

Reconcilliation – The railwaymen of Coesfeld, Germany.[7]

In the most part this book has concerned the British Railway and British railwaymen engaged in the Great War. Nearly 100 years on it is fitting to remember that our enemy was made up of fellow human beings, engaged in the same range of jobs, trades and professions, who volunteered or were called up, and who experienced the same privations, risks, injuries and death.

The railwaymen's association book from the town of Coesfeld in Westphalia lists 54 railwaymen who were killed in the Great War. In recognising the loss of Germany and particularly German railwaymen in the Great War, one in particular is recognised.

Theodor Hörnemann and two of his brothers worked for the Royal Prussian State Railway until he joined the 3rd Queen Elizabeth's Guard Grenadier Regiment which was part of the 5th Guard Infantry Division of the 7th German Army. On 21 July 1917 he was wounded in the head and right arm by artillery fire, having been fighting the French at the 'Chemin des Dames', or 'Way of the Ladies'. He was evacuated to No 8 Field Dressing Station at Chivres where he died three days later. He was buried in the Sissonne German War Cemetery.

---

7   Information provided by The Rev Dr Daniel Hornemann. See www.hellfirecorner.co.uk/theodor.htm

Name	Died	Age	Name	Died	Age
Ahlers, Bernard	09.06.1916		Plesker, Heinrich	25.05.1915	32
Bäumer, Heinrich			Rathmann, Heinrich		
Böckenberg, Anton			Relt, Bernhard	18.03.1918	
Boll, Heinrich	27.09.1914	23	Rier, Anton		
Brüggemann, Heinrich	03.09.1915	27	Roesmann, Wilhelm		
Brüning, Bernhard			Rößmann, Josef		
Burhoff, Josef	15.07.1918		Roters, Heinrich		
Dapper, Hermann	21.03.1918		Scharlau, Heinrich		
Demmer, Hubert			Schichte, Josef		
Drees, Bernhard	14.06.1918		Schlottbohm, Johann	19.08.1916	
Ebbing, Johann	31.05.1919	35	Schmees, Paul		
Festring, Bernhard			Schoppen, Heinrich		
Flecksig, Karl	17.09.1916	26	Schöttler, Heinrich	03.1918	23
Frieling, Heinrich	11.06.1915	23	Schüer, Josef	20.09.1915	23
Gerdes, Josef	probably 1917		Schulz, Bernhard		
Grüter, Heinrich	29.06.1917		Sicking, Anton		
Hagedorn, Bernhard			Stahlhauer, Wilhelm	05.11.1917	
Heggelmann, August	1916		Sühling, Heinrich	13.06.1918	
Hörnemann, Theodor	24.07.1917	23	Terwei, Wilhelm	23.08.1914	
Hummelt, August	29.10.1914	24	Uesbeck, Felix	01.01.1915	
			Wahlers, Bernhard		
Hummelt, Heinrich	(07.10.1918)	19	Weitenberg, August	06.10.1914	
Kerkeling, Anton	23.04.1918		Wiesweg, Ludger	12.04.1917	
Kestermann, August	12.06.1915				
Kramer, Theodor					
Logermann, Johann					
Möllers, Paul					
Nieland, Wilhelm					
Nienhaus, Heinrich	21.08.1917	36			
Ordes, Josef					

Shot at Dawn

Private Albert Ingram	Private Alfred Longshaw
18th Manchester attached to 90th Machine Gun Company Ex Clerks at Salford Goods Yard Lancashire and Yorkshire Railway Shot by firing squad 1.12.1916	
Aged 24 Son of George & Eliza Ingham Atherton Cottage Lower Kersal Manchester	Aged 21 Son of Charles and Elisabeth Longshaw Pendleton, Manchester Husband of Mary Longshaw 21 Milnthorpe Street, Pendleton

Albert and Alfred were arrested in civilian clothes whilst trying to board a Swedish ship in Dieppe harbour in November 1916, having deserted the previous month when they were about to go into the trenches. They were court-martialled and shot on 1 December 1916. Ingram's parents were told that he had 'died of gun shot wounds' and Longshaw's that he had 'died of wounds'. Both accounts factually correct but not a full account of what had happened. Presumably these words were carefully chosen perhaps to save the family any dishonour from having their offspring executed. They were buried in a small graveyard in the village of Bailleulmont just south of the Arras to Doullens road along with about 30 other soldiers who died in the Great War, some of whom were also executed.

Neither Albert nor Alfred were inexperienced soldiers who panicked at the crucial moment, they had both been in France since November 1915. They had decided to desert at the point that they were told they were going back into the line, and perhaps crucially being detached from their pal's battalion to the 90th Machine Gun Company. The 18th Manchesters spent most of July 1916 on the Somme in the line, attacking Montauban on 1 July, Trones Wood on 7th, and Guillemont on 30th.

They were finally withdrawn on 31 July; they didn't return until 4 October. The two men deserted the following day. Presumably the two could not cope with the prospect of another period of bloody annihilation as the Somme was still consuming humanity on an industrial scale.

Having disappeared for at least a month before they were discovered, they could not blame their actions directly on the shock of war. They were presumably of sufficiently sound mind to take their uniform off, to acquire civilian kit, and to leg it several hundreds of miles. This perhaps differentiates them from those temporarily, or permanently 'maddened' by the violence. Nonetheless, had they had a defence, and to be realistic, they probably didn't have one that was listened to, then they perhaps would have claimed it was lunacy to return to that supreme violence. But that didn't cut any mustard at the time. They had deserted, and to the powers that be this was probably at the severe end of the desertion scale. They had conspired, and they had rationally acted to dodge their duty. The only sanction available would have been execution as a clear example to others who might consider such a path.

The only defence made by Albert Ingram was, 'I was worrying at the time through the loss of my chums. Also about my mother at home, being upset, through learning bad news of two of my comrades. I plead for leniency on account of my service in France of 12 months and previous good conduct. I beg for a chance to make amends. I left with my chum firstly to see those at home and then to try and get into the Navy along with his brother who is serving there.'[8]

---

8   http://blindfoldandalone.worldpress.com/2012/11/06/115/

The graves of Privates Ingram and Longshaw, Bailleulmont Communal Cemetery, France.

There wasn't much sympathy or compassion from the Commander of 90th Infantry Brigade Brigadier, J H Lloyd, who said, 'In the case of No. 10495 Pte Ingham a well thought out plan of escape from service is disclosed – and a man who commits such a crime deserves the extreme penalty.'[9] The two men were sentenced to death by firing squad.

How would the firing party have felt on that cold pre-dawn morning on the first day in December? Of course it is impossible to know. I have tried to imagine how I might feel, as a soldier, preparing my rifle in the darkness, stripping, lightly oiling, re-assembling. Hanging around until the condemned man arrived. Getting lined up, standing at ease, magazine of one round in my hand. Watching as the condemned man was tied to the execution post. Probably trying to put him out of my mind, concentrating on my job. Waiting for the words of command, 'Load, ready', and then whatever the order is to execute one of your fellow soldiers. Then 'unload' and march off. Leaving the doctor to confirm death and do his business. Clinical! Such a contrast to the mud of the Somme. Perhaps a 20 minute wait in some nearby shed, perhaps a brew, then march on again and next 'detail' as the army can refer to a duty. Alfred or Albert. It is impossible to know how a soldier felt executing a fellow soldier. Of course they wouldn't know whether the miscreant was a battle weary infantryman, or a profiteering deserted murderer from the rear echelon. Perhaps to reconcile it, it was made easier if

9   http://blindfoldandalone.wordpress.com/2012/12/03/the-fgcm-of-10502-private-alfred-longshaw-18manchester-regiment-attd-
     90th-coy-mgc/ which itself quotes The National Archives WO71/525 as the source.

you could differentiate the individual from your type. If you thought this guy was an infantryman like you, who had been through so much, like you, then perhaps there was a chance that you might end up like this. Perhaps, on reflection, it was better not to think at all. Load. Aim. Fire. At least these don't fire back, and a day shooting deserters is better than fatigues and better than advancing to contact against heavily defended positions.

Des Browne, defence minister in August 2006, said, 'I do not want to second guess the decisions made by commanders in the field, who were doing their best to apply the rules and standards of the time. But the circumstances were terrible, and I believe it is better to acknowledge that injustices were clearly done in some cases, even if we cannot say which – and to acknowledge that all these men were victims of war.'[10]

After the War

On Wednesday, 14 May 1919, a service of remembrance was held in St Paul's Cathedral 'In memory of the railwaymen of Great Britain and Ireland who have died in the service of their country during the war 1914–1918'.[11] According to the service, 186,475 railwaymen joined His Majesty's forces and 18,957 died. However, an analysis of the individual company's rolls of honour and memorials, and excluding those from Ireland and London Underground, total more than 20,000. Furthermore, some railwaymen who died do not feature on either. It is now impossible to know quite how many railwaymen died in the Great War.

Memorial

After the war in villages, towns and cities across the country and indeed the empire, local people created lasting memorials to the men who had died. The Network Rail database records over 440 railway memorials. Some are impressive and quite majestic such as the Waterloo Arch and the list of names at Liverpool Street Station and Manchester Victoria.

On page five of *The Times* dated 22 October 1921, is an article concerning the unveiling of the L&NWR memorial at Euston station, headed 'Lord Haig's debt to the Railways. Loyalty unsurpassed'.[12]

'Lord Haig after unveiling the memorial expressed the thanks of the old army he commanded to the railways of the country, and not least among them the North-Western for their splendid conduct and loyal support throughout the great struggle. The development of modern war had given an enormous importance of the completeness and efficiency of railway communicaiton. It was scarcely an exaggeration to say that without adequate railways to serve it the modern army could neither move, feed nor fight.

Before the end of the war, the whole area behind our front line was so linked with railways that a big offensive might have been mounted without much further construction at almost any point. This has been accomplished in the midst of the dangers and vicissitudes of unrelenting war. There was little of the heavy excitement of the battle about that work, but it was patient, steady, courageous labour under shell-fire.

10 Des Browne
11 St Pauls
12 *The Times* October 22nd 1921, 5.

In 1918 alone, we built or reconstructed in France 2,340 miles of broad gauge track and 1,348 miles of narrow gauge railway. In six months of that year the average weekly load carried by our railway system out there amounted to 530,000 tons each week employing 1,200 locomotives and 52,600 trucks. The feat could not have been accomplished but for the loyalty and unselfishness and efficiency of the railways at home, none of which had a finer record than the North-Western. He imagined the figure of 31,000 sent to the front was unsurpassed.

He had a special debt of his own to acknowledge, for it was a London and North-Western train, engine and staff which carried him about in France during the critical days of 1918 which formed his advance headquarters and then finally steamed to Metz, Strasbourg and Cologne.' (Cheers).

Field Marshall Earl Haig was the Commander in Chief of the BEF and a somewhat controversial figure for many years after his death in 1928. Happily, recently historians seem to be rehabilitating his reputation. At the time of the unveiling of the Euston memorial he remained one of the most famous personalities in the country. Haig's speech clearly demonstrates the importance with which he held the railway in enabling him to fight successfully. The focus of his speech, perhaps understandably, is on the achievements of an industry and not on the individuals that the memorial was built to remember. It seems odd looking back that there was no mention of the loss, but at the time it may have been so obvious that there was no value in mentioning it. It may have been that it was felt to be more positive to celebrate success than to mourn the loss.

The memorial erected at Euston station was designed by L&NWR architect Mr R Wynn Owen. It is an obelisk 43 ft high with four bronze figures representing the Navy, the Infantry, the Artillery and the Flying Corps. The choice of the four bronze guards with 'bowed heads and arms reversed' is interesting. Presumably the designer wanted to record the service in the three forces, but there was a problem with what to do with the fourth corner. Logically this should have been a Royal Engineer since the Rail Operating Division came under the engineers. Also more L&NWR men died as Sappers than Gunners. The choice of artillery may have been in the perception that it was artillery that won the war, which neatly links back to the railway, as artillery could not have performed without the constant supply of shells. If the decision was being made purely on those who died, the four soldiers would have come from the Royal Engineers, Artillery (Royal Horse Artillery, Royal Field Artillery and Royal Garrison Artillery), The London Regiment and the Kings (Liverpool) Regiment.

Most of the memorials are smaller and less grand. Many are more personal affairs, local to specific stations or particular workshops. Those that are located on the busy stations are prominent, but in all likelihood, rarely seen by busy commuters. Many are tucked away, in Newcastle, for example, one was in a quiet stairwell of a former railway building (now being renovated for the local constabulary), and another sits somewhat out of place in a posh entrance hall for a children's nursery, looking down on a parking area for pushchairs. In Attenborough under a bridge sits a small memorial to the few men who died at what is today two unmanned platforms. Hopefully the railwaymen of today will ensure that every one of those 440 memorials are cherished.

The railwaymen only had a small part to play in the Great War, but the scale of the campaign, logistics, fighting and slaughter is overall so enormous as to be hard to comprehend, and so hopefully by concentrating on just this small group it is possible to gain some understanding of the contribution of the manpower of one industry and the sacrifice can be more easily comprehended and understood.

Although this is a book about railwaymen, it is primarily about people. It is fitting, therefore, that the contributions of those who gave their lives for King and Country and who had worked for the railway are remembered in a way that is more than a name etched in brass or carved in stone.

Horwich Locomotive Works. NRM 1997_7059-HOR_F_3212

Conclusion

As I mentioned at the start I have been driven by a dual purpose, to tell the story of fellow railwaymen who went to war, and also to raise money for the Railway Benefit Fund and the Army Benevolent Fund (The Soldiers' Charity). Everyone mentioned in this book was part of the railway industry, the railway family, and today I am delighted that the railway industry has embraced this work and before a single copy has been sold raised over £30,000 for those charities. By purchasing this book you have also made a charitable contribution. Thank you.

This book is based upon 12,500 of the 20,792 railwaymen who were known to have died in, or as a result of, the Great War. As there are still over 8,000 railwaymen to trace it remains incomplete. The quest will continue to identify as many as possible and to provide a full picture of the railway contribution throughout the war. Men like P W Adams, Private in the Duke of Wellington's Regiment and a former porter with Midland Railway at Apperley Bridge and Charles Blythman an ex-carter for Caledonian Railway still need to be located. As do some 28 Campbells, 42 Evans, 34 Halls and 194 Smiths.

Little mention has been made of the 160,000 railwaymen who, upon completion of their service, returned home. Some of these men died in the following years to be commemorated on no memorial, the vast majority returned to the railway, back to the work they had done before the war carrying on with their lives, no doubt repressing many of the experiences they had encountered during the horror of what was their war. Some were too horrifically injured ever to return to work, and never had the chance to bring home a wage packet, and it is these men who the Railway Benefit Fund may have helped 100 years ago. Today there are people who work or have worked for the railway and the army who need help, who have served this nation well and it is fitting that this book recognises the contribution of the railwaymen who served in the Great War by raising money to help support those in need today.

Lest we forget.

Paddington Station 11.11.1919 Armistice day. 2 minutes Silence. NRM 1995_7233_GWR_B_ 2082

'There were no heroes and no cowards once you left England. If you had never seen war before once you stood in those front line trenches and had a smashing and bashing of shell fire you weren't human again after that, your mind went…You didn't know what you were doing half the time or you wouldn't have done it'. [13]

Hawtin Mundy, ex-railwayman, volunteered at the start of the war, was wounded three times, captured and a POW for 20 months and survived.

---

13   IWM Sound Archive, Hawtin Mundy, 5868.

THANKS AND ACKNOWLEDGEMENTS

Top of my list of acknowledgements is Royal Leamington Spa Station, the idea came whilst standing on the platform of what is quite a wonderful Art Deco station, tastefully restored by the team at Chiltern Railways. My thanks must also go to the Friends of Leamington Spa Station who maintain a fantastic garden on platform 2, a source of reflection, motivation and inspiration. Thanks to the team at the Search Engine at The National Railway Museum, York, a fantastic national asset, especially to Tim Proctor and Alison Kay but also to Martin Bashforth, formerly of the NRM, who helped to develop the idea and encouraged me to write. Special thanks go to all at the Commonwealth War Graves Commission, not that I have ever met any of them in person, but they have quite an amazing website! Thanks to the incredible but slightly bonkers Pam and Ken Linge, they were truly inspirational as is their search for all of the 72,000 'Missing of the Somme'. Thanks to Wikipedia, FirstWorldWar.com and Thelonglongtrail (and to Chris Baker), and the worldwideweb!

I couldn't have got this far if it wasn't for Peter Hart, author, and frustrated punk musician. Thanks Pete! Matthew Payne helped me to see the wood from the trees. Thanks to everyone at CrossCountry Trains and Arriva who, sometimes unwittingly, supported me throughout this campaign, special thanks to Andy Cooper and Noelle Partington who brought so much energy just when mine was flagging. This project would not have happened if Chris Gibb, then my boss at Virgin Trains had not, with undue haste, agreed for my release to be mobilised to serve in Iraq, without that experience I would not have had the inspiration in the first place.

This statue topped the war memorial at Horwich Locomotive works, unveiled on 27 August 1921.
1997-7059_HOR_F_3057

More than anyone else I must thank Rebecca Grier for being a constant support through the long and often fruitless hours of developing the massive database (currently though incomplete amounting to 245,850 individual pieces of information) and in then helping fashion the countless iterations consigned to the bin in order to get to what you read today.

Finally, as well as there being 8,000 individuals still to research, there are bound to be some mistakes in the 12,500 completed, so if anyone has any better information, or any history surfacing from attics or the back of drawers, please feel free to drop me a line so that the history of the railwaymen in the Great War can be improved. Of particular interest is information of those who having served returned to the railway. Also, if you want any information on anyone who died serving in the railway during the Great War then do please drop me a line at Jeremy-higgins@hotmail.co.uk.

APPENDICES

APPENDIX I

THE METHODOLOGY

This project gradually grew legs. Initially on each commute into Birmingham from Leamington Spa I jotted down a few names and locations from the Great Western memorial at the station and began to amass a list. Eventually I worked out that the internet was a better place to begin my search and located lists of most of the railway companies which individuals and railway societies had transcribed. Each entry was entered into a database to include all the details of the war memorial or roll of honour, such as, name, rank, regiment, railway place of work and job. There was no consistency of railway company, some for example Great Western and Midland Railways had fuller records, however, the information was more limited for Scottish companies. Lacking basic information made it more difficult to 'find' the railwaymen when cross-referencing with the Commonwealth War Graves database. This was the next step. Without the CWGC database this research would not have been possible. As it is, finding the railwayman has taken many hundreds, if not thousands, of man hours. The greater the detail or the more unusual the name, generally the easier it has been to locate but for common names or more limited records, such as no home location, regiment or full name has made it difficult to accurately identify the individual from the CWGC database. For that reason this project is far from complete and represents only 12,500 of the 20,000 or so who died. It remains work in progress. During the research I located a copy of a fantastic book the *St Paul's book* (The St Paul's Railway Service, Naval & Military Press & IWM) which, reprinted by the Imperial War Museum included a record of 'every' railwayman who died during the Great War. This was a very useful aid.

By combining the War Memorials/Rolls of honour (and/or) *St Paul's book* with the CWGC information I was able to synthesise complimentary information.

For example, J A Farr appeared on the Great Western Railway roll of honour as a clerk in the Goods Department at Cardiff. By using the CWGC website I searched J A Farr and only one name was returned, James Alfred Farr who served in the 6th Kings Own Scottish Borderers. If further assurance is required that this is J A Farr from GWR in Cardiff, the CWGC website also shows that he was the son of James Farr of 74 Mardy Street, Cardiff. The CWGC website informs that he died on 9 July 1916 in the battle of the Somme, and is buried in the Peronne Road CWGC Cemetery. This cemetery was used by field ambulances indicating that James Farr was not killed in action but was evacuated wounded.

From the fantastically detailed book by Ray Westlake *Tracing British Battalions on the Somme*, (Pen and Sword 2009) I was also able to establish that the 6th Kings Own Scottish Borderers had been fighting in Bernafay Wood on that day. This battle was taking place some 2 to 3 km north of Maricourt.

However, for most of the railwaymen who died I have not yet established where they were injured, and have concentrated on trying to marry up the details of the various rolls of honour with the CWGC. This in itself has been diffcult, especially with common names, Davis, Smith, Jones and many Mcs of Scotland. Tracking down the Scottish railwaymen has been more tricky than the English or Welsh, as the Scottish tended not to record the full names or where the man worked or which regiment they served in.

In an effort to reduce the list of 'unfound' railwaymen I have consulted the National Archive, the Scottish National Archive and the Trade Union records of Warwick University.

There have been a number of methodological issues, not least the scarcity of some information, also there are examples of people on the railway databases who don't appear on the CWGC, often this is because they died sometime after the war and aren't considered as war dead. In some cases there is mention of railway workers who died and yet are not on any of the railway company rolls of honour. Given the throughput of men throughout the war this may be understandable. For example, Albert French, believed by the BBC to have been the youngest soldier to die in the Great War, and widely reported to have been an apprentice engineer at the LNWR engineering works at Wolverton, yet there is no record of him on the LNWR roll of honour. Some companies recorded their maritime employees within their roles of honour and others didn't. In the case of the merchantile marine I have shown those I believe to have died serving on the ships, but they are not counted within the 12,500 unless the names also appear on their role of honour. You can begin to understand why there might be discrepancies and no certainty as to how many railwaymen died during the Great War.

The *St Paul's book* states that 18,957 died serving, whereas my summation of the various rolls of honour totals 20,792 and I do not include those of the Metropolitan railway (now the Metropolitan line of the London Underground or any of the Irish Railways) and that does not include all of those, such as those mentioned above, who do not feature on the rolls of honour!

At the point when I had 'found' 12,500 names (of the 18,957 or 20,792) I decided to pull together the themes from that database. If ever I locate all of the names the story could be quite different. There is clearly still much work to do.

Since completing my initial research the NRM has included an online database of those who died on their online 'search engine' this, interestingly, amounts to 20,320 names.

The only names recorded as 'railway dead' on the database are those shown as railwaymen on the company rolls of honour. However, in this section where there are merchant seamen who were serving on railway ships which were lost, it seems likely that they had been railway employees (indicated perhaps by their home eg Hull).

APPENDIX 2

RAILWAY DEAD IN THE GREAT WAR AND WHERE THE 12,500 CAME FROM

All of the railway companies contributed volunteers and later conscripts into the armed forces.

	Served	% total staff at Aug 14	Died	% of served who died	Researched	% researched of those who died
Alexandra (Newport & South Wales Docks) Rly	416	33	39	9	14	36
Barry	791	26	65	8	65	100
Belfast & County Down Rly			10		1	10
Bishops Castle Rly			2			0
Brecon & Merthr railway	103	15	13	13		0
Caledonian Railway	5229	22	706	14	117	17
Cambrian	452	22	48	11	25	52
Cardiff	713	30	56	8	16	29
Cheshire Lines Committee	1279	25	107	8	33	31
Cleator & Workington Junction Rly	50	29	5	10	2	40
Clogher Valley Railway			2			0
Cokermouth, Keswick, & Penrith Rly	39	30	7	18	5	71
Colne Valley	35	20	5	14	1	20
Easingwold Rly	2	18	1	50		0
East and West Yorkshire Union	17	22	2	12	1	50
East London Rly Joint Committee	49	54	4	8	0	0
Felixstowe Dock & Railway			2		2	100
Freshwater, Yarmouth & Newport Railway			1			0
Furness	515	18	68	13	68	100
Glasgow & South Western Rly	2458	23	302	12	66	22
Great Northern Railway	9691	28	938	10	255	27
Great Central Railway	10135	29	1310	13	1005	77
Great Eastern Railway	9734	29	1155	12	1150	100
Gt North of Scotland Railway	609	22	93	15	91	98
Great Western Railway	25460	33	2575	10	1964	76

	Served	% total staff at Aug 14	Died	% of served who died	Researched	% researched of those who died
Highland Rail Company	668	25	86	13	7	8
Hull & Barnsley Rly	1381	40	169	12	78	46
Isle of Man			3			0
Isle of Wight	59	40	2	3	1	50
Isle of Wight central Railway	67	32	5	8	2	40
Knott End Railway	7	20	1	14	1	100
London and North Western Railway	31744	34	3719	12	2062	55
Lancs and York Railway	10453	28	1465	14	344	23
London & South West Rly	6621	27	585	9	304	52
London Bri & S Coast Rly	5207	32	626	12	306	49
Maryport & Carlisle	135	26	17	13	6	35
Mersey	158	24	14	9	5	36
Mid Suffolk Light			2		1	50
Midland	22441	29	2833	13	1868	66
Neath & Brecon	64	22	1	2		0
North Eastern Railway	18339	34	1994	11	1969	99
North British Railway	4554	18	775	17	66	9
North Staffs	1372	23	147	12	147	100
Port Talbot Railway & Docks	139	34	11	8	1	9
Railway Clearing House	1314	45	135	10	115	85
Rhondda & Swansea Bay Coy	51	18	1	2		0
Rhymney Railway	399	23	31	8	12	39
South Eastern and Chatham Railway	5074	24	556	11	372	67
Taff Vale	1085	22	89	8	37	42
Wirral	56	17	9	16	2	22

APPENDIX 3

List of Railway Companies recorded in the St Pauls Cathedral Service in Memory of Railwaymen Wednesday 14th May 1919. 'Dedicated to 188,475 Railwaymen of Great Britain and Ireland, 18,957 of whom died'.

Name	Abbreviation	Died (St Pauls)	Died (other refs)
Alexandra (Newport and South Wales) Docks and Railway		39	39
Barry Railway		60	60
Belfast and County Down Railway*		10	N/A
Bishops Castle Railway*		2	N/A
Brecon & Merthyr Railway		14	13
Caledonian Railway		630	706
Cambrian Railways		48	48
Cardiff Railway		56	56
Cheshire Lines Committee		106	107
Cleator and Workington Junction Railway		5	5
Clogher Valley Railway		2	
Cockermouth, Keswich and Penrith Railway		7	7
Colne Valley Railway		5	5
Cork Brandon and South Coast Railway*		1	N/A
County Donegal Railways*		7	N/A
Dublin and South Eastern Railway*		14	N/A
Easingwold Railway		1	1
East London Railway Joint Committee*		4	N/A
East and West Yorkshire Union		2	2
Felixstowe Dock and Railway		2	2
Freshwater, Yarmouth and Newport Railway		1	1
Furness Railway		63	68
Glasgow and South Western Railway	G & SWR	290	302
Great Central Railway	GCR	1200	1310
Great Eastern Railway	GER	1024	1155
Great Northern Railway	GNR	854	938
Great North of Ireland Railway*		87	N/A
Great North of Scotland Railway	GNSR	83	93
Great Southern and Western Railway		1	
Great Western Railway	GWR	2081	2575

Name	Abbreviation	Died (St Pauls)	Died (other refs)
Highland Railway		73	86
Hull and Barnsley Railway		168	169
Isle Of Man Railway		3	3
Isle of Wight Railway		2	2
Knott End Railway		1	1
Lancashire and Yorkshire Railway	L&Y	1385	1465
London and North Western Railway	L & NWR	3212	3719
London and North Western and Furness Joint Railway		4	
London and South Western Railway	L & SWR	561	585
London Brighton and South Coast Railway	LB&SCR	513	626
Manx Electric Railway		2	N/A
Maryport and Carlisle Railway		17	17
Mersey Railway		14	14
Metropolitan Railway*		129	N/A
Midland Railway		2324	2833
Midland Railway (Northern Counties Committee)*		44	N/A
Midland Great Western Railway of Ireland*		47	N/A
Midland and South Western Junction Railway		18	
Mid-Suffolk Light Railway		2	2
Neath and Brecon Railway	NBR	1	1
North British Railway	NER	752	775
North Eastern Railway		1979	1994
North Staffordshire Railway		115	147
Port Patrick and Wigtownshire Joint Railway		11	
Port Talbort Railway and Docks		11	11
Railway Clearing House		135	135
Rhondda and Swansea Bay Railway		1	1
Rhymney Railway		31	31
Sligo, Leitrim and Northern Counties*		4	N/A
South Eastern and Chatham Railway	SECR	472	556
Southwold Railway		1	
Stratford-upon-Avon and Midland Junction Railway		8	
Taff Vale Railway		90	89
Underground Electric Railways of London*		11	
Wirral Railway		355	

* Excluded: Does not currently form part of this research project.

APPENDIX 4

THE 12,500 AND WITH WHOM THEY SERVED

Cavalry

1st Dragoon Guards	1
2nd Dragoon Guards (Royal Scots Greys	5
3rd Dragoon Guards (Queens Bays)	5
4th Royal Irish Dragoons	4
6th Inniskilling Dragoon Guards	5
7th Princess Royals Dragoon Guards	2
3rd Hussars	1
4th Hussars	1
5th Lancers	3
7th Hussars	1
8th Hussars	2
9th Lancers	3
10th Hussars	3
11th Hussars	1
12th Lancers	5
16th Lancers	5
17th Lancers	5
18th Hussars	3
19th Hussars	3
20th Hussars	3
21st Lancers	1
Reserve Cavalry Regiment	5
	67

Yeomanry

Ayrshire	1
Bedford	2
Berkshire	5
City of London	1
County of London (Westminster Dragoons)	11
Derbyshire	3
East Riding	1
Essex	1
Hampshire	4

Yeomanry (cont)

Hertfordshire	1
Lincolnshire	4
Middlesex Hussars	2
North Somerset	1
Northamptonshire	
Queens Own Worcester Hussars	8
Queens Own Oxford Hussars	1
Royal Buckinghamshire Hussars	6
Royal East and West Kent	2
Royal Gloucestershire Hussars	1
Royal North Devon	1
Fife and Forfar	14
Royal Wiltshire Hussars	1
Scottish Horse	2
Sherwood Rangers	2
South Nottinghamshire Hussars	2
Staffordshire	3
Westmoreland & Cumberland	1
Worcestershire	1
Yorks Dragoons	1
Yorks Hussars	2
	90

Guards

Life Guards	6
Royal Horse Guards	2
Grenadier Guards	123
Coldstream Guards	88
Scots Guards	23
Irish Guards	6
Welsh Guards	18
Household Battalion	11
	265

Infantry

Bedfordshire	134
Border	112
Cambridgeshire	16
Cheshire	151
Devonshire	110
Dorset	34
East Kent	101
East Lancs	45
East Surrey	84
East Yorks	214
Essex	192
Gloucestershire	153
Hampshire	82
Herefordshire	10
Hertfordshire	17
Kings Own Royal Lancs	105
Kings	161
Lancashire Fusiliers	119
Leicestershire	112
Lincoln	191
London	506
Loyal North Lancs	67
Manchester	201
Middlesex	181
Monmouth	37
Norfolk	108
North Lancashire	1
North Staffordshire	69
Northamptonshire	150
Northumberland Fusiliers	416
Notts & Derbyshire	313
Royal Fusiliers	232
Royal Berkshire	136
Royal Warwickshire	169
Royal West Kent	98
Royal West Surrey	81
Royal Lancs	1
Royal Sussex	57

Infantry (cont)	
South Lancs	57
South Staffordshires	79
Suffolk	103
West Riding (Duke of Wellingtons)	84
West Yorks (Prince of Wales's own)	277
Wiltshire	275
Worcestershire	157
Yorkshire & Lancashire	163
Yorkshire	137
	6307

Scottish	
Argyll & Sutherland Highlanders	20
Black Watch	24
Cameron Highlanders	27
Cameronians	34
Royal Scots Fusiliers	20
Royal Scots	54
Seaforth Highlanders	76
Gordon Highlanders	63
Kings Own Scottish Borderers	51
	369

Welsh	
Royal Welsh Fusiliers	90
Royal Welsh	88
South Wales Borderers	84
	262

Irish	
Connaught Rangers	3
Royal Irish Fusiliers	20
Royal Inniskilling Fusiliers	29
Irish Rifles	1
Leinster	9
Royal Dublin Fusiliers	21
Royal Irish	14
Royal Irish Regiment	11
Royal Munster Fusiliers	13
	121

Light Infantry	
DCLI	62
DLI	291
HLI	47
KOYLI	168
KRRC	229
KSLI	78
Oxfordshire & Buckinghamshire	154
Royal Guernsey LI	2
Rifle Bde	186
Royal Irish Rifles	12
Somerset LI	97
	1326

Army cyclist corps	14
Huntingdon Cyclist Battalion	3
General List	2
Machine Gun Corps	263
Tank Corps	16
	298

Artillery	
HAC	11
RHA	19
RFA	608
RGA	240
	878

Engineers	
Royal Monmouthshire Royal Engineers	1
Royal Engineers	478
Rail Operating Division RE	482
Rail Transport Executive RE	1
	963

Other	
RAOC	11
Army Service Corps	96
Military Police	9
RAMC	143
Training Reserve	5
Labour Corps	21
Army Gymnastics Staff	1
Army Musketry School	1
Army Vet Corps	2
Royal Defence Corps	4
	293

Royal Flying Corps	26
Royal Air Force	67
	93

Canadian	2
French	1
Egyptian Labour Corps	1
Imperial Camel Corps	1

Royal Navy	384
Royal Naval Division	143
Royal Marines	55
Merchant Navy	84
	666

APPENDIX 5

The top 18 cemeteries where 5,212 of the 12,500 are commemorated.
(M = memorial to the missing).

		Total Rail	GWR	GCR	GER	L&NW	L&SW	Lanc &York	LB & SCR	Mids	NER	SECR	Total
YPRES													
Lijssenthoek		121	15	7	9	26	8	4	0	18	22	4	9,877
Menin Gate	M	657	104	54	50	141	13	12	7	103	84	27	54,405
Ploegsteert		213	42	14	20	39	4	4	1	43	28	4	11,383
Tyne Cot		557	64	57	50	90	12	14	9	106	91	15	43,035
FRANCE													
Arras	M	461	45	37	46	56	18	11	9	95	68	17	34,724
Cambrai		110	25	7	9	17	4	3	5	18	10	5	7,602
Etaples		152	20	15	8	26	3	6	2	21	21	8	10,816
Le Touret		229	58	9	14	41	7	5	8	42	18	8	13,393
Loos	M	320	56	33	30	53	6	3	4	47	36	15	20,616
Pozieres		258	35	1	25	32	4	8	8	54	53	6	14,657
St Sever		180	27	13	13	29	5	4	5	23	38	7	11,727
Thiepval	M	1051	146	127	104	158	19	31	18	177	160	29	72,195
Vis-en-Artois		168	21	12	22	27	1	7	2	36	28	4	7,833
OTHER													
Basra	M	102	38	3	6	15	3	4	2	17	3	3	40,626
Helles	M	314	43	38	34	68	2	13	9	39	36	3	20,878
ROYAL NAVY													
Chatham	M	115	9	4	30	14	2	1	5	8	23	15	8,517
Plymouth	M	98	22	3	14	18	5	10	0	7	9	3	7,251
Portsmouth	M	106	7	4	4	20	8	2	8	17	19	3	10,000
Total		5212	777	438	488	870	124	142	102	871	747	176	

APPENDIX 6

THE WORST DAYS FOR RAILWAYMEN

Date	No	Campaign
25.9.15	134	Battle of Loos
26.9.15	55	Battle of Loos
27.9.15	31	Battle of Loos
1.7.16	242	Battle of The Somme (opening day)
2.7.16	25	Battle of The Somme
3.7.16	36	Battle of The Somme
7.7.16	41	Battle of The Somme
14.7.16	44	Battle of The Somme
15.7.16	30	Battle of The Somme
19.7.16	32	Battle of The Somme
20.7.16	31	Battle of The Somme
23.7.16	31	Battle of The Somme
30.7.16	33	Battle of The Somme
15.9.16	72	Battle of The Somme
16.9.16	46	Battle of The Somme
25.9.16	34	Battle of The Somme
26.9.16	28	Battle of The Somme
13.11.16	53	Battle of The Somme
9.4.17	63	Arras & Vimy Ridge
31.7.17	90	Passchendaele – Day 1
21.3.18	130	Ludendorffs Offensive, Day 1, Operation Michael
22.3.18	66	Ludendorffs Offensive.
23.3.18	43	Ludendorffs Offensive.
24.3.18	33	Ludendorffs Offensive.
25.3.18	33	Ludendorffs Offensive.
26.3.18	36	Ludendorffs Offensive.
27.3.18	32	Ludendorffs Offensive.
28.3.18	65	Ludendorffs Offensive

APPENDIX 7

Those railwaymen who died on 1st July 1916 at the Battle of The Somme

Surname	First name	Rank	Btn	Regt	Age	CWGC	Company	Location	Job
Atkins	EW	L/Cpl	7th	Bedfords		Dantzig	Midland	St Albans	Porter
Sibthorpe	Joseph	Cpl	7th	Bedfords	22	Dantzig Alley	GER	Hertford	Cleaner
Gaughy	A	Pte	11th	Border		Thiepval	L & NWR	Carlisle	Carriage Cleaner
Grisedale	Thompson	Cpl	1st	Border	28	Thiepval	L & NWR	Workington	Ticket Collector
Slack	Samuel	Pte	1st	Border	35	Thiepval	GCR	Gorton Shed	Shunter
Beavis	Arthur	Pte	2nd	Cameronians		Thiepval	Midland	Derby	Labourer
Northcott	Frank	Pte	2nd	Devons		Thiepval	Gt Western	Devonport	Porter
Older	Edgar	Pte	2nd	Devons	24	Thiepval	SECR	Labourer	Labourer
Connett	RV	Pte	8th	Devons		Devonshire Cem Mametz	Gt Western	Exeter	Engine Cleaner
Best	Wilie	Pte	9th	Devons	22	Devonshire Cem	GCR	London	Clerk
Bill	Horace	CSM	9th	Devons		Devonshire	Gt Western	Hockley	Carman
Forrester	Henry	L/Cpl	9th	Devons	25	Thiepval	GER	Police Dept	Police Constable
Opie	John	Pte	9th	Devons		Thiepval	Gt Western	Plymouth	Porter
Orsman	Reginald	Pte	9th	Devons	19	Devonshire Cem	Caledonian	Dumbarton & Balloch	Lampman
Weston	Alfred	Pte	9th	Devons		Devonshire ametz	GER	Stratford C&W Dept	Painter
Cook	Robert	Pte	10th	DLI	21	Faubourg	NER	Darlington	Greaser
Skinner	John	Pte	15th	DLI	32	Norfolk	NER	West Hartlepool	Gangman
Telford	Francis L	Pte	15th	DLI		Thiepval	NER	Darlington	Porter
Clarke	CJ	L/Cpl	1st	Dorset		Lonsdale Authuille	L & NWR	Aston	Porter
Smith	Edwin	Pte	1st	E Lancs		Thiepval	Lancs & Yorks		Colliery Prev Cleaner
Dunkley	Fred	Pte	7th	East Kent	25	Thiepval	GER	Ilford	Porter
Lomax	Charles	Sgt	7th	East Kent	21	Serre	Midland	London (St Pancras)	Van Guard
Courtney	Lindsay	Pte	8th	East Surrey	19	Thiepval	GER		Smith
Fairman	John	Pte	8th	East Surrey		Thiepval	LB & SCR		Cleaner
Hague	Kenneth	Pte	1st	East Yorks		Thiepval	NER	Hull	Dredgerman
Lythe	Richard W	Pte	1st	East Yorks	22	Thiepval	NER	Malton	
Mann	Charles	Pte	1st	East Yorks		Thiepval	NER	Hull	Gangman
Mulvey	James	Pte	1st	East Yorks		London Cemy	NER	Hull	Assistant Boilersmith
Wells	William	L/Cpl	10th	Essex	20	Thiepval	GER	Parkeston Quay	Boiler-maker's assistant
Hasler	John	Pte	1st	Essex	20	Thiepval	GER	Squirrels Heath	Labourer
Auker	George	Pte	2nd	Essex	21	Thiepval	GER	Liverpool St, CTMO	Clerk
Blyth	WG	Pte	2nd	Essex	32	Thiepval	GER	Bishopsgate Goods	Porter
East	William	Pte	2nd	Essex	20	Serre Road no 1	GER	Ongar	Porter
Oakman	George	Pte	2nd	Essex	26	AIF Burial Ground, Flers	GER	Stratford	Carriage Washer
Allsworth	Frederick	Sgt	1st	Hampshire	42	Redan Ridge	Gt Western	Oxford	Labourer
Budd	A G	Sgt	1st	Hampshire		Redan Ridge 2	L & SWR		Labourer
Toomer	Harry	Pte	1st	Hampshire		Thiepval	L & SWR		Platelayer
Baxter	David	Pte	17th	HLI	20	Thiepval	North British		Striker
Coote	Richard	Rfrn	2nd	KOR Lancs	20	Maroc	GCR	Gorton Works	Apprentice Rivetter
Catherall	Edward	Pte	14th	Kings	20	Thiepval	Gt Western	Chester	Carriage Cleaner
Blinkhorn	Humphrey	Pte	18th	Kings		Thiepval	L & NWR	Park Lane	Goods Porter
Wake	George	Pte	18th	Kings	22	Thiepval	GNR		Acting Junior Clerk
Keough.	Joseph	L/Cpl	1st	KOR Lancs		Thiepval	L & NWR	Walsall	
Scanlan	Michael	Pte	1st	KOSB	37	Thiepval	NER	Percy Main	Platelayer
Hodgkinson	John	Pte	10th	KOYLI		Thiepval	GCR	Stockport	Carter
Jeffrey	John	Pte	10th	KOYLI	30	Thiepval	GCR	Doncaster	Asst Shunter
Jeeves	Claude	L/Cpl	2nd	KOYLI		Thiepval	L & NWR	Rugby	Cleaner (Loco.)
Wainman	Arthur	Pte	8th	KOYLI		Thiepval	NER	Goole	Porter
Warren	Harold	Pte	8th	KOYLI	28	Serre 2	Gt Western	West London	
Woodhouse	Benjamin	Pte	8th	KOYLI	26	Thiepval	Midland	Leeds	steam raiser
Almond	Arthur	L/Cpl	9th	KOYLI	24	Thiepval	GCR	Wombwell	Platelayer
Cooper	John	Pte	9th	KOYLI		Thiepval	Midland	Sheffield	Labourer
Johnson	Robert	L/Cpl	9th	KOYLI	23	Thiepval	NER	Hull	Carriage cleaner
Fisher	G	Sgt	2nd	KRRC		Maroc	Midland	Plaistow	Lifter
Core	Alfred	Sgt	15th	Lancs Fus		Thiepval	Lancs & Yorks		Carter
Alford	Charles	Pte	19th	Lancs Fus	24	Thiepval	Glasgow & SW		

Surname	First name	Rank	Btn	Regt	Age	CWGC	Company	Location	Job
Burrell	Henry	Pte	10th	Lincoln	27	Thiepval	GCR	Immingham	Cook
Coupland	William	Pte	10th	Lincoln		Thiepval	GCR	Ulceby	Assistant Loader
Grant	Allan	Pte	10th	Lincoln	18	Thiepval	GCR	Grimsby Docks	Clerk
Hempstock	Jesse	Pte	10th	Lincoln	21	Thiepval	GCR	Grimsby Docks	Clerk
Marshall	Christopher	Pte	10th	Lincoln		Thiepval	GCR	Grimsby Docks	Fish Porter
Oxley	Percy	Pte	10th	Lincoln	19	Thiepval	GCR	Grimsby Docks	Clerk
Pearson	Maurice	Pte	10th	Lincoln	21	Thiepval	GCR	Grimsby Docks	Clerk
Russell	John	Pte	10th	Lincoln		Thiepval	GCR	Grimsby Docks	Fish Porter
Walker	Percy	Pte	10th	Lincoln	21	Ovillers	GCR	Grimsby Docks	Clerk
Ward	George	Pte	10th	Lincoln		Thiepval	GCR	Grimsby Docks	Goods Porter
White	George	Pte	10th	Lincoln		Thiepval	GCR	Grimsby Docks	SS Porter
Ayres	Joseph	Pte	2nd	Lincoln	32	Blighty Valley	Midland	Lincoln	Checker
Barnard	WH	Pte	2nd	Lincoln	20	Lonsdale	GCR	Keadby	Cleaner
Fearn	Harry	Pte	2nd	Lincoln	23	Thiepval	Midland	Derby	Labourer
Hulme	Charles	Pte	2nd	Lincoln		Thiepval	GCR	Langwith Junct	App Fitter
Benbow	George	L/Cpl	1/14th	London	20	Thiepval	L & NWR	Bletchley	Parcel Porter, Junior
Beer	David	Pte	1/16th	London		Thiepval	Gt Western	Chief Managers Office	Clerk
Love	Vincent	Rfn	1/16th	London		Thiepval	SECR	Clerk	Clerk
Loynes	Edward	Rfn	1/16th	London	26	Thiepval	Gt Western	Smithfield	Clerk
Farley	Frederick	2/Lt	1/2nd	London	25	Thiepval	LB & SCR		Erector
Ilsley	Cyril	L/Cpl	1/2nd	London		Thiepval	L & SWR		Clerk
Tarbox	Reginald	Pte	1/2nd	London		Thiepval	L & NWR	Camden	Cleaner (Loco.)
Batchelor	William	Rfn	1/5th	London	17	Thiepval	LB & SCR		Clerk
Cook	George	Rfn	1/5th	London		Thiepval	L & SWR		Clerk
Marsh	Harold	Rfn	1/5th	London	18	Thiepval	GER	Stratford CME	Clerk
Reeves	Ernest	Rfn	1/5th	London	25	Thiepval	LB & SCR		Clerk
Stewart	Edward	Rfn	1/5th	London		Thiepval	Gt Western		Clerk
Buckland	Richard	Cpl	1/9th	London	20	Thiepval	L & NWR	Euston	Clerk
Collis	Leonard	Rfn	1/9th	London	26	Gommecourt	Gt Western		Clerk
Dawkes	Albert	Pte	1/9th	London		Thiepval	GCR	London	Clerk
Kerr		Rfn	1/9th	London		Gommecourt 2	L & NWR	Euston	Clerk
Whitehouse	Sid	Rfn	1/9th	London		Thiepval	Gt Western	Paddington	Messenger
Lawrence		Pte	14th	London		Gommecourt Wood	L & SWR		Clerk
Bamford	John	Pte	12th	Manchester		Thiepval	GCR	Manchester	Porter
Green	Stanley	L/Cpl	16th	Manchester	22	Thiepval	GCR	Manchester	
Green	Stanley	L/Cpl	16th	Manchester	22	Thiepval	GCR	Manchester	Clerk
Mainwaring	Ernest	Pte	16th	Manchester	19	Thiepval	GCR	Manchester	Clerk
Butterworth	William	Sgt	17th	Manchester	24	Thiepval	Lancs & Yorks		Clerk
Byrne	Frank	Pte	17th	Manchester		Thiepval	L & NWR	Longsight	Fireman
Birdsall	E	Pte	18th	Manchester	20	Peronne Road	Lancs & Yorks		Clerk
Shaw	Allen	Pte	20th	Manchester	28	Dantzig Alley	GCR	Manchester	Clerk
Birtwistle	William	Pte	21st	Manchester		Dantzig Alley	L & NWR	London Road	Goods Porter
Kemp	Harold	Pte	21st	Manchester	20	Thiepval	GCR	Manchester	
Russell	Edward	Pte	21st	Manchester	20	Thiepval	Gt Western	Manchester	Clerk
Davies	Edward	Pte	22nd	Manchester		Thiepval	GCR	Ashburys	Platelayer
Entwistle	Henry	Pte	22nd	Manchester	23	Dantzig Alley	Lancs & Yorks	Wigan	Clerk
Heaps	George	Pte	22nd	Manchester	25	Thiepval	GCR	Manchester	Clerk
Knowles	Frederick	Sgt	22nd	Manchester	40	Thiepval	GNR		Drayman
Nadin	William	Pte	22nd	Manchester	26	Thiepval	GCR	Guide Bridge	Shunter
Redfern	W	Pte	22nd	Manchester		Mametz Alley	GCR	Gorton Works	Labourer
Worthington	George	Pte	22nd	Manchester	19	Thiepval	GCR	Gorton Works	Brass Dresser
Yardley	Joseph	Cpl	2nd	Manchester		Thiepval	L & NWR	Crewe	Labourer, Temporary
Walton	George	Pte		MGC		Thiepval	GCR	New Holland	Passenger Porter
Pluck	Frederick	Pte	11th Coy	MGC	26	Serre Road No 2	GER	Lowestoft	Acting fireman
Cornall	George	Pte	12th Coy	MGC		Thiepval	Lancs & Yorks		Labourer
Taylor	Jesse	CQMS	12th Coy	MGC		Bertrancourt	Furness		Shunter
Rudd	Ernest	l/Sgt	1/8th	Middlesex		Thiepval	Gt Western	Southall	Clerk
Milne-Mills	Kenneth	Pte	16th	Middlesex	26	Hawthorn Ridge No 1	LB & SCR		Clerk

Surname	First name	Rank	Btn	Regt	Age	CWGC	Company	Location	Job
King	Arthur	Sgt	26th	Middlesex	30	Hawthorne Ridge No 1	Railway Clearing House		Clerk
Bruce	Herbert	Pte	2nd	Middlesex	29	Thiepval	GER	Spitalfields	Porter
Coulson	J	Pte	2nd	Middlesex		Ovillers	Midland	London (St Pancras)	Goods guard
Rackley	Edwin	Pte	2nd	Middlesex		Thiepval	L & NWR	Watford	Porter
White	George	Cpl	4th	Middlesex		Gordon Dump	SECR	Porter	Porter
Howells	Charles	Rfn	1st	Monmouth	23	Thiepval	Gt Western	Newport	Fireman
Small	William	Rfn	1st	Monmouth	27	Foncquevillers	Gt Western	Bassaleg	Packer
Beman	Percival	Pte	8th	Norfolk	19	Thiepval	GER	Norwich Goods	Porter
Price	Edwin	Pte	1/6th	North Staffs	39	Gommecourt Wd	Gt Western	Hockley	Packer
Stait	George	Pte	1/6th	North Staffs		Thiepval	L & NWR	Walsall	Labourer
Griggs	WE	Cpl	6th	North Staffs		Gommecourt Wd	Midland	Burton	Ticketer
Dunglinson	Dan	Cpl	16th	Northumb Fus	26	Thiepval	NER	Newcastle Forth	Clerk
Sharpe	W D	Pte	16th	Northumb Fus		Lonsdale	NER	Tyne Dock	fireman
Simpson	A H	Sgt	16th	Northumb Fus	28	Ovillers	NER	Newcastle Eng	Clerk
Waugh	William	Pte	16th	Northumb Fus	24	Thiepval	NER	Accountants Dept	Clerk
Baldwinson	Tom	Cpl	17th (NER)	North Fus	34	Bouzincourt	NER	Leeds Wellington St	Porter
Bays	F	Pte	17th (NER)	North Fus		Authuile	NER	York Wagon Works	Wagon repairer
Dalby	E	Pte	17th (NER)	North Fuss		Blighty Valley	NER	Middlesbrough	Underman
Staples	Joseph	Pte	17th (NER)	North Fus	22	Bouzincourt	NER	Heslerton	Porter
Thompson	Roderick	Pte	20th (TS)	North Fus	30	Thiepval	NER	Monkseaton	Platelayer
Barclay	John	Pte	21st (TS)	North Fus	34	Thiepval	NER	Heaton Junction	Coalman
Chadwick	James	Pte	21st (TS)	North Fus		Thiepval	NER	Gateshead	Labourer
Nugent	George	Pte	22nd (TS)	North Fuss	28	Ovillers Mil Cemy	NER	Newcastle	Porter
Healy	James	Pte	24th (TI)	North Fus		Thiepval	NER	Darlington	Labourer
Matthewson	William	Pte	24th (TI)	North Fus		Ovillers Mil Cemy	NER	Blyth	Platelayer
Railton	Alexander	Pte	24th (TI)	North Fus		Thiepval	NER	Gateshead	Apprentice
Bowes	Joseph	Pte	27th (TI)	North Fus		Thiepval	NER	Shildon Works	Labourer
McHugh	Thomas	L/Cpl	27th (TI)	North Fus		Thiepval	NER	Tyne Dock	Fireman
McKeown	William	Pte	27th (TI)	North Fus		Thiepval	NER	Walker Gate	Assistant Painter
Tompkin	Stanley	Pte	2nd	R Fus		Thiepval	L & NWR	Coventry	Clerk
Streeter	John	Pte	1st	R Innis Fus		Thiepval	Barry Rail		Fitters Apprentice
Byfield	Henry	Pte	9th	R Innis Fus	23	Thiepval	Midland	Liverpool (sandon & c dock)	Number taker
Shields	Ernest	L/Cpl	12th	R Irish		Thiepval	Gt Western	Port Talbot	Packer
Taylor	Samuel	Pte	15th	R Scots		Thiepval	Lancs & Yorks	Radcliffe	Platelayer
Adams	Herbert	Pte	1/8th	R Warwicks	23	Thiepval	L & NWR	Wolverton	Underman
Hughes	James	Spr	122nd Fd Coy	RE		Thiepval	SECR	Fitter's Apprentice	Fitter's Apprentice
Whitcut	H	Spr	2/1 N Mids Bde	RE	18	Foncquevillers	N Staffs		
Best	T	Spr	2nd Coy	RE	36	Aveluy Wood	GCR	Mexborough	Sp Driver
Gedge	David	Spr	8th Sig Coy	RE		Thiepval	L & SWR		Office Porter
Bratby	Alec	Gnr	North Mids Bde	RFA	24	Foncquevillers	Midland	Derby	Labourer
Brockwell	John	Gnr	P 34 TM Bty	RFA		Thiepval	Midland	Nottingham	Porter
Cooper	John	Rfn	1st	Rifle Bde	28	Serre Road No 2	GER	Bishopsgate	Goods Porter
Girling	Thomas	Bugler	1st	Rifle Bde	28	Serre Road No 2	GER	Ipswich	Signal-fitter's labourer
Lovatt	Thomas	Rfn	1st	Rifle Bde		Serre Road	Midland	Burton	Labourer
Buckley	Albert	Rfn	2nd	Rifle Bde		Thiepval	NER	Haverton Hill	Fireman
Maunsell	Edwin	Capt	1st	Royal Dublin Fus	25	Auchonvillers	L & SWR		Assistant Foreman
Harrison	Frank	Cpl	15th	Royal Scots	26	Gordon Dump	L & NWR	London Road	Clerk
Meadowcroft	Fred	Pte	15th	Royal Scots	18	Gordon Dump	Lancs & Yorks		Clerk
Begbie	J	Pte	16th	Royal Scots		Gordon Dump	North British		Surfaceman
Spencer	Edward	Pte	2nd	Royal Scots Fus	44	Thiepval	Midland	Derby	Ganger
Jones	EC	L/Cpl	1/6th	Royal Warwicks	23	Thiepval	L & NWR	Curzon Street	Clerk
Nash	Charles	Pte	1/6th	Royal Warwicks		Thiepval	L & NWR	Aston	Porter
Adams	Herbert	Pte	1/8th	Royal Warwicks	23	Thiepval	L & NWR		
Woodman	Alfred	Pte	1/8th	Royal Warwicks	20	Serre Road	Gt Western	Swindon	Apprentice
Alldred	FA	Pte	1/5 th	Sherwood For	24	Thiepval	Midland	Derby	Labourer
Derbyshire	Ernest	Pte	1/5 th	Sherwood For		Thiepval	Midland	Derby	Labourer

Surname	First name	Rank	Btn	Regt	Age	CWGC	Company	Location	Job
Dumelow	William	L/Cpl	1/5th	Sherwood For	22	Thiepval	Midland	Derby	Coach body makers boy
Frost	Frank	Pte	1/5th	Sherwood For		Thiepval	Midland	Derby	Coach Trimmer
Goodwin	Thomas	CSM	1/5th	Sherwood For	32	Thiepval	Midland	Derby	Labourer
Harrison	Victor	L/Cpl	1/5th	Sherwood For	21	Thiepval	Midland	Derby	Coach Finishers boy
Hunt	George	Pte	1/5th	Sherwood For		Thiepval	Midland	Chaddesden	Shunter
Bancroft	Joseph	Pte	1/5th	Sherwood For		Thiepval	GCR	Nottingham	
Bickerton	A	Pte	1/5th	Sherwood For	26	Gommecourt Wd	Midland	Derby	Wagon repairer
Holmes	Joseph	Pte	1/5th	Sherwood For	30	Thiepval	Midland	Derby	Labourer
Lewes	Frederick	Capt	1/5th	Sherwood For	29	Thiepval	Midland	Hazelwood	Cadet
Poyser	F	Pte	1/5th	Sherwood For		Thiepval	Midland	Derby	Wagon repairer
Rose	RE	L/Cpl	1/5th	Sherwood For		Gommecourt Wd	Midland	Derby	Porter
Shaw	H	Sgt	1/5th	Sherwood For	21	Foncquevillers	Midland	Hucknall	Porter
Smith	James	Pte	1/5th	Sherwood For	19	Gommecourt	Midland	Derby	Machine Boy
Webster	George	Pte	1/5th	Sherwood For		Thiepval	Midland	Derby	Hammerman
Webster	William	Pte	1/5th	Sherwood For	23	Thiepval	Midland	Derby	Demurrageman
Whittingham	Frederick	Pte	1/5th	Sherwood For	28	Thiepval	Midland	Westhouses	Holder up
Wilcox	Antony	Pte	1/5th	Sherwood For	25	Thiepval	Midland	Derby	Striker
Gibbons	GF	L/Cpl	1/6th	Sherwood For		Gommecourt	GCR	Chesterfield	Stores Labourer
Maha	Frederick	Sgt	1/7th	Sherwood For	26	Thiepval	L & NWR	Netherfield & Colwick	Fireman
Bacon	Albert	Pte	11th	Sherwood For	20	Thiepval	GCR	Annesley	
Ford	George	Sgt	11th	Sherwood For		Thiepval	Midland	Derby	Labourer
Fulcher	John	L/Cpl	11th	Sherwood For	23	Thiepval	Midland	Derby	Cupolaman
Gibbons	Arnold	Pte	11th	Sherwood For		Thiepval	Midland	Derby	Labourer
Gibson	Walter	Pte	11th	Sherwood For	39	Blighty Valley	GCR	Arkwright town	
Gibson	Walter	Pte	11th	Sherwood For	39	Blighty Valley	GCR	Arkwright Town	Sub-Ganger
Hawkins	B	Pte	11th	Sherwood For		Blighty Valley	Midland	Langley Mill	Ganger
Pymm	Sidney	Cpl	11th	Sherwood For	23	Blighty Valley	Midland	Spondon	Porter
Guest	Henry	Cpl	1st	Somerset LI		Serre Rd 2	Gt Western	Taunton	Labourer
Spiller	William	L/Cpl	1st	Somerset LI	26	Thiepval	Gt Western	Yeovil	Carman
Stead	P	Pte	1st	Somerset LI		Thiepval	Midland	Fo?dridge	Porter
Moger	Bertie	L/Cpl	8th	Somerset LI	23	Thiepval	Gt Western	Pensford	Slip Labourer
Churm	John	Sgt	1st	South Staffs		Thiepval	L & NWR	Walsall	Labourer
Upton	Walter	Cpl	2nd	South Wales Borderers	26	Y Ravine	Gt Western	Shifnal	Porter
Baines	Francis	Pte	11th	Suffolk	19	Thiepval	GER	Murrow	Gate Lad
Speed	Charles	L/Cpl	11th	Suffolk	23	Thiepval	GER	Whittlesford	Porter
Atkinson	William	Pte	10th	West Yorks	33	Thiepval	NER	Leeds	
Godwin	Joseph	Cpl	10th	West Yorks	37	Thiepval	Gt Western	Hockley	Hydraulic Labourer
Hodgson	Henry	Pte	10th	West Yorks		Thiepval	NER	Leeds	Parcels Porter
MacCabe	Albert	Pte	10th	West Yorks		Thiepval	NER	Neville Hill, Leeds	Engine Cleaner
Richmond	John	Pte	10th	West Yorks	20	Fricourt New Military Cemetery	NER	Erimus	Greaser
Scott	William	Pte	10th	West Yorks		Fricourt New Military Cemetery	NER	Sunderland	Fireman
Stowe	Ernest	Pte	10th	West Yorks	26	Fricourt	Midland	Leeds	Labourer
Bond	Percy	Pte	15th	West Yorks	28	Thiepval	Midland	Leeds	Clerk
Gurmin	George	Sgt	15th	West Yorks		Thiepval	Midland	leeds	Clerk
Redfern	Harry	L/Cpl	15th	West Yorks		Thiepval	Midland	Leeds	Clerk
Swindells	Thomas	Pte	15th	West Yorks	18	Thiepval	Midland	Leeds	Train Recorder
Wilkinson	Gerald	L/Cpl	15th (Leeds Pals)	West Yorks		Thiepval	NER	Leeds	Clerk
Wilkinson	Reginald	Pte	15th (Leeds Pals)	West Yorks		Thiepval	NER	Ulleskelf	Clerk
White	William	Pte	1st/7th	West Yorks	20	Thiepval	NER	Leeds	
Berry	Harold	Pte	2nd	West Yorks		Thiepval	NER	Darlington	Erector
Brophy	Ernest	2/Lt	2nd	West Yorks	27	Bouzincourt	Railway Clearing House		Clerk

Surname	First name	Rank	Btn	Regt	Age	CWGC	Company	Location	Job
Hooley	Arthur	Pte	2nd	West Yorks	22	Thiepval	Midland	Leeds	Labourer
Jowett	Arthur	Pte	2nd	West Yorks		Thiepval	Midland	Colne	Dray loader
Slater	Joseph	L/Cpl	2nd	West Yorks	22	Thiepval	Midland	Leeds	Carriage cleaner
Fuller	Phillip	Pte	10th	Yorks	34	Thiepval	NER	Middlesbrough	Labourer
Major	A E	Sig	10th	Yorks	20	Gordon Dump Cemetery, Ovillers-La Boiselle	NER	Scarborough	Cleaner
Murton	R W	Pte	7th	Yorks		Fricourt British Cemetery	NER	Shildon Works	Furnaceman
Beaumont	Douglas	Pte	12th	Yorks & Lancs	24	Queens Cemy, Puisieux	Midland	Sheffield	Clerk
Burgon	John	Pte	12th	Yorks & Lancs		Thiepval	GCR	Mexborough	Sp Fireman
Stothard	Edwin	Pte	12th	Yorks & Lancs		Thiepval	GCR	Sheffield	Clerk
Watkins	Francis	Cpl	12th (Sheffield City Btn)	Yorks & Lancs	32	Thiepval	Midland	She	Clerk
Hepplestone	John	Pte	14th	Yorks & Lancs		Thiepval	GCR	Worsborough	Platelayer
Cropley	Charles	L/Cpl	8th	Yorks & Lancs	22	Thiepval	Midland	Wombwell	Sidings porter
Depledge	Fred	L/Cpl	8th	Yorks & Lancs	25	Thiepval	GCR	Mexborough	Boilermakers Assistant
Harwood	J	Pte	8th	Yorks & Lancs		Blighty Valley	GCR	Wath	Goods Guard
Teat	Harry	Pte	8th	Yorks & Lancs	23	Thiepval	GCR	Conisborough	Checker
Worker	Harry	Sgt	8th	Yorks & Lancs		Thiepval	Midland	Masboro	Passed cleaner
Brook(e)s	William	Pte	9th	Yorks & Lancs		Thiepval	GCR	Mexborough	Washer Out
Jennings	RH	Pte	9th	Yorks & Lancs		AIF Burial Ground Flers	Midland	Sheffield	Porter
Saunderson	Walter	L/Cpl	9th	Yorks & Lancs	33	Serre Rd No 2	Midland	Sheffield	Porter

APPENDIX 8

LAST RESTING PLACES OF THE 240 RAILWAYMEN
WHO DIED ON THE FIRST DAY OF THE BATTLE OF THE SOMME

CWGC	No	CWGC	No
AIF Flers	2	London Road	1
Auchonvillers	1	Lonsdale	3
Authuille	1	Mametz Alley	1
Bertancourt	1	Norfolk	1
Blighty Valley	7	Ovillers	5
Bouzincourt	3	Peronne Road	1
Dantzig Alley	5	Queens Cemetary	1
Devonshire Trench	4	Redan Ridge	2
Foncquevillers	4	Serre 1 and 2	10
Fricourt	4	Y Ravine	1
Gommecourt	9	Thiepval	161
Gordon Dump	5		
Hawthorn Ridge	2		

APPENDIX 9

ROYAL NAVY VESSELS SUNK WITH RAILWAYMEN ON BOARD

Date	HMS	Cause	Railwaymen	Total
22 Sept 1914	Aboukir	Torpedoed U9	15	527
22 Sept 1914	Cressy	Torpedoed U9	12	560
22 Sept 1914	Hogue	Torpedoed U9	8	373
1 Nov 1914	Good Hope	Gunfire	27	900
26 Nov 1914	Bulwark	Unknown (exploded)	4	738
1 Jan 1915	Formidable	Torpedoed	6	550
8 Mar 1915	Lord Airedale	Wrecked	2	14
11 Mar 1915	Bayano	Torpedoed U27	3	195
13 May 1915	Goliath	Torpedoed	10	570
30 Dec 1915	Natal	Unknown (exploded)	4	400
5 May 1916	Hampshire	Torpedoed U75	7	643
31 May 1916	Ardent	Gunfire	3	78
31 May 1916	Black Prince	Gunfire	9	857
31 May 1916	Broke	Gunfire (damaged)	2	47
31 May 1916	Defence	Gunfire	6	903
31 May 1916	Indefatigable	Gunfire	7	1017
31 May 1916	Invincible	Gunfire	9	1026
31 May 1916	Tipperary	Gunfire	4	197
31 May 1916	Tiger	Damaged	1	
31 May 1916	Turbulent	Gunfire	1	90
31 May 1916	Queen Mary	Gunfire	7	1266
19 Apr 1917	MV Star of Freedom	Torpedoed	1	10
9 July 1917	Vanguard	Unknown (exploded)	11	800
9 Aug 1917	Recruit	Torpedoed	3	54
24 Dec 1917	SS Daybreak	Torpedoed	1	21
12 Jan 1918	Narborough	Run aground	4	188
18 Jan 1918	Gambri	Mine	3	21
20 Jan 1918	Raglan	Gunfire	3	127
4 Apr 1918	Bittern	Collision	3	63
23 Apr 1918	Vindictive	Scuttled	1	
4 Oct 1918	L10	Gunfire	2	38
15 Oct 1918	J6	Friendly fire	1	16
			234	12,289

APPENDIX 10

RAILWAY MARITIME SHIPS

	Ship	Owner	Date lost	Fate	Casualties	Notes
	Roedean ex Roebuck	GWR	13 Jan 15	Collision with HMS Imperieuse.		Result of dragging anchor whilst at Scapa Flow
	Char (ex Stranton)	NER	16.1.15	Lost when rammed by a trawler.	8	Off Orkney
	Duke of Lancaster	L & Y	8.5.15	Torpedoed in the North Sea		
	Don	L & Y	8.5.15	Torpedoed off Blyth		
	Immingham	GCR	12.6.15	Sunk in collision off Lemnos		Date unclear could be 12.6.18
HMS	Hythe	SECR	29.9.15	Collision with Sarnia	9+144	Serving as a minesweeper but at the time of the collision was carrying troops.
HMS	Tara (ex Hibernia)	L & NWR	5.11.15	Sunk by U35 off Libyan coast	10	Remaining crew captive and marched across North Africa until rescued by the Duke of Westminster some months later.
HMHS	Anglia	L & NWR	17.11.15	1 mile East of Folkestone struck a mine	120-160	Hospital Ship
HMS	Duchess of Hamilton	Caledonian	29.11.15	Mined and sunk near Harwich Longsand	9	Minesweeper
SS	Dearne	L&Y	22.12.15	Detained at Hamburg at outbreak of war & lost whilst in enemy hands		
SS	Leicester	GCR	21.2.16	Sunk by a mine from U6 2.5 miles from Folkestone	17	From Portsmouth to Cromarty with general cargo.
SS	Chesterfield	GCR	18.5.16	Torpedoed in the Mediterranean	?	
HMS	Brussels	GER	23.6.16	Captured by enemy in North Sea		
HMS	Clacton	GER	3.8.16	Torpedoed by U73, Kavalla Bay, Aegean	5	Minesweeper
SS	Duke of Albany	L & Y	25.8.16	Torpedoed by U27, 20 miles east of Pentland Skerries, Orkney	24	Armed Boarding Vessel
SS	Colchester	GER	21.9.16	Captured by enemy in North Sea. Sunk while in enemy service	?	
SS	The Queen	SECR	26.10.16	Captured by German destroyer S60 and sunk	?	Merchant ship
	Copenhagen	GER	5.3.17	Torpedoed in North Sea	?	
HMS	Duchess of Montrose	Caledonian	18.3.17	Mined off Dunkirk	5	Minesweeper
SS	Achille Adam	SECR	23.3.17	Torpedoed by U39 31 Miles from Beachy Head	6	Merchant ship

	Ship	Owner	Date lost	Fate	Casualties	Notes
HMHS	Donegal	Midland	17.4.17	Torpedoed	11	Hospital ship sunk mid channel en route for Southampton.
	Neptune	G&SWR	20.4.17	Mined in English Channel	?	
SS	Hebble	L & Y	6.5.17	Struck a mine laid by U32 off Sunderland	5	
SS	Cito	NER	17.5.17	Sunk by Torpedo Boat Destroyers S53 and V70	10	Including Master
	Newmarket	GER	July 17	Believed to have been sunk by U38	All Hands	Minesweeper went missing in the eastern Med last reported on 16th July 1917.
	Anjou	LBSCR	18.7.17	Mined Bay of Biscay		
	Maine	LBSCR	21.11.17	Torpedoed between Newhaven and Dieppe whilst loaded with Ammunition	?	
HMS	Louvain	GER	21.1.18	Torpedoed in the Aegean by U22	224	Armed Boarding Steamer
	Normandy	South Western	25.1.18	Torpedoed off Cape La Hague Channel.	4	Merchant ship.
	South Western	South Western	16.3.18	Torpedoed. English Channel	24	Merchant ship
	Slieve Bloom	L & NWR	30.3.18	Collision with USS Stockton a light cruiser	0	All cargo including railway rolling stock and 370 cattle lost.
SS	Rye	L & Y	7.4.18	On Passage from Newhaven to Rouen when sunk by U 74	2	
SS	Unity	L & Y	2.5.18	On passage from Newhaven to Calais torpedoed by U57	12	
	Wrexham	GCR	19.6.18	Struck rock and wrecked in White Sea, Murmansk.		
HMS	Sarnia	South Western	12.9.18	Sunk by torpedo off Port Said when escorting troopship.	58	Collision with auxilliary minesweeper Hythe off cape Helles (see below).
	Onward	SECR	24.9.18	Caught fire and burnt out at Folkestone		Merchant ship
HMS	Mars	G &SWR	18.11.18	Sunk in collision off Harwich		Known as HMS Marsa

HMS = Royal Navy – His Majesty's Ship
HMHS=Royal Navy-His Majesty's Hospital Ship
SS = Steam Ship

ABBREVIATIONS

A/S	Able Seaman
Btn	Battalion
CWGC	Commonwealth War Graves Commission
DST	Divisional Supply Train
G & SWR	Glasgow & South Western Railway
GCR	Great Central Railway
GER	Great Eastern Railway
GNR	Great Northern Railway
GNSR	Great North Of Scotland Railway
GWR	Great Western Railway
KRRC	Kings Royal Rifle Corps
L/S	Leading Seaman
L & NWR	London and North Western Railway
L & SWR	London and South Western Railway
L & Y	Lancashire and Yorkshire Railway
LB & SCR	London, Brighton and South Coast Railway
LROC	Light Railway Operating Company
L/Sgt	Lance Sergeant
NBR	North British Railway
NER	North Eastern Railway
Pte	Private
Regt	Regiment
Rfn	Rifleman
ROC	Railway Operations Company
RTO	Railway Transport Officer
SECR	South Eastern and Chatham Railway
Sgt	Sergeant
Spr	Sapper

BIBLIOGRAPHY

Books

Astill, E., (2005) *A History of 1st Battalion Wiltshire Regiment*, RBGW Salisbury Museum, Salisbury.

Aves, W.A.T., (2009) *The ROD on the Western Front 1915–1919*, Shaun Tyas, Donnington.

Barker, A.J., (2009) *The First Iraq War 1914–1918 Britains Mesopotamian Campaign*, Enigma Books, New York.

Brown, I.M., *British Logistics On The Western Front. 1914–1919.*

Buchan, J., (ed), (1920) *Long Road to Victory.* Thomas Nelson & Son, London.

Carver, Lord., (1998) *Britain's Army in the 20th Century*, Macmillan, London

Corrigan. G., (2003) *Mud, Blood and Poppycock*, London.

Dane, E., (1919) *British Campaigns in the Nearer East 1914–1918 Vol 2*, Hodder & Stoughton. London.

Darroch, G.R.S., (1920) *Deeds of a great railway.* A record of the enterprise and achievements of The London and North Western Railway Company during the Great War. John Murray, London.

De Grace, L.W., *The History Of The Fifth Battalion The Sherwood Foresters Notts and Derby Regiment. 1914–1918.*

Davies, W., (1988) *The sea and the sand: the story of HMS Tara and the western desert force*, Gwynedd, Archives and Museums Service.

Davies, W.J.K., (1967) *Light Railways of WWI*, David & Charles.

Earnshaw A., (1990) *British Railways at War 1914–1918*, Atlantic, Penryn, Cornwall.

Evans, A.S., (2010), *Beneath The Waves.* A History of HM Submarine Losses, 1904–1971. Pen & Sword, Barnsley.

Farndale, M., (1986) *History of the Royal Regiment of Artillery –Western Front 1914–1918*, Royal Artillery Institution.

Fawcett, H.W., and Hooper, G. W. W., (ed) (1921) *The Fighting At Jutland.* The Personal Experiences of Forty–five Officers and Men of the British Fleet, Macmillan, London.

Forbes, A., (1929) *A History of the Army Ordnance Services*, reprinted, The Naval and Military Press Uckfield, East Sussex.

Gilbert, M., (1994), *First World War.* Weidenfeld and Nicholson, London.

Gittins, S., (2010), *The Great Western Railway in the First World War*, The History Press, Stroud.

Hart, P., (2008), 1918. *A Very British Victory*, Weidenfeld and Nicholson, London.

Haslam, M.J., *The Chilwell Story: VC Factory and Ordnance Depot.*

Hastings, M., (2014), *Catastrophe. Europe Goes To War, 1914.* William Collins, London.

Henshaw, T., (1995), *The Sky Their Background. Air Fighting And The Complete List of Allied Air Casualties From Enemy Action in the First War.* Grub Street, London.

Heritage, T.R., *The Light track from Arras.*

Hills, J.D., *The Fifth Leicestershire.* A record of the 1/5th Battalion the Leicestershire Regiment T. F., during the war, 1914–1919.

Holt, T. & V., (1995), *Battlefields of the First World War – a Travellers Guide Place*, Pavilion Books , London.

Keegan, J., (1998), *The First World War*, Hutchinson, London.

Lewis–Stempel, J., (2010), *Six Weeks.* The Short and Gallant Life of the British Officer in the First World War. Weidenfeld and Nicholson, London.

Liddell Hart, B.H., (1930), *History of the First World War,* Cassell, London.

Livesey, A., (1994) *The Viking Atlas of WWI*, Viking, London.

Lock, H.O., (1919) *With the British Army in the Holy Land.* Robert Scott. London.

Maggs, C., (1983), *Rail Centres; Swindon*, Ian Allen, London.

Massie, R.K., (2004) *Castles of Steel. Britain, Germany and the winning of the Great War at sea.* Jonathan Cape, London.

Matrix Evans, M., (1996), *The Battles of the Somme*, Orion, London.

McCarthy, C., (1996), *The Somme The Day By Day Account*, GE New Orchard, London.

McDonald, A., (2008) *A lack of offensive spirit?* The 46th (North Midland) division at Gommecourt 1 July 1916, Iona Books.

McGreal S., The War on Hospital Ships 1914–1918.

Mitchell, T.J., (1931), History Of The Great War based on Official Documents. Medical Services, Casualties and Medical Statistics.

Mullay, A.J., (2008), *For the King' Service Railway Ships at War*, Pendragon, York.

Neilson, K., and Otte, T.G., (2006), *Railways And International Politics. Paths of Empire, 1848–1945*. Routledge, Abingdon.

Perry, P., (2007) *A History of the 5th (Service) Battalion Wiltshire Regiment 1914–1919*, Rifles Wardrobe Museum Trust, Salisbury.

Pratt E.A., (1921) *British Railways and the Great War*. Selwyn and Blount, London.

Priestley, R.E., (1919) *Breaking the Hindenburg Line*. The story of the the 46th (North Midland) Division T. T. Fisher Unwin Ltd, London.

Prior. R., and Wilson. T., (2004), *Command On The Western Front*. The Military Career of Sir Henry Rawlinson 1914–1918. Pen & Sword Barnsley.

Radford, B., (1986) *Rail Centres: Derby*, Ian Allen, London.

Regimental History Committee (2005) *The Northamptonshire Regiment 1914–1918*, Naval & Military Press, Uckfield.

Rogerson, S., (1933/2006) *Twelve Days on the Somme*, Greenhill Books, London.

Roosevelt, K., (1919) *War in the Garden of England*, Charles Scribner's Sons, New York.

Rolls, S.C., (1937 reprinted 1988), *Steel chariots in the desert*: the story of an armoured car driver with the Duke of Westminster in Libya and in Arabia with T. E. Lawrence, Jonathan Cape, London (reprinted by the Rolls–Royce Enthusiasts Club, 1988).

Sandilands, J.W., & Macleod, N., (1922) *The History of the 7th battalion Queens Own Cameron Highlanders*.

Scott Shepherd, W., (1927) *The 2nd Battalion the Wiltshire Regiment 1914–1918*, 2nd Edition,The Rifles Wardrobe and Museum Trust, Salisbury.

Shakespeare, Lt Col., *A record of the 17th and 32nd Battalions Northumberland Fusiliers 1914–1919*, Naval & Military Press, Uckfield.

Thompson, J., (1991), *The Lifeblood of War Logistics in Armed Conflict*. Brassey's, Oxford.

Van Bergan. L., (2009) *Before My Helpless Sight*. Suffering, Dying and Military Medicine on the Western Front, 1914 –1918, Ashgate, Farnham.

Weetman, W.C.C., (1920), *The Sherwood Foresters in the Great War 1914–1919*. History of the 1/8th Battalion. Thos Forman & Son, Nottingham.

Westlake, R., (2009) *Tracing British Battalions on the Somme*, Pen & Sword, Barnsley, South Yorkshire.

Wheeler, H.F.B., *Daring Deeds of Merchant Seamen in the Great War.*

Williams, A., (1915/2010) *Life in a Railway Factory*, Amberley, Chalford, Gloucestershire.

Official Documents

A brief record of the advance of the Egyptian Expeditionary Force July 1917 to October 1918. (1919)   Official sources HMSO.

Investigation into Quintinshill rail crash, Railway Department, Board of Trade, Lt Col E Druitt, 17.6.1915.

Railway Manual (WAR) 1911, reprinted by IWM

Statistics of the Military effort of the British Empire during the Great War 1914–1920, (1920), HMSO

Transportation on the Western Front – Henniker. The Battery Press/IWM

The St Pauls Cathedral Railwaymen Service 14th May 1919, Naval and Military Press & IWM.

War Diary 1 Wiltshires, August 1914– May 1919.

War Diary 5 Wiltshires

War Diary 5th Sherwood Foresters. WO/95/2695/1. The National Archives.

War Diary Number 20 Ambulance Train. WO/95/4136. The National Archives.

Women's War Work in Maintaining the Industries and Export Trade Of The United Kingdom, War Office, Sept 1916, HMSO.

Articles

Anderson EP (1927) The Railway Organisation of an Army in War. RUSI Journal 72 1927.

Bonham–Smith R, (1916) Railway transport arrangements in France. RUSI Journal 61. 1916.

Ellis H, (1991) July 1st 1916 – a surgical catastrophe. The Ulster Medical Journal Vol 60 April 1991.

Gullace, NF, (nk) Female Patriotism in the Great War. NF Gullace University of New Hampshire. Women, War & Society 1914–1918 a Gale Digital Collection.

Jeremy, DJ (1991) 'The hundred largest employers in the united kingdom , in manufacturing and non– manufacturing industries in 1907, 1935 and 1955. Business History 33 (1990–91) 93–111

Lindsell, WG (1926) Administrative lessons of the Great War. RUSI journal 71, 1926

Morley, R., Earning their Wings: British Pilot Training 1912–1918.

Napier CS (1935) Strategic movement by rail in 1914. RUSI Journal 80. 1935.

Singleton, J (nk) Britain's Military Use of Horses 1914–1918. Downloaded from oxfordjournals. org

Stevenson, D., War By Timetable? The Railway Race Before 1914, Past and Present, No 162 (February, 1999).

South Eastern & Chatham Railway London District –War period 4th August 1914 to 11th November 1918. Issued from London Bridge Station 12th November 1918. NRM. 42. (SECR report). From The Search Engine, NRM.

The work of the German Military railway staffs before and after the outbreak of war, 1914–1915 (translated) RUSI Journal 66, 1921.

The Great Eastern Railway Magazine 1914–1919.

The Great Western Railway Magazine 1914–1919.

The Great North of Scotland Railway War Memorial booklet.
The North Eastern Railway Magazine 1914–1919.

Map Book

1 Cemeteries & Memorials in Belgium and Northern France. (2008) CWGC. Maidenhead,

IWM Sound Archive

6,638	Frank Gillard	1980
6,649	Sid Coles	1981
10,939	Harold Pendleton	1977
11,042	Eric Potten	1989
11,963	Hardie Henderson	1990
12,850	Harry Sharratt	1966
7,310	Monty Cleeve	1983
39	Walter G Ostler	1973
9,420	Walter Gillman	1986
10,408	Charles Minter	1988
11,458	Herbert Verrity	?

Website

http://www.cwgc.org/
http://1914–1918.invisionzone.com/forums/index.php
http://www.firstworldwar.com/
http://www.nationalarchives.gov.uk/pathways/firstworldwar/service_records/sr_soldiers.htm
http://www.mkheritage.co.uk/la/ (for Albert French)
http://www.greatwar.co.uk/people/albert–french.htm (for Albert French)
http://blindfoldandalone.wordpress.com/2012/11/06/115/ (for shot at dawn)

INDEX

Italic text is used for the names of ships and publications. The publications are also indicated by (publication) after the name. **Bold** text is used to indicate the pages where illustrations occur. The index is in word-by-word sorting order so that "Air Force Cross" comes before "aircraft carriers".

INDEX OF NAMES